EMS Quality Management and Research

Bruce E. Evans, BS, MPA, NREMT-P

Fire Chief

Upper Pine River Fire Protection District

Bayfield, Colorado

EMS Management Series

Series Editor, *Jeffrey T. Lindsey, PhD, PM, EFO, CFO*

Distance Education Coordinator for the Fire and Emergency Services Programs

University of Florida

Gainesville, Florida

PEARSON

Boston Columbus Indianapolis New York San Francisco Upper Saddle River
Amsterdam Cape Town Dubai London Madrid Milan Munich Paris Montreal Toronto
Delhi Mexico City São Paulo Sydney Hong Kong Seoul Singapore Taipei Tokyo

Publisher: Julie Levin Alexander
Publisher's Assistant: Regina Bruno
Editor-in-Chief: Marlene McHugh Pratt
Product Manager: Sladjana Repic
Program Manager: Monica Moosang
Development Editors: Kay S. Peavey and Allison Murray, iD8-TripleSSS
Editorial Assistant: Daria Galbo Ballard
Director of Marketing: David Gesell
Executive Marketing Manager: Brian Hoehl
Marketing Specialist: Michael Sirinides
Project Management Lead: Cynthia Zonneveld
Project Manager: Julie Boddorf
Full-Service Project Manager: Munesh Kumar, Aptara®, Inc.
Editorial Media Manager: Amy Peltier
Media Project Manager: Ellen Martino
Creative Director: Jayne Conte
Cover Designer: Suzanne Behnke
Cover Image: Shutterstock/B Calkins
Composition: Aptara®, Inc.
Text Font: Times Ten LT Std

Credits and acknowledgments borrowed from other sources and reproduced, with permission, in this textbook appear on the appropriate pages within the text.

Library of Congress Cataloging-in-Publication Data
Evans, Bruce E., author.
EMS quality management and research / Bruce E. Evans, BS, MPA, NREMT-P, Fire Chief, Upper Pine River Fire Protection District.
pages cm.—(EMS management series)
ISBN-13: 978-0-13-815281-9
ISBN-10: 0-13-815281-0
1. Emergency medical services—Quality control. 2. Emergency management—Research. 3. Total quality management. I. Title.
RA645.5.E92 2015
362.18—dc23

2014000582

PEARSON

ISBN 13: 978-0-13-815281-9
ISBN 10: 0-13-815281-0

14 2023

Dedication

For my first experience with quality improvement (QI) in EMS, I am grateful to my mother the late Sandra Laidlaw one of the first EMT's with West Des Moines EMS and responsible for the quality assurance (QA) committee. While I was an EMT-I with West Des Moines EMS, she fostered my understanding of quality in EMS. It started me on a path toward excellence in service that I continue to travel. To the University of Iowa Hospitals and Clinics EMSLRC, thank you for allowing me to be part of the research on defibrillation by EMTs in the early 1980s that opened my eyes to the science of EMS. To Mike Taigman and Dave Williams, I am forever one of your disciples who is thankful for your teachings in health care quality. To Mike Stern, EMS Program Chair at the National Fire Academy, I appreciate the opportunity to develop, teach, and experiment with quality topics in the EMS Quality Management Course. I am grateful to my wife Debora, who is always there with a cup of coffee on those early Sunday mornings dedicated to writing this text. I also acknowledge my son Oliver and the missed opportunities to build Legos—I hope when you are old enough to read and understand this text, you will look for ways to make things better and further develop your inquisitive mind.

Contents

Chapter 3

Domains of a QI System 43

Chapter 4

Defining Quality 60

Chapter 5

Measuring Quality 89

Chapter 6

Databases and Data Collection 115

Chapter 7

Data and Quality Analysis 143

Chapter 8

Chapter 9

Preface

This text was prompted by the death of a special needs child who, despite the struggle to overcome the physiological consequences of his existence, succumbed to an iatrogenic death. Witnessing a life-robbing error after a difficult battle to stabilize this child left a lasting impression. Shortly after this event, *EMS Agenda for the Future* (National Highway Traffic Safety Administration, 1996) was released and *Leadership Guide to Quality Improvement for Emergency Medical Services Systems* (National Highway Traffic Safety Administration, 1997) hit the streets. In the late 1990s, EMS waded into the world of QI. Mike Taigman and Dave Williams initiated a series of 3-day seminars to teach the principles of the *Leadership Guide to Quality Improvement for Emergency Medical Services System.* The lore of high-performance EMS systems became buzzwords of the profession. The skills and abilities needed to capture the impact of EMS and define quality had begun to develop. The move to ensure a level of quality was reinforced a few years later, when the Institute of Medicine published *To Err Is Human* (1999), calling national attention to medical errors.

Two decades later as a company officer and paramedic, I stood in the kitchen recording medications on the clipboard at 3:00 a.m. It was a busy shift, and my crew was assessing and treating a patient in the next room. I heard the EMT—the only one on a crew of five other paramedics—say, "Are you sure you want to do that?" Before I could comprehend these words, a medication that had not been indicated was administered to the patient. We were fortunate that there was no negative outcome; however, the system had failed to afford the patient the proper care. A combination of fatigue and reliance on equipment—rather than on assessment skills, training, and communication procedures—had placed this patient at risk. This type of error would be prevented in the future by better system design, just culture, and the advent of crew resource management, all fostering a culture of safety for the patient.

EMS entails matters of life and death. As medical professionals, we are entrusted with responsibilities and obligations. Carelessness, inadequate skill, and breach of ethics cannot be tolerated; we must be ultimately accountable for the quality of the care we provide. EMS must have mechanisms in place to reinforce and ensure adherence to this principle in the system design, procedures, and actions of its members. Professionals render specialized services based on theory, knowledge, and skills that are often peculiar to their profession and generally beyond the understanding and/or capability of those outside of the profession. It is our responsibility to ensure the public trust by creating a safe, quality, and efficient experience for patients.

ORGANIZATION OF THIS TEXT

Chapter 1 details developments that have fostered quality, such as important issues in the field of EMS and the current health care reform movement.

Chapter 2 chronicles the history of EMS QI and builds on terminology necessary for a knowledge base of QI principles.

In Chapter 3, the domains of EMS QI are defined. Structure, process, and measuring outcomes are all addressed.

Chapter 4 defines quality through benchmarking and creating indicators.

Chapter 5 discusses capturing information and data for quality measurement.

Chapter 6 presents databases and how they can relate to each other.

The focus of Chapter 7 is analysis of data, employing mathematical assessments, and simple conclusions of charted data.

In Chapter 8, such management processes as root cause analysis and project management are discussed.

Chapter 9 discusses how to facilitate change or create a "culture of quality."

Chapter 10 presents legal aspects of EMS, including sample legislation and sample cases on protecting information.

FEATURES

Chapter Objectives: Objectives are identified at the beginning of each chapter and outline the material the reader should understand upon completion of the chapter.

Key Terms: Key terms are listed at the beginning of each chapter and are bold upon introduction in the chapter. Each chapter's terms are defined at the end of the chapter, and all terms are included in the comprehensive glossary at the end of the book.

What Would You Do? Case Study: Every chapter starts with an EMS manager tackling some issue related to quality management that is related to the content of the chapter. How he resolved the issue based on information in the chapter is presented in the **What Would You Do? Reflection** feature at the end of the chapter.

Best Practice: Every chapter includes a real-world example that illustrates information from the chapter having been used successfully by an EMS agency.

Side Bars: This feature relates interesting information that corresponds very closely to text discussion.

Review Questions: Students are required to draw on the knowledge presented in the chapter to answer the questions.

References: A list of bibliographical references appears at the end of each chapter.

ROAD MAP/HOW TO USE THIS TEXT

This text is designed as a starter manual for building comprehensive knowledge of QI. It is ideally studied within a committee, since QI should never be the responsibility of a single person. Each chapter is populated with best practices and organizational stories. As a practical guide, the text goes far beyond theory and review of journal material. Frontline supervisors and EMS providers who are interested in QI should experiment with adapting the best practices and practical applications to their agencies.

TEACHING AND LEARNING RESOURCES

For information on instructor resources, including PowerPoint presentations and assessment tools, as well as student resources, please contact your Brady sales representative.

ACKNOWLEDGMENTS

The author would like to thank the Henderson (Nevada) Fire Department, Memphis (Tennessee) Fire Department, West Des Moines (Iowa) EMS, Centura Health's Littleton Adventist Hospital, and Firstwatch San Diego (California).

Reviewers

Chris Harris, SPHR
Human Resource Manager
Hutchinson Community College
Wichita, KS

George Hettenbach, BBA, MS
Adjunct Professor
Delaware County Community College
Havertown, PA

Steven E. Lynn BS, EMTP
Paramedic/Firefighter/Adjunct Instructor
Southwestern Illinois College
Belleville, IL

M. Ryan Maloney, BS, EMT-P
San Diego, CA

Geoffrey L. Shapiro
Coordinator, Operational Medicine Program
The George Washington University Emergency Health Services Program
Washington, DC

Brad Van Ert
Fire Captain
Downey Fire Department
Downey, CA

David M. Williams, PhD
Improvement Advisor
Institute for Healthcare Improvement
Austin, TX

About the Author

Bruce E. Evans

Bruce E. Evans, BS, MPA, NREMT-P Bruce Evans is the Fire Chief at the Upper Pine River Fire Protection District and has an Appointment to the Institute of Medicine's Preparedness Committee. He previously served as the EMS Chief and as an Assistant Chief at the North Las Vegas Fire Department in Southern Nevada.

Chief Evans started his fire service career at the Henderson (Nevada) Fire Department as a firefighter/paramedic, EMS captain, and engine company captain at Henderson's busiest station. He has over 30 years of experience in a variety of EMS settings, including private ambulance, helicopter, hospital, and third-service EMS agencies. Chief Evans is the 2010 recipient of the International Association of Fire Chiefs James O. Page Award for Leadership in EMS.

Chief Evans has served as a program coordinator and faculty member at the College of Southern Nevada's Fire Technology program, teaching various fire and EMS topics, for 21 years. He is an adjunct faculty for the National Fire Academy (NFA) in the EMS, safety, incident management, and quality and research programs. Chief Evans is also a certified faculty for the International Public Safety Leadership & Ethics Institute training program.

Chief Evans holds an M.A. in Public Administration, a B.S. in Education, and an A.A. in Fire Management. He is currently on the board of directors for the National Association of EMTs, representing Region IV. Chief Evans also is on the board of directors for the National EMS Management Association.

Chief Evans has served as a technical writer for several of the courses at the NFA. He also wrote the bi-monthly column EMS Viewpoints in *Fire Chief* magazine for over a decade and is on the editorial board for the *Journal of Emergency Medical Services*. Chief Evans has co-authored several textbooks, including *Crew Resource Management* with Jones and Bartlett, *Management of EMS* with Brady/Prentice Hall, and *High-Rise Firefighting* for the Structural Fire Fighting series of the International Fire Services Training Association (IFSTA). He also is one of the authors of the National Association of EMT's Safety Course.

Chief Evans, his wife, Debora, and their son, Oliver, have lived in Southwest Colorado since 2008. Chief Evans is an avid railroad fan and enjoys the whitewater.

About the Series Editor

Jeffrey T. Lindsey, PhD, PM, EFO, CFO

Dr. Jeffrey Lindsey has served in a variety of roles in the fire and EMS arena for the past 30 years. He has held positions of firefighter, paramedic, dispatcher, educator, coordinator, deputy chief, and chief. He started his career in Carlisle, Pennsylvania, as a volunteer firefighter/EMT. In 1985 Dr. Lindsey pioneered the first advanced life support service in Cumberland County, Pennsylvania. He is retired as the Fire/EMS Chief for Estero Fire Rescue, where he served as the South Division Incident Commander during major events. He was also part of the Area Command for Lee County EOC. Currently he is the Distance Education Coordinator for the Fire and Emergency Services Programs at the University of Florida.

He has served as an inaugural member on the National EMS Advisory Council, representing fire-based EMS, and is a past member of the State of Florida EMS Advisory Council, where he served as the firefighter/paramedic representative. He currently serves as representative to the Fire and Emergency Services Higher Education EMS degree committee. He has been active in the IAFC, serving as liaison to ACEP and attending various meetings representing fire-based EMS, and as the inaugural chair of the Community Paramedic committee, and he is an associate member of the Prehospital Research Forum.

He was a monthly columnist on product reviews for 3 years for *The Journal of Emergency Medical Services (JEMS)*, a national EMS journal. He is a columnist for Firerehab.com and has authored numerous fire and EMS texts for Brady/Pearson. He is currently the Chief Learning Officer for the Health and Safety Institute, which produces *24-7 EMS* and *24-7 Fire* videos. He also was an EMS professor for St. Petersburg College (Florida).

Dr. Lindsey has been involved in a number of large events and has served within the incident command system at the upper level, including during a number of wildland fires and Hurricane Charley. He has also been involved in the preparations for a number of other hurricanes and tropical storms.

He holds an associate's degree in paramedicine from Harrisburg Area Community College, a bachelor's degree in Fire and Safety from the University of Cincinnati, a master's degree in Instructional Technology from the University of South Florida, and a Ph.D. in Instructional Technology/Adult Education from the University of South Florida.

In addition, Dr. Lindsey has completed the Executive Fire Officer Program at the National Fire Academy. He has designed and developed various courses in fire and EMS. Dr. Lindsey is accredited with the Chief Fire Officer Designation. He also is a certified Fire Officer II, Fire Instructor III, and paramedic in the state of Florida; holds a paramedic certificate for the state of Pennsylvania; and is a certified instructor in these and a variety of other courses.

Dr. Lindsey has an innate interest in alternative health. He is a certified nutritional counselor, a master herbalist, and a holistic health practitioner.

About FESHE

FESHE (Fire and Emergency Services Higher Education) is a dedicated group of individuals from around the country. It is hosted by the United States Fire Administration through the National Fire Academy. The mission of this group is to develop a uniform model curriculum for associate's, bachelor's, and master's degrees. In December 2006, a group of EMS educators convened as the inaugural EMS committee for FESHE. The mission was to develop a model curriculum in EMS management at the bachelor's level. It was the consensus of the leaders across the United States that the committee focus on the management issues of EMS. The clinical portion of the industry is addressed through the National EMS Education Standards and is mainly focused at the associate's level.

This text is written to meet the needs of the national model curriculum for EMS management at the bachelor's level. The EMS management curriculum includes six core courses and seven elective courses. Following are titles in Brady's *EMS Management Series*, designed to meet the FESHE curriculum.

CORE

- Foundations of EMS Systems
- Management of EMS
- EMS Community Risk Reduction
- EMS Quality Management and Research
- Legal, Political and Regulatory Environment in EMS
- EMS Safety and Risk Management

ELECTIVE

- Management of Ambulance Services
- Foundations for the Practice of EMS Education
- EMS Special Operations
- EMS Public Information and Community Relations
- EMS Communications and Information Technology
- EMS Finance
- Analytical Approaches to EMS

Why Quality?

1 CHAPTER

Objectives

After reading this chapter, the student should be able to:

1.1 Identify the need for quality improvement.
1.2 Recognize the current status of medical errors.
1.3 Engage in quality activities and offer quality initiatives.
1.4 Analyze the current state of medicine and issues in quality.
1.5 Locate and identify the source of current medical errors information.
1.6 Compare and contrast the need for quality.

Key Terms

accountable care organizations (ACOs)
iatrogenic
managed care
medical errors
medication errors
normalization of deviance
patient-safety incidents (PSIs)
patient-safety organizations (PSOs)
performance-based reimbursement
quality
quality improvement (QI)
quality improvement system
quality gap
quality of health care

WHAT WOULD YOU DO?

The operations supervisor from Lifeline ambulance received a letter from the local medical center with a comprehensive cardiac center. The outreach coordinator for the cardiac care program identified that the paramedic crews were only administering aspirin to patients in which an alert was triggered for ST elevation myocardial infarction (STEMI) in 54 percent of the patients arriving at its hospitals. Aspirin 160–325 mg in the first 20 minutes of an STEMI has a Class I recommendation for which there is evidence for and/or general agreement that a given procedure or treatment is beneficial, useful, and effective. The "ACC/AHA Guidelines for the Management of Patients with Acute Myocardial Infarction" were approved by the American College of Cardiology Board of Trustees on July 10, 1996, and by the American Heart Association Science Advisory and Coordinating Committee on June 20, 1996, after an exhaustive review of the science and outcome of myocardial infarction patients. After the evidence was presented to a quality improvement committee, a suggestion was made to attach the nitroglycerin bottle with a rubber band to the aspirin bottle in the approach bag. (See Figure 1.1.) The idea was trialed on one medic unit on one shift; after a month, it was confirmed to work. The solution was implemented into the rest of the system, and compliance rose to 95 percent within the following month.

Questions

1. How does this scenario reflect the growing movement toward quality?
2. What makes this a cost-effective solution that relates to a national standard of care?
3. What type of error or classification does this incident appear to be?

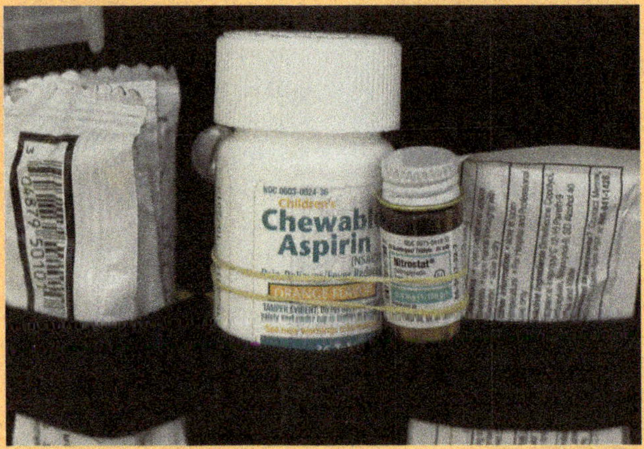

FIGURE 1.1 Nitroglycerine can be attached with a rubber band to an aspirin bottle. *Source: Courtesy Bruce Evans*

INTRODUCTION

When the word **quality** is used, we think immediately of products. Lexus, Craftsman, and Ethan Allan are all brand names with products recognized for quality. Yet, recognition of quality also applies to services, such as Southwest Airlines, Starbucks, and Ritz-Carlton hotels. In the profession of medicine and emergency services, it is expected that services must be of good quality since they deal with the most precious situations of care and healing of human lives. Yet, few quality initiatives exist in the field of prehospital medicine. It is only in the last decade that major quality control efforts have been initiated in hospitals and physician practices. In this chapter, problems related to quality are reviewed. The underlying question is defined as "Why is quality so important?" In sharing numbers and financial costs, the need for EMS to develop processes and programs to promote and ensure quality will be paramount.

THE MOVE TO QUALITY

When a person puts on a public safety uniform and walks out the door to an assignment, it is likely that he has every intention to do the best job possible for the public. The thought is often to perform some miraculous outcome that gives rise to the folklore that surrounds EMS and builds the public's perception that EMS saves everyone. EMS is a complex operation; some cases involve over 300 separate decisions that must be made on a single call in a very compressed amount of time. Compared to other health care professions that often include better training, accredited education, closer supervision, and a more controlled environment, EMS has substantially less training and education. But, it still faces the same level of decision making. It is this dynamic—sense of duty, public expectation, and limited training—that fuels the need for quality.

Every other aspect of mainstream medicine is now subject to the scrutiny of a comprehensive quality initiative. In hospital systems, quality is measured in processes, outcomes, errors, and customer satisfaction. National certification agencies, such as the Joint Commission, have launched efforts to track sentinel events and have rolled out comprehensive patient safety initiatives. The Institute of Medicine (IOM) has defined **quality of health care** as the degree to which health services for individuals and patient populations increase the likelihood of desirable health outcomes and are consistent with current professional knowledge. The American College of Emergency Physicians (ACEP) devotes a significant amount of attention to **quality improvement (QI)** and patient safety. ACEP produces a monthly safety newsletter and, in 2010, was awarded the National EMS "Culture of Safety" Strategy Project to raise awareness of safety in EMS. The differences between health care processes or outcomes observed in practice and those thought to be achievable with the most current and effective professional knowledge comprise the **quality gap**.

Patient safety is defined by the absence of the potential or an occurrence of a health care system injury to a patient and differs from QI in that QI encompasses the entire patient experience, regardless of an error and more focused on outcome. Patient safety is created by avoiding **medical errors** as well as taking action to prevent errors from causing injury. Patient safety is an emerging concept in EMS; however, it is a major effort in health care that includes more than **medication errors**. It includes missed opportunities, wrong procedures, patient restraint, and many other specifics that could injure or kill a patient in the health care setting. QI in EMS has long been thought of as being compliant with paperwork and ensuring the boxes are all filled out on the patient care report. Often what is lacking is the identification of medical errors and sentinel events as outliers to normal operations and patient care. This is much different from most other industries, which look at defects in products as quality issues. Changes in outcome and cost are seen in other health care industries as variation or influencing quality. In EMS the crossover between public safety and medicine often leaves the focus of quality in an undefined area.

Insurance companies and **accountable care organizations (ACOs)** are now beginning to base reimbursement on proper procedures and outcomes verses effort. A new level of accountability is emerging, in which the extent of reimbursement for medical services will be based on outcome. Medicare, Medicaid, and insurance companies are emphasizing outcomes and patient safety. EMS is very likely to see a change in the reimbursement model that is based on quality determined by outcomes and customer experience.

THE INSTITUTE OF MEDICINE

The IOM published a text called "To Err is Human: Building a Better Health System" in 1999 and published "Crossing the Quality Chasm: A New Health Care System for the 21st Century" in 2001 (Wolfe, 2001). These documents set in motion a national effort to improve the quality of medical care in the United States. In April 2007, the National Academies of Science and the Institute of Medicine released a report entitled "Emergency Medical Services: At the Crossroads" as part of the *Future of Emergency Care* series. This report was highly critical of the current state of EMS in the United States. It cited the lack of evidence and little scientific basis for many practices routinely used by EMS. It also listed a wide variety of performance outcomes. The quality and effectiveness of EMS care varies widely by location and by provider, with no accountability or public awareness.

The printing of the IOM report is a sentinel event for EMS. The attention of the National Academies as it relates to EMS is important for the following reason. The National Academies is a private, nonprofit institution that advises the nation on scientific and technical matters. It is made up of the National Academy of Sciences, National Academy of Engineering, Institute of Medicine, and National Research Council. The IOM process is an independent view; it lacks the bias or conflicts of interest often voiced by interest groups. The IOM reports are confidential and peer reviewed using expert presentations, commissioned papers, and literature review. Most important, the reports are well received by Congress and tend to direct policy and funding.

A medical error could mean a health care provider chose an inappropriate method of care, such as giving a patient a certain asthma drug without knowing that he was allergic to it. However, the wrong care is only part of the picture; failing to provide care and preventing harm are key components of patient safety under a quality program. A medical error could also mean that the health care provider chose the right course of care but carried it out incorrectly, such as intending to administer a lidocaine drip to a patient but inadvertently administering a concentrated, lethal overdose. Medical errors happen when the wrong plan was used or when something that was planned as part of medical care does not work out. Medical errors can occur anywhere in the health care system, as depicted in Figure 1.2.

Medical errors are typically classified in six categories. Although it is common that errors in medications, procedures, and diagnosis result in some of the most catastrophic outcomes, equipment failures can have a similar impact. Medical failures in devices or adverse medication effects often go unreported. Some common errors in medical reports—for example, a dose described in milligrams rather than

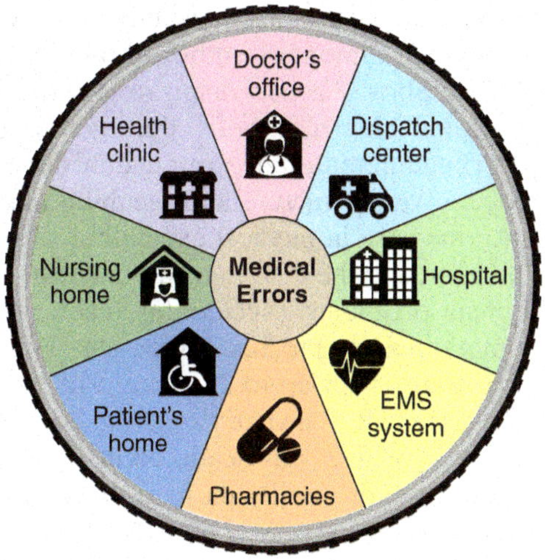

FIGURE 1.2 Medical errors occur in various locations. *Source: Author drawing*

micrograms—are being lessened by technology. In addition, errors of omission can occur when the provider does not carry out a function or process to provide service or treatment to the patient.

Errors can occur during even the most routine tasks, such as when a patient allergic to latex is placed on a nasal cannula made of latex. Most errors result from problems created by today's complex health care system. Errors also happen when doctors and their patients have problems communicating. For example, a study supported by the Agency for Healthcare Research and Quality (AHRQ) and conducted by the RAND Corporation in 2003 found that doctors often do not do enough to help their patients make informed decisions (Farley, Morton, Damberg, Ridgely, Fremont, Greenberg, et al., 2007). Uninvolved and uninformed patients are less likely to accept the doctor's choice of treatment and less likely to do what they need to do to make the treatment work. Similar decisions in EMS—such as hospital destination, directions surrounding a nontransport, medications, or procedures to be performed in the back of the ambulance—are rarely explained fully to the patient (or, similar data confirming the practice of informed consent have never been published).

The statistics in the 1999 IOM report *To Err Is Human*, which was based on two large studies, suggest that medical errors are the eighth leading cause of death among Americans, with error-caused deaths each year in hospitals alone exceeding those from motor vehicle accidents (43,458), breast cancer (42,297), or AIDS (16,516). Attention to medical errors escalated after the release of *To Err is Human*, which found that between 44,000 and 98,000 Americans die each year in U.S. hospitals due to preventable medical errors. The IOM estimates that hospital errors occur in 5 percent to 10 percent of patients admitted to hospitals. These numbers may understate the problem because they do not include preventable deaths due to medical treatment outside of hospitals. The IOM estimates that medical errors cost $37.6 billion each year and $17 billion is directly related to preventable errors. About 1.14 million **patient-safety incidents (PSIs)** occurred among the 37 million hospitalizations in the Medicare population over the years 2000 to 2002.

The numbers in the IOM report do not tell the whole story. People in the hospital are just a small proportion of those at risk. Doctors' offices, clinics, and outpatient surgical centers treat thousands of patients each day; retail pharmacies fill countless prescriptions; and nursing homes and other institutional settings serve vulnerable patient populations. The Canadian Patient Safety Institute Report (Bigham, Morrison, Maher, Brooks, et al., 2010) states that there are no studies on the error rates in EMS.

As its title suggests, the IOM report supports moving away from the traditional culture of "naming, shaming, and blaming" individual health providers who make mistakes. Instead, the IOM believes that preventing future errors is best achieved by designing a safer overall system. To build a safe system in EMS, we must first obtain data and establish baselines on EMS system performance. As EMS managers wade into such a project, employees must feel they have nothing to fear by engaging the **quality improvement system**.

Emerging quality practices show much to be gained by employing a "just culture" concept rather than mandating medical error reporting. It is imperative that a culture of fear be removed or an agency will not overcome the hesitancy of EMTs, paramedics, or firefighters to self-report errors. Although more than twenty states currently have mandatory reporting systems, state officials know that underreporting persists. It is then that QI becomes either mandated or the responsibility of the management team.

MEDICAL ERRORS, COST, AND OUTCOMES

The Institute of Health Improvement launched a campaign to reduce harm and death. Over 33 million errors have been recorded, and it has been determined that 44,000 **iatrogenic** (caused by the health care system) deaths occur annually—confirming the IOM report that determined medical errors to be the eighth leading cause of death. EMS has to look to the hospital industry for comparable numbers due to the lack of data and systems in place within EMS. Like a hospital, an ambulance is a place of healing or providing lifesaving care. It can also be a place of injury. A 2008 article from the *Healthcare Economist* reported that in the United States 2.9 percent of people who enter the hospital are actually harmed by the care they receive. What are the costs of these injuries? A February 2009 study conducted by the *Healthcare Economist* (Shafrin, 2009) looked at attempts to estimate the cost of hospitals failing to prevent adverse medical outcomes. The authors examined fourteen patient safety indicators (PSIs): anesthesia complication, accidental laceration, foreign body left in, iatrogenic pneumo-thorax, transfusion reaction, infections due to medical care, sepsis, pulmonary embolism and deep vein thrombosis, acute respiratory failure, physiologic and metabolic derangements, hemorrhage/hematoma, wound dehiscence, postoperative hip fracture, and decubitus ulcer.

An increase in medical expenditures that are attributed to the PSIs ranged from $646 for technical problems (accidental laceration, pneumothorax, etc.) to $28,218 for acute respiratory failure, with up to 20 percent of these costs incurred after the patient left the hospital. With a third of all 90-day deaths occurring after discharge from the facility, the excess death rate associated with PSIs ranged from 0 to 7 percent. The 90-day readmission rate associated with PSIs ranged from 0 to 8 percent. Overall, 11 percent of all deaths, 2 percent of readmissions, and 2 percent of expenditures were likely due to these 14 PSIs. These numbers could be applied to EMS for conditions created similar to those in the hospital setting, such as aspiration during an attempted intubation resulting in respiratory failure or a gurney drop that results in a back injury (*Source:* Excerpt from The Impact of Medical Errors on Ninety-Day Costs and Outcomes: An Examination of Surgical Patients by William E. Encinosa and Fred J. Hellinger from HEALTH SERVICES RESEARCH JOURNAL 43(6): 2067–2085. Published by John Wiley & Sons, Ltd., © 2008).

In addition to the harm caused to patients, medical errors are expensive: The Institute of Medicine has estimated that medical errors cost $17 billion to $29 billion per year. Since most of these costs are shifted to outside sources such as Medicare and private insurance, there is no strong incentive for health care organizations to improve patient safety. It is only recently that reimbursement has begun to adjust or deny payment for cost incurred by a health care organization.

Medicare and Quality Initiative

Healthgrades, a U.S. company that develops and markets quality and safety ratings of health care providers, including hospitals, nursing homes, physicians, and dentists, highlights the findings of safety and quality in U.S. hospitals. Of the total 323,993 deaths among Medicare patients who had experienced one or more PSIs between 2000 and 2002, 263,864, or 81 percent, of these deaths were directly attributable to the incident(s). One in every four Medicare patients who were hospitalized from 2000 to 2002 and experienced a PSI died. Fewer PSIs in the best-performing hospitals resulted in a lower cost of $740,337 per 1,000 hospitalizations as compared to the bottom 10th percentile of hospitals. Medicare has identified that patients who were admitted to the bottom 10th percentile of hospitals compared to those admitted to the "best" hospitals had much higher complications and death rates. By identifying the facilities and investigating the causes, approximately 4,000 lives and $580 million would have been saved. One estimate shows these errors cost taxpayers $30 million a year (Zhan and Miller, 2003).

The sixteen PSIs over the 3 years studied accounted for $8.54 billion in excess for inpatient costs to the Medicare system. Extrapolated to the entire United States, an extra $19 billion was spent and more than 575,000 preventable deaths occurred from 2000 to 2002. PSIs with the highest rates per 1,000 hospitalizations were failure to rescue, decubitus ulcer, and postoperative sepsis, which accounted for almost 60 percent of all PSIs that occurred.

Performance-based reimbursement will drive QI initiatives. Insurance and payment for EMS services will be based not just on outcomes but on quality outcomes. In the future, we could see reimbursement for a single event, such as chest pain with a myocardial infarction or a stroke, distributed from the Centers for Medicare and Medicaid Services (CMS) to an ACO. The ACO would then have to pay all of the providers that have extended services to that patient's event. Reimbursement may depend on providing care that is evidence based and has a measure of quality assessed. Health economics will force us to abandon long-accepted treatments for what science tells us. As Medicare and Medicaid funding becomes smaller or overburdened by the aging population, money will be paid only for those medical activities that have a measurable outcome.

THE PROBLEM

Many forces work against quality. Installing and maintaining a quality program has a cost. Although start-up costs can be significant, it is generally accepted and well documented that process improvement results in cost savings. Many costs within an EMS organization are the result of unreliable processes, waste, and rework due to a lack of process improvement and reliability. Few agencies have looked at the cost to build and maintain a QI program in comparison to what has or could have been saved by reduction in errors.

For QI to be successful, an operating strategy or approach has to be used throughout the organization. Improvement systems can have a wide range of structures. In its simplest form, QI can be accomplished with existing people, structure, and the spreadsheet tool available in Microsoft Excel. Often, as larger systems or agencies become more intrigued with their processes and outcomes, QI will require human resources and a substantial outlay for computers. A limited number of EMS agencies in the United States understand the mechanics of conducting QI. Few have a written plan. Feedback to crews is often blocked by a lack of communication or perceived barrier due to privacy laws. In addition, many organizations lack the culture to have quality. You may have heard the descriptor "good enough for government work."

Organizations that do not measure the quality of their products or services run the

FIGURE 1.3 This EMS worker is talking to a father holding his child. *Source: Essentials of Paramedic Care 2nd Edition from Bledsoe, Cherry, Porter ISBN 0-13-171163-6*

risk of loss due to what is known as **normalization of deviance.** This condition develops when an organization becomes so complacent or comfortable that it deviates from the standard of care or practice, thereby offering substandard care or assessments. When these actions do not result in consequences, substandard care becomes more common and quality further diminishes until a catastrophic event occurs. For example, an EMS crew may release a child with a febrile seizure to the parents for transport to a pediatrician 99 times. Following the 100th time that the child is released by EMS, the child does not visit the doctor for one reason or another and winds up with a fatal infection. (See Figure 1.3.) Essentially, this occurs due to EMS's lack of accountability, lack of feedback, and the fact that the crew had left a similar patient before without a bad outcome. Perception and an approach to patient care that uses a rule out method working backward from the possible worst case scenario to least seriousness possibility can help avoid a missed diagnosis. Often, this is reflective of leadership failing to focus on outcomes and or to design reliable processes to achieve those outcomes. Not measuring or focusing on reliability can result in normalization of deviance and in this scenario the same patient in the hospital would be required to have certain processes and procedures via a checklist which may not allow the physician to clear or discharge the patient without completion. Normalization of deviance can come from poor leadership, lack of training, overutilization, or skill degradation. The root causes of these symptoms are lack of measurement and process reliability.

CAUSES OF MEDICAL ERRORS

The causes of medical errors are multifaceted and not yet completely understood. Some causes that have been identified include the following:

- *Communication Errors*—A widely publicized case from 1994 involved the death of a Boston newspaper columnist from an overdose of chemotherapy for breast cancer due to misinterpretation of the doctor's prescription. The patient was given four times the correct daily dose, when what the doctor had intended was for the dosage to be administered over a 4 day period. Other cases involve medication mix-ups due to drugs with very similar names. The Food and Drug Administration (FDA) has identified no fewer than 600 pairs of look-alike or sound-alike drug names since 1992.

- *The Increasing Specialization and Fragmentation of Health Care*—The more the number of people who are involved in a patient's treatment, the greater the possibility that important information will be missing along the chain. Since EMS has been slow to get involved with electronic reporting, key information is often neglected. Often, EMS is not seen as part of the profession and opinions or diagnosis of EMS personnel are discounted.
- *Human Errors Resulting from Overwork and Burnout*—For some years, hospital interns, residents, nurses, and EMS providers have attributed many of the errors made in patient care to the long hours they are expected to work, many times with inadequate sleep. With the coming of **managed care**, many hospitals, and health care facilities have cut the size of their staff and require those who remain to work mandatory overtime shifts. A study published in the *Journal of the American Medical Association* in October 2002 found a clear correlation between higher-than-average rates of patient mortality and higher-than-average ratios of patients to nurses (Agency for Healthcare Research and Quality, 2013).
- *Manufacturing Errors*—Instances have been reported of products being mislabeled during the production process, resulting in patients being given the wrong medication or concentration. Frequently, an error in manufacturing has placed a contaminant in the medication.
- *Equipment Failure*—A typical example of equipment failure might be an EKG machine with a malfunctioning software package, which would misdiagnosis, underdiagnosis, or wrongly diagnose a heart condition.
- *Diagnostic Errors*—A misdiagnosed illness can lead the doctor to prescribe an inappropriate type of treatment. Errors in interpreting diagnostic results have resulted in paramedics treating the wrong illness, such as treating what is incorrectly diagnosed as congestive heart failure with Lasix when the correct diagnosis is pneumonia. Another common form of diagnostic error is failure to act on abnormal test results.
- *Multiple Choices for Care*—An EMS provider is allowed to use more than one procedure rather than a singular evidence-based approach. For example, in a patient with shortness of breath the paramedic may have an option of intubation, CPAP, or any number of bronchodilator, steroids, and smooth muscle relaxing medications.
- *Poorly Designed Vehicles, Buildings, and Facilities*—Hallways that end in sharp right angles, for example, increase the likelihood of falls or collisions between people on foot responding to calls. Another example is an ambulance in which the patient is not accessible by a provider who is restrained in a seat belt.

EMS-RELATED ERRORS

EMS has suffered somewhat from an identity crisis. Whereas EMS leadership regards EMS as part of the medical hierarchy, others deem it as belonging in public safety. This lack of identity could be the reason EMS has been late to embrace the initiation of comprehensive QI plans. Regardless of uniform or who issues the paycheck, EMS personnel are providing health care. The IOM report *Emergency Medical Services: At the Crossroads* (Institute of Medicine of the National Academies, 2006) described EMS at the intersection of public safety, public health, and health care. All of these disciplines are essentially "health care." Some limited information is emerging on key areas to focus on in EMS:

- Airway choice and placement
- Medication errors
- Missed diagnosis
- Early recognition and communication of signs and symptoms

AIRWAY CHOICE AND PLACEMENT

Paramedics are thought to provide lifesaving emergency medical care to patients in the out-of-hospital setting, but only selected emergency interventions have proven to be safe or effective. (See Figure 1.4.) Endotracheal intubation is an important and high-profile procedure performed by paramedics and often thought of as one of the most important skills in the Paramedic's skills set. Several studies continue to find that errors occur in 22 percent of intubation attempts, with a frequency of up to 40 percent in selected ambulance systems (Wang, Lave, Sirio, and Yealy, 2009). A large study on intubation found that errors are more common in children under 6 years and less likely to occur in EMS systems with a smaller number of paramedics doing a high number of intubations. These findings indicate frequent errors associated with what is supposed to be a lifesaving technique. These events are problematic of larger issues in the structure and delivery of out-of-hospital emergency care.

MEDICATION ERRORS

Since 1992, the FDA has received about 20,000 reports of medication errors. These are voluntary reports, so the number of medication errors that actually occur is thought to be much higher. There is no "typical" medication error, and health professionals, patients, and their families are all involved. U.S. Pharmacopeia is a nonprofit public health group that maintains one of the largest databases on medication errors. Medication errors involve the wrong dose, medication, route, and concentration. One San Diego study identified that 9.1 percent of the paramedics surveyed admitted to medication error (Vilke, Tornabene, Stepanski, et al., 2007). The federal system MedMARX is an anonymous

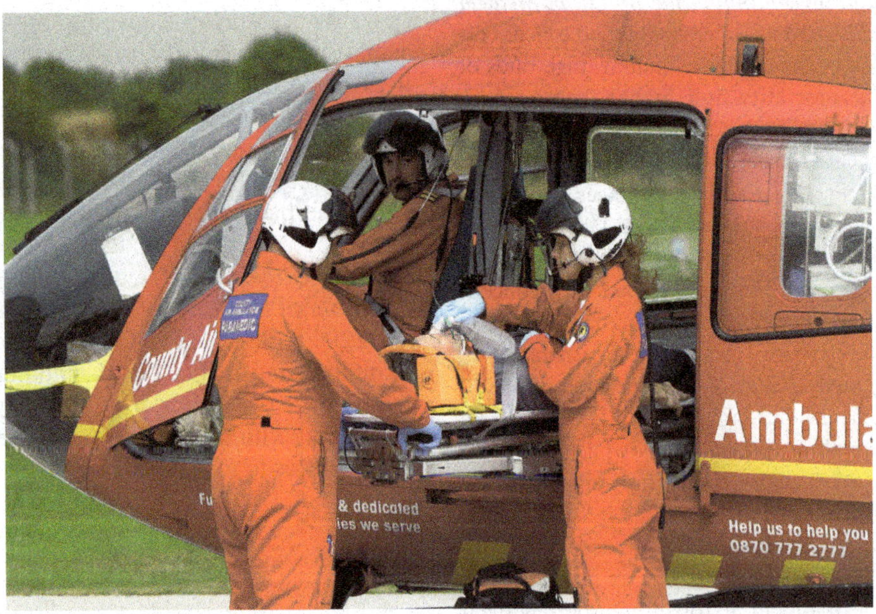

FIGURE 1.4 These paramedics are attempting to secure a difficult airway. *Source:* Colin Bennett/Alamy.

medication error reporting program used by hospitals, but no such system is targeted to collect EMS data. The FDA accepts reports from consumers and health professionals about products regulated by the FDA, including drugs and medical devices, through MedWatch, the FDA's safety information and adverse event reporting program. To date MedWatch serves as the common ground between EMS and the rest of the medical community when it comes to reporting medical errors.

Several other organizations collect data on medical errors. The Department of Health and Human Services (HHS) issued the Patient Safety and Quality Improvement Final Rule (Patient Safety Rule) to implement the Patient Safety and Quality Improvement Act of 2005 (Patient Safety Act), which authorizes the creation of **patient-safety organizations (PSOs)**. The Agency for Healthcare Research and Quality administers the provisions of the Patient Safety Act and Patient Safety Rule. AHRQ is responsible for maintaining a list of those entities whose PSO certifications have been accepted in accordance with Section 3.104(a) of the Patient Safety Rule. In addition, AHRQ maintains a publicly available list of entities whose certifications as PSOs have been accepted as required by Section 3.104(d) of the Patient Safety Rule.

The Institute for Safe Medication Practices is a listed PSO and also accepts reports from consumers and health professionals related to medication error or reactions. The Institute publishes *Safe Medicine*, a consumer newsletter on medication errors. Each state maintains a list of PSOs with various affiliations.

ERRORS IN PEDIATRICS

A study reviewing the science pediatric medication errors in the December, 2010 *Journal of Pediatric Nursing* (Gonzales, 2010) found that problems due to medications occurred in 11 percent of children who were in the hospital and that 22 percent were preventable. Another study in the *Journal of the American Medical Association* found a rate of 55 medications errors per 100 pediatric admissions with three or more errors in 64 out of the 320 patients who had a medication error (Kaushal, Bates, Landrigan, et al., 2001). Children are also the victims of diagnostic errors, incorrect procedures or tests, infections, and injuries. Medical errors pose a greater threat to children than to adults for a number of reasons. Children are physically small, and their kidneys, liver, and immune system are still developing. Even a tiny increase in the dose of medication can have serious effects. When children take a turn for the worse, they can deteriorate more rapidly than adults. (See Figure 1.5.) Children also are less able to communicate what they are feeling, making it difficult to diagnose their problem or know when a symptom or complication develops. Adult medications are prepackaged and have standardized doses, but pediatric medications vary, based on the child's weight and sometimes height, requiring EMS providers and health care workers to make calculations. It is easy to misplace a decimal point—a tenfold error.

Best Practice

MedWatch

One best practice is to report malfunctions in EMS equipment or side effects from medications given in the prehospital setting through the FDA's MedWatch, which is available at 1-800-332-1088.

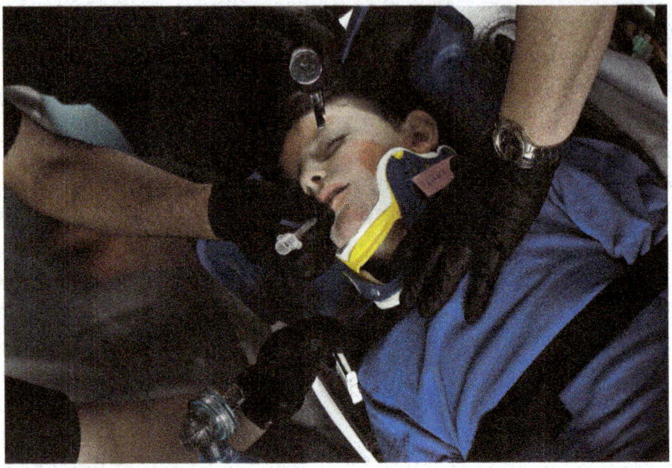

FIGURE 1.5 A paramedic intubates a child. *Source: Essentials of Paramedic Care 2nd Edition from Bledsoe, Cherry, Porter ISBN 0-13-171163-6*

CHAPTER REVIEW

Summary

It has been a long journey for EMS to arrive at a place in the medical hierarchy where we are being held to a set of performance standards and processes designed to create quality. Quality improvement is an organizational strategy with a clear focus on its purpose, a vector of measures on outcomes, and a leadership focus on creating and sustaining reliable processes that achieve desirable outcomes for the patient. Building and managing a quality improvement system is a mandated component in most EMS systems. Many oversight agencies, such as state, county, or local health districts or boards of health, require some sort of quality initiatives as a condition of accreditation or authorization to operate. Without measuring, EMS agencies cannot assess their effectiveness. In a modern EMS system, quality improvement must be linked to the education program. A medical error can occur without causing patient harm. Patient safety in EMS must be based on diagnosis and reliability of care through evidence-based protocols and continuous measurement of performance. Consider the adage "You can't manage what you don't measure." Quality improvement systems are a measure for proving that EMS gets it done.

WHAT WOULD YOU DO? Reflection

This scenario reflects the growing movement toward quality triggered by *To Err Is Human*, which encouraged all aspects of medicine to initiate quality improvement programs. Medical errors are common and have significant human and financial costs. A quality improvement program looks for causes and trends instead of identifying individual people.

In this scenario, applying a committee approach to find the solution and measuring the before and after effects provide validation. Often a team can find a better or optimal solution that is better than what management may identify. As the leader or manager responsible for quality, I would ensure that an educational program is tied to the data retrieved before and after performance once the employee-formulated solution was introduced. In addition, I would include the use of a checklist for chest pain, train on the five R's (right medication, right dose, right route, right indication, and right patient) of medication administration, and ensure performance through simulation. The checklist would follow the American Heart Association guidelines for what should occur with chest pain.

Many standards are now supported by evidence-based medicine. Encouraging employees to find solutions is often the most practical and most cost-effective route. Quality could be improved by providing information and then acting on it.

This is a diagnostic, fragmentation, and communication error. A treatment regimen was discounted, and the appreciation of the diagnosis was not communicated.

Review Questions

1. What simple solutions can an organization use to get started on a quality improvement initiative?
2. List the classifications of errors.
3. List the locations where a medical error may occur.
4. What are the key focus areas that emerging information indicates EMS needs to address?
5. What organizations collect error information and promote patient safety?
6. Identify operational areas in your organization that demonstrate normalization of deviance.

References

Agency for Healthcare Research and Quality. (2013, March). "Making Health Care Safer II: An Updated Critical Analysis of the Evidence for Patient Safety Practices." Rockville, MD: Author. Evidence Reports/Technology Assessments, No. 211.

Bigham, B. L., L. Morrison, J. Maher, S. C. Brooks, et al. (2010). "Patient Safety in Emergency Medical Services: Advancing and Aligning the Culture of Patient Safety in EMS." Edmonton, Alberta, Canada: Canadian Patient Safety Institute.

Bradley, E. H., L. Curry, and I. Horwitz. (2012, August 14). "Contemporary Evidence About Hospital Strategies for Reducing 30-Day Readmissions: A National Study." *Journal of the American College of Cardiology 60*(7), 607–614.

Encinosa, W. E., and F. J. Hellinger. (2008). "The Impact of Medical Errors on Ninety-Day Costs and Outcomes: An Examination of Surgical Patients." *Health Services Research 43*(6), 2067–2085.

Farley, D. O., S. C. Morton, C. L. Damberg, M. S. Ridgely, A. Fremont, M. D. Greenberg, et al. (2007). *Assessment of the AHRQ Patient Safety Initiative: Moving from Research to Practice Evaluation Report II (2003–2004).* Santa Monica, CA: RAND Corporation.

Gonzales, K. (2010, December). "Medication Administration Errors and the Pediatric Population: A Systematic Search of the

Literature." *Journal of Pediatric Nursing 25*(6), 555–565.

Institute of Medicine. (1990). *A National Strategy for Quality Assurance*, vol, II. Washington DC: National Academies Press.

Institute of Medicine. (1999). "To Err Is Human: Building a Safer Health System." Washington, DC: National Academies Press.

Institute of Medicine of the National Academies. (2006). *Future of Emergency Care: Emergency Medical Services at the Crossroads.* Washington, DC: National Academies Press.

Kaushal, R., D. W. Bates, C. Landrigan, et al. (2001). "Medication Errors and Adverse Drug Events in Pediatric Inpatients." *JAMA 285*(160), 2114–2120.

Lemonick, M. D. (1999, December 13). "Doctors' Deadly Mistakes." *Time 154*(24), 74–76.

Liberman, M. (1999). "Cardiopulmonary Resuscitation: Errors Made by Pre-hospital Emergency Medical Personnel." *Resuscitation 42*(1), 47–55.

McGlynn, E., S. Asch, J. Adams, et al. (2003). "The Quality of Health Care Delivered to Adults in the United States." *New England Journal of Medicine 348*, 2635–2645.

Ryan, T. J., J. L. Anderson, E. M. Antman, B. A. Braniff, N. H. Brooks, et al. "ACC/AHA Guidelines for the Management of Patients with Acute Myocardial Infarction: A Report of the American College of Cardiology/ American Heart Association Task Force on Practice Guidelines (Committee on Management of Acute Myocardial Infarction)." *Journal of the American College of Cardiology 28*, 1328–1428.

Shafrin, J. (2009, February 6). "Medical Errors and Ninety-Day Cost and Outcomes." *Healthcare Economist.*

Stella, J., A. Davis, P. Jennings, and B. Bartley. (2008). "Introduction of a Prehospital Critical Incident Monitoring System: Pilot Project Results." *Prehospital Disaster Medicine 23*(2), 154–160.

Van Rosse, F., B. Maat, C. M. Rademaker, A. J. Van Vught, A. C. Egbert, et al. (2009, April). "The Effects of Computerized Physician Order Entry on Medication Prescription Errors and Clinical Outcomes in Pediatric and Intensive Care: A Systematic Overview." *Pediatrics 123*(40), 1184–1190).

Vilke, G. M, S. V. Tornabene, B. Stepanski, and H. Shipp. (2006, October–December). "Paramedic Self-Reported Medication Errors." *Prehospital Emergency Care 10*(4), 457–462.

Vilke, G. M, S. V. Tornabene, B. Stepanski, et al. (2007). "Paramedic Self-Reported Medication Errors." *Prehospital Emergency Care 11*(1), 80–84.

Wang, H., J. Lave, C. Sirio, and D. Yealy. (2009). "Errors in Prehospital Endotracheal Intubation." Paper presented at the annual meeting of the National Association of EMS Physicians, Registry Resort, Naples, FL.

Wang, H. E., T. A. Sweeney, R. E. O'Conner, and H. Rubinstein. (2001, April–June). "Failed Pre-Hospital Intubations: An Analysis of Emergency Department Courses and Outcomes." *Prehospital Emergency Care 5*(2), 134–141.

Wolfe A. (2001, August). "Institute of Medicine Report: Crossing the Quality Chasm: A New Health Care System for the 21st Century." *Policy, Politics & Nursing Practice 2*, 233–235. doi:10.1177/152715440100200312

Zhan, C., and M. R. Miller. (2003). "Excess Length of Stay, Charges, and Mortality Attributable to Medical Injuries During Hospitalization." *Journal of the American Medical Association 290*(14), 1868–1874. doi:10.1001/jama.290.14.1868.

Key Terms

accountable care organizations Combinations of hospitals, primary care physicians, and possibly specialists associated with a defined population of patients accountable for the total Medicare spending of that patient population.

iatrogenic Induced inadvertently by the medical treatment or procedures or activity of a health care provider. The term is now applied to any adverse condition in a patient occurring as the result of treatment by a physician, nurse, or other health care professional, especially infections acquired by the patient during the course of treatment.

managed care Systems and techniques used to control the use of health care services, including reviews of medical necessity, incentives to use certain providers, and case management. It is a body of clinical, financial, and organizational activities designed to ensure the provision of appropriate health care services in a cost-efficient manner.

medical errors Errors or mistakes committed by health care professionals that result in harm to the patient. They include errors in diagnosis (diagnostic errors), delivery of drugs and other medications (medication errors), performance of procedures, use of other types of therapy, use of equipment, and interpretation of laboratory findings. Medical errors are differentiated from malpractice in that the former are regarded as honest mistakes or accidents, whereas the latter is the result of negligence, reprehensible ignorance, or criminal intent.

medication errors Any preventable events that may cause or lead to inappropriate medication use or patient harm while the medication is in the control of the health care professional, patient, or consumer. Such events may be related to professional practice, health care products, procedures, and systems, including prescribing; order communication; product labeling, packaging, and nomenclature; compounding; dispensing; distribution; administration; education; monitoring; and use.

normalization of deviance A long-term phenomenon in which individuals or teams repeatedly accept a lower standard of performance until that lower standard becomes the norm. Usually, the acceptance of the lower standard occurs because the individual or team is under pressure (budget, schedule, etc.) and perceives it will be too difficult to adhere to the expected standard.

patient-safety incidents (PSIs) Any unintended or unexpected incidents that could have or did lead to harm for one or more patients receiving health care.

patient-safety organizations (PSOs) Established under the Patient Safety and Quality Improvement Act of 2005, Pub. L. 109-41, 42 U.S.C. 299b-21—b-26 (Patient Safety Act). The Patient Safety and Quality Improvement final rule (Patient Safety Rule) establishes a framework by which hospitals, doctors, and other health care providers may voluntarily report information to PSOs, on a privileged and confidential basis, for the aggregation and analysis of patient safety events.

performance-based reimbursement Financial incentives based on the utilization of resources and application of procedures or medications as indicated by evidence-based medicine.

quality Subjective term for which each person has his own definition. In technical usage, quality can have two meanings: (1) the characteristics of a product or service that bear on its ability to satisfy stated or implied needs and (2) a product or service free of deficiencies.

quality improvement (QI) Actions taken to increase the value to the customer by improving the effectiveness and efficiency of processes and activities throughout the organizational structure.

quality improvement system A formalized system that documents the structure, process, and responsibilities required to achieve effective customer satisfaction or the delivery of quality products and services to the patient or the public.

quality gap Differences between health care processes or outcomes observed in practice and those thought to be achievable with the most current and effective professional knowledge.

quality of health care The degree to which health services for individuals and patient populations increase the likelihood of desirable health outcomes and are consistent with current professional knowledge.

CHAPTER 2

History of Quality in EMS

Objectives

After reading this chapter, the student should be able to:

2.1 Identify historical figures who have contributed to modern quality improvement initiatives.

2.2 Identify government structures that support and facilitate quality in EMS.

2.3 Create and identify the components of a key indicator.

2.4 Defend the use of or share quality improvement initiatives with private industry or trade groups.

2.5 Locate and review five major trade or government projects fostering quality improvement projects.

Key Terms

American National Standards Institute (ANSI)
DMAIC
DMADV
indicators
International Organization for Standardization (ISO)
metric
National Quality Forum (NQF)
peer review organizations (PROs)
quality assurance system
quality control
quality council
quality improvement (QI)
quality improvement organizations (QIOs)
quality management
quality planning
quantitative approach
Six Sigma
special cause variation
standard
Vital Few

WHAT WOULD YOU DO?

Justin Hemp is an EMS supervisor at the Trinity River Fire Department, which is a rural/suburban department providing advance life support ambulance service. Twice now his EMS chief has called to his attention that EMS supplies were not ordered on time. A recent call involving a sick child required an intraosseous (I/O) needle to gain vascular access. The first on-scene fire engine did not have the needle that showed on the inventory for the pediatric bag. Fortunately, the transport unit had the required equipment and arrived only a few minutes after the engine. Immediately, the I/O line was accessed and the child received the necessary medication and fluid.

After investigating the event, it turned out that the engine crew had used the equipment a week before and had not restocked the equipment. Furthermore, another crew had noticed it missing, but the supply cache at the station did not have an extra. A request had gone in for another needle, but the e-mail notification went to an EMS field supervisor who had been on vacation. The I/O needle is an expensive item available only through special order from an exclusive vendor.

Now in a shift meeting with his paramedics, Justin is detailing the problems with the supply chain. The chief had authorized a committee to streamline the supply chain and asked Justin to coordinate the efforts. Three paramedics on the shift volunteered to help: Eddie, who had been a supervisor at a Levi Strauss distribution center prior to his employment at the fire department; Mark, a former logistics officer in the military; and Scott, who had been a logistics section chief for Type III incident management and had worked several large wildland fires.

Within a month, each station had standardized vehicle and station inventories established as draft standard operating procedures (SOPs). A minimum and maximum amount of each product was listed with a computerized inventory that automatically e-mailed supply requests to a redundant chain of command. Redundancies in the supply chain were established, and mission-critical backup equipment was supplied in the EMS supervisor vehicles and the battalion chief office.

Questions

1. What do fire and EMS companies have to learn from other organizations' quality initiatives?
2. Do you know your staff members' experience with quality from other work venues?
3. What is the history of quality initiatives in your organization, your local government, and fire or EMS services?

INTRODUCTION

There is an increasing focus on quality throughout the United States. When talking about Total Quality Management, Continuous Quality Improvement, or any other name given to the quality movement, the common thread is meeting the needs of those who pay for and use the services and products provided by an organization. All types of industries, including health care, have lowered costs and improved the quality of their operations and products by working to meet the needs of the people they serve.

Many books have been written describing the philosophy and methods used in the quality movement. This section is not intended to be a substitute for those works but, rather, to provide a brief overview of **quality management** principles by reviewing the work of three leaders (Shewhart, Deming, and Juran) who have shaped the discipline. These three pioneers all stressed the importance of management awareness and leadership in promoting quality. Shewhart helped us understand variation, Deming provided the system of profound knowledge, and Juran introduced the concept of the quality trilogy.

> **Side Bar**
>
> **Westinghouse Studies**
>
> Beginning in the 1920s, physicists Walter Shewhart and W. Edward Deming, along with engineer Joseph Juran, developed the groundwork for modern quality improvement. They looked to improve American manufacturing by streamlining processes, minimizing errors, and creating new concepts such as data-driven decision making, reducing human error, and finding ways to get workers to commit to the quality of their processes. Walter Shewhart's work inspired Deming, and the two worked together in 1925 at Westinghouse.

ORIGINS OF QUALITY MANAGEMENT

The Industrial Revolution triggered the beginning of the study of management and the process of formalizing management theories and processes. By the early 1900s, many professors of modern management were advancing and proving theories of management. Fredrick Taylor's *Principles of Scientific Management* secured a place in history by becoming the mainstay of modern management. However, scientific management's sole focus on productivity (as exemplified by the Westinghouse studies) soon failed due to the lack of consideration of creativity and commitment on behalf of the employees. In most cases, it was found that people under scientific management produced more just because they were being watched. Productivity was the focus, and as soon as the employees realized that they were not being watched, production returned to the level prior to Taylor's inspection. Soon, specialties of management based in humanistic or behavioral science moved to the forefront. An entire generation of students in these studies was spawned.

Current efforts in quality management have their origins in the **quantitative approach** to management. Often called operations management, the quantitative approach uses information models, computer simulation, optimization models, and the application of statistics. Quantitative managers were developed during World War II to help maximize aircraft production and antisubmarine warfare. After the war, many of these managers went to work for major industries in the United States, bringing those principles from the military to the business world.

By the late 1960s, courses in operations management and statistics had become required in business schools and universities around the world. The work on quality of Joseph Juran and W. Edward Deming started to change business and government. Quality management and continuous improvement had entered the mainstream. As quality principles began to be taught and employed in business, industry, and the public sector, they became necessary for survival in a competitive environment.

WALTER SHEWHART

The American Society for Quality's first honorary member was Walter Shewhart, an engineer who successfully introduced into production the concept of variation. He brought together engineering, statistics, and economics to develop what is known today as quality control. Early on, Shewhart identified common cause variations or normal differences in production that often were time consuming, costly, and wasteful, yet not exactly worth management effort. More important, he described **special cause variation**. Special cause variation is a difference in outcome of a process that required investigation in order to ensure quality and maximize productivity. The lasting tool Shewhart gave to the field of quality was the control chart, which is often referred to as the Shewhart chart. The control chart is a statistical tool used to distinguish between process variation resulting from common causes and variation resulting from special causes. Control charts help in monitoring process variation over time, differentiating between special cause and common cause of variation, and communicating process performance. Shewhart was a statistician at Bell Laboratories, and he also held academic appointment and consulting positions with many educational and government institutions.

Shewhart was Deming's colleague and created the PDCA cycle: *P*lan, *D*o, *C*heck, and *A*ct. PDCA can be implemented in an EMS operation to improve quality and/or decrease the cost of providing services. After the plan is developed (Plan), it is put into action (Do), and then assessed to see if it worked (Check). The last step is to stabilize the improvement that occurred or to determine what went wrong if the anticipated gains do not materialize (Act). PDCA is a continuous cycle; any improvement realized by carrying out one PDCA cycle will become the baseline for an improvement target on the next PDCA cycle. The process of improvement is never ending, although the dramatic improvements of initial PDCA efforts may be hard to sustain. Shewhart's work on variation strongly influenced Deming, Juran, and Philip Crosby.

W. EDWARDS DEMING

Deming promoted his ideas of accuracy and obtaining quality data while working at the U.S. Census Bureau. His work in Japan in 1950 was instrumental in building the Japanese industry into an economic world power. His strongly humanistic philosophy is based on the idea that problems in a production process are due to flaws in the design of the system, as opposed to being rooted in the motivation or professional commitment of the workforce. Under Deming's approach, quality is maintained and improved when leaders, managers, and the workforce understand and commit to constant customer satisfaction through continuous quality improvement (QI). From his book *The New Economics*, Deming's approach became known as the System of Profound Knowledge. The system focused on understanding systems and variation, with psychological factors of change and incentives being core to Deming's approach and legacy.

Deming enhanced the PDCA cycle by substituting *S*tudy (S) for *C*heck (C), thereby creating the PDSA Cycle. Modern QI is still based on this cycle. Additional processes, such as performing a root cause analysis or studying variations in quality, now complement the PDSA cycle. Reviewing processes after the fact is seen predominantly as a quality assurance tool. Studying an item or process for variation has become the *S*tudy step, replacing the *C*heck step in the process of QI. The PDSA cycle, often called the Shewhart-Deming cycle, is now the mainstay in health care QI. Deming's famous 14 principles for transforming management practices can be applied to almost every aspect of EMS operations. (See Figure 2.1.)

Deming advocated using simple statistical techniques as the primary approach to

1. Create constancy of purpose for improvement of product and service.
2. Adopt the new philosophy of Total Quality.
3. Cease dependence on mass inspection.
4. End the practice of awarding business on price tag alone.
5. Improve constantly and forever the system of production and service.
6. Institute training.
7. Institute leadership
8. Drive out fear.
9. Break down barriers between staff areas.
10. Eliminate slogans, exhortations, and targets for the workforce.
11. Eliminate numerical quotas.
12. Remove barriers to pride of workmanship.
13. Institute a vigorous program of education and retraining.
14. Take action to accomplish the transformation.

FIGURE 2.1 Deming's Principles of Quality Management. *Source: Fire Administration by Bruegman & Lindsey, Figure 3.7 on pgs. 124–125*

improving performance. Shewhart later collaborated with Deming to measure data over time to identify common and special cause variations. This became one of Deming's key techniques for measuring and managing the two common types of variation.

When problems arise in EMS delivery, the causes should be verified by data. All human activity will contain variations in performance and some simple statistical analysis can reduce the inaccuracies. Random variations must be established for every EMS procedure or service.

JOSEPH JURAN

Joseph Juran was a Romanian immigrant who attended the University of Minnesota and obtained a degree in electrical engineering. While working, in 1936 he completed a law degree from Loyola University. Juran became interested in quality management. His approach was based on the idea that QI programs must reflect the strong interdependency that exists among all of the operations of an organization's production process. Juran wrote *The Quality Control Handbook*, which focused on freedom from deficiencies and product features that meet the customer's needs. To meet those goals, Juran outlined three concepts known as the Juran Trilogy that included quality planning, quality control, and quality improvement:

- **Quality planning** is a process in which the organization seeks to understand what the customer needs and designs all aspects of a system that is able to meet those needs reliably. Designing an EMS system to do anything less is wasteful because it does not meet patient needs.
- Once the system is put into operation, **quality control** is used to constantly monitor performance for compliance with the original design or performance standards. If performance falls short of the **standard**, plans are put into action to deal quickly with the problem. Quality control puts the system back into a state of control—that is, the way it was designed to operate.
- **Quality improvement** occurs when new, previously unattained levels of performance are achieved.

QI, as described by Juran, is about continuous QI throughout an organizational system. Juran also developed the idea of the **Vital Few** and the Useful Many, which helps prioritize the QI projects that should be undertaken. This concept was influenced by the work of an Italian economist named Vilfredo Pareto, who identified that the majority of the wealth is held by a minority of people. This became known as the Pareto Principle. Juran applied this principle to identify what to improve to make the biggest impact. In any organization, there will be a lengthy list of possible ideas for improvement. Resources to actually implement new ideas are limited; leaders must choose those vital few projects that will have the greatest impact on improving the ability to meet customer or system needs. The criteria for selecting QI projects includes the potential impact on meeting customer needs, cutting waste, or adding required resources vital to the project.

Juran also developed the idea of instituting a leadership group or quality council, consisting of the organization's senior executive staff. The **quality council** is typically charged with the responsibility of designing the overall strategy for quality planning, control, and improvement. Senior leadership involvement is a must since QI activities are as important as other management tasks (e.g., budgeting, human resource management, purchasing, and training). Leaders can integrate QI into every aspect of EMS operations.

OTHER EARLY CONTRIBUTORS TO THE FIELD

Phil Crosby was a hospital corpsman for the U.S. Navy. He was originally trained as a podiatrist, and then went to the Marines as a corpsman. After leaving the military, he worked for the Bendix Corporation as a quality engineer and joined the American Society of Quality. Crosby wrote a text, *Quality Is Free*, about the absence or lack of quality being costly to an organization—for example, in money spent on doing things wrong or inefficiently or in litigation. Crosby advocated that quality should occur primarily at the design phase. Instead of spending time and money on finding and fixing errors, organizational changes should encourage doing a job right the first time. Crosby developed an organizational approach that thinks about how processes can be designed or redesigned to reduce errors and defects to reach a goal of zero defects. Crosby believes managers' policies and actions indicate their commitment to quality. He also advocates a step-by-step approach for educating the entire workforce about quality principles, extensive measurement to document system failures, and formal programs to redesign faulty production processes. He developed pragmatic concepts, including his Four Absolutes of Quality Management, which are considered foundational elements of the body of quality knowledge. (See Figure 2.2.)

- Quality means conformance to requirements, not goodness.
- Quality is achieved by prevention, not appraisal.
- Quality has a performance standard of zero defects, not acceptable quality levels.
- Quality is measured by the Price of Nonconformance,™ not indexes.

FIGURE 2.2 Crosby's Four Absolutes of Quality Management. *Source: Text compiled by author*

One of Deming's colleagues in Japan was Kaoro Ishikawa, a management analyst who insisted that quality could always go one step further. According to Ishikawa, quality was a continuous process. Ishikawa developed the cause-and-effect diagram that is often called a fishbone diagram or Ishikawa diagram. It allows a user to see all of the potential causes of a result and hopefully find the root cause of the process's lack of quality. This provided quality from the bottom up. Ishikawa focused on seven quality tools: a cause-and-effect diagram, control chart, run chart, histogram, scatter chart, Pareto chart, and flowchart. Ishikawa noted that quality must be focused on the life cycle of the product or service.

SIX SIGMA

Six Sigma is a methodology that provides tools to improve the capability of business processes or EMS operations. It is based on an increase in performance and a decrease in variations, which lead to defect reduction and improvements in employee morale and the quality of the product or service. Sigma is the name of the Greek symbol for standard deviation around the mean of a population. Six Sigma is a measurement-based strategy for process improvement and problem reduction completed through the application of improvement projects. This is accomplished through two Six Sigma models:

- **DMAIC** (*D*efine, *M*easure, *A*nalyze, *I*mprove, *C*ontrol) is an improvement system for existing processes falling below specification and seeking incremental improvement.
- **DMADV** (*D*efine, *M*easure, *A*nalyze, *D*esign, *V*erify) is an improvement system used to develop new processor products at Six Sigma quality levels.

The origins of Six Sigma as a measurement standard for quality can be traced back to Carl Gauss. Gauss introduced the concept of the normal curve in which 65 percent of the measurements should fall within a standard deviation of the center of the normal curve. This is known as a Gaussian distribution. This distribution relies on two parameters that relate to EMS quality or overall quality: a location on a control chart, most commonly the mean, and a scale, most commonly the variance.

Six Sigma as a measurement standard in product variation can be traced back to the 1920s when Walter Shewhart first showed that three sigma from the mean is the point where a system requires correction in the process and then tied this to an economic model. Although an interesting economic model for quality and measuring variation, it did not take hold in industry until 1986 when it was adopted with success at Motorola.

Hundreds of organizations around the world have adopted Six Sigma as a way of doing business. Several EMS organizations have embraced the Six Sigma concept for emergency operations. Six Sigma has evolved over time and is more than just a quality system, like total quality management (TQM) or **International Organization for Standardization (ISO)**. Six Sigma can be a vision, philosophy, symbol, **metric**, goal, or methodology.

Best Practice

Memphis Fire Department and FedEx

In 1992, the Memphis Fire Department's EMS division began its journey with state-mandated quality assurance. This type of quality enhancement tool was regarded by field providers as punitive in nature, rather than as a tool for assurance and not improvement. This Memphis FD quality improvement system was dysfunctional: It had no field supervision, no active education or training dedicated to improving the providers identified in the quality assurance process, and no active medical direction.

With new leadership in place, Memphis Fire reanalyzed and overhauled its quality improvement efforts. Mike Taigman, an EMS leader in quality improvement, was consulted and provided advice on restructuring processes and developing a quality vision. Memphis Fire was providing service to its citizens that seemed to improve on the surface, but data continued to show that efforts were not equating to system change. A piece of the puzzle was still missing.

The answer was discovered right in Memphis's own backyard. FedEx is a leader in quality customer service and the first service-based recipient of the Malcolm Baldrige Award. With some facilitation by Taigman, Memphis Fire soon was at the table and briefing the FedEx team on its processes. Each month, the Memphis Fire QI team would gather data, identify issues, consult with providers, and share information with the EMS field officers, yet it had reached an unsurpassable ceiling. FedEx conveyed the same experience with some of the obstacles early on in its quality model.

FedEx's solution was to procure buy-in from the top down to facilitate ownership. The CEO required each division to bring its data related to that month's quality indicator. At each meeting, the division and data were revealed for each area's productivity and customer satisfaction. The CEO asked the divisions to take the information back to their areas and return to the next meeting with root causes for deficiencies and solutions for improvement. The FedEx QI team working with the Memphis Fire QI team was able to increase protocol compliance by 30 percent in less than 3 months. Combined efforts between Memphis Fire and FedEx continue, demonstrating what a fire department can learn from a private industry that has a long history of developing quality service.

LEAN

Regardless of the approach to QI, the underlying theory of the system of profound knowledge remains a constant since the 1950s. Lean as a quality process came on the scene in 1990 in a book entitled *The Machine That Changed the World*. In 1996, it was developed into a book entitled *Lean Thinking* (Womack and Jones, 1996). Five core principles translate into the Lean process:

1. Specify the value desired by the customer.
2. Identify all the steps in the value stream for each product or service, eliminating whatever steps do not necessarily create value or quality.
3. Make the product or service flow smoothly through the remaining value-added systems.
4. As the flow of the process is introduced, allow the customer to pull between all steps where continuous flow is possible in the process.
5. Manage toward perfection so that the number of steps and the amount of time and information needed to serve the customer continuously falls.

> **Side Bar**
>
> **Six Sigma**
>
> Six Sigma is a federally registered trademark of Motorola. The process was named by Bill Smith, an engineer at Motorola. Although the principles and concepts were developed by Gauss and Shewhart, it was Motorola that made it work and patented the process.

A value stream is a sequence of activities required to design, produce, and provide a specific good or service, and along which information, materials, and worth flow.

Lean is used by Toyota in the assembly process; however, it has become an excellent tool for the service industry and translates well into health care and government.

NATIONAL MOVEMENTS

Quickly, industry and government recognized the need to produce quality goods and services to ensure the best possible product or service. It became expensive to recall a product and even worse to be sued or have litigation due a service or product of poor quality. Many organizations, trade groups, or standard-setting organizations began to develop quality processes and standards often very specific to the their trade, product line, or service.

INTERNATIONAL ORGANIZATION FOR STANDARDIZATION

A series of important standards known as ISO 9000 originated within the British defense procurement system as an inspection-oriented system. In 1968, the British Ministry of Technology, which handled defense material specifications and procurement, produced one of the most innovative quality systems designed to ensure a reduction in variations in the process of specification of military parts and supplies. This was done to standardize and ensure quality in NATO military equipment. Known as AvP92, the system covered the entire spectrum of the contractor's operation, from design to delivery. When it became apparent that European manufacturers were positioned to gain from a standardized system of quality, the United States entered into the system. The result was ISO 9000, first published in 1987 by ISO. The **American National Standards Institute (ANSI)** is the U.S. member body to ISO. Standards developed by ISO are voluntarily adopted. There are no legal requirements for countries to adopt them. These generic standards for quality management and quality assurance are applicable to all types of companies—large and small—in all sectors of the economy.

> **Side Bar**
>
> **ISO 9000**
>
> The letters in "ISO 9000" should not be confused as an acronym for "Insurance Services Organization," which is an organization that rates fire protection in communities.

The five documents of the ISO 9000 series are internationally recognized, fostering both common language and global trade. As of 1994, seventy-four countries had adopted the ISO 9000 series as a national standard. In addition, government agencies around the world are beginning to use the ISO 9000 series. ISO clarifies terms that are often used interchangeably, such as the following:

- *Accreditation*—procedure by which an authoritative body gives formal recognition that a body or person is competent to carry out specific tasks
- *Certification*—procedure by which a third party gives written assurance that a product, process, or service conforms to specific requirements
- *Registration*—procedure by which a body indicates relevant characteristics of a product, process, or service, or particulars of a body or person, and then includes or registers the product, process, or service in an appropriate publicly available list

The Role of ISO 9000

The ISO 9000 series standards provide direction for suppliers of all types of products who want to put into practice effective quality systems in their organizations or to improve their existing quality system. In December 2000, the ISO merged ISO 9001, ISO 9002, and ISO 9003 into a revised ISO 9001 standard. The latest standard is the ISO 9001:2008. Everything from ambulance construction to the delivery of EMS in the field to the procurement of communication equipment has an ISO 9000 application. The standards also provide common requirements against which an EMS provider, community, or patient can evaluate the adequacy of a supplier's quality system. As a general rule, all of the standards related to quality are commonly referred to as the ISO 9000 series.

The ISO 9000 Series and Standards

The basic ISO 9000 series and supporting standards consist of the following documents:

- *ISO 9001:2008*—Quality management systems. Requirements.
- *ISO 9004:2009*—Managing for the sustained success of an organization. A quality management approach.
- *ISO 10005:2005*—Quality management systems. Guidelines for quality plans.
- *ISO 10007:2003*—Quality management systems. Guidelines for configuration management.

The 9001:2008 standard encompasses five sections. Because the standard is for any operation providing services or products, the concepts are broad. These concepts can thus serve as a framework for providing confidence to customers or the public that the EMS organization serves. The following are the major sections in the ISO 9001 standard:

- *Section 1: Quality Management Systems*—This section identifies processes and the sequence for their interaction. It outlines how these should be measured and controlled, with an emphasis on supporting and monitoring processes for continuous improvement.
- *Section 2: Management Responsibilities*—This section details the management necessary for supporting quality and reinforcing the processes that the organization has adopted for quality. This includes establishing responsibilities and assigning authority.
- *Section 3: Resource Management*—This section defines resources (e.g., training, facilities, and equipment) necessary for quality systems.
- *Section 4: Product Realization*—This section explores the sequence of processes and subprocesses required to achieve the products or services. This includes how design, implementation, and testing meet the needs of the customer or the system.
- *Section 5: Measurement, Analysis, and Improvement*—This section outlines the audits, monitoring, and collection of facts that outline the quality of the service or product. These processes must be defined, planned, and implemented.

The ISO 9001:2008 guidelines ensure that EMS organizations provide a satisfactory product or service. Standards 9001, 9004, 10005, and 10007 are guidance standards. They are descriptive documents, not prescriptive requirements, providing guidance to all organizations for quality management purposes. The documents are used for internal quality assurance to support activities aimed at providing confidence to the management of an organization that the intended quality is being achieved.

The ISO series supports a definition of quality that refers to "fitness for use" or "fitness for purpose" in a product or service. The ISO 9000 standards indicate that a quality system is the organizational structure, responsibilities, procedures, processes, and resources needed to implement quality management. The ISO 9000 series is based on the idea of building quality into every aspect of the enterprise with an integrated quality management system.

Under the ISO 9000 standard, quality management is referred to as "all activities of the overall management function that determine the quality policy, objectives, and responsibilities and implement them by means such as quality planning, quality control, quality assurance, and quality improvement within the quality system" (Stamatis, 2003, p. 518). The ISO 9000 series indicates that quality assurance includes well planned and systematic activities implemented within the quality system and demonstrated as needed to provide adequate confidence that an entity will fulfill requirements for quality. An entity can be a process, a product, an organization, a system, a person, or any combination of these. The purpose of the **quality assurance system** is to prevent problems from occurring, detect them when they do occur, identify causes, remedy causes, and prevent reoccurrence. Standards in the ISO 9000 series are not product standards. The series does not include any technical requirements. The standards are considered complementary to, but not substitutes for, distinct product technical requirements.

Supporting ISO Standards

The ISO 9001:2008 standard requires an organization to document what it does, do what it documents, review the process, and change it when necessary. These requirements do not constitute a full-fledged TQM system; rather, they provide the building blocks for such a system. ISO 9004:2009 *Managing for the Sustained Success of an Organization* is a supporting document that helps an organization define a quality management approach.

ISO 10005:2005 *Quality Management Systems—Guidelines for Quality Plans* is for organizations looking to make a complete plan for implementation of processes that support a comprehensive plan. ISO 10007:2003 *Quality Management Systems—Guidelines for Configuration Management* outlines the management structure necessary for implementing and supporting a QI plan and process.

HISTORY OF EMS-RELATED QI

The push for quality in EMS has largely been driven by physician groups affiliated with EMS. To date, most EMS organizations operate as chart reviewers; rarely are they looking at variations or trending the activities. Real QI has escaped EMS for decades. The National Highway Traffic Administration (NHTSA) and a few academic centers, such as the David Geffen School of Medicine at UCLA, have striven to take EMS QI to the next level by teaching and promoting research in EMS.

PHYSICIAN GROUPS

Physician groups have a long-standing history of developing and participating in EMS quality initiatives. Physician medical directors are commonly responsible for quality in most EMS organizations. Many of the policies and national initiatives are generated by one of three physician associations or by research generated by medical directors.

National Association of EMS Physicians

Since 1984, the National Association of EMS Physicians (NAEMSP) has been the largest contributor to the field of QI in EMS. In 1991, NAEMSP sponsored a conference on quality assurance in EMS to examine EMS quality activities. As a result of this conference, the first textbook on EMS quality, *Quality Assurance in Pre-Hospital Care*, was published (1983). For over a decade, NAEMSP has updated and published the textbook *Improving Quality in EMS*.

NAEMSP has been on the forefront of the many procedural and data collection processes associated with EMS. Major projects on airway management, cardiac and stroke care, and emergency medical dispatch have been started by NAEMSP. The key research material presented to the EMS community has been distributed through *Prehospital Emergency Care*, the official journal of NAEMSP. This journal presents several topics that are related to or are direct processes that apply to QI processes in every aspect of EMS. NAEMSP also produces a medical directors' course intended to promote quality management in clinical operations.

American College of Emergency Physicians

The American College of Emergency Physicians (ACEP) has maintained a long-standing section and committee within ACEP focused on the study of the delivery of quality medicine. ACEP published one of the first textbooks on quality in EMS, *Continuous Quality Improvement in EMS*. ACEP's Quality and Performance Committee develops and submits recommendations to the ACEP board of directors that protect and enhance those areas of emergency medicine impacted by quality of care/performance measures. ACEP participates in developing quality measures that have relevance to the practice of emergency medicine. ACEP works to educate members regarding the Physician Quality Reporting Initiatives (PQRI) and other federally based programs affecting emergency physician reimbursement. The Quality and Performance Committee (QPC) works with the Quality Improvement and Patient Safety Section (QIPS) to develop a curriculum for teaching quality to emergency medicine residents and medical students. QIPS also works to improve the quality of patient care and patient safety in local hospitals and communities across the United States.

Society for Academic Emergency Medicine

The Society for Academic Emergency Medicine (SAEM) was formed in 1989 by a group of physicians with strong research backgrounds to improve the care of acutely ill and injured patients. SAEM is a combined effort of the University Association for Emergency Medicine (UAEM) and the Society of Teachers of Emergency Medicine (STEM). For over twenty years, STEM and UAEM have helped shape the field of emergency medicine by shaping education and investigation in this dynamic field.

Much of SAEM's activities are devoted to improving research and education. SAEM influences health policy, publications, interorganizational collaboration, policy development, and services for physicians, teachers, researchers, and students. SAEM represents excellence and leadership in academic emergency medicine. Its values include idealism and quality in all endeavors; nurturing, camaraderie, and diversity among members; and creative and symbiotic interactions with other organizations. SAEM publishes a peer-reviewed journal, *Academic Emergency Medicine* (AEM) that provides information relevant to the practice, educational advancement, and investigation of emergency medicine.

GOVERNMENT EMS QUALITY

Since the enactment of the National Highway Safety Act of 1966, EMS has been designed to deliver quality care and to reduce death and disability. The Malcolm Baldrige National Quality Award was established in 1987 through federal legislation to promote the awareness of quality and foster best practices. In 1994, the Baldrige Award launched a special initiative in 1994 to extend the program to health care. Further government efforts, as detailed in the Patient Protection and Affordable Care Act Health Care and Education Reconciliation Act of 2010, look to link reimbursement to quality medicine and patient outcomes.

U.S. PUBLIC HEALTH SYSTEM

The U.S. Public Health Service Act (Section 1201(1)) defines an emergency medical services system as "a system that provides for the arrangement of personnel, facilities, and equipment for the effective and coordinated delivery in an appropriate geographic area of health care services under emergency conditions (occurring either as a result of the patient's condition or of natural disasters or similar conditions) and which is administered by a public or nonprofit private entity which has the authority and the resources to provide effective administration of the system."

When it became apparent that it was necessary to improve emergency medical services, Congress added the Emergency Medical Services (EMS) Systems Act of 1973 (42 U.S.C. 300d) to the Public Health Service Act. The EMS Systems Act promoted development of comprehensive regional EMS systems. The act also provided that all federal EMS-related programs be coordinated through the Interagency Committee on Emergency Medical Services. Under the act, comprehensive regional systems were to have adequate medical staff, emergency facilities, transportation equipment, and other resources to provide needed emergency care to all persons in the system's service area. EMS systems were to be administered by a single public or nonprofit private entity. Requests for emergency care were to be handled by a central communications system that linked all of the system's resources. To receive federal funding under

- Communications
- Training
- Manpower
- Mutual aid
- Transportation
- Accessibility
- Facilities
- Critical care units
- Transfer of care
- Consumer participation
- Public education
- Public safety agencies
- Standard medical records
- Independent review and evaluation
- Disaster linkage

FIGURE 2.3 Original components of an EMS system (1973). *Source: EMS Systems Act*

- Integration of health care services
- EMS research
- Legislation and regulation
- System finance
- Human resources
- Medical direction
- Education systems
- Public education
- Prevention
- Public access
- Communication systems
- Clinical care
- Information systems
- Evaluation

FIGURE 2.4 Fourteen attributes of emergency medical services. *Source: EMS Agenda for the Future (1996).*

the EMS act, regional systems were required to meet certain requirements regarding fifteen mandatory system elements. (See Figure 2.3.)

DEPARTMENT OF TRANSPORTATION/ NATIONAL HIGHWAY TRAFFIC SAFETY ADMINISTRATION

A more modern view of the components of an EMS system were updated by the Department of Transportation (DOT) and the National Highway Traffic Safety Division in 1996. This was a significant step in integrating EMS into the health care system and designing the system for a quality approach to EMS. The *EMS Agenda for the Future* narrowed the focus of the national EMS activities from the EMS Systems Act's fifteen components to fourteen attributes. (See Figure 2.4.) This was based on redesigning EMS to more fully integrate into the health care system and making it a more community-based organization. All of these functions integrate in the system design through the phases of an EMS response.

As EMS systems are modified for the future, they will look longitudinally at the patient. The effectiveness of an EMS system is to be measured in a research phase at the beginning of the system and in an evaluation phase at the end of the system. Quality of the system is measured by the impact it has on the movement of the patient through the health care system.

To address the mechanics of that quality, the NHTSA published *A Leadership Guide to Quality Improvement for Emergency Medical Services (EMS) Systems* (1997). This was the first document detailing the process for QI in the EMS. NHTSA sponsored several training session to spread learning about QI based on the guide.

Given the rate of expansion in health care cost and the lack of data regarding the effectiveness of EMS practices, emphasis has been placed on demonstrating which clinical and operational interventions can be shown to improve patient outcomes in EMS systems. NHTSA funded a study to examine patient outcomes within EMS systems. In 2001, NHTSA's Office of EMS and the Health Resources and

Services Administration (HRSA) together sponsored the development of the *National EMS Research Agenda.* This report highlighted the lack of evidence available to validate many clinical practices in the field and detailed an agenda for building the research base.

The NHTSA's Office of EMS also currently funds two key research initiatives, one of which is the Emergency Medical Services Outcomes Project (EMSOP), a study on developing metrics for use in EMS-related research. EMSOP was designed to develop a foundation and framework for out-of-hospital outcomes research—a branch of clinical research that focuses on determining whether interventions performed in clinical practice actually work. EMSOP's work resulted in a series of four journal articles outlining the key components of the framework for outcomes research:

1. Specific patient conditions that should take precedence in EMS outcomes research
2. Methodologically acceptable outcome models, including the Episode of Care model
3. Core risk-adjustment measures
4. Specific issues related to pain measurement

The Emergency Medical Services Cost Analysis Project (EMSCAP) is another study that develops metrics for assessing the costs and benefits of EMS.

NHTSA and HRSA also co-sponsor the National EMS Information System (NEMSIS), which is a national database on EMS systems and outcomes. NHTSA's Office of Human-Centered Research sponsors the Crash Injury Research and Engineering Network (CIREN), which collects and shares detailed research data on automobile crashes and patient outcomes.

EMS FOR CHILDREN

Under the supervision of the EMS for Children (EMS-C) is the National EMSC Data Analysis Resource Center NEDARC, a technical resource for EMS-C grantees and state EMS offices. This center focuses on developing organizational capabilities to collect, analyze, and utilize EMS and other health care data, with the ultimate goal of improving the quality of care provided by state EMS and trauma systems. Established in 1995, NEDARC assists EMS offices in establishing research designs, determining what data to collect, selecting a collection tool, storing the data, overcoming barriers to collection, coordinating data from other systems or agencies, converting data to a standard dictionary, formatting data to conform to a data model, and cleaning or standardizing and aggregating them. NEDARC also assists in disseminating model data systems from states that have developed such systems.

AGENCY FOR HEALTH CARE RESEARCH AND QUALITY

The Agency for Healthcare Research and Quality (AHRQ) was created in 1989 as the lead federal agency charged with improving the quality, safety, efficiency, and effectiveness of health care for all Americans. As one of twelve agencies within the Department of Health and Human Services (HHS), AHRQ supports health services research that will improve the quality of health care and promote evidence-based decision making. The goal of the AHRQ is to promote measurable improvements in the quality of health care in America, gauged in terms of improved quality of life and patient outcomes, lives saved, and value gained for what is spent in the health care system. The AHRQ was reauthorized in 1999 and tasked with the following strategies:

- Support improvements in health outcomes
- Strengthen quality measurement and improvement
- Identify strategies that improve access, foster appropriate use, and reduce unnecessary expenditures
- Improve the quality of health care

- Promote patient safety and reduce medical errors
- Advance the use of information technology for coordinating patient care and conducting quality and outcomes research

Within the umbrella of the AHRQ is the Quality Interagency Coordination Task Force (QuIC). The QuIC was established in 1998 in accordance with a presidential directive during the Clinton administration. The purpose of the QuIC was to ensure that all federal agencies involved in purchasing, providing, studying, or regulating health care services were working in a coordinated manner toward the common goal of improving quality care. The QuIC was directed to collaborate on goals, models, and timetables that are consistent with the Quality Commission's six National Aims for Improvement:

- Reducing the underlying causes of illness, injury, and disability
- Reducing health care errors
- Ensuring the appropriate use of health care service
- Expanding research on effectiveness of treatments
- Addressing oversupply and undersupply of health care resources
- Increasing patient participation in their own care

INSTITUTE OF MEDICINE

The Institute of Medicine (IOM) is an independent, nonprofit organization that works outside of government to provide unbiased and authoritative advice to decision makers and the public. The IOM was established in 1970 as the health arm of the National Academy of Sciences, which was chartered under President Abraham Lincoln in 1863. A series of reports from the IOM have addressed quality issues in EMS. The IOM defines quality as the degree to which health services for individuals and populations increase the likelihood of desired health outcomes and are consistent with current professional knowledge.

In 1999, the IOM produced a book entitled *To Err is Human*, which detailed the problem of human errors in medicine. Congress soon launched a series of hearings on patient safety, and in December 2000 it appropriated $50 million to the AHRQ to support a variety of efforts targeted at reducing medical errors. The AHRQ already has made major progress in developing and implementing an action plan. Efforts under way include these:

- Developing and testing new technologies to reduce medical errors
- Conducting large-scale demonstration projects to test safety interventions and error-reporting strategies
- Supporting new and established multidisciplinary teams of researchers and health care facilities and organizations, located in geographically diverse locations, that will further determine the causes of medical errors and develop new knowledge that will aid the work of the demonstration projects
- Supporting projects aimed at achieving a better understanding of how the environment in which care is provided affects the ability of providers to improve safety
- Funding researchers and organizations to develop, demonstrate, and evaluate new approaches to improving provider education in order to reduce errors.

NATIONAL EMS INFORMATION SYSTEM

The National Association of State EMS Directors, in conjunction with its federal partners at the NHTSA and the Trauma/EMS Systems program of the HRSA's Maternal Child Health Bureau, in 2001 began to develop the national EMS database known as NEMSIS. NEMSIS resides or is controlled at local, state, and national levels. The purpose of NEMSIS is to evaluate patient and EMS system outcomes, facilitate research, and develop nationwide EMS training curriculum.

This system is easily integrated with EMS patient/run records and can be routinely used for performance measurement and EMS research. NEMSIS starts by collecting data from medical devices such as cardiac monitors, 9-1-1 computer systems, and patient monitors (e.g., implantable defibrillators and insulin pumps). Information is then collected from local agency patient care reports (PCRs) and keyed into XML or Health 7-standard software that is compatible with the state's EMS database. The state database then can either transfer the data back to the agency or up to a national database in the same XML format. EMS services and hospitals can be linked with local, state, and national databases and the trauma registry to enable data to flow both ways. Even the smallest EMS agency can report in by phone or online. This type of pooled data can be used to evaluate the clinical care provided to the patients. NEMSIS uses performance **indicators** defined in NHTSA's *Guide to Performance Measures*, which is based on the Uniform Prehospital Dataset definitions. Version 3.3.0 is the latest data set available, as of 2013, in a computer format in Health Level 7. The NHTSA uniform data set version 2.2 or 3.3 is available through various venders and has fifty-two participating states and U.S. territories. NHTSA, HRSA (EMSC), and the Centers for Disease Control and Prevention (CDC) provide funding to create the NEMSIS Technical Assistance Center. Through a contract, the University of Utah School of Medicine operates the NEMSIS Technical Assistance Center. Utah partners with the University of North Carolina to handle all customer service needs.

REIMBURSEMENT, PATIENT SAFETY, AND OUTCOMES

There is much federal activity surrounding performance improvement, QI, benchmarking, and indicator development. There is also some activity within EMS in these arenas with development of NEMSIS and the National EMS Performance Measures Project. However, EMS is behind the curve when compared to other sectors of the health care community.

In March 2005, the Medicare Payment Advisory Commission (MedPAC) advised Congress that it needs to adopt "pay for performance" programs for hospitals and other specified care providers, stating, "Medicare payment systems are neutral and sometimes negative toward quality" (Milgate and Cheng, 2006). It advises Congress to support methods that measure quality-enhancing activities that are supported by information technology. MedPAC did not, at that time, include the EMS industry within the list of providers to move to pay for performance.

The 2005 meeting focused on identifying a limited set of performance measures for the EMS industry. A pilot set of indicators that can be derived from the data elements included in the NEMSIS data set was established. It encouraged the National EMS Performance Measures Project, the Open Source EMS Initiative, and other similar efforts to continue to develop EMS industry consensus on additional clinical and operational performance indicators. In May 2012, a report from the National EMS Advisory Council warned of the impending influence of MedPAC on ambulance reimbursement and lack of a clear path to assess quality as it had been applied to other aspects of medicine.

MALCOLM BALDRIGE AWARD

The highest standard of performance in medical quality is acknowledged each year. The Malcolm Baldrige Quality Award is bestowed on four different industries: manufacturing, health care, education, and service. Modeled after Japan's famous Deming Prize, this national award recognizes achievements in quality and is the model for most state quality awards. The award is managed by the U.S. Department of Commerce's National Institute of Standards and Technology and is presented by the president of the United States. The Baldrige program identifies seven key action areas or categories:

- *Leadership* involves senior leadership and management leading by example to integrate QI into the strategic planning process and throughout the entire organization and to promote quality values and QI techniques in work practices.
- *Information and Analysis* addresses managing and using the data needed for effective QI. Since QI is based on management by fact, information and analyses are critical to QI success.
- *Strategic Quality Planning* involves three major components: (1) developing long- and short-term organizational objectives for structural, performance, and outcome quality standards; (2) identifying ways to achieve those objectives; and (3) measuring the effectiveness of the system in achieving quality standards.
- *Human Resource Development and Management* works toward developing the full potential of the EMS workforce. This effort is guided by the principle that the entire EMS workforce is motivated to achieve new levels of service and value.
- *EMS Process Management* focuses on the creation and maintenance of high-quality services. Within the context of QI, process management refers to the improvement of work activities and work flow across functional or department boundaries.
- *EMS System Results* entails assessing the quality results achieved and examining the organization's success at achieving QI.
- *Satisfaction of Patients and Other Stakeholders* ensures ongoing satisfaction by those internal and external to the EMS system.

Side Bar

State Quality Awards

The Emergency Medical Service Authority of Tulsa and Oklahoma and Sunstar in Florida have won state quality awards similar to the Malcolm Baldrige National Quality Award.

Health care organizations that follow the Baldrige program can ask for an external review of their progress. Applying the Baldrige guidelines and recommendations can result in improvements in service and patient care delivery; economic efficiency and/or profitability; patient and community satisfaction and loyalty; and health outcomes. For more information regarding the Malcolm Baldrige National Quality Award, contact the National Institute of Standards and Technology.

TRADE GROUPS AND QUALITY

Several trade groups have weighed in on EMS quality. Labor groups also have an interest in EMS quality as it relates to working conditions and potential discipline. Several associations that specify standards have encompassed quality within larger standards dealing with overall EMS operations, with ambulance or fire service accreditation, and in attempts to define working conditions in EMS. Many of the measurements have been well developed. Trade and association groups have made significant contributions to EMS quality standards and measurements.

INTERNATIONAL ASSOCIATION OF FIREFIGHTERS

The International Association of Firefighters (IAFF) and the International Association of Fire Chiefs funded a 4-year study to define quality indicators and field-test a set of performance indicators. The system outcomes to be measured assess if the components of the EMS system function in an integrated manner so as to achieve outcomes for the patient. An example of a patient may be that a chest pain patient reports pain relief and normal vital signs upon arrival at the hospital. The IAFF conducted a focus group to identify sixteen key performance indicators with twenty-seven different measures.

Response times have been defined by the National Fire Protection Association in NFPA 450 Guide for Emergency Medical Services and Systems; NFPA 1710 Standards for the Organization and Deployment of Fire Suppression Operations, Emergency Medical Operations, and Special Operations to the Public by Career Fire Departments; and the Committee on Accreditation of Ambulance Services. Each of these indicators has a definition, key terms relevant to the definition of the indicator, and the basis for why each indicator is linked to a specific concept of quality. The rationale is included to help to validate the indicator. A goal was set for each of the indicators. Its process was validated, field-tested, and edited by a consensus group.

NFPA 450

The NFPA 450 Guide for Emergency Medical Services and Systems, 2013 Edition, addressed quality management, clinical quality, and data reliability in Chapter 8. Within Chapter 8 of NFPA 450, a primary focus calls for a quality management program and performance objectives to be established and include a complete system review. Benchmarking is to be based on public health outcomes with physician participation. Patient confidentiality and Health Insurance Portability and Accountability Act (HIPAA) are important components of the QI system. The standard also details how to process complaints. Participating in studies and research is required in the NFPA standard. Unique to the standard is the standardization of the clocks involved with an EMS response. All of these subsections in the quality management chapter require adequate documentation.

VOLUNTEER AND COMBINATION OFFICERS SECTION

The Volunteer and Combination Officers section (VCOS) of the International Association of Fire Chiefs (IAFC) has also produced a document that includes the basics of QI. Very little information or research is available on QI activities. The Rural Health Care Association is also attempting to increase the QI initiatives for rural EMS providers. In very simplistic terms, a clear distinction is made between quality assurance and QI and how to transition a combination department's strategic plan for EMS response.

NATIONAL ASSOCIATION OF EMS OFFICIALS

The National Association of EMS Officials (NAEMSO) has been a leader in creating a common set of performance measures. In 2002, NAEMSO (then known as the National Association of State EMS Directors) and the National Association of EMS Physicians (NAEMSP) held a leadership forum sponsored by NHTSA and HRSA to facilitate the EMS Outcomes project. The goal of the project was to develop a common set of specifically defined measures. The task was to distill over 125 proposed performance standards and what those measures would be. The results were thirty-five consensus-based measures.

Each measure is presented in a format developed to be comparable somewhere else in the health care system, which is anticipated to assist EMS providers and systems with future performance reporting, research, and reimbursement issues. Users are encouraged to focus on the measures, formulas, and data elements necessary to implement the measures. The measures have been categorized by characteristic or operational area (e.g., "finance and funding" and "response") for reference purposes. The following is a list of the categories:

- System Design and Structure
- Human Resources (culture, training, safety, credentialing, etc.)
- Clinical Care and Outcome
- Response
- Finance/Funding
- Quality Management
- Community Demographics

Three of the thirty-five measures are awaiting future development and one, though immediately implemental, requires further coordination of data elements between two ongoing processes: the EMS prehospital data set and the nationally standardized field trauma triage criteria. Figure 2.5 is a performance measure example for assessing the consistency of chest pain patients receiving a 12-lead EKG.

NATIONAL EMS MANAGEMENT ASSOCIATION

The National EMS Management Association (NEMSMA) is a supporting agency to the National EMS Performance Measures Project. Membership in NEMSMA provides access to a repository of performance standards and other QI documents. NEMSMA and the North Central EMS Institute jointly operate a national business data benchmarking program. Unlike other programs that measure clinical activities, this one provides comparative information about business processes, such as fleet cost per mile and best practices. NEMSMA joins forces with EMS Best Practices, Inc., to help facilitate the analysis of best practices and provide a forum for EMS management activities that revolve around QI.

THE JOINT COMMISSION

Formerly known as the Joint Commission on Accreditation of Healthcare Organizations (JCAHO), since 1951 The Joint Commission has been the national leader in setting standards for health care organizations. When a health care organization seeks accreditation, it demonstrates commitment to giving safe, high-quality health care and to continually work to improve that care. The history of The Joint Commission is rooted in performance measurement and dates back to Ernest A. Codman and the development of his "end results thesis," which proposes that patient decision making be based on data. This goal is consistent with The Joint Commission's mission to continuously improve the safety and quality of care provided to the public through the provision of health care accreditation and related services that support performance improvement in health care organizations.

During the 8-year period from 1986 to 1994 of planning for the accreditation process advocated by the *EMS Agenda for Change*, The Joint Commission engaged in a continuing process to develop, test, and implement sets of standardized performance measures. In 1995, The Joint Commission revised its original measurement strategy by employing several external measurement systems. External measurement systems use an array of existing or emerging measures. The Joint Commission developed an electronic system called the ORYX initiative. ORYX is a software and management system used by hospitals to gather and process QI data under Joint Commission standards. This growing movement for health care reform ultimately led to the creation, in 1999, of the **National Quality Forum (NQF)**. The NQF is a nonprofit organization that aims to improve the quality of health care for all Americans through fulfillment of its three-part mission:

- Setting national priorities and goals for performance improvement

1. Indicator ID	7(CC)
2. Question	What percentage of patients over 35 years of age with suspected cardiac chest pain received a 12-lead ECG?
3. Indicator Name	12-Lead Performance Rate
4. Key Process Path	Clinical Care: ACS > 12-Lead Performance Rate
5. Patient/Customer Need	Early performance of diagnostic EKG can accelerate definitive care
6. Type of Measure	Process
7. Objective	Increase rate in appropriate patients
8. Indicator Formula	Number of cardiac chest pain patients having 12-lead EKG in a given period divided by total chest pain patients in that period
9. Indicator Formula Description	Percentage of patients having a recorded NHTSA E09-15 "provider primary impression" or E09-16 "provider secondary impression" value of 1785 "786.50- chest pain/discomfort" and have an E19-03 "procedures performed . . ." value 89.820 "12-lead ECG"
10. Denominator Description	Number of patients creating a provider impression of chest pain/discomfort
10.a Denominator Inclusion Criteria	Patients with NHTSA E09-15 or E09-16 value 1785 "786.50- chest pain/discomfort"
10.b Denominator Exclusion Criteria	Patients with NHTSA E06-14/E06-15 "age/age units" values, or NHTSA E06-16 "date of birth" value minus E05-07 "arrived at patient data/time" value indicating patient less than 35 years of age
10.c Denominator Data Sources	NEMSIS state level
11. Numerator Description	Number of patients creating a provider impression of chest pain/discomfort who have 12-lead EKG performed
11.a Numerator Inclusion Criteria	Patients having a recorded NHTSA E09-15 "provider primary impression" or E09-16 "provider secondary impression" value of 1785 "786.50- chest pain/discomfort" and have an E19-03 "procedures performed . . ." value 89.820 "12-lead ECG"
11.b Numerator Exclusion Criteria	
11.c Numerator Data Sources	NEMSIS state level
12. Sampling Allowed	No
13. Sampling Description	NA
14. Minimum Number of Data Points	Seven plus agency/locale and time/date identifiers
15. Suggest Reporting Format: Numerical	Percentage

FIGURE 2.5 Sample quality performance indicators. (*Continued*)

16.	Suggest Reporting Format: Graphical	
17.	Suggest Reporting Frequency	
18.	Testing	
19.	Stratification	
20.	Stratification Options	
21.	Current Development Status	
22.	Additional Information	Proxy for Chicago meeting "ALS performed" indicator
23.	References	
24.	Contributors	

FIGURE 2.5 Sample quality performance indicators. (*Continued*) *Source: National Highway Traffic Safety Administration (2009), p. 23.*

- Endorsing national consensus standards for measuring and publicly reporting on performance
- Promoting the attainment of national goals through education and outreach programs

A nonprofit health care safety agency, the NQF has created a list of avoidable things that should never happen in medicine. As you read through this partial list, think about how this could be modified to be more specific to EMS:

- Patient death or serious disability associated with the use of contaminated drugs, devices, or biological preps
- Patient death or serious disability associated with the misuse or malfunction of a device
- Patient suicide or attempted suicide resulting in serious disability
- Patient death or serious disability associated with a medication error
- Maternal death or serious disability associated with labor or delivery in a low-risk pregnancy
- Patient death or serious disability associated with hypoglycemia
- Patient death or serious disability associated with an electric shock
- Any incident in which a line designated for oxygen or other gas to be delivered to a patient contains the wrong gas or is contaminated
- Patient death or serious disability associated with a burn
- Patient death or serious disability associated with a fall
- Patient death or serious disability associated with the use of restraints
- Any care ordered or provided by an impostor
- Abduction of a patient
- Sexual assault on a patient
- Death of a patient or staff member resulting from a physical assault

NQF's mission includes a wide variety of health care stakeholders, including consumer organizations, public and private purchasers, physicians, nurses, hospitals, accrediting and certifying bodies, supporting industries, health care research, and **quality improvement organizations (QIOs)**. NQF's structure enables private and public sector stakeholders to work together to create and implement solutions to drive continuous QI in the U.S. health care system. NQF has now come to be acknowledged as the final common pathway for review and approval of performance measures. In addition, **peer review organizations (PROs)**, renamed and commonly called quality improvement organizations, have assumed expanded performance measurement responsibilities, and the IOM's *Crossing the Quality Chasm* report laid out national measurement and improvement objectives.

The Joint Commission's future measurement objectives are continuously adapting to the rapidly changing health care environment and ongoing performance measurements. To facilitate achievement of these objectives, The Joint Commission has developed a set of principles to guide this work. The Joint Commission continues to refine the process for gathering of high-quality standardized performance information in the practice of medicine. The Joint Commission will collect data from all aspects of patient care delivery across the various types of health care organizations, including EMS. This will result in the creation of sophisticated applications of data use for accreditation, accountability, and public reporting. Coordination activities will focus on the amalgamation of data demands by large national entities such as the IOM. Successful achievement of these long-term goals should eventually result in demonstrable improvements in health care quality and patient safety.

Many Joint Commission principles have been applied to EMS, and it is a natural migration for Joint Commission standards to find their way from a physician medical director to an EMS agency. Joint Commission ratings are based on twenty-two measurements in five categories:

- Heart attack
- Heart failure
- Pneumonia
- Surgical care
- Children's asthma

A Joint Commission *standard* is a generalized goal that is an achievable model of excellence and is used to define expectations. An *indicator* is an objective behavior or outcome that can be measured to determine compliance with a standard. A *threshold* is an established level or percentage of acceptable compliance that indicates when further evaluation should be initiated. When care drops below the threshold, it is considered a sentimental event.

The Joint Commission also requires a root cause analysis on sentinel events as part of the accreditation process. Any unexpected death or serious physical or psychological injury that results in a chance of an adverse outcome must be investigated. The root cause analysis and an action plan must be submitted within 45 days of the event or awareness of the event. This same concept is applicable to EMS systems, and often EMS regulatory agencies require similar time frames to report errors or serious compromises in quality.

INSTITUTE FOR HEALTHCARE IMPROVEMENT

The Institute for Healthcare Improvement (IHI) was founded in 1991 after a national demonstration project on health care quality was launched. Founder Dr. Don Berwick has often been described as the rock star of QI. The IHI was instrumental in the IOM's reports on the quality of medicine. The IHI has been involved in EMS quality in several other countries and safety projects. At least two EMS projects from the IHI include a communication tool for paramedics when they arrive at hospitals and a tool for reducing emergency department diversion. The IHI provides education, best practices, and tremendous support, including mentorship for agencies looking to embrace the QI process.

CONSULTANTS AND CONFERENCES

QI is a difficult and complex study to undertake. The lack of a formal education or college program on QI techniques makes an excellent environment for consultants and trainers who create quality programs. A number of consulting teams now specialize in developing QI programs and training staff to function in environments attempting to achieve continuous QI. QI is becoming a common topic in EMS professional development conferences and trainings.

CONSULTING

QI in EMS is in the early stages of attaining the same significance in U.S. businesses and hospitals. Relatively few organizations in EMS have achieved a sophisticated level of QI. It is for this reason that consultants in EMS management have a history in EMS QI that is as long as the movement to bring modern QI efforts to EMS.

Fitch and Associates is a long-standing recognized expert in modern QI. It hosts the annual Pinnacle Conference, which includes detailed EMS QI activities and has attempted to change the momentum in EMS. TriData is a corporation with a fire-and-emergency services division that is commonly hired by municipal governments to measure, consult, or report on quality activities.

Two not-for profit-organizations consult for EMS services. International City/County Management Association (ICMA) and the National League of Cities helps communities solve critical problems by providing consulting support in police, fire, and EMS issues, including staffing, scheduling, and workload analysis. Emergency Services Consulting International operates as a for-profit subsidiary of the IAFC and draws from a variety of fire and EMS providers to manage consulting contracts.

Agencies or organizations with limited organizational knowledge on QI should give serious thought to utilizing the services of a consultant. "Stumbling out the starting gate" with a QI program typically sets back organizations and hampers QI processes and agency buy-in. Any consulting contract for QI should be researched for the bidders' past performance. Deliverables and important benchmarks the consultant must have include timelines and due dates for the organization to set the standard for project management and future programs.

ACCREDITATION AGENCIES

Accreditation in EMS is commonly provided by the Commission on Accreditation of Ambulance Services (CAAS) for ambulance operations and the Centers for Public Safety Excellence (CPSE) for fire and public safety organizations.

In 1990, CAAS was incorporated, bringing together a board of representatives from the American Ambulance Association, the Emergency Nurses Association, the International Association of Fire Chiefs, the National Association of Emergency Medical Technicians, the National Association of EMS Physicians, and the National Association of State EMS Directors. In 1993, the first agencies were accredited by CAAS. Both CAAS standards sections 201 and 204 include requirements for comprehensive QI programs for clinical and emergency medical dispatch operation. The CAAS standards are incorporated in the Centers for Public Safety Excellence's accreditation for fire-based EMS providers. Section 5 of the CPSE accreditation of fire departments requires extensive reports and programs in place to measure and promote quality in emergency services delivery.

In 1986, the IAFC and ICMA met to develop the concepts and design for continuous improvement of the fire services industry. On December 13, 1996, the IAFC and ICMA executed an Agreement and Declaration of Trust for the Commission on Fire Accreditation International and Commission on Chief Fire Officer Designation, formally known as the Master Trust Agreement. The Commission on Fire Accreditation International was created to award accreditation to fire and emergency service agencies and to pursue scientific research and educational purposes in the public interest. In November 2001, the original trust was dissolved and the Commission on Fire Accreditation International was incorporated as a nonprofit 501(c)(3) corporation. It is governed by a board of directors that oversees two commissions—the Commission on Fire Accreditation International (CFAI) and the Commission on Professional Credentialing (CPC).

CHAPTER REVIEW

Summary

The history of QI is rooted in scientific management and was influenced early on by experts such as Deming, Juran, and Crosby. A natural progression from modern business and health care has prompted several efforts by trade organizations, and NHTSA's EMS division has placed QI on the main stage for EMS. It is essential that PDSA (*P*lan, *D*o, *C*heck, and *A*ct) be the baseline for EMS QI, focusing on understanding variation and using run and statistical control charts. ISO 9000, Malcolm Baldrige, and other awards serve as incentives for EMS. Several organizations and associations are utilizing private industry models, and national processes for EMS QI are evolving. The National Association of EMS Physicians and the American College of Emergency Physician were the early pioneers of EMS QI. Consensus standards and accrediting agencies are establishing guidelines for the measurement of quality in EMS. The use of consulting services can be helpful for new QI operations in a service.

WHAT WOULD YOU DO? Reflection

The case of Memphis Fire and FedEx provides an excellence example for people to seek in their own communities. What can you learn about customer service from a hotel, fast-food restaurant, or hardware chain? Brainstorm with a local establishment that has great service or a local manufacturer that employs quality programs. Many of the principles and ideas can cross- pollinate organizations. It save time and efforts to model behavior and improve on existing programs.

Take a quick survey of your employees and staff to learn where they worked before and whether they recognized or participated in previous QI projects. Conversation and assessment of the successes and failures of those programs can work in an EMS manager's favor to plug in key personnel for EMS QI activities.

Chronicle the history of QI in your organization. Accreditation organizations require an organization to document its QI efforts. Not only reports on clinical performance, but meeting minutes and change that is facilitated by the QI process will need to be documented. Because so few are trained in QI, the need for an accurate history of the activities must be kept for succession planning. Most governments are participating in some form of quality process in which EMS can participate.

Review Questions

1. Based on the work of the National Quality Forum, what would you include in a list of things that should never happen in medical transportation?
2. Place the origins of and current efforts toward EMS quality improvement on a timeline.
3. Identify national efforts that are underway to facilitate EMS QI.
4. Name four organizations or agencies with which an EMS organization might interact regarding comprehensive QI activities in medicine.
5. Identify components of the key indicator or EMS performance measure.
6. What are key indicators of the IAFF performances measures?
7. Where does legal or legislative authority come into play in the origins of EMS QI?
8. Compare and contrast two of the models of QI mentioned in this chapter. Which one appeals to you? Why?
9. What QI programs can you identify in business, industry, or government related to EMS, both nationally and internationally?
10. Select one of the Malcolm Baldrige Award criteria and make an outline of how your organization could meet such an objective.

References

Balestracci, D., and J. Barlow. (1996). "Quality Improvement: Practical Applications for Medical Group Practice." Englewood, CO: Center for Research and Ambulatory Health Care Administration.

Berwick, D. M. (1990). *Curing Health Care: New Strategies for Quality Improvement.* San Francisco: Jossey-Bass, Inc.

Crosby, P. B. (1979). *Quality Is Free: The Art of Making Quality Certain.* New York: McGraw-Hill.

Deming, E. W. (1994). *The New Economics: For Industry, Government, Education*, 2nd ed. Cambridge, MA: Massachusetts Institute of Technology, Center for Advanced Educational Services.

Eastman, J. (1997, July). "A Leadership Guide to Quality Improvement for Emergency Medical Services (EMS) Systems." Washington, DC: U.S Department of Transportation, National Highway Traffic Safety Administration.

"Emergency Medical Services Outcomes Project (EMSOP): Application in Future Performance Measurement Systems." Presented at A Leadership Forum on Performance Measures in EMS, Arlington, VA, March 20, 2002.

Gygi, C., N. DeCarlo, et. al. (2005). *Six Sigma for Dummies.* Hoboken, NJ: Wiley.

Harbour, J. L. (1997). *The Basics of Performance Measurement.* New York: Quality Resources.

Huge, E. C. (1989). *Total Quality: An Executive's Guide for the 1990's.* Chicago: Irwin Professional Publishing.

Ishikawa, K. (D. J. Lu, trans.). (1985). *What Is Total Quality Control?* Englewood Cliffs, NJ: Prentice-Hall Inc.

Juran, J. M. (1988). *Juran on Planning for Quality.* Mankato, MN: The Free Press.

Kuehl, A. E., ed. (2002). *Prehospital Systems and Medical Oversight.* Lenexa, KS: National Association of EMS Physicians.

Langley, G. J. K. M. Nolan, et al. (2009). *The Improvement Guide: A Practical Approach to Enhancing Organization Performance.* San Francisco: Jossey-Bass.

Medicare Payment Advisory Commission. (2003, June). "Report to the Congress: Variation and Innovation in Medicare." Washington, DC: MedPAC.

Milgate, K., and S. B. Cheng. (2006). "Pay-for-Performance: The MedPAC Perspective." *Health Affairs 25*(2), 413–419.

Moore, L. (2003). *IAFF/IAFC EMS System Performance Measures Tool Operations Manual.* Washington, DC: IAFF.

National Highway Traffic Safety Administration. (1996). *Emergency Medical Services Agenda for the Future* (No. DOT HS 808 441). Washington, DC: U.S. Department of Transportation.

Peach, R. W. (ed.). (1994). *The ISO 9000 Handbook.* Fairfax, VA: Ceem Information Services.

Shewhart, W. (1931). *Economic Control of Quality of Manufactured Product.* New York: Van Nostrand.

Singhal, D., and K. R. Singhal. (2012). *Implement ISO 9001:2008 Quality Management System: A Reference Guide*. New Delhi, India: PHI Learning Pvt. Ltd.

Stamatis, D. H. (2003). *Six Sigma and Beyond: Foundations of Excellent Performance.* Boca Raton, FL: CRC Press.

Swor, R. A. (1993). *Quality Management in Pre-hospital Care*. St. Louis, MO: Mosby.

Swor, R. A., and R. G. Pirallo, eds. (2005). *Improving Quality in EMS.* Lenexa, KS: National Association of EMS Physicians, 2005.

U.S. Department of Transportation, National Highway Traffic Safety Administration. (2009). *Emergency Medical Services Performance Measures*. See the NASEMSO website.

Womack, J. P., and D. T. Jones. (1996). *Lean Thinking: Banish Waste and Create Wealth in Your Corporation.* New York: Simon & Schuster.

Key Terms

American National Standards Institute (ANSI) A private, nonprofit organization that administers and coordinates the U.S. voluntary standardization and conformity assessment system. It is the U.S. member in the International Organization for Standardization.

DMAIC An improvement system (*D*efine, *M*easure, *A*nalyze, *I*mprove, *C*ontrol) for existing processes falling below specification and looking for incremental improvement.

DMADV An improvement system (*D*efine, *M*easure, *A*nalyze, *D*esign, *V*erify) used to develop new processor products at Six Sigma quality levels.

indicators Objective behaviors or outcomes that can be measured to determine compliance with a standard.

International Organization for Standardization (ISO) A network of national standards institutes from 148 countries working in partnership with international organizations, governments, industry, and business and consumer representatives to develop and publish international standards.

metric Standard for measurement or evaluation method.

National Quality Forum (NQF) A unique, multi-stakeholder organization that has been instrumental in advancing efforts to improve quality through performance measurement and public reporting.

peer review organizations (PROs) Individuals or organizations who review projects or performance. They have equivalent knowledge and background but do not hold a superior position or role to the person or operation being reviewed.

quality assurance system All of the planned and systematic activities and related results to comply with planned arrangements and whether these arrangements are implemented effectively and are appropriate to achieve the objectives.

quality control All the planned and systematic activities implemented within the quality system that can be demonstrated to provide confidence that a product or service will fulfill requirements for quality.

quality council Group driving the quality improvement effort that usually has oversight for the implementation and maintenance of the quality management system; operates in parallel with the normal operation of the business; also called quality steering committee.

quality improvement (QI) The formal approach to the analysis of performance and systematic efforts to improve it.

quality improvement organizations (QIOs) Organizations that represent, promote, and/or validate the actions taken to increase the value to the customer by improving the effectiveness and efficiency of processes and activities throughout the organizational structure.

quality management Oversight and application of quality principles in a management system used to guide overall operational process to achieve maximum customer satisfaction at the lowest overall cost to the organization while continuing to improve the process.

quality planning Establishing and developing objectives and requirements for quality and the requirements for application of the quality system. According to Juran, these steps should include a quality council, quality policies, strategic quality goals, deployment of quality goals, resources for control, measurement of performance, and quality audits.

quantitative approach A systems approach to quality that is continuous and designed to keep a process within a range.

Six Sigma A model for improvement deriving from the statistical use of the Greek letter sigma to denote standard deviation from the mean. Six sigma is equivalent to 3.4 defects or errors per million.

special cause variation Difference in outcome of a process that required investigation in order to ensure quality and maximize productivity.

standard A generalized goal that is an achievable model of excellence and is used to define expectations.

Vital Few Term coined by Joseph Juran to describe his use of the Pareto principle. This principle suggests that most effects come from relatively few causes; that is, 80 percent of them come from 20 percent of the possible causes. The 20 percent of possible causes are referred to as the "vital few."

Domains of a QI System

3 CHAPTER

Objectives

After reading this chapter, the student should be able to:

3.1 Define the three domains of quality improvement in EMS.
3.2 Identify the three components of EMS quality management.
3.3 Apply a strategy for each domain of quality.
3.4 Apply an appropriate technique to the proper domain of EMS quality, given a list of QI processes.
3.5 Differentiate the levels of measurement on outcomes for EMS patients.
3.6 Identify how an outcome in the system is influenced by structure or process.

Key Terms

benchmarking
best practices
causation
death
disability
discomfort
disease
dissatisfaction
destitution
flowchart
indicators
outcomes
process
system
trending

WHAT WOULD YOU DO?

It was dark and the Engine 16 crew was making its way to the back of a home, responding to a reported overdose. Found lying on the floor in a bedroom was a young female with agonal respirations. Bystanders and evidence on a small table in the cramped room indicated heroin. A quick assessment indicated an immediate need to assist ventilations and a declining heart rate from hypoxemia, which confirmed the crew's initial assessment of an opiate overdose. The call was made to administer Narcan to reverse the effects of the opiate. After placing an intravenous line, the paramedic removed the medication bag from the approach bag and retrieved a vial from the flap on the pouch. The medication was quickly drawn up into a syringe while the captain was obtaining medical history and the firefighter was providing respiratory support with a valve mask to the patient.

As 1 cc went into the patient's IV, the crew waited for the anticipated sudden increase in level of consciousness and return of normal respirations. Instead, what was immediately noticed was a rapid increase in heart rate. The paramedic looked at the medication vial and realized a medication error had occurred. Epinephrine 1:1000 had been administered instead of Narcan.

Questions

1. How had this medication error occurred?
2. What aspects of the structure and process failed?
3. How would your organization handle this incident?
4. What is the best practice for how to handle this?

INTRODUCTION

Components of any **system**, whether it is for diagnosis and treatment of a medical problem or the making of widgets, must be defined. Prior to learning or understanding the details of a quality improvement (QI) system, it is important to understand the framework of the system. The framework of a system details a group of independent but interrelated elements comprising a set of unified whole components of a system.

The origins of QI being based on structure, **process**, and **outcomes** are a result of the works of Avedis Donabedian. Donabedian was an Armenian-born physician who studied at Harvard School of Public Health and wrote a tremendous amount on quality. For over 30 years, he advocated the basic system for QI in health care. Several of the programs and architecture of the Institute of Medicine (IOM) and the Joint Commission's efforts on QI in medicine apply Donabedian's approach to analyzing quality.

Donabedian advocated that three areas or domains affect quality: structure, process, and outcome. First, the structure in which QI will occur must be defined. The next step is to improve process reliability and reduce variations. This will result in quality outcomes.

QUALITY IS MANAGEMENT'S PROBLEM

W. Edward Deming, the American statistician known for the *P*lan, *D*o, *C*heck, *A*ct (PDCA) cycle, argued that 94 percent of what goes wrong with a system is within management's domain, and only 6 percent lies with the individual or thing. Kaoru Ishikawa from the University of Tokyo and creator of quality circles and the fishbone diagram, along with New York University professor Joseph Juran, who founded the Pareto principle, reported different figures. They identified 75 percent to 80 percent and 20 percent to 25 percent, respectively, as falling within management's control by adjusting the system. The root cause of the failure in quality might be determined through the use of a fishbone diagram. (See Figure 3.1.) Management defines material specifications, equipment standards, and personnel practices; shapes the working environment; and dictates production processes or service delivery. All of these factors contribute to product and service variations. At a strategic level, failure of management to plan for the future and to foresee problems brings about waste of manpower, materials, and time, all of which raise the agency's cost and price of providing EMS.

EMS QI VERSUS MAINSTREAM QI

Traditionally, QI in EMS has consisted of someone reviewing a patient care report and sending some sort of communication to the writer of that report. More often than not, this provokes a negative opinion of quality activities. Other than completed paperwork, no real results are produced. This can lead to two poor assumptions: that the issue is at the provider level, and that provider feedback or education—versus improvement to the whole process—will fix a quality problem. This approach only looks at one part of the system, versus the entire process, which may yield a variety of ideas or adjustments to be made to improve care and service. More comprehensive methods of QI have begun to surface in every aspect of EMS as the result of viewing the EMS QI process as a system.

In almost every other aspect of medicine, QI is part of the mainstream. For example, outcome surveys and consistency in diagnosis now reward physicians with additional reimbursement. Incentive pay is also being based on how quickly a patient is moved to appropriate care. The principles of quality cannot be achieved with incentives. In fact, some science documents that the psychological impact of incentive pay can corrupt QI (Jennings, 2007). Very sophisticated processes are in place to monitor the delivery of care in hospitals, with structures for both supplies and people to be processed in a way to control for errors and make efficient use of time and people.

As EMS begins to be held more accountable and employs more complex QI activities, the system should focus on the six principles of quality that most health care agencies are seeking to encompass. The six principles of EMS quality require that EMS care is characterized by the following attributes:

- Safe
- Effective
- Patient centered
- Timely
- Efficient
- Equitable (*Source:* Excerpt from "Crossing the Quality Chasm: A New Health System for the 21st Century" from INSTITUTE OF MEDICINE: Shaping the Future for Health, March 2001. Published by the National Academy of Sciences, © 2000).

DOMAINS OF QUALITY

When looking at a QI system with a framework of structure, process, and outcome, each of the domains needs a definition. *Structure* is defined as the environment in which health care is provided or will occur, including the characteristics of the care of providers, their tools and resources, and physical and organizational settings. *Process* is both the interpersonal and technical aspects of treatment. *Outcome* is the change

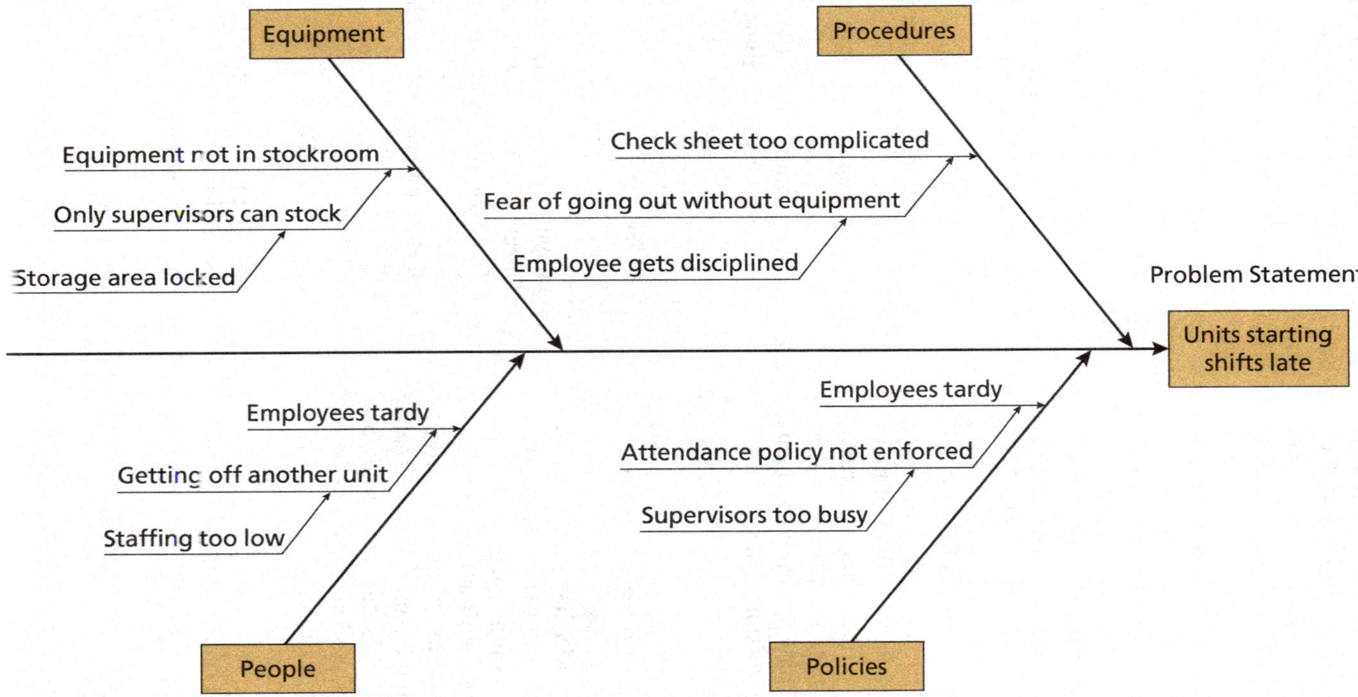

FIGURE 3.1 Example of a fishbone diagram. *Source: "Figure 35.4—Cause and Effect Diagram: Units Starting Shifts Late" from CRITICAL CARE PARAMEDIC by Bryan E. Bledsoe and Randall W. Benner. Copyright © 2006 by Pearson Education. Used by permission of Pearson Education.*

in the patient's symptoms and functioning. As a result, quality is the relationship between quality **indicators** (structure and process) and quality validators (i.e., outcomes).

The Joint Commission is a national certifying body that accredits and certifies hospitals and other health care organizations in the United States. Payment from government and insurance services often requires certification from the Joint Commission. The Joint Commission helps to ensure that people receive the safest, highest-quality, and best-quality health care. Founded in 1951, the Joint Commission has accredited more than 20,000 health care organizations.

According to the Joint Commission, an indicator is a quantitative performance measure that can be used as a tool to monitor performance and direct attention to potential performance issues that may require more intensive review within an organization. An EMS indicator measures the degree of conformance to a reasonable expectation as defined by the community served. Indicators may be related to the structure (people, places, and things) or the processes (activities occurring in a system) and ends in outcomes (the results of the structures and activities within a system). In fact, the types of indicators (structure, process, and outcome) are all related and dependent on one another. Therefore, the following equation becomes the golden rule for QI:

$$\text{Structure} + \text{Process} = \text{Outcome}$$

Changes in structure may affect the process and the outcome. Likewise, changes in the process may affect the structure and outcome. Indicators, in short, are a way to simplify information so that data can be digested more efficiently and in a significant way.

STRUCTURE

Structure is comprised of people, resources, and an environment. For a QI system to work and be efficient, there must be structure to keep processes organized. As with any QI system, involvement is key for success. Without a map detailing the structure, it is easy for those affected or wanting to participate to become lost in the process. Of critical importance is identification of who is responsible for each of the processes. This should be clearly and graphically articulated. The more detailed the system, the more structure is required.

In a QI program, people are one key component of the structure of a QI system. EMS is a team approach, and the people within the structure of the QI system ideally consist of a team within the EMS system or the authority managing the QI process. This is the current model in many EMS organizations, where quality is a business strategy. A QI department cannot create sustainable organizational improvement. It must be imbedded in the structure, processes, and people. The makeup of the QI system's structure will be created according to the size and responsibility of the organization. A state EMS QI structure will vary greatly from a smaller, rural ambulance service.

A simple organizational chart and flow map are important parts of a QI program's structure. It is mandatory that a record of the structure detailing who is responsible for what and how the information flows be displayed graphically. The team's organizational chart should reflect the integration of the EMS QI program into an EMS organization. The organizational chart also helps determine access points into the system for QI activities. More important, the organizational chart should identify linkages, processes, or information channels.

An EMS QI team should be under the direction of a program director. Members of the organization's EMS QI team should have expertise in administration, management, or knowledge of an EMS system. EMS QI programs require knowledge by managers, to some limited degree, in the areas of EMS evaluation and QI, data systems, biostatistics, and the clinical aspects of EMS. As we place people in the organizational structure, it is important that they receive education and training in QI processes.

State EMS systems, large corporate EMS or metropolitan fire departments, and hospital corporations require a more complex structure. Often, the QI advisory group with statewide representation should include, but not be limited to the following:

- Local EMS agency administrator(s) or designee
- Local EMS agency medical director(s)
- EMS service provider medical director(s)
- EMS educator(s)
- EMS receiving facilities
- EMS personnel
- EMS service provider EMS QI program representative(s)
- Public representative(s)

The structure of EMS QI programs must establish and maintain relationships with everyone who interacts with EMS. The quality of a service is also measured in terms of relationships and feedback about the level of service provided to agencies that are coordinating, cooperating, or assisting with EMS. Many of these agencies also supply resources. For example, the services of a heavy rescue are often a limited resource in an EMS system. This is an area where the interactions among the people, resources, and processes should be monitored for improvement. The care of a patient trapped in a motor vehicle requires a coordinated effort that is often time sensitive. The measurement of time and outcome should be shared by two agencies cooperating within the structure of the system. Some other agencies commonly associated with the structure of a QI system include, but are not limited to the following:

- Local EMS agencies
- EMS service provider(s)
- EMS receiving facilities
- Base hospital(s)
- EMS dispatch center(s)
- Labor and management
- Local department of health
- Law enforcement
- Public safety answering point(s) (PSAP(s))
- Constituent group(s)
- Specialty center(s)
- Poison control
- Public organization(s)

Side Bar

Improvement Map Software

The Institute for Health Improvement, in conjunction with Microsoft, has created "Improvement Map" software designed to apply structure to a QI initiative. The software lists resources and objectives and then rates the cost, time, difficulty, and evidence for implementing the structure.

Best Practice

The Value of Feedback

As part of the Palm Beach Fire Rescue (PBFR) EMSCQI program, there was a desire to close the loop. PBFR arranged with Palm Beach Gardens Medical Center (the hospital to which 95 percent of the patients are transported) to provide a spreadsheet listing all patients transported to its facility each month. The spreadsheet includes patient name, age, date of transport, what the paramedics treated, and the hospital's admitting or discharge diagnosis.

When there is a discrepancy between the prehospital diagnosis and the hospital's admitting or discharge diagnosis, the EMS captain in charge of QI pulls up the patient care report (PCR). The hospital's diagnosis is then written on the PCR. A QI cover sheet is attached to the report, which is forwarded to the treating paramedics so that they can see what they treated versus what the patient was admitted or discharged with.

The purpose is twofold. First, the treating paramedics can put a clinical picture together as to how the patient presented and how that clinical picture fit the hospital's diagnosis or, just as important, how it did not fit the hospital's diagnosis. When the clinical presentation is similar for the prehospital and hospital diagnosis, the medic gets a better understanding of differential diagnosis. The elements of the history and physical exam or diagnostics that supported the hospital's diagnosis are included, with the hope that in the future the paramedics will be better able to recognize and treat the patient correctly. The other reason is to track the data for possible trends of medics missing particular diseases. If this proves to be the case, training in that area is provided. For instance, several stroke alerts were actually incidents of Bell's palsy. So an in-service on differentiating between a stroke and Bell's palsy was conducted. The percentage of correct versus incorrect prehospital diagnoses and which area (neurological, cardiac, respiratory, etc.) is weakest are also being tracked.

The medics really like the feedback, and it prompts them to research unfamiliar but specific diseases. They can email the medical director with specific questions. Input from the prehospital provider is returned to be included in the review of protocols and process for treating patients to see if more improvements should be made. The training can be tailored to address specific problems.

It took some groundwork and several meetings to get the ball rolling, but now feedback on both cardiac and stroke alerts is received within 24 hours. As with most QI, this is not punitive in any way. Once the medic reviews the report, it is destroyed.

UNDERSTANDING PEOPLE, PROCESS, AND OUTCOMES

The theory or knowledge on how to build a system is important when designing a QI program. A system is a network of interdependent components. All of the components must be defined. The system must have an aim. Most EMS systems have focused on changes to the system designed to accommodate responding to cardiac arrest with an aim to produce a neurologically intact outcome. More specifically, an aim would be, for example, to increase from 20 percent to 35 percent by December 31 the number of patients discharged alive and neurologically intact following witnessed VF/VT sudden cardiac arrest. Responses set to the high standard and efficiency to produce a positive outcome for cardiac arrest sets up the system for other true emergencies, such as stroke or trauma. When building a system or employing a QI strategy, ask the following questions:

- What is it that needs to be accomplished?
- What change can result in potential improvement?
- How will it be known that the change resulted in improvement?

Employing a QI system using science can create a system of profound knowledge. Deming described that achieving a system reliant on a system of profound knowledge first starts with changing the individual. Once individuals change, they have an appreciation for the system knowledge of variation, theory of knowledge, and psychology as a large part of managing a QI system, including EMS. The system provides the knowledge necessary to spark ideas. Ideas ultimately lead to changes being made in the system. A variation, in turn, can trigger an idea to change the system. Messages that come from the work environment or convey ideas or report variations should be catalogued and processed. It is important to understand the nature of variation to determine if it is a special or common cause. The point is that systems are dynamic and interrelated.

Often, we create systems to account for the worst-case scenario. Relating back to the principles that should be incorporated into a QI system, safety must be ensured. If we build a system for the worst-case scenario, the system will be able to respond to lesser events with the same efficiency. This may even allow for changes in the system that will ultimately benefit the goal of the system. For example, most EMS systems are designed to meet the challenges of responding to and caring for a cardiac arrest. The system is built to ensure that the time to CPR from time of collapse to response is four minutes. The patient gets a 15 percent increase in probability of survival under the 4-minute standard with rapid dispatch, aggressive CPR, and protocol-based dispatch process for pre-arrival instructions. When the time increases to 5 minutes, the chance of a successful resuscitation drops to 10 percent; at 6 minutes, it is 5 percent. Several factors, other than response time, have been identified through QI systems to have similar influence on patient outcomes. Patients in cardiac arrest have a 5 percent increase in survival with a skilled paramedic, a 5 percent increase in survival with CPR and immediate defibrillation, and with hypothermia another 5 percent increase in survival if applied within 2 hours. All of these processes and the time frames in which the system is built allow the EMS system to respond to other emergencies with the same efficiencies.

PROCESS

A process is a set of interrelated work activities involving people, materials, machines, methods, energy, and environment. A process is characterized by a set of specific inputs and value-added tasks that make up a procedure for a set of specific outputs. A **flowchart** is a graphic representation of a process. The mechanics of a flowchart use different shapes to indicate the different actions in the process and is different from a process map. (See Figure 3.2.)

Within a flowchart, shapes depict certain actions. The majority of flowcharts use just four of the process symbols: terminator, process, decision, and connector. Most people are unfamiliar with the other flowcharting shapes, and it is common for an agency to add a shape symbol key or legend to its flowchart. One shape that EMS processes use, as an alternative to the normal processes or predefined process, is a rectangle with divisions on both sides. An upside-down triangle indicates a merging of multiple processes into one. A hexagon calls for preparation or a set-up process step. A trapezoid requires data input. A rectangle cut in half horizontally with a wave-like line symbolizes the need for documentation. Figure 3.3 depicts common shapes that could be used to create flowcharts for EMS and QI processes. A graphic depiction of a process resonates with employees who typically do not read the fine print and are often visual learners.

Process Application

Process analysis is the measurement of four factors: approach, deployment, learning, and integration. The first factor is an organization's approach, which evaluates the methods used

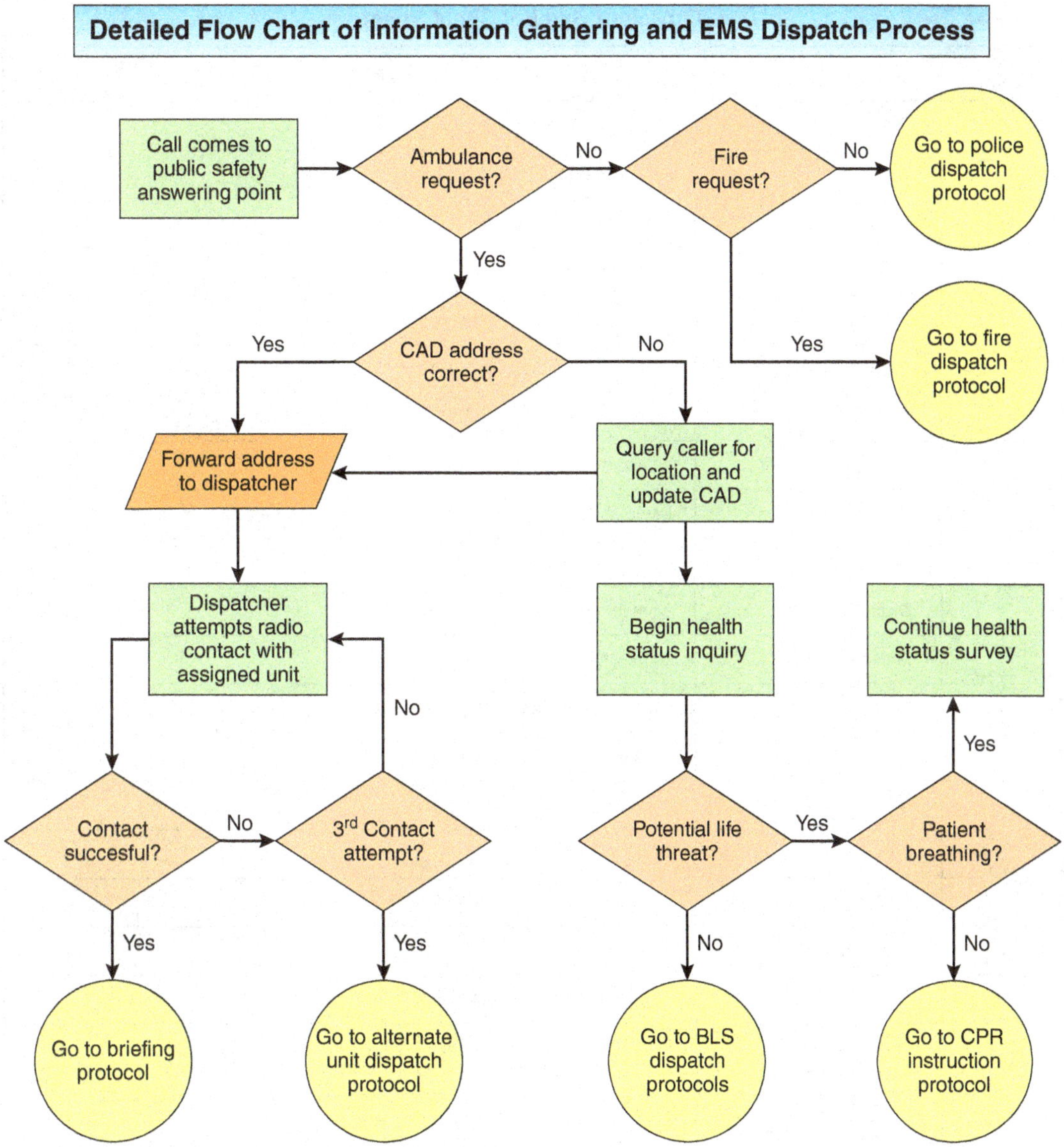

FIGURE 3.2 Example of a flowchart. *Source: Paramedic Emergency Care by Bledsoe, Porter & Shade*

to accomplish the processes and the appropriateness of the methods used in the organization's operating environment. The effectiveness of methods and the degree to which the approach is repeatable and based on reliable data and information are fundamental to process analysis. The use of various techniques to control an airway in a patient is an example of an approach to process. Success rates using various techniques or devices applied to certain scenarios constitute an approach measurement.

Flowchart Symbol Cheat Sheet

Flowchart symbol	Name (alternates)	Description
	Process	An operation or action step.
	Terminator	A start or stop point in a process.
	Decision	A question or branch in the process.
	Delay	A waiting period.
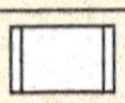	Predefined process	A formally defined sub-process.
	Alternate process	An alternate to the normal process step.
	Data (I/O)	Indicates data inputs and outputs to and from a process.
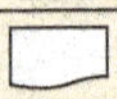	Document	A document or report.
	Multi-document	Same as document, except, well, multiple documents.
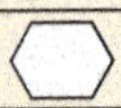	Preparation	A preparation or set-up process step.
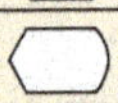	Display	A machine display.
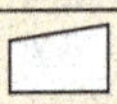	Manual input	Manually input into a system.
	Manual operation	A process step that isn't automated.
	Connector	A jump from one point to another.
	Off-page connector	Continuation onto another page.
	Transfer	Transfer of materials.
	Or	Logical OR
	Summing junction	Logical AND
	Collate	Organizing data into a standard format or arrangement.
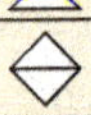	Sort	Sorting into some pre-defined order.
	Merge (storage)	Merge multiple processes into one. Also used to show raw material storage.
	Extract (measurement) (finished goods)	Extract (split processes), or more commonly, a measurement or finished goods.
	Magnetic disk (database)	A database.
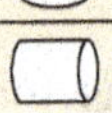	Direct access storage	Storage on a hard drive.
	Callout	One of many callout symbol used to add comments to a flowchart
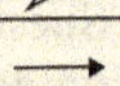	Flow line	Indicates the direction of flow for materials and/or information

FIGURE 3.3 Flowchart symbols and definitions. *Source: public domain*

Deployment is the next factor and the extent to which the organization requirements are relevant and important to the organization's operations. The core process in deployment is in the way the organization supplies resources to the system. This includes consistency in the approach to processes and the approach used by all employees. Routine vehicle checkouts, the deployment of response vehicles, and the impact to response times are examples of deployment analysis.

Learning within the organization is measured by the approach the organization takes through cycles of evaluation and improvement. Learning as a process level also involves encouraging innovation and refining processes within the organization. Learning analysis requires the ability to embrace change and reward attempts to improve that may indeed fail. A system that punishes or applies negative consequences to failed attempts to improve or modify the service will suppress innovation.

The final analysis is integration. This level is achieved by aligning the organizational processes with the organization's profile and other processes in emergency service and mobile health care, both inside and outside. For example, an EMS organization may need to measure chest pain care between crews and shifts within the organization and then benchmark it against regional providers outside the organization. It measures information and improvement that is complementary for work units and processes within the organization. Integration among plans, processes, results, analysis, learning, and other actions that harmonize processes becomes the highest level of process measurement.

The process by which an EMS organization uses a heavy rescue is an example of integration. A heavy rescue is a specialty resource that often responds from another organization required to integrate with first responders and often advanced life support providers to administer care during the rescue operation. Removing a victim from a vehicle crash is a time-sensitive operation, and the clinical care provided is an area to be monitored for quality. Even the timeliness of the dispatch of a specialty resource is a process to be measured for integration.

Analysis of Processes Activity

The analysis of activity within a process commonly measures time, quality or accuracy, and cost at the process level. Time and cost are relatively easy to define and measure. Quality and accuracy require industry standards and **best practices** to be employed with correct applications of medical processes and procedures without error. The key to defining quality measures is in knowing the purpose of process steps that lead to outcomes. Defining these purposes operationally yields quality measures. Evaluation of data by using graphic representations of activities that depict trends and variations over time are types of process analysis. The following are common methods used to help evaluate an activity:

1. **Trending**—the process of showing, by plot or process control chart, the upward, downward, or level movement of an activity over a specified period of time.
2. **Causation**—the results of tests applied to a set of data points plotted on a process control chart. The tests determine whether or not a "special cause" exists within the data set and can explain unusual character or nature of undesirable results.
3. **Benchmarking**—using known results of similar data measurements or tests as an impetus for achieving or surpassing a desired goal for improvement.
4. **Best practices**—using the best known results of similar data measurements of similar tests for similar systems or operations as an impetus for achieving or surpassing a desired goal for improvement.

5. **Published referencing**—using published results of similar data measurements or tests as a beginning or starting reference point for achieving or surpassing a desired goal for improvement.

An example of applying process and process analysis is the use of applying a checklist and procedural steps to facilitated intubation. Placing an endotracheal tube in a breathing patient with a pulse to control or protect the airway is a high-risk, low-frequency process. Errors can be catastrophic. Even when the process is done correctly, the patient often experiences a period of low oxygenation that can result in further injury. A study appeared in the *Journal of Trauma* (Davis, Hoyt, Poste, et al., 2004) on the incidence of oxygen desaturation during intubation and corresponding lower survival rates associated with desaturation.

The Henderson (Nevada) Fire Department used the published reference from the San Diego study to develop a specific process to apply to a patient scenario that requires facilitated intubation. Using the principles of crew resource management, Henderson Fire created a process in which a checklist, position-specific tasks, and a set goal for a desired outcome using a team approach became a best practice for airway management. Identifying a problem and making a simple design and process change (configuring a practice to monitor the oxygen and carbon dioxide trending) achieved a better outcome. (See Figure 3.4.)

OUTCOMES

Outcomes are the result of structure and process. There are six D's in the outcome domain: death, disability, disease, discomfort, dissatisfaction, and destitution. (See Figure 3.5.)

In medicine and EMS, an outcome classified as **death** is that the patient did not survive to hospital discharge or was pronounced at the scene of the incident. The measure of death in EMS has had some variation. For example, a child who drowns in a pool and is pronounced dead at the emergency room is counted somewhat differently than a child who survives the first 24 hours and then expires. The former is classified as a drowning; the other is classified as a near drowning. Although the child is a recorded death, the category in which the event gets placed is dependent on how the process and outcomes are defined. Again using the drowning scenario, if the child succumbs to an infection from the aspiration of water during the incident, the death is considered a result of the infection.

There are several ways in which outcome assessments can be made for **disability**. Disability is defined as the patient's level of function as a result of the injury or as a result of the patient care rendered. The most common measurement in EMS is the Glasgow Coma Scale (GCS). Often, GCS is measured with EMS's initial encounter, when the patient is transferred at the emergency room or released, or when a change occurs during the EMS encounter. Often, GCS is measured again by hospital staff 24 hours after arrival, at intervals of 30 or 90 days, and at 1 year following discharge from the hospital.

Another commonly used assessment measure is the Cerebral Performance Category (CPC), which is used to determine a valid neurological score. For example, did the application of hypothermia in a cardiac arrest victim result in the decrease in disability from a hypoxemic brain injury resulting in limited disability?

An outcome measuring **discomfort** is assessing whether there was an improvement in the patient's symptoms (e.g., alleviation of pain, improved breathing). Discomfort is commonly measured on pain scales by asking patients to rate their own pain. Modifications have been made to numerous pain scales for pediatric patients. Most are ratings that are on

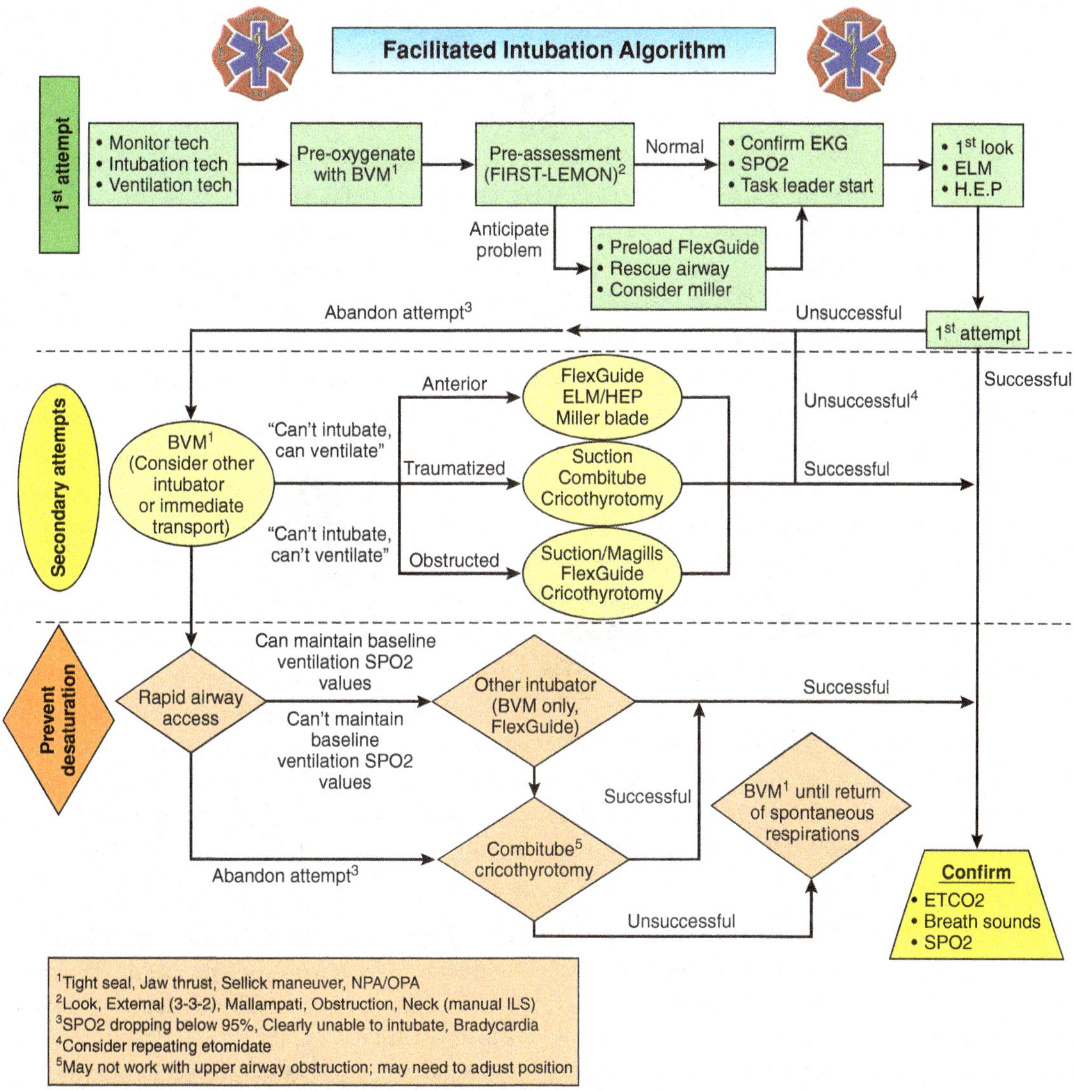

FIGURE 3.4 Facilitated intubation task standards from Henderson Fire Department. *Source: "Facilitated Intubation Task Standards" from Henderson Fire Department. Copyright © Henderson Fire Department. Used by permission of Henderson Fire Department.*

a scale of one to ten with one being the least and ten being the worst.

Disease is an outcome measure that is focused on the symptoms, physical findings, and diagnostic assessments or abnormalities. This measurement ensures a quality outcome by making the correct diagnosis of the patient's illness and applying the correct treatments. It is often a measure of the provider's clinical competency. Accuracy in disease identification is paramount for a correct therapy to be applied. For example, the diagnosis of congestive heart failure versus pneumonia in a patient with rales or crackles is

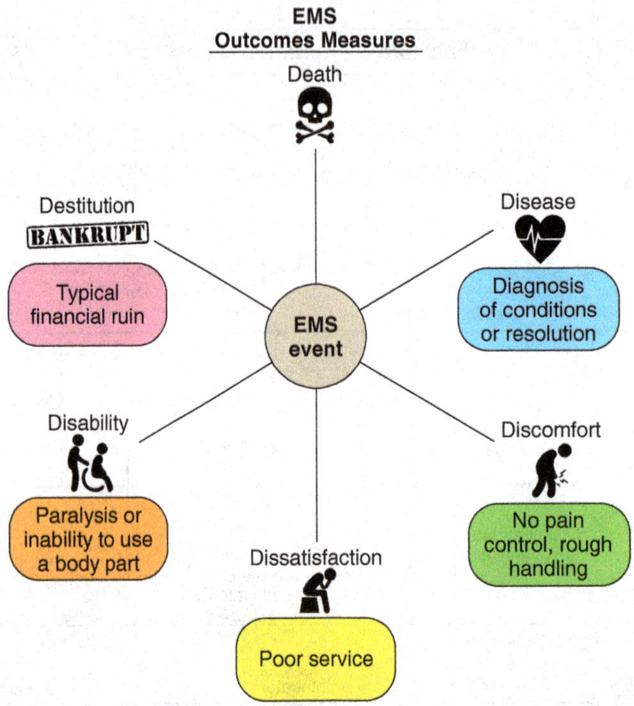

FIGURE 3.5 Graphic of the 6 Ds. *Source: Author drawing*

often a missed diagnosis. These conditions have two opposite treatments required, which can be detrimental to the survival of the patient if not correctly administrated to the right condition.

Dissatisfaction or satisfaction assesses whether the patient (and/or family) was satisfied with service rendered. This is often a perception or subjective rating based on courtesy and compassion, since few patients or their families understand the level of care they receive by EMS. This outcome can be biased, as some medical outcomes are out of the hands of EMS providers, as in the case of a spinal cord injury.

Destitution is a monetary measurement for the patient and for the service. Was the treatment provided at the lowest cost to the patient, the payer, and society as a whole? For example, evidence suggests that smoke inhalation victims suffer from cyanide poisoning from chemicals in the smoke. An effective antidote is available; however, the cost is $700 to $800 per dose. This single medication exceeds the reimbursement most insurance will pay for an ambulance transport. The medication is often not administered until the patient arrives at the emergency room. In comparison, EMS systems provide a very low-cost delivery of emergency care to diabetics with little or no reimbursement.

The six D's or outcomes need to be measured based on four factors: performance, trending, deployment and use, and comparison. It is best to establish a baseline and measure against that baseline. Each of the six outcomes can be measured based on the level of performance—for example, a quantitative number, trends in the rate of sustainability of good performance or consistency in process, and the extent of the deployment or use once a baseline is established (even it is a referenced baseline from another study). Comparison is another form of evaluation of the domains of outcomes. This occurs when the performance is measured comparatively to appropriate competition or similar organizations. This may also be a comparison against industry benchmarks and or leaders. The highest level of outcome evaluation is integration. Integration occurs when results are measured at each segment or episode and subsequently addressing important patient and stakeholder health care service, process, and action plans. This includes valid indicators of future performance and should be harmonized across work processes to support the organization's goals.

Side Bar

IHI

The Institute for Health Improvement (IHI) is a nonprofit organization that promotes the Institute of Medicine (IOM) and other initiatives to improve health care. The website contains tools and information on quality and background material on processes.

CHAPTER REVIEW

Summary

The basic components of a QI program or system include structure, processes, and measurement of outcomes. Structure is required to organize the people, resources, and processes in a QI program. Flowcharts are excellent tools to illustrate processes. Processes must be defined and analyzed over time to understand the reliability of trends. Best practices and published research may provide insight to a level of performance that is achievable. It is important to measure outcomes so the EMS systems can adjust or determine performance. Outcomes in EMS are measured in one of six categories: death, disability, discomfort, disease, dissatisfaction, and destitution.

WHAT WOULD YOU DO? Reflection

The crew immediately realized that the paramedic had grabbed the epinephrine, which was packaged in a vial of the same color as the Narcan. The vials look the same, particularly in low-light conditions, and are shaped the same. The distractions in the room and in the environment contributed to the error.

Both structural and procedural failures occurred in this scenario. First, no medication should look like or seem like another. Labels, containers, or placement in the bag should be different to ensure that medications are not confused. Many approach bags have medications randomly placed in pouches, instead of having a specific place labeled for the medication. A four-person crew instead of a three-person crew would allow an additional person to focus on the process of medication administration, thereby minimizing the possibility of error.

In addressing this type of incident, most agencies respond with disciplinary action and involvement of the medical director or regulatory agency. The paramedic will be held accountable for not following the 5 R's: right medication, right dose, right patient, right route, and right time or frequency.

A best practice for this scenario is to analyze the supply chain to explore the possibility of replacing the vial with a difficult color, size, or other type of administration device that differentiates the two drugs. A procedure that uses verbalization to another crew member and is acknowledged by that crew member on the accuracy of the medication prior to administration is known as a closed feedback loop. Additional procedures to consider include requiring four people on scene before evasive procedures or medication administrations are performed and instigating a procedural change requiring that patients be moved to a well-lit, distraction-free environment.

Review Questions

1. List and define the three domains of quality discussed in this chapter.
2. List the six principles of EMS quality.
3. What four factors should be measured in the system?
4. List the six D's in the outcome domain.
5. What is benchmarking?
6. What is a flowchart?

References

Christoffel, K., and M. Longjohn. (2002). "Standardized Outcomes Measurements in Emergency Medical Services for Children Research." *Ambulatory Pediatrics 2*(4), 315–318.

Davis, D. P., J. V. Dunford, J. C. Poste, et al. (2004). "The Impact of Hypoxia and Hyperventilation on Outcome After Paramedic Rapid Sequence Intubation of Severely Head Injured Patients." *Journal of Trauma 57*(1), 1–10.

Donabedian, A. (1980). *The Definition of Quality and Approaches to Its Assessment.* Ann Arbor, MI: Health Care Administration Press.

Donabedian, A. (1988). "The Quality of Care: How Can It Be Assessed?" *Journal of the American Medical Association 260*, 1743–1748.

Dunford, J., D. Davis, M. Ochs, D. Doney, and D. Hoyt. (2003) "Incidence of Transient Hypoxia and Pulse Rate Reactivity During Paramedic Rapid Sequence Intubation." *Annals of Emergency Medicine 42*(6), 721–728.

Eisenburger, P., F. Sterz, M. Haugk, M. Scheinecker, M. Holzer, et al. (2006). "Cardiac Arrest in Public Locations: An Independent Predictor for Better Outcome?" *Resuscitation 70*(3), 395–403.

Henderson Fire Department. (n.d.)., "EMS Task Standard 01: Facilitated Intubation Task Standard." See the organization website.

Institute of Medicine, Committee on Quality of Health Care in America. (2001). "Crossing the Quality Chasm: A New Health System for the 21st Century." Washington, DC: The National Academies Press.

Jennings, B. (2007). *Health Care Quality Improvement: Ethical and Regulatory Issues.* Garrison, NY: Hasting Center.

Kohn, A. (1993, September–October). "Why Incentive Plans Cannot Work." *Harvard Business Review*.

McLean, S., F. Maio, D. Spaite, and H. Garrison. (2002). "Emergency Medical Services Outcomes Research: Evaluating the Effectiveness of Prehospital Care." *Prehospital Emergency Care 6*(2), S52–S56.

Ouchs, M., D. Davis, D. Hoyt, et al. (2002). "Paramedic-Performed Rapid Sequence Intubation of Patients with Severe Head Injuries." *Annals of Emergency Medicine 40*, 159–167.

Key Terms

benchmarking Using known results of similar data measurements or tests as an impetus for achieving or surpassing a desired goal for improvement.

best practices Using the best known results of similar data measurements of similar tests for similar systems or operations as an impetus for achieving or surpassing a desired goal for improvement.

causation The results of tests that are applied to a set of data points plotted on a process control chart. The tests determine whether or not a "special cause" exists within the data set and can explain unusual character or nature of undesirable results.

death The patient did not survive to hospital discharge or was pronounced at the scene of the incident.

disability The patient's level of function as a result of the injury or as a result of the patient care rendered.

discomfort Accessing whether there was an improvement in the patient's symptoms (e.g., alleviation of pain, improved breathing).

disease A pathological condition of a part, organ, or system of an organism resulting from various causes, such as infection, genetic defect, or environmental stress, and characterized by an identifiable group of signs or symptoms.

dissatisfaction Negative assessment by the patient (and/or patient's family) of services rendered.

destitution A monetary measurement for the patient and for the service.

flowchart A schematic representation of a sequence of operations, as in a manufacturing process or service.

indicators A structure (people, places, things), processes (activities occurring in a system), or outcomes (the results of the structures and activities within a system) used to help organizations define and evaluate how successful they were in making progress toward goals and objectives.

outcomes Results of structure and process.

process A set of interrelated work activities involving people, materials, machines, methods, energy, and environment.

system A network of interdependent components.

trending The process of showing by plot or process control chart, the upward, downward, or level movement of an activity over a specified period of time.

CHAPTER 4

Defining Quality

Objectives

After reading this chapter, the student should be able to:

4.1 Create a standard within his or her organization.

4.2 Identify quality standards in the EMS industry and profession.

4.3 Match organizational performance with national standards for clinical care.

4.4 Map and define quality using a variety of management tools, diagrams, and other processes.

4.5 Differentiate between a performance measure, indicator, and benchmark.

Key Terms

benchmark
benchmarking
external benchmarking
indicators
internal benchmarking
outcome indicator
process indicator
sentinel event
standards
structural indicator

WHAT WOULD YOU DO?

When Cerro Gordo County Medic 11 showed up at the call for leg pain and shortness of breath, the patient was all too familiar. Thomas had been a fixture in the system for years. He was a skinny African American with a history of sickle cell and a frequent user of the 9-1-1 system. Most crews had written him off as a drug seeker. He had a history of opiate abuse with IV heroin when he was young. Now at age 38, he looked 60. The senior paramedic immediately sighed and copped an attitude: "What is it tonight, Thomas? Out of Lortab?" The crew continued to belittle Thomas and told him to walk to the ambulance. No vital signs were taken, and Thomas opted out of the transport after repeated suggestion of other options. An hour later, the Medic 11 crew sees Thomas on the gurney with Medic 5 who had started an intravenous line and run at least 800 ccs into Thomas. A nebulizer with Albuterol® was also being administered to Thomas. The cardiac monitor showed ST elevation in leads two and three and AVF. The crew from Medic 5 was conversing with the doctor about refilling their morphine and the mechanism that had made Thomas's sickle cell crisis a risk for myocardial infarction.

Questions

1. What aspect of quality care failed here?
2. How is *quality* defined for this type of patient?
3. What types of errors were experienced here?
4. What type of key indicator could be created or already exists for this patient?

INTRODUCTION

EMS must apply business principles the way that other government or private industry providers have. Every business or organization must define what it does. EMS can benefit from reviewing processes to identify opportunities for improving reliability in all aspects of its operation. Among the reasons to define quality are to focus membership on organizational goals, to jump-start change initiatives, and to energize improvement initiatives. Before this can happen, quality must be defined, the level of quality desired must be determined, and how quality will be measured must be considered. The most comprehensive and, perhaps simplest, definition of quality is that used by advocates of total quality management: "Doing the right thing right, right away" (Deming, 1982).

Determining causes of deficiency involves determining who or what is expected to change; taking corrective actions involves determining who is responsible for implementing action to bring about change. An organization must also determine when change is expected to occur. Another essential feature of Continuous Quality Improvement (CQI) is the concept of continuously seeking improvement in quality by eliminating all activities that do not add value to the process of providing quality. Non-value activities are considered "waste" under CQI and are candidates for elimination. A *P*lan, *D*o, *S*tudy, *A*ct (PDSA) cycle should be used to enhance a reliable, reproducible, and waste-free process. Synergistic and systematic thinking by providers, hospitals, regulatory agencies, and other interest groups are additional key components of CQI. Thinking and planning in terms

Best Practice

STEMI to Reperfusion

Getting door-to-balloon time under 90 minutes 90 percent of the time in preidentified ST segment elevation myocardial infarction (STEMI) risk situations is a well-recognized standard by the American Heart Association and the American College of Cardiology. Several EMS systems list this definition as a quality goal. However, few systems make this standard. Recently, the application of a prehospital 12-lead was shown to significantly reduce the door-to-drug time. This illustrates several changes in the existing standard of door-to-balloon time versus door-to-drug time. Both of these processes could produce favorable outcomes, and each has a different structure. Instead of measuring from door to drug as the time interval, a more effective definition (according to research) is STEMI to reperfusion. This definition of quality helps define quality based on science and a more accurate measurement of cardiac care. Although door-to-drug time is common if one drug does not work and alternative therapy is required, the destination choice may change the outcome. It is reperfusion that ideally ends the emergency.

of the big picture and seeing how all the EMS system components are aligned and balanced are functions of CQI.

QUALITY IMPROVEMENT DEFINED

The overall concept of quality improvement (QI) begins with the idea that all members of the team or organization want to do well and continues with an assessment of the system to determine how it can be structured to achieve this goal. The theories of CQI look at what was done and what was done right so that the members can learn from both. The program must define *quality* and also take into consideration what is timely (mandated), efficient, and effective. In most EMS organizations, there is a degree of fiscal uncertainty so it is pragmatic to consider those areas that will meet mission goals without compromising budgetary constraints. When a quality manager is examining and defining quality, it is necessary to consider all the system resources, including personnel, facilities, equipment, and financing. Some of the variables that need quality measures and definitions include communications, clinical procedures, financial processes and customer expectations, education, and expectations. Quality should always be customer focused and employ a system of improvement, orientation, and elimination of any culture of blame.

CQI should encompass the entire organization's goals or mission and not just the organizational structure, processes, and outcomes of the service or product that the organization exists to deliver. Total Quality Management (TQM) encompasses several aspects of quality. Each aspect requires the EMS organization to outline the standard or **benchmark** for the level of service or activity in each category. There are five areas of organizational quality:

- *Reputation Quality*—Does the organization enjoy respect among peers for doing what it says it does?
- *Image Quality*—Is the agency brand identifiable? Is the staff considered professional?
- *Service Quality*—Is the overall experience of the customer, patient, or public perceived as a quality experience?
- *Technical (Clinical) Quality*—Was the clinical care competent, appropriate, and evidence based?

- *Operational Quality*—Did a well-stocked vehicle with working equipment arrive in a timely manner?

PUBLIC/PATIENT EXPECTATIONS

One of the most essential variables that is often neglected is what the public expects (or, in some cases, demands) of EMS as a public agency or EMS provider. This is often referred to as the "voice of the customer." The public expects that EMS will respond in a timely and competent manner when called. Therefore, it is up to EMS managers and leadership to examine an agency's inner strengths and weaknesses and make the modifications necessary to meet public demand. It should be the goal of the program to meet the expectations of the public and the patient through team building and by defining quality in an EMS system. Without this definition, there can be no direction to achieve the goals or direct QI efforts.

An organization may have goals, but it may be unclear or lack focus. A focus group is often convened to identify trends and needs. The FOCUS method is used to process a CQI topic by a focus group trying to pin down QI definitions taken from the PDSA cycle. The FOCUS method (Institute of Medicine, 2001) for defining a quality initiative includes the following:

- *F*ind a process to improve.
- *O*rganize an effort to work on improvement.
- *C*larify current knowledge of the process.
- *U*nderstand process variation and capability.
- *S*elect a strategy for further improvement.

What Does the Customer Want?

It is important to recognize that information, compassionate care, and preservation of dignity are what most customers or patients are expecting. EMS providers are taught the mechanics of providing emergency and nonemergency care; however, some of the other needs of the patient may not be met. Often, quality is about perception. How people are treated and first impressions made by EMS crews often set the tone for the remainder of the response and the patient/customer perception of care or service received. Introducing oneself, offering a blanket, and handling people gently are just some ways that can make a huge difference in the perception of the care provided.

THE CUSTOMER IS ALWAYS RIGHT!

Everyone has encountered patients or customers who are wrong. Customers are not always right, but they are always the customers and should be treated with respect and dignity. Regardless of right or wrong, the emergency responder's attitude toward the patient and family is what matters most.

It is important to know what the customer wants, which begins with defining the customer. Customers in a prehospital setting include, but are not limited to, the following:

- Patient
- Patient's family
- Employers
- Field supervisors
- Employees
- Other emergency responders
- Nurses
- Doctors
- Hospitals

In a restaurant setting, for example, the server will almost always ask, "Is everything okay?" shortly after serving the meal. This provides an opportunity for the customer to recognize excellence or encourage change, thereby increasing the likelihood of a satisfactory experience. Similarly, EMS providers are providing a service and need to determine how customer service will be assessed. The key is to treat customers the way you expect you and your family to be treated. EMS should develop a standard set of questions that assess customer service and satisfaction. Open-ended questions may lead to long responses, so it may be more appropriate to use close-ended questions with responses of objective or numerical value. Asking patients/customers questions about the care and attention they received will indicate that the emergency responder cares about their well-being. Here are some examples:

- Has the service met your expectations?
- Did you receive and understand the information provided to you?
- Do you have any questions about the care you have received or will receive?

DEVELOPING A STRATEGIC QUALITY PLAN

When developing a strategic quality plan, an organization should create long-, medium- and short-term organizational objectives. Short-term objectives can range from days, weeks, or months. In a large organization, short-term objectives commonly project 1 to 3 years into the future. Medium-term objectives are most commonly geared to 3 to 5 years. Long-term objectives are commonly 5 years or more and can sometimes last 10 to 20 years. Objectives and ideas that extend beyond 5 years are considered part of an organization's vision. Whatever the duration, the length of goals should be defined by the organization.

The length of a goal or objective is related to the rate of change of the information available to the organization or the ability of the organization to muster resources to make change. Each objective should identify the ways to achieve those objectives and measure their effectiveness. EMS organizational objectives should focus on ensuring customer, patient, and stakeholder satisfaction. This includes satisfaction both external and internal to the organization. Developing and defining quality in a strategic plan requires the utilization of information and analysis. Decisions on the development of quality **standards** in a strategic plan must be made based on valid data. The goal of QI is to manage with facts, ideally eliminating speculation or organizational stories that are not accurate.

As part of the strategic plan, the organization should provide for human resource development, with the intent to develop the full potential of the EMS work force. It is important to understand and improve on processes by ensuring good relationships between internal and external customers and focusing on system results. An organizational assessment of quality looks at the results of an organization's success at achieving quality. Benchmarks, processes, or goals should be placed in a strategic plan. Strategic plans must identify key processes or key performance indicator(s). QI strategies should be planned by measuring and initiating improvements and then remeasuring to identify gain in key processes or performance indicators.

Side Bar

Recipe for Strategic Planning

This recipe for strategic planning is based on years of wisdom from a Paramedics Plus supervisor.

1 percent	Plan (structure for getting there)
1 percent	Knowledge (teams, tools, methods)
1 percent	Commitment (leadership and employee buy-in)
1 percent	Communication (Intra- and interagency)
1 percent	Recognition (mission, customers, consumers)
1 percent	Respect (for job, for co-workers)
94 percent	Common Sense (How would you like to be serviced?)
100 percent	Customer, Employee, and Manager Satisfaction

PERFORMANCE INDICATORS

In modern QI, there are three types of performance **indicators** used to measure quality in patient care: structural, process, and outcome indicators. A **structural indicator** consists of data or attributes involving the setting in which care is provided. These usually refer to the characteristics of the different components of an EMS system, including facilities, equipment, staffing, and the knowledge base of providers, credentialing, and deployment. Most structural indicators reflect standards developed at a local, regional, or national level through consensus building or by EMS organizations, administrators, or authorities. These indicators provide an indirect measure of quality and are difficult to relate to outcomes in patient care. Since EMS system designs are diverse, these indicators may not be applicable to all systems. The emergency vehicle response time standard is the most commonly used structural measure in EMS. The goal is to respond to 90 percent of the priority 1 responses (life threatening and highly time dependent) in less than 9 minutes. Several EMS systems designed ambulance deployment strategies to meet this standard despite conflicting results from several studies about the effect of short response times on patient outcome in trauma and the need for even shorter EMS times (around 4 minutes) to impact survival in out-of-hospital cardiac arrest (El Sayed, 2011). In the United Kingdom, the adoption of a similar time target structure measure (8-minute response time for 75 percent of category A or emergency calls) by the National Service Framework for coronary artery disease as the main performance indicator was criticized and described by the paramedics as a poor quality indicator that is "too simplistic and narrow" and that is putting patients and ambulance crews at risk (Bevan and Hamblin, 2009).

Another type of measure is the **process indicator**. A process indicator measures ways in which program services and goods are provided (i.e., error rates). These are the components of the encounter between the prehospital provider and the patient. It is an evaluation of the steps of the care provided. A process is the repeatable sequence of actions used across all EMS levels to produce good patient outcome. Process indicators measure more sensitive differences in quality of care. In contrast to structural and outcome measures that provide an indirect approach to quality measurement, process measures allow for a direct assessment of quality of care. The inputs from process measures are very useful for QI programs since they are easy to interpret and act on. One disadvantage of using process measures to monitor quality is that they can become very complex with increased clinical sophistication of the medical services provided in the prehospital setting. In the United States, EMS medical directors commonly use process measures when performing a structured implicit review of prehospital records (run sheets) to evaluate compliance with medical protocols and appropriateness of the treatment provided. One example would be collecting specific data points on the process of endotracheal intubation performed by EMS providers to monitor the success rate of this procedure. A medical director can evaluate the technical skill of providers performing this procedure and their compliance with preestablished criteria and decide which specific elements will need improvement, such as mandating tube placement verification with End Tidal CO_2 waveform documentation.

A third type of measure is outcome data. These evaluate the change in patient's subsequent health status in response to a clinical intervention. Numerous prehospital interventions are not yet evidence based. An **outcome indicator** is a quantitative or qualitative measure that provides information about whether or not an outcome has been accomplished. An outcome indicator is the measurable evidence or information. In many cases, more than one indicator may be necessary to measure an outcome—for example, discharge rate and Glasgow Coma Scale on discharge. Outcome research in EMS focuses on determining the effectiveness of some of these interventions and showing the true value of an EMS system since it offers feedback on all aspects of care. Outcome data are easy to interpret and easily understood by the different stakeholders (policymakers, patients, EMS providers, public, etc.) and can be used to compare EMS systems. The adoption of pure outcome data as performance indicators is not, however, straightforward. For outcome data and, more specifically, clinical outcome data to be relevant, performance indicators, accurate risk adjustment, standardization of definitions, and development of research models for each measured outcome are required

DEFINING A THEME AND VALUES

As a start to defining quality, several themes must be incorporated into EMS operations. EMS managers can look at other industries and develop tools and methods based on quality management principles. Similarities or universal principles are the same for organizations, independent of the type of service or industry being studied. These universal principles of quality can then be applied to EMS and health care systems. Four core principles have emerged to guide quality in EMS and health care:

- *Focus on the Patient/Public*—Services must be designed to meet the needs and expectations of patients and communities.
- *Focus on Systems and Processes*—Providers must understand the service delivery system and its key service processes in order to improve them.
- *Focus on Measurement*—Data are needed to analyze processes, identify problems, and measure performance.
- *Focus on Teamwork*—Quality is best achieved through a team approach to problem solving and QI.

STRATEGIC PLANNING

An understanding of the strategic planning process is essential for today's EMS organization. EMS organizations defining quality need to integrate quality goals, develop short- and long-term organizational goals, and measure the success of the organization—essentially creating a seamless integration of QI initiatives into all aspects of EMS operations.

BENCHMARKING

Benchmarking is a common process used to perform self-evaluation and begin the strategic planning cycle. It can take many forms, but it is viewed as the ongoing and systematic process for measuring and comparing the work process of one organization to those of another, most often a peer, by bringing an external focus to internal activities, functions, or operations. Benchmarking either compares performance of an indicator or establishes a level of performance that should be reached for a given indicator of structure, process, or outcome of the EMS service. The goal of benchmarking is to provide EMS managers with a standard for measuring the quality and cost of internal activities, to help identify where opportunities for improvement can be made, and should be conducted internally before going outside to compare performance.

Internal benchmarking involves two-way communication and sharing opinions between departments within the same organization or between areas of the organization operating as a different shift, crew, or station.

Once any part of an organization has a better performance indicator, others can learn how this was achieved. Findings of internal benchmarking can then be used as a baseline for extending benchmarking to include external organizations.

All benchmarking processes should start by dealing with internal benchmarking because this requires an organization to examine itself, and this provides a baseline for comparison with others. Among advantages of internal benchmarking are the ability to deal with employees, collaborating agencies, and a management team who share a common language, culture, and systems; having easy access to data; and being able to establish a baseline for future comparisons. Thus, the outcomes of internal benchmarking can be developed more quickly.

Asking the following questions, and reacting positively to the answers, provides decision makers with the opportunity to strive for improvement and promote healthy competition. This approach perpetuates constant improvement as agencies continually try to surpass each other's accomplishments, and over time an entire region can be operating at peak efficiency. The self-assessment for internal benchmarking may involve the following questions:

- How well are we doing compared to others?
- How good do we want to be?
- Who is doing it the best?
- How do they do it?
- How can we adapt what they do to our organization?
- How can we be better than the best?

External benchmarking requires the organization to turn its focus to outside organizations. It requires a comparison of work with external organizations in order to discover new ideas, methods, products, and services. The objective is to continuously improve one's own performance by measuring it, comparing it with other EMS organizations, and determining how the others achieve their performance levels. External benchmarking provides opportunities for learning from the best practices and experiences of others who are at the leading edge of the EMS industry.

The National Highway Traffic Safety Administration (NHTSA) recommends the following developmental stages in building a framework for quality. First, the EMS manager must build potential for success by developing awareness throughout the organization that QI is a meaningful endeavor. Then the organization must expand agencywide knowledge of, and capability in, QI practices and techniques. Finally, the EMS organization must integrate the strategic quality planning process and related actions into daily EMS operations.

It is important to realize that there is a difference between benchmarking and benchmarks. Benchmarking is an improvement process by which an EMS agency measures its performance against the best in class of other companies, agencies, or organizations; determines how those groups achieved that level of excellence or performance; and then applies or uses that information to improve its own performance.

A set of common benchmarks remains the challenge to EMS. Due to the differences in systems that influence outcomes, benchmarking must have an appreciation for variety. EMS commonly uses lateral benchmarking through processes suggested by the Committee on Accreditation of Ambulance Services (CAAS), the Coalition of Advanced Emergency Medical Systems (CAEMS), or the Centers for Public Safety Excellence (CFSI). Sequential benchmarking is an internal approach that is often a more effective long-term approach of measuring against internal processes. Best-practice benchmarking is described in many cases. In one instance, FedEx helped Memphis establish benchmarks by applying FedEx supply chain quality initiatives to Memphis Fire Department EMS processes.

For benchmarking to be worthwhile, an organization needs to understand the gap between its own performance and best practices and to take actions to close that gap. Competitive benchmarking requires a comparison with direct competitors only. This is the most sensitive type of benchmarking activity because it is very difficult to achieve a healthy collaboration and cooperation with direct competitors and reach primary sources of information. It is often easier for larger organizations than for smaller ones, as the former have the infrastructure to support quality and continuous improvement and often have a market or service area secured.

Any aspect of an EMS operation can be benchmarked. In EMS, benchmarking involves searching for and copying new ideas and best practices for the improvement of processes, products, and services. Benchmarking can be done by conducting a literature review, consulting experts, identifying current practice, or replicating another agency's best practices

BENCHMARKS

A benchmark is a standard against which something is measured. In most cases, there is a reference point or organization that has been identified as "best in class." Benchmarks can cover all aspects of EMS and encompass the operational, clinical, and business processes of an EMS organization. Generic benchmarks are comparisons of EMS with business functions that are the same regardless of business. This means, for example, that an EMS organization's accounting department would look at the accounting department of a trucking organization that has been identified as having the fastest operations. It is believed to be easier to obtain data, or to benchmark designs or definitions, when establishing generic benchmarks as organizations that are ranked as best in class are more likely to share their experiences. However, generic benchmarks can take a long time to complete, and research outcomes may need a lot of modification in order for organizations to set their own standards.

Operational Benchmarks

Operational benchmarks include those measurements against everything that affects the field operations of an EMS operation. Operational items can be any process, procedure, or action that involves the support of the clinical applications of EMS. It is *not* the practice of medicine.

The North Central EMS Institute is conducting a lateral benchmarking process that includes twenty-five agencies and five states. Staff are looking at traditional clinical aspects of EMS and assessing EMS business processes. Specifically, they are looking at EMS processes that involve the following:

- General business
- Business office
- Dispatch
- Fleet management
- Response times (first response on scene and ALS on scene)
- Unit-hour utilization
- Time to generate a bill
- Work-related injuries
- Motor vehicle accidents
- Staffing
- Coverage
- System status management use
- Transports/10,000 population
- Cost/unit hour
- Number of certifications per staff member
- Fractal response data
- Cardiac arrest survival rates
- Dollars in community subsidy required

Clinical Benchmarks

A clinical benchmark is established using process and outcome indicators. Using the example of door-to-reperfusion time for an acute myocardial infarction, measuring the time from the door to the catheterization lab may reveal factors that influence the speed of this process. The survival rate and the damage or lack of damage to the heart are outcome-based indicators used in conjunction with the process indicators to help establish a clinical benchmark, such as the following:

- Cardiac arrest process and outcome
- Intubation success
- Pain control
- System trauma outcomes
- Patient's subjective opinion on improvement of pain relief

Business Benchmarks

As the QI process evolves, EMS agencies should be encouraged to measure other areas of organizational efficiency. Quality definitions should be established for other processes, including (but not limited to) these:

- *Ratio of In-Service to Out-of-Service Hours for Apparatus and Ambulances*—This would include how often a unit is out of service for training, maintenance, or various other reasons. This should also include a registry of how often the unit is taken down for staffing and other reasons (e.g., nonovertime, sick call, person of sufficient rank unavailable). This is a structural indicator as it looks at how often a component of the EMS system will be available. It is influenced by processes such as how a unit is taken out of service for education or how an employee uses sick or vacation time.
- *Staffing Pattern-to-Peak Call Volume Intervals* — This indicator measures how well an agency matches the unit hours to the call volume. In a quality measure, peak volumes should be identified and how often mutual aid or automatic aid occurs should be determined. This should also include any time when the EMS system overloads and a unit is unavailable.
- *Customer Satisfaction*—This should include assessments of internal and external customers. A Likert scale provides respondents an opportunity to judge a variety of different customer experiences on a 1 to 5 scale: 1 = poor, 2 = below average, 3 = average, 4 = good, 5 = very good.
- *Vehicle Performance/Reliability*—A quality definition should be developed to keep track of the cost involved with vehicle repair and preventative maintenance schedules.
- *Availability of Provider Educational Opportunities*—This quality indicator requires a definition and benchmark. For example, will the agency provide continuing education classes and to what level? A quality definition may be to what extent classes are offered to meet National Registry requirements.
- *Emergency Department Turnaround Times*— A quality definition should be benchmarked for what the expected time is to clear an ambulance from the hospital. This is often called drop time or time until available.
- *Recruitment and Retention of Members*—The reasons that people leave the organization should be categorized and tracked as a quality item. Is it a voluntary or nonvoluntary separation? The job satisfaction of current employees is a common benchmark related to internal quality. The number of people screened or tested for a new position versus being actually hired is a business process that can be very expensive.
- *Employee Absenteeism*—Sick leave, long-term injuries, and the amount of time it takes to return people to duty from work-related injuries are measures of quality and should be trended. High numbers in this category may indicate unsafe conditions and/or a need for programs or equipment to be changed to reduce injuries.
- *Workforce Relationships*—The number of grievances and the resolution of grievances or other disputes should be a quality definition. What is

an acceptable number of disputes? How much staff time or additional cost is needed to resolve issues with workforce relations?

- *Compliance with OSHA Standards*—As a measure of quality, OSHA standards protect employees. Loss to an organization due to noncompliance should be seen as a quality item.
- *Billing and Collection Processes*—Several quality definitions are required for billing operations. The payer mix determines which type of insurance and collections, and what has been billed versus what has been collected. The time it takes to process and get a bill in the billing cycle is a key indicator.
- *Safe Community's Initiatives/Injury Prevention Strategies*—Program evaluation should be monitored for effectiveness in reducing injuries targeted by programs designed to meet the needs of these strategies. For example, has the helmet program reduced the number of head injuries in children in the community?

FUNCTIONAL BENCHMARKING

Conducting a functional benchmark refers to comparative research and attempts to seek world-class excellence by comparing EMS agency performance not only against competitors but also against the best health care organizations operating in similar fields and performing similar activities or having similar problems, but in a different industry.

COMMON REGIONAL BENCHMARKS

Often, benchmarks are established for EMS agencies as regional efforts by a regulatory or administrative authority. This is common in EMS systems that have a single, advanced life support (ALS) provider umbrella over several other basic life support providers. On a regional level, benchmarks may include the following:

- Adherence to regional or state medical protocol
- Adherence to regional or state standard operating procedure or policy
- Comparison of prehospital impression to hospital diagnosis
- Comparison of prehospital presentation to outcome
- Emergency medical dispatch (EMD) priority call criteria compliance
- Statistical analysis of critical skills
- Appropriateness of selection of destination hospital
- Resource allocation
- Effects of prehospital patient care activity on length of hospital stay
- Cardiac arrest survivability
- Emergency medical dispatch and prearrival instructions
- Public access to EMS

PLANNING FOR TYPES OF ERRORS

Quality also means operating without errors. Any organization looking to maintain a high level of quality needs to identify and employ techniques to reduce errors. Errors must be analyzed to establish the cause. Then, a failure mode and effect analysis (FMEA) process or a root cause analysis can be applied to the error. An organization needs to define quality by categorizing the kind of errors. Errors generally fall into one of four categories: diagnostic, treatment, preventive, and other.

- Diagnostic
  - Error or delay in diagnosis
  - Failure to employ indicated tests, equipment, or assessments
  - Use of outdated tests, assessments, or therapy
  - Failure to act on results of monitoring or testing
- Treatment
  - Error in the performance of a procedure or test
  - Error in administering the treatment
  - Error in the dose or method of using a drug
  - Avoidable delay in treatment or in responding to an abnormal test or physical exam findings
  - Inappropriate (not indicated) care

- Preventive
  - Failure to provide prophylactic treatment or an injury-prevention scheme
  - Inadequate monitoring or follow-up of treatment
- Other
  - Failure of communication
  - Equipment failure
  - Other system failure

The know-how already exists to prevent many mistakes and errors. The Institute of Medicine's (IOM) report *To Err is Human: Building a Safer Health System* sets a minimum goal of a 50 percent reduction in errors. In its recommendations for reaching this goal, the IOM strikes a balance between regulatory and market-based initiatives and between the roles of professionals and organizations.

One of the report's main conclusions is that the majority of medical errors do not result from individual recklessness or the actions of a particular group. More commonly, errors are caused by faulty systems, processes, and conditions that lead people to make mistakes or fail to prevent them. For example, stocking EMS units with certain drugs in the same containers or with similar color schemes has resulted in deadly mistakes and medication errors. Thus, mistakes can best be prevented by designing the EMS system to make it safer at all levels—to make it more difficult for people to do something wrong and easier for them to do it right. This does not mean that individuals can be careless. They still must be vigilant and held responsible for their actions. But when an error occurs, blaming an individual does little to make the system safer and prevent someone else from committing the same error.

ADVERSE EVENT AND NEAR-MISS REPORTING SYSTEMS

Significant knowledge has been developed in other high risk industries, such as aviation, power generation, and the military, which allows problems to be reported and system safety interventions and solutions to be implemented and studied. These initiatives have focused on system problems, as opposed to the failings of any one individual as the root cause of adverse events. This method is applicable to EMS for the characterization and analysis of hazards and errors, as well as the ultimate improvement of EMS patient safety. Without knowledge of what types of errors and hazards exist, a system cannot be designed to protect the patient from an adverse outcome as a result of these hazards. There are several ways to investigate the nature of error, but event reporting systems have been shown to identify problems and trends that can otherwise go unnoticed. This allows an EMS organization to define the number of these events that drop the organization below the organization's definition of quality.

There are two main types of event-reporting systems: mandatory and voluntary. Mandatory reporting systems have two major downfalls: (1) They are often punitive in nature (a barrier to self-reporting), and (2) their reporting criteria select for accidents and errors, which result in harm. Thus, near-miss data, known to be extremely important for predicting future problems, are absent from the database. The importance of near-miss reporting and analysis has been emphasized by the IOM. In medicine, near misses are thought to occur 300 to 400 times more often than actual adverse events. This higher rate allows for more powerful analysis.

Nonpunitive or voluntary reporting systems have a high degree of acceptance among system participants and therefore capture a much larger proportion of actual errors. Such systems also permit participants to report near-miss events, increasing the total amount of analyzable information that is captured.

The IOM, Agency for Healthcare Research and Quality, American College of Emergency Physicians, and other prominent medical organizations all support standardized systems of event reporting as a method for improving patient safety. Some states, such as Pennsylvania, and some local EMS systems, such as Houston Fire, have developed their own confidential, nonpunitive event-reporting systems for EMS.

Three national EMS reporting systems are known to exist. The Medical Errors Prevention and Reporting System (MEPARS), originally called the Medical Errors Reporting System, is a privately held domain for several types of error-reporting systems. It has a system that is based on NASA's near-miss and adverse-events system that has resulted in hundreds of systems improvements.

Side Bar

Error-Reporting Systems

MEPARS conducts a more formal analysis and plans to publish results to be shared among agencies. This program is operated out of the University of Pittsburgh's Center for Emergency Medicine.

EMS Close Calls operates in conjunction with the International Association of Fire Chiefs and Firefighter's Close Calls. It records near-miss events related to EMS operations among all EMS agencies.

The National Firefighter Near Miss program is operated by the International Association of Fire Chiefs, International Association of Firefighters, and the Fire Act Grants program. It encourages EMS providers to report events, including medical errors. All EMS agencies are encouraged to participate in near-miss and error-event reporting systems in order to contribute to data collection as well as to learn from the past experiences of others.

Side Bar

Near Miss

The National Firefighter Near Miss reporting system is a voluntary, confidential, nonpunitive reporting system with the goal of improving fire and EMS safety. Submitted reports are reviewed by EMS professionals. Identifying factors are removed to mask the identity of the reporting agency. Reports are posted on the website for other firefighters and EMS workers to use as learning tools.

In 2013 the Center for Leadership, Innovation and Research in EMS with sponsorship from the North Central EMS Institute, National EMS Management Association, Emergency Medical Services Chiefs of Canada, National Association of EMTs, and National Association of State EMS Officials created the EMS Voluntary Event Notification Tool (E.V.E.N.T). E.V.E.N.T is designed to improve the quality and consistent delivery of emergency medical services.

Side Bar

E.V.E.N.T.

The EMS Voluntary Event Notification Tool (E.V.E.N.T.) website is home to the EMS voluntary notification tool. This EMS near-miss reporting website shares stories that are individually submitted by a provider or agency. This site allows for anecdotal and experiential data to be collected and acts as a compass for further quality issues that relate to patient safety and QI by identifying near misses or mishaps in EMS. The E.V.E.N.T. system collects near-miss events, patient safety events, and line-of-duty deaths.

INTERNAL QUALITY

In an EMS agency, management must understand that the EMS provider is, in a sense, one of the customers. Personnel relations are a key quality indicator. An organization must define the level of quality that it will provide to internal customers. Feedback to the EMS provider is always necessary. Negative feedback should be given only during appropriate times and never in front of a patient. Telling a patient that the EMS provider is wrong without investigation will damage the relationship between the provider and supervisor, preceptor, or whoever provides such feedback. Opportunity should also be available for personnel to rate the leadership.

Providers look for consistency in their supervisors. A sense of fairness and equal treatment is required to ensure consistent progress in the quality of care. Inconsistent application of discipline, remediation, or praise can affect the quality of patient outcomes. It is difficult to have a functional organization driven to provide excellent patient care and customer service when the providers do not feel that they themselves are treated well. Therefore, internal quality should be defined and measured based on the consistency of rules and how they are applied as well as processes and rewards.

Effective personnel development and succession planning focused on producing providers should be the responsibility of EMS management and developed as quality measures. Not all personnel want to develop or promote, yet every effort should be made to provide development sessions and plan succession within the organization. Most continuing medical education is structured around patient care, not people care. Emphasis should be placed on the entire organization, not just the clinical aspects.

An organization also must have fun. The responsibilities of patient care and giving direction in patient care environments come with enormous pressures. The supervisor should remain cognizant of this and, from time to time, attempt to organize social opportunities. Laughter is good and healthy. However, this must not occur in patient-care scenarios or at the expense of the personnel or organization.

Recognition is equally important in defining an internal quality process to highlight outstanding customer service activity. This recognition will demonstrate the agency's mission to go beyond *having* a customer service goal to actually *meeting* that goal.

A customer service program provides many benefits in an EMS agency. From a public service perspective, patients hold the providing agency or region accountable under the guise of a public trust issue. The public can seek to demand change through the legislature or city/county council. Mergers or disbanding agencies can affect the provider's livelihood. Often communities that contract for EMS services can simply choose a competitor for alternative service. The quality of customer service can often be the deciding factor. Simple examples of customer service standards for which EMS providers should strive include the following:

- Making everyone feel at home
- Smiling and introducing themselves
- Being courteous and going the extra mile
- Being professional and dressing the part

EMS professionals should always remember to handle patients with care and dignity. An old saying in EMS asks providers to put themselves in the shoes of the patient and family. Respecting privacy is not only mandated but also necessary for maintaining the confidence of the patient. Customer service means anticipating a customer's needs and doing what you say you will do.

SETTING GOALS OR STANDARDS —

Defining quality is a step toward developing expectations or quality standards. Standards can be developed for inputs, processes, or outcomes; they can be clinical or administrative. Standards can be applied at the level of an individual, facility, or system. A good standard is explicit, reliable, realistic, valid, and clear. Defined standards or definitions of quality are prerequisites for measuring quality. If standards are not established, they must be developed. Standards of quality can be defined according to certain dimensions of quality and should be based on the best scientific evidence available. Stakeholder (including client and community) expectations of quality should also be incorporated into quality standards.

Experts generally recognize several distinct dimensions of quality that vary in importance, depending on the context in which a QI effort takes place. The following nine dimensions of quality have been developed from the technical literature on quality and ideas from various QI experts:

1. *Technical Performance*—The degree to which tasks carried out by health workers and facilities meet expectations of technical quality (i.e., adhere to standards)
2. *Access to Services*—The degree to which health care services are unrestricted by geographic, economic, social, organizational, or linguistic barriers
3. *Effectiveness of Care*—The degree to which desired results (outcomes) of care or emergency services are achieved
4. *Efficiency of Service Delivery*—The ratio of the outputs of services to the associated costs of producing those services; typically, unit hour cost and utilization
5. *Interpersonal Relations*—Trust, respect, confidentiality, courtesy, responsiveness, empathy, effective listening, and communication between providers and clients
6. *Continuity of Services*—Delivery of care by the same health care provider throughout the course of care (when appropriate) and appropriate and timely transfer and communication between providers
7. *Safety*—The degree to which the risks of injury, infection, or other harmful side effects are minimized
8. *Physical Infrastructure and Comfort*—The physical appearance of the facility or emergency vehicles, cleanliness, comfort, privacy, and other aspects that are important to patients
9. *Choice*—As appropriate and feasible, patient choice of provider, insurance plan, or treatment

Together, these dimensions provide a useful framework that helps health teams define, analyze, and measure the extent to which they are meeting program standards for clinical care and for management services that support service delivery. Although all of these nine dimensions are relevant to all settings, not all of them deserve equal weight in every program. Each should be defined according to the local context and specific programs. Universally accepted standards are often a good starting point for developing local standards. Often, standards must also be refined to make them usable by health workers.

DEVELOPING AND COMMUNICATING STANDARDS

Standards are clear statements of expected quality in the performance of EMS activity. Standards may take the form of procedures, clinical practice guidelines, treatment protocols, critical paths, algorithms, standard operating procedures or guidelines, and expected outcomes, among other formats. Standards communicate expectations for how a particular EMS activity will be performed so that it achieves the desired results and defines, for both EMS workers and patients, what is needed to produce quality services. Performance in accordance with standards is thus the cornerstone of QI in health care and the end result to which a wide range of QI activities lead, including accreditation of health facilities, external quality evaluation, and performance improvement. The field of quality assurance is also focused on performance according to standards because adherence to evidence-based standards has been shown to be associated with improved outcomes. Moreover, failure to provide clinical care in accordance with standards has serious negative effects on patient outcomes.

Standards may be implicit (understood) or explicit (written). Implicit standards derive from the expertise of professionals who work in a specific environment. For example, a crew working on a pediatric patient may know the treatment that a dehydrated child needs but may have different ideas about the most appropriate way to provide the treatment (e.g., dosage, duration, and frequency). Converting implicit standards to explicit standards provides consensus on the way to provide quality care, reduces variation among health care providers, and allows a baseline measure for monitoring quality.

Explicit standards appear in a variety of forms, such as procedures, protocols, or clinical practice guidelines. Process reliability relies on clear explicit standards. In the preceding example of a dehydrated child, the explicit standard is 20 cc of normal saline per kilogram, as set forth in pediatric ALS training and other standardized courses. These standards for EMS-related professional organizations can come from government agencies (e.g., Centers for Disease Control and Prevention, EMS Division of the NHTSA, or state EMS authorities), national organizations (e.g., National Association of EMTs, International Association of Fire Chiefs, National Fire Protection Association, National EMS Management Association, and American Society for Testing and Materials [ASTM]), accrediting organizations (e.g., Joint Commission International, Committee of Accreditation of Ambulance Services, and Centers for Public Safety Excellence), or by an EMS agency itself. To achieve expected patient or customer outcomes, standards must be developed in such a way that they have these characteristics:

- *Realistic*—The standards can be followed or achieved with existing resources.
- *Reliable*—Following the standards for a specific intervention results in the same outcome (all factors being equal).
- *Valid*—The standards are based on scientific evidence or other acceptable experience.
- *Clear*—The standards are understood in the same way by everyone concerned and are not subject to distortion or misinterpretation.
- *Measurable*—Performance according to the standards must be able to be assessed and quantified.

EMS performance according to standards is foundational for producing reliability and quality, but QI can be used both to take an organization from not meeting standards to meeting standards and from meeting standards to new levels of performance. QI is a continuous process, not a destination. Quality assurance is the process of confirming a performance meets specifications, not trying to improve performance.

There is no single best method for developing standards that meet these criteria. The six-step Standards Development Cycle provides a process for setting standards that can be adapted to each specific clinical, operational, and business situation. Standards should be made as lean and simple as possible with clear decision making. Sometimes it is better to define a choice versus giving options to increase reliability. The process for setting standards will be very different depending on the level and scope of the work, resources available, and complexity of the process. Standards should be designed not for all hazards but for the majority with guidance for cases that are outside the norm. The focus is on 80 percent of cases that are in the norm.

THE STANDARDS DEVELOPMENT CYCLE

The U.S. Agency for International Development (USAID) Health Care Improvement Project has found that there is no single best method for developing standards. Instead, a menu of six steps called the Standards Development Cycle provides a flexible process for setting standards that can be adapted to each specific situation. The process for setting standards will be very different, depending on the level and scope of the work, resources available, and complexity of the topic. These are the six steps:

- Step 1: Define and agree.
- Step 2: Select who should be involved.
- Step 3: Gather information.
- Step 4: Draft standards.
- Step 5: Test the standards.
- Step 6: Communicate the standards.

Step 1: Define and Agree

In this step, the goal is to define and agree on several areas and issues that will define the standards development task:

- Define the area or topic for which standards are being developed (for more limited, facility-level activities, skip the next two bullet points).
- State the scope of care and identify the most important aspects of care, if needed, to focus standard setting where it can have the greatest impact.
- State the level of the health care system for which the standards are being developed (e.g., national, regional, or facility).
- Clarify the consensus process, both for topic selection and approval.
- Clarify the approval process for the standards.

Step 2: Select Who Should Be Involved

Identify, at the outset of the process, all stakeholders (i.e., those individuals or groups with a vested interest in the successful development of the standards). Learning the stakeholders' expectations should be incorporated into the consensus and approval process of standards development. A determination should also be made regarding whether experts will be required. When developing clinical standards experts may be invited to participate in a working group (e.g., pediatric physicians, trauma surgeons). Depending on the scope of the task, additional technical experts may be required as the work progresses and issues arise. The last part of step 2 is to organize the working group that will develop the standards and to develop a management action plan that provides the parameters for successful completion of the task and the process by which it is achieved. Key items that should be addressed in the plan are these:

- Selection of a team leader
- Definition of the lines of authority and communication, resources available, and the process for working together (including clarifying tasks, roles, and responsibilities of team members)
- The approval process for the standards developed
- Specifications for the desired product and the deadline for completion

Step 3: Gather Information

In this step, the working group gathers information about the topic under review and other resources that can help define the key elements that should be included in the standards. A flowchart may be developed to better understand the points in the current process requiring the development of standards. Even if there are no resources for extensive research, here are some areas to consider before launching into drafting standards:

- Are existing standards related to the topic?
- Are any laws and regulations related to the topic?
- What current practices related to this topic should be considered?

- Is clinical evidence available for best practices in this topic? Does the team have access to someone with knowledge or access to such information?
- What is the technology base available in the health system in this topic area? How does it limit or facilitate the development of standards?
- What resources are available for research, drafting, testing, and communicating these standards?

Step 4: Draft Standards

There are several components to drafting standards:

- Decide the structure and format of the standards, depending on their purpose.
- After the format is decided, the working group drafts the standards, developing key indicators to measure performance.
- Prior to field testing, the draft standards should be evaluated internally for quality.

Step 5: Test the Standards

Once indicators are developed, the working group must decide whether a field test is needed. This step might be skipped, for example, if testing has already been done on another level. If a test is needed, a testing plan should be developed. Testing informs the wording and presentation of the standards, improves their quality, increases credibility, and continues the consensus-building process. Following an evaluation of the field test, revisions, if needed, should be made to the standards and the revised standards field-tested again. The process of field testing, revision, and field testing continues until revisions are no longer needed and standards are submitted for approval.

Step 6: Communicate the Standards

Although the standards-setting process might be completed with the approval of the standards, the impact of well-developed standards depends on EMS providers using the standards. Standards communication and implementation strategies are critical to achieving EMS provider performance according to the standards. A well thought-out communication plan is needed to identify how the correct people will receive the correct information so they will perform the correct tasks related to the standards. Key elements of the communications plan may need to be tested. For example, if a job aid will be used to support implementation of standards, it should be tested to ensure that it is clear and reliable. If new standards are expected to change current practices significantly, testing the communications strategy will help develop the most acceptable message and identify the best messenger to ensure that providers and health administrators will modify their practices to perform according to the standards. Rolling out the communication plan might include presenting or publicizing the standards, training health workers in the standards, and distributing job aids. The communication process should allow opportunities for feedback, both on the standards and the communication process itself.

QUALITY DESIGN

Quality design involves EMS providers, patients/public, and EMS managers in a structured process to explicitly identify patient/public needs and design service processes with key features to meet those needs. In the context of designing quality, the features of a QI system require a practical assessment of the patient and public needs, desires, and expectations. Although quality design is often applied to develop an entirely new process or service where a comparable one does not exist, it may also be used to substantially redesign an existing process or service. A QI process developed by the Joint Commission has a ten-step systematic approach to quality design:

1. Select the process to be designed or modified.
2. Define objectives/aims of the new process.

3. Identify the customer, patient, and stakeholders (both external and internal) of the selected process.
4. List and prioritize the patient's needs and requirements.
5. Create a flowchart of the new process with main activity blocks.
6. Link the patient, customer, and public's needs with each activity block in the flowchart.
7. Identify key features in the new design that respond to priority needs and requirements of patient, customer, and the public. Link key features with activity blocks.
8. Design the new process incorporating the key features.
9. Test the new design for robustness (i.e., reliability, feasibility).
10. Plan, implement, and monitor the new process. (O'Leary and O'Leary, 1992)

SENTINEL EVENTS

A **sentinel event** is an unexpected occurrence involving death or serious physical or psychological injury, or the risk thereof. Serious injury specifically includes loss of limb or function. The phrase *or the risk thereof* includes any process variation for which a recurrence would carry a significant chance of a serious adverse outcome. Such events are called sentinel because they signal the need for immediate investigation and response. When a sentinel event happens, there should be an analysis and action plan to correct the causes within 7 to 14 days. When defining what a sentinel event is as a quality indictor, the following should be considered:

- Type of sentinel event
- Setting of sentinel events
- Source(s) for how a sentinel event is identified
- Outcome(s) of sentinel event
- Self-reported sentinel events by year
- Method for review of EMS management's response to sentinel event

The following tools should be available to EMS field supervisors and QI coordinators. Part of the QI process involves the agency having a reporting mechanism for sentinel events that should be monitored. Each of the following instances requires a mandatory response in the form of QI indicators that point to a possible loss to the organization or a catastrophic outcome:

1. Cardiac arrest of a patient after being embarked on an ambulance.
2. A unit that upgrades to emergency that started enroute non-emergent
3. Any use of a helicopter for a scene call
4. Any critical pediatric patient
5. A return to the same address by an EMS unit within 24 hours of the original call.
6. Any EMS vehicle crash
7. Any transport of public safety professional.
8. Any equipment failure related to patient care.

Although not every EMS system has a roving or immediately available EMS supervisor or officer to monitor for sentinel events, the use of technology can help overcome the challenges to real-time monitoring in the system. With use of a system called FirstWatch, data can be monitored in a computer-aided dispatch center for sentinel events, such as an EMS unit returning to the same address within 24 hours or an ambulance breakdown. Both are extremely high-risk events for an organization. Data-mining software systems can help define and monitor quality in a system.

EMS PERFORMANCE MEASURES

The EMS Performance Measures Project began in 2002 and concluded in 2006. It provided an additional tool with which to gauge and report the environment and performance of EMS agencies and systems. This was a consensus-building effort with stakeholders from various EMS and fire trade groups. The EMS

Performance Measures Project was coordinated by the National Association of State EMS Officials (NASEMSO), in partnership with the National Association of EMS Physicians (NAEMSP) and supported by the NHTSA and the Health Resources and Services Administration (HRSA). The EMS Performance Measures Project tool offers improvement through common measures comparable nationwide, regardless of service-sponsor type or system con-figuration. (See Figure 4.1.)

The goals of the project, addressed in two distinct phases, were to determine whether the country's EMS leadership desired a common set of specifically defined measures and, if so, what those measures would be. Each measure is presented in a format developed to be comparable with a measures format used elsewhere in the health care system, which is anticipated to assist EMS providers and systems with future performance reporting, research, and reimbursement issues. It is best to focus on the measures portrayed and the formulas and data elements necessary to implement them.

STANDARDIZED DEFINITIONS OF PERFORMANCE INDICATORS

Several attempts have been made to establish a national set of performance standards. Some of the first performance indicators advocated on a national level were produced by the International Association of Firefighters. The latest and most expansive system of performance indicators is from NASEMSO and by the Northwest EMS Consortium. (See Figure 4.2.)

STATE EMS DIRECTORS PERFORMANCE INDICATORS

In an attempt to incorporate a larger number of services in QI activities, the state EMS directors and EMS managers have begun an initiative to define performance indicators that complement the International Association of Firefighter (IAFF) QI indicators. The state EMS directors look to incorporate an approach to quality from a traditional health care model that may be measured and improved in the following six dimensions:

1. Competency and credentialing on both a professional and/or organizations level
2. Appropriateness/accessibility
3. Resource utilization and cost efficiency
4. Effectiveness by assessing desired outcome, quality assurance
5. Safety/risk management (medical/legal)
6. Customer satisfaction

The performance indicators were blended with the results from focus groups of paramedics that revealed fifteen EMS quality indicators that are important to providers.

Other performance indicators suggested by paramedics in various focus groups include research activities, crew and equipment appearance, accuracy of communication, and public confidence. Most of these suggested that key indicators do not have established measurements or identified ways of being measured accurately. Valid performance measures are necessary and cannot be substituted for when improving quality in EMS systems. It is important to adopt validated criteria or to conduct research for validating new performance indicators. Each of the performance indicators is formatted and has a standardized definition. The following is a list of the components of a key indicator:

- *Indicator/Attribute Name*—Name or title of the performance indicator.
- *Key Process Path*—Starting with one of the predefined key process names, this item shows which key process and sub process that the indicator reflects.
- *Patient or Customer/Need*—Indicators are designed to reflect how well and/or how efficiently a given patient or customer need is being met. This item shows what patient or customer need the indicator reflects.

Performance Measure Definitions

Last Modified January 2014

Operations

	MEASURE	GOAL	STANDARD	DEFINITION
A	Emergency calls responded to in 9 minutes or less	90% or Greater	NFPA 1710	From the time Harvest Junction Fire Receives the call to the time a HJFD vehicle arrives on scene on code one calls
1	Transporting ambulance on scene in 10 minutes or less	90% or Greater	NFPA 1710	From the time of call receipt until a Harvest Junction Fire ambulance is on scene for Code 1 calls
2	ALS on scene within 9 minutes or less	90% or Greater	NFPA 1710	From the time of call receipt until any ALS responder is on scene on Code 1 calls
3	Amount of road coverage while system is at rest	90% in 8 minutes	NFPA 1710	A measure of readiness: The percent of geographical addressed area covered by ALS in 8 minutes or less when the system is at rest
4	Number of emergency calls per month	new measure	Internal	The number of unique emergency events responded to in a month
B	Field positions filled	95% or >	Internal	A measure of retention ability and hiring process (FF, EMT PM, Lt., Cpt., BC)
D1	Daytime Chute Time	90% less than 90 seconds	Internal	Measured as time from receipt of emergency call to responding for calls that originate between 0800 and 2200 for Code 1 calls.
D2	Nighttime Chute Time	90% less than 120 seconds	Internal	Measured as time from receipt of emergency call to responding for calls that originate between 2200 and 0800 for Code 1 calls.
E	Acute Coronary Syndrome Advanced Patient Protocol Compliance	≥ 70 pts	Internal	Compliance with the Acute Coronary Syndrome protocol, max score 90 pts
H	Patients surveys rated highest possible (Very Satisfied)	≥ 85%	IAFF PM's	A random measure of patient satisfaction
I	Lost time work related employee exposure, illness or injury	≤ 2 events a month	Internal	Number of work related injury or illness events during the given month causing lost days of work that cause medical expense or lost time
J	Hire date until 2 person crew status	85% in 105 days	Internal	Date of hire until employee is cleared to serve a two person crew, in calendar days

FIGURE 4.1 Sample performance indicators from Harvest Junction Fire. *Source: Emergency Medical Services Performance Measures by NFTSA.*

Performance Measure Definitions

Last Modified January 2014

		MEASURE	GOAL	STANDARD	DEFINITION
	1	Experienced new hire	65 days or <	Internal	Date of hire until new hire with experience is on a two person crew, in calendar days
	2	No experience new hire	105 days or <	Internal	Date of hire until new hire with no experience is on a two person crew in calendar days
Education	**L**	% of cardiac arrest with AED deployment prior to ALS	25%	Healthy People 2010	Defined as deployed by fire, police or general public
	L1	% Adult cardiac arrest with pulse @ ER	32% or Greater	Internal	% of Adult cardiac arrest with a pulse upon arrival @ ER
	M	Cardiac Arrest with bystander CPR	25% or Greater	Internal	Defined as civilian CPR prior to the arrival of a professional rescuer
	N	Number of original content CEU's offered in last 24 month	≥ 72	NREMT	Output measure: Number of unique CE hours offered during the past 24 months
Admin.	**Q**	% of time emergency vehicle fleet is available	95%–98% (min-max)	Internal	A measure of fleet readiness: percent of time the fleet is available for use; no less than 95% and no more than 98%
	R	Critical Emergency Vehicle Failures	Max of 1/month	Internal	A responding unit (BC, PAR, or Ambulance) is unable to complete a call due to vehicle failure
	1	Total Emergency Vehicle Miles Driven		Internal	Number of miles driven by ambulances, PAR's and BC's
	2	Maintenance Cost per Unit Mile per month (Ambulances only)	per month	Internal	Total maintenance expenditures divided by unit mile for ambulances
	S	Percent of calls audited by Medical Director	3% or >	NAEMSP	Percent of calls reviewed by the medical director

FIGURE 4.1 (*Continued*)

Patient satisfaction
Managerial satisfaction
Patient outcomes
Dispatch accuracy
EMS crew satisfaction
Call quality
Partner performance
Response times
Complaints
Paramedic wellness/occupational illness
Equipment practicality
EMS cost-effectiveness
Public confidence
Crew and equipment appearance
Innovations/research

FIGURE 4.2 State EMS officials quality indicators. *Source: Emergency Medical Services Performance Measures by NHTSA.*

- *Type of Measure*—Structural, process, or outcome.
- *Objective*—Describes why an indicator is useful in specifying and assessing the process or outcome of care measured by the indicator.
- *Indicator/Attribute Formula*—The equation for calculation of the indicator. If applicable, separate sections will separately address the numerator and denominator of the indicator equation.
- *Indicator/Attribute Formula Description*—Explanation of the formula used for the indicator. Where applicable, separate descriptions detailing the numerator and denominator will be provided.
- *Denominator Description*—Description of the population being studied or other denominator characteristics, including any equation or other key aspects that characterize the denominator.
- *Denominator Inclusion Criteria*—Additional information not included in the denominator statement that details the parameters of the denominator population.
- *Denominator Exclusion Criteria*—Information describing criteria for removing cases from the denominator.
- *Denominator Data Sources*—Sources for data used in generating the denominator.
- *Numerator Description*—Description of the subset of the population being studied or other numerator characteristics, including any equation or other key aspects that characterize the numerator.
- *Numerator Inclusion Criteria*—Additional information not included in the numerator statement that details the parameters of the numerator population.
- *Numerator Exclusion Criteria*—Information describing criteria for removing cases from the numerator.
- *Numerator Data Sources*—Sources for data used in generating the numerator.
- *Sampling Allowed*—Indicates if sampling the study population is or is not allowed in calculation of this indicator.
- *Sampling Description*—If sampling is allowed, this will describe the sampling process to be used for this indicator.
- *Minimum Number of Data Points*—Tells how many data points are needed, at a minimum, for calculation of this indicator.
- *Suggest Reporting Format: Numerical*—The suggested way in which the numerical results should be expressed (e.g., decimal minutes, percentages, ratios).
- *Suggest Reporting Format: Graphical*—The suggested way in which reports should be presented in graphical format (e.g., pie charts, statistical process control charts).

- *Suggest Reporting Frequency*—Time frame, number of successive cases, or other grouping strategies by which cases should be aggregated for calculating and reporting results.
- *Testing*—Indicates if a formal structured evaluation has been performed on the various scientific properties of the indicator, such as its reliability, validity, and degree of difficulty of data collection.
- *Stratification*—Indicates if stratification has been applied to the indicator.
- *Stratification Options*—Suggested stratification criteria for use with this indicator.
- *Current Development Status*—Describes the amount of work completed to date relative to the final implementation of the indicator.
- *Additional Information*—Further information regarding an indicator not addressed in other sections.
- *References*—Citations of works used for development of the indicator.
- *Contributors*—Listing of persons or organizations used in development of and refinements to this indicator.

NASEMSO created eighteen standard performance indicators, which are categorized into seven types. (See Figure 4.3.)

One of the most important of the NASEMSO indicators is the completion of what can be classified as a successful intubation. The performance indicator for intubation is an example of a performance standard that defines an often confusing benchmark. For example, what counts as an intubation attempt? The standard defines an attempt as any time that the laryngoscope passes the plane of the teeth. The performance indicator also lists how the skill should be recorded.

S	System Design and Structure
HR	Human Resources (culture, training, safety, credentialing, etc.)
CC	Clinical Care and Outcome
R	Response
F	Finance/Funding
Q	Quality Management
CD	Community Demographics

FIGURE 4.3 Key to category abbreviations.
Source: National Association of State EMS Officials (2009).

Side Bar

Defining QI Goes Global

The European Union (EU) Project is looking at clinical outcomes. The EU Project involves thirteen agencies and thirteen countries, all which have significantly different structures. The EU is specifically looking at cardiac arrest outcomes, intubation success rates, pain control, systematic trauma care, and outcomes. Improvement is based on opinions from quality circles that have identified key processes.

IAFF PERFORMANCE INDICATORS

The EMS system performance indicators of the International Association of Firefighters are a specific set of measurable processes. The application of the IAFF definitions should be adjusted for system demographics. The IAFF also separates performance indicators into three categories (structure, process, and outcome) with specific definitions.

QI measurements that focus on the system structure focus on the attributes with which the care is provided and seek to measure patient outcomes. For example, the resource deployment for each response area and the percentage of life-threatening calls that are met within 8 minutes or less 90 percent of the time is a system measurement. The interrelated components forming a prehospital system and what is actually done when care is being provided are part of a system process that should be monitored.

One aspect of EMS systems is call-processing time. Can a 9-1-1 operator process a call in less than 30 seconds and get the call to the first-due basic life support (BLS) unit so it can be at the patient's side within 4 minutes? The outcomes of the system should be measured to assess if the components of the EMS system functioned in an integrated manner so as to achieve outcome for the patient. An outcome that demonstrates patient outcome may be that a chest-pain patient reports pain relief and normal vital signs upon arrival at the hospital.

Using a focus group, the IAFF identified sixteen key performance indicators with twenty-seven different measures.

Response times have been defined by the National Fire Protection Association (NFPA) and the Committee of Accreditation of Ambulance Services (CAAS). Although the time intervals are identified, compliance to the standard is not. The requirement to meet a certain time interval within a specified percentage in a phase of the standard is typically a contractual issue or objective set as part of process improvement in a QI plan. Response time is made up of four components: call processing time, turnout time, travel time, and staffing

- Call processing is the time from call intake by unit dispatching agency until unit notification, including answering the phone or alarm, gathering information, and initiating a response by dispatching appropriate units. The measurement for this indicator is to assess the number of EMS calls that are processed in 90 seconds or less.
- Turnout time is the time from response unit notification to the vehicle's "wheels rolling" toward the incident location. This includes personnel preparation for response, boarding the responding vehicle, placing the apparatus in gear for response, and wheels rolling toward the emergency scene. The percentage of all EMS calls in which turnout is 60 seconds or less should be measured.
- Travel time is the time from the responding vehicle's wheels rolling toward the incident location until the arrival or "wheels stop" of the vehicle on scene at the incident location. The measure of performance for travel time is what percentage of all EMS calls achieve first-responding unit travel time of 4 minutes, 0 seconds or less. What percentage of all EMS calls achieves transport unit travel time of 8 minutes, 0 seconds or less? In addition, what percentage of all EMS calls achieve an ALS unit travel time of 8 minutes, 0 seconds or less?
- Staffing should include both the number and level of training of personnel deployed in the system. What percentage of ALS calls receives a response of two EMTs and two paramedics within 8 minutes or less? What percentage of BLS-level calls receive a response that in-cludes two EMTs within 4 minutes? Is the deployment effective to ensure that EMS response units are staffed and equipped to respond immediately to a request for emergency medical assistance at all times of the day. For what percentage of EMS calls is an EMS unit immediately available to be dispatched and how many incurred a delayed response or required assistance from form a neighboring auto-aid or mutual aid agency? How effective is the road capability—the capacity to provide equality of response to all features of the street network within the jurisdiction? Road structure is an identifiable data point in most communities, as compared to a more unreliable proportion of the population served. This indicator is measured by what percentage of the jurisdiction's road miles has projected coverage by a first-due response unit within specified response time frames. Percentages for first responders should be 5 minutes, 0 seconds, and a transport capable unit should be 9 minutes, 0 seconds. In some fire and EMS systems, a fractal time measurement is used. For example, instead of a flat 5-minute response, the performance measure may be 4 minutes, 59 seconds or 5 minutes, 59 seconds. Each could be considered a 5-minute response time.

Patient care protocol compliance is achieved when EMS-trained personnel operated or performed according to established protocol for patient care. The measurement should be the percentage of ALS and BLS calls for which EMTs and paramedics followed an appropriate recognized protocol. Patient outcomes relate to protocol compliance and patient status following prehospital treatment and/or care relative to the patient's signs and symptoms. Outcomes should be measured based on the status of the patient at first contact and following the EMS experience. What percentage of patients encountered improved, what percentage had no change, and what percentage got worse or died after interfacing with EMS?

The availability of defibrillation will have a substantial impact on patient outcomes. The availability of defibrillator-trained emergency response personnel and use of a defibrillator within 5 minutes of a call is a key indicator. This should be measured by the percentage of calls needing defibrillation that has the first shock delivered within 5 minutes from the time of collapse.

Getting an extrication tool and a trained rescuer to the scene is another key performance indicator. A hydraulic extrication or specialized rescue tool should be available for the rescue of injured people trapped or confined in an area from which they cannot readily be removed. Trauma victims require scene time of 10 minutes or less; however, for a pinned or trapped victim, 20 minutes is the performance goal. The percentage of calls that needed a hydraulic extrication tool to remove a victim or injured person is part of the performance indicator. In most systems, a benchmarked standard for a call requiring extrication equipment is to have a tool available on scene within 8 minutes of the initial responding unit getting notification.

Measuring personnel illness and injury as a result of participating in an EMS encounter, including personnel exposures requiring evaluation and medical follow-up, has been identified as a key performance indicator. This is measured by recording what percentage of EMS calls resulted in reported personnel injury and illness. Personnel turnover is defined as any person leaving the department for any reason (thus no longer participating in the EMS system) and is a key indicator for the health of the EMS system. Annual turnover is calculated by the total number of EMTs or paramedics leaving the organization in 1 year divided by the total number of personnel in the agency.

Training and the amount of continuing medical education (CME), including opportunities for outside training, are key indicators in the system. Training indicators should be tied to a quality management program. Another indicator is if the agency has a comprehensive quality management program. A quality program is one that includes total quality management, continuous QI, and quality assessments. Such programs also include direct field observation by a designated medical quality officer or medical director. Measures include ongoing, well-defined programs with trained observers. System user opinion is another key indicator that identifies system and process performance. A percentage of users who are satisfied with the system should be identified by friends and family of the patient and by other agencies, such as law enforcement. This includes patients of nontransport calls. The last performance indicator under the IAFF program is the presence of a department-specific disaster and multi-casualty plan.

The IAFF has spent considerable expense to validate its version of performance indicators and has participated in many national forums for establishing EMS performance indicators and correlating them to the Department of Transportation's National EMS Information System (NEMSIS) database. The IAFF system offers the likelihood of buy-in from labor. The power behind this system is the ability to benchmark performance of fire-based EMS on a national basis.

LOCAL AND REGIONALLY CREATED PERFORMANCE STANDARDS

Many EMS organizations have chosen to create their own performance measures. Some areas have adopted the NASEMSO format and added more defined performance standards.

The West Des Moines Emergency Medical Services Quality Improvement Program's use of indicators is one very effective way to monitor the quality of patient care in the EMS arena. The West Des Moines EMS and the Iowa Health Alliance QI program develops and uses standardized indicators as defined by local agency. Others are based on those found at the State level. For example the Santa Clara County EMS uses the State of California Quality Improvement Guidelines that allow agencies to uniformly review aspects of patient care, some of which may identify potential risk. Other indicators can guide targeted studies to assess the effectiveness of new processes (e.g., stroke centers, cardiac centers, trauma centers).

CHAPTER REVIEW

Summary

Defining quality starts with the incorporation of quality initiatives into the strategic plan. As part of a strategic plan, benchmarking to measure one's organization against the best in the EMS field helps an organization create its own benchmarks. Creating benchmarks is a process that must follow consistent steps. Benchmarking requires that customers, both internal and external, be considered. An EMS organization's effort to define quality also needs to prepare and define adverse or sentinel events in the system. Once a benchmark has been established, the standard for which the organization will perform to achieve that benchmark needs to be created. Creating a standard requires a step-by-step process and may encompass operational, clinical, or business processes. Once a standard is created, performance indicators need to be created to highlight the detail of a standard.

Two systems of performance indicators for EMS exist as national projects. They are from the National Association of State EMS Officials and the International Association of Firefighters. A national definition of performance indicators has been created by state EMS officials in conjunction with the NEMSIS project. Other local and state systems have similar performance indicators.

WHAT WOULD YOU DO? Reflection

In this scenario, the key indicator of customer satisfaction failed. For this type of patient, quality is defined using both clinical and business process indicators: one for pain control and shortness of breath and the other for patient satisfaction. Errors in diagnostics and treatment occurred in this scenario. Developing a key indicator or protocol for a sickle cell crisis as a general item or creating a detailed option to query sickle cell events using two generic indicators for shortness of breath and the use of pain control medications could help identify the level of care or the performance of the organization.

Review Questions

1. What are the four core principles discussed toward the beginning of this chapter?
2. What are the two main types of event-reporting systems? Provide brief descriptions.
3. List simple examples of customer service standards with which EMS providers should comply.
4. Describe the Standards Development Cycle in detail.
5. What is the goal of benchmarking?
6. What are the three different types of indicators discussed in this chapter?

References

Bevan, G., and Hamblin, R. (2009). "Hitting and Missing Targets by Ambulance Services for Emergency Calls: Effects of Different Systems of Performance Measurement Within the UK." *Journal of the Royal Statistical Society: Series A* (Statistics in Society) *172*(1), 161–190.

California Code of Regulations (Title XXII Social Security), Division 9 Pre-hospital Emergency Medical Services, Chapter 12: EMS Systems Quality Improvement.

Curtis, J. P., E. L. Portnay, Y. Wang, R. L. McNamara, J. Herrin, et al. (2006). "The Pre-Hospital Electrocardiogram and Time to Reperfusion in Patients with Acute Myocardial Infarction, 2000–2002: Findings from the National Registry of Myocardial Infarction. Journal of the American College of Cardiology *47*, 1544–1552.

Deming, E. W. (1982, 1986). "Out of the Crisis." Cambridge, MA: MIT Center for Advance Educational Services.

Eisenberg, M. S., L. Bergner, and A. Hallstrom. (1979a). "Cardiac Resuscitation in the Community: Importance of Rapid Provision and Implications for Program Planning. *JAMA 241*, 1905–1907.

Eisenberg, M. S., L. Bergner, and A. Hallstrom. (1979b). "Paramedic Programs and Out-of-Hospital Cardiac Arrest: I. Factors Associated with Successful Resuscitation." *American Journal of Public Health 69*, 30–38.

El Sayed, M. J. (2011). "Measuring Quality in Emergency Medical Services: A Review of Clinical Performance Indicators." *Emergency Medicine International*. doi: 10.1155/2012/161630.

Institute of Medicine (IOM). 2001. *Crossing the Quality Chasm. Crossing the Quality Chasm: A New Health System for the 21st Century.* Washington, DC: National Academies Press.

International Association of Fire Fighters and International Association of Fire Chiefs. (n.d.). "EMS System Performance Measurement." See the organization website.

International City/County Management Association. (1993). "Benchmarking: Achieving Superior Performance in Fire and Emergency Medical Services." Washington, DC: ICMA.

Leape, L., A. G. Lawthers, T. A. Brennan, et al. (1993). "Preventing Medical Injury." *Quality Review Bulletin 19*(5), 144–149.

McLaughlin, C. P., and A. D. Kaluzny. (2006). *Continuous Quality Improvement in Health Care*, 3rd ed. Sudbury, MA: Jones & Bartlett.

Mohr, P. (2000, May 26). "Rural Emergency Medical Services Issues," presented at the National Rural Health Association conference, Walsh Center for Rural Health Analysis, Project HOPE, Bethesda, Maryland.

National Association of State EMS Officials. (2009). "Performance Measures." See the organization website.

O'Connor, R., C. E. Slovis, R. Hunt, R. G. Pirrallo, and M. R. Sayre. (2002). "Eliminating Errors in Emergency Medical Services: Realities and Recommendations." *Prehospital Emergency Care 6*(1), 107–113.

O'Leary, D. S., and M. R. O'Leary. (1992, August). "From Quality Assurance to Quality Improvement: The Joint Commission on

Accreditation of Healthcare Organizations and Emergency Care." *Emergency Medical Clinics of North America 10*(3), 477–492.

O'Leary, M. R., et al. (1994). *Lexikon: Dictionary of Health Care Terms, Organizations and Acronyms for the Era of Reform.* Chicago: Joint Commission on Accreditation of Healthcare Organizations.

Pande, P., and L. Holpp. (2002). *What Is Six Sigma?* New York: McGraw-Hill.

Roush, W. R., and R. M. McDowell. (1989). "Emergency Medical Services Systems." In W.R. Roush, ed., *Principles of EMS systems: A Comprehensive Text for Physicians*. Dallas, TX: American College of Emergency Physicians.

Key Terms

benchmark A standard against which something is measured. In most cases, there is a reference point or organization that has been identified as "best in class."

benchmarking A common process used to perform a self-evaluation and begin the strategic planning cycle. This is an ongoing and systematic process for measuring and comparing the work process of one organization to that of another, by bringing an external focus to internal activities functions or operations.

external benchmarking A process that requires a comparison of work with external organizations in order to discover new ideas, methods, products, and services.

indicator A quantitative performance measure. An EMS indicator measures conformance with a reasonable expectation as defined by the community served.

internal benchmarking Involves two-way communication and sharing opinions between departments within the same organization or between work areas of the organizations operating as different units.

outcome indicator The measurement of the sum of structural and process indicators within a system. Changes in structure and/or processes have direct effect on outcomes.

process indicator Measurements of activities occurring within a system.

sentinel event An unexpected occurrence involving death or serious physical or psychological injury, or the risk thereof.

standards Can be developed for inputs, processes, or outcomes; can be clinical or administrative.

structural indicator Measurement of an expectation of people, places, or things within a system.

Measuring Quality

5 CHAPTER

Objectives

After reading this chapter, the student should be able to:

5.1 Recognize areas of EMS attributes that need quality improvement activities.
5.2 Identify the components of a service audit.
5.3 Extrapolate the out-of-hospital unit-of-service model.
5.4 Apply a mathematical tool as a decision-making strategy for EMS QI projects.
5.5 Define the intervals for measuring quality.
5.6 Apply techniques on how to make accurate observations and measure field activities.
5.7 Describe the challenges of measuring EMS activities.
5.8 Identify how measurements can be collected from episodic points of field care.
5.9 Identify technology that assists in data measurement.

Key Terms

activity
anecdotal
assessment
blanket sampling
check sheet
controlled variable
dependent variable
differential measurements
independent variable
invalid code
measure
null code
random assignment
randomization
risk adjustment
service audit
temporal analysis
variable
wrong code

WHAT WOULD YOU DO?

A large metropolitan fire department had twenty personnel assigned to the EMS quality assurance division under the EMS bureau. Five of those sit in an office all day and review 9-1-1 tapes using a checklist to gauge whether the dispatcher and call taker followed procedures step by step. The other fifteen personnel were given staff cars to patrol the city, following EMS crews to various calls. At 9:00 a.m., each person carried a clipboard with a generic checklist and hit the streets with instructions to produce ten to twelve audits per day. The firefighter or firefighter paramedic often hung back in the shadows, checking off such things as "Did the crew apply oxygen or a c-collar, when appropriate?" At 4:30 p.m., the crews would return to the office and file the reports.

Personnel arrive in this position either by bid or after being placed there due to a work-related injury or a light-duty assignment. The next day, the same routine was repeated and so on. Every month, complaints would continue to pour in from the medical community and the public. Several times a year major errors would occur, resulting in substantial litigation and poor outcomes despite a large amount of money and personnel assigned to the quality division.

Questions

1. How does this system fail to meet the needs of a modern quality improvement initiative?
2. How can the resources be deployed to make a more significant impact on quality?
3. Identify what aspects of information collection could lead to an error in measurement or unreliable data.

INTRODUCTION

As the old saying goes, "What is not measured is not done." The importance or the mere act of measuring a process, attitude, or outcome often brings about changes in quality. A **measure** is a criterion, metric, or means by which a comparison is made with outputs. **Assessment** of quality must be impartial and neutral without a predisposed assumption of the outcome. When measuring quality, it is important to maintain the confidentiality of the patient and protect the dignity of the provider. Data and quality measurements occur at national, state, community, hospital, agency, and individual provider levels.

Capturing a measurement is a science and requires knowledge of techniques and systems that are or can be put in place to obtain the data. The quality of health care can be defined and measured with a degree of scientific accuracy similar to that of most analytic measures used in clinical medicine. Correct measurement also depends on correct systems being put in place to assess the actions in the system. A quality improvement (QI) manager must have an understanding of a system's **activity** to determine when and where a data point should be pulled out of the process. As with any product or service, the increments of time, units, and actions all have to be measured.

THEORIES OF MEASUREMENT

When tackling the task of measuring EMS activity, it is paramount that you get things right the first time. Capturing the actions and data the first time is important because it accurately influences the cost and effectiveness of QI. Errors in data that require remediation can be costly and unduly influence statistics that can erode the confidence of the statistics. Separating measurements into smaller and more manageable increments can aid in eliminating errors.

RISK ADJUSTMENT

A well-accepted model for establishing health care outcomes is to focus on each aspect of measurement. Richard Kane's model of health care outcomes research is based on the assessment of several interrelated measurements. Kane (1998) focuses on measurements of those characteristics that can be dissected, such as demographics, severity, or co-morbidity. This type of health care research looks for the relationship between the outcome and the treatments by controlling or isolating the variables or measurements. A **variable** is a characteristic of a unit being observed that may assume more than one of a set of values to which a numerical measure or a category from a classification can be assigned. A relatively new term in the health care field is **risk adjustment**. Although risk adjustment is a complicated topic, it is basically a corrective tool used to level the playing field regarding the reporting of patient outcomes, adjusting for the differences in risk among specific patients. Risk adjustment also makes it possible to compare performance fairly. Comparing unadjusted event rates for different EMS providers would unfairly penalize those providing services to higher-risk patients.

For example, if an 86-year-old female with diabetes is seen by EMS for low blood sugar, there is less chance for a good outcome when compared with a healthy 40-year-old male being seen for the same issue. To take factors that influence outcomes into account—for example, advanced age, experience and qualifications of emergency personnel, previous visits—a risk-adjusted model is used to report treatment outcome, cost-benefit, and mortality results. Often, multiple adjustments for risk must be made due to the fact that multiple interventions are needed. For example, a critical trauma patient who is delivered with good blood pressure, immobilization, and a controlled airway may need multiple surgeries to correct the injuries, each one exposing the patient to a complication or infection that may cause death. Therefore, the risk adjustment increases the value and quality of the EMS response by assigning the risk to the hospital course.

Hospital databases are not robust enough to provide answers to many of the research or QI questions that EMS as an industry is asking. The measurement of variables by the hospital only identifies results and misses the assessment of processes. More measurable intervals—such as autopsy, dispatch data, and other operational processes that are not associated with the EMS event—will be needed to link the patient's experience or to make a risk adjustment. Because the interventions delivered along the patient's entire course of treatment have the potential to affect the outcomes, it is hard to identify the effects EMS has on the patient. The EMS phase of a patient's care is usually less than an hour, compared to the days and sometimes weeks in the hospital or in rehabilitation that account for more time proportionally but are usually less critical or more controlled. The EMS phase has so many variables and is so often conducted in a dangerous environment that it is hard to take an accurate or timely measurement without compromising safety.

The measure of quality in EMS most often involves quality assurance that is primarily chart review with little measurement in other aspects of the EMS response. In 1998, the President's Advisory Commission on Consumer Quality in the Health Care Industry offered general recommendations for quality measurement and reporting in health care (Figure 5.1).

- Identify sets of quality measures for standardized reporting by each sector of the health care industry.
- Develop a framework for quality measurement and reporting and standardization of quality reporting.
- Support the development of quality measures to enhance the ability to evaluate and improve health care.
- Determine stable mechanisms for quality measurement and reporting.
- Ensure that information about health care quality is valid, reliable, comprehensive, and available to the public.

FIGURE 5.1 Recommendations for Quality Measurement and Reporting in Health Care. *Source: Agency for Healthcare Research and Quality (1998).*

Keeping these basic principles in mind, the EMS QI staff and administrators must now begin the practice of selecting proper measurements from the definitions of quality. EMS administrators cannot manage what is not measured. The *EMS Agenda for The Future*, produced by the National Highway Traffic Safety Administration (1996), listed fourteen attributes in an EMS system that should have QI measurements. Over the last decade, several projects have been undertaken to clarify and define the measurements. Figure 5.2 presents areas requiring measurement.

SERVICE AUDIT

Fire-based, municipal EMS services and private or other not-for-profit EMS providers should begin a QI movement by first assessing all aspects of emergency services they provide. Often, the focus is only on emergency services and not on the service as a whole, yet it is necessary to begin measuring a baseline of all services at the current level. A good place to start a measurement is to make an analysis of the EMS system for strengths and weaknesses, assessing what is being done and what level of performance or quality is being delivered. This is known as a **service audit**. Often this is done as a Strengths/Weaknesses/Opportunities/Threats (S.W.O.T.) analysis. QI activities can begin without a service audit. However, in the face of multiple priorities, a service audit helps to prioritize tasks. A service audit determines if EMS is

Attribute	Example
• Clinical Care	Intubation success, Correct diagnosis
• Communication Systems	Call processing time, Accuracy in call coding
• Education Systems	National Registry Pass Rates
• EMS Research	Comparison and national data submissions
• Evaluations	Customer service assessments
• Human Resources	Turnover rate
• Information Systems	Completion of patient care reports
• Integration of Health Services	Transmission of EKGs
• Legislation and Regulation	Protocol compliance
• Medical Direction	Physician Review of charts, infield observations
• Prevention	Car seat checks, helmet distribution
• Public Access	AED use, CPR performed by bystanders
• Public Education	CPR classes given
• System Finance	Reimbursement Rates

FIGURE 5.2 EMS attributes recommended by the National Highway Traffic Safety Administration for inclusion in continuous QI programs. *Source: National Highway Traffic Safety Administration (1996).*

meeting national standards, assesses structure, and determines if EMS is effective and efficient. Any measurement must begin with a baseline, and a service audit measures what is currently being done. This is even more important when budget request and efficiency questions are posed to an agency and the EMS provider. It is incumbent upon EMS leaders and managers to conduct a service audit on a periodic basis. A service audit is a measurement of all services being provided by the organization and is detailed in Figure 5.3.

- ALS first responses
- BLS first responses
- ALS transports
- BLS transports
- Auto extrications
- Rescues
  - Water
  - Below grade
  - High angle
  - Hazardous materials
  - Confined space
- Special events response and standby
- Wilderness EMS and searches
- Tactical EMS callouts
- Hazardous materials responses
- Aero medical evacuations
- Disaster response
- Shelter EMS
- MCI responses
- CPR training
- CERT training
- EMS education
- All personnel trained as EMTs and paramedics
- Sports EMS and standbys
- ALS engine responses
- CISD call outs
- Injury risk management and prevention

FIGURE 5.3 Components of EMS service audit assessment. *Source: "Figure 13.9—Components of an EMS Service Audit" from MANAGEMENT OF EMS by Bruce E. Evans and Jeff T. Dyar. Copyright © 2009 by Pearson Education. Used by Permission of Pearson Education.*

A service audit is a measurement that usually signifies the beginning of a strategic plan. Service audits also aid in accreditation and budgeting. The service audit serves as a reference point to begin a quality measurement. If the goal of quality management is to improve on a structure, process, or outcome, you must have a starting point. Service audits help to focus measurements by understanding existing structure, process, and desired outcomes.

The federal EMS initiative conducted through the National Highway Traffic Safety Administration (NHTSA) includes an ongoing effort to establish quality measurements. Starting with the EMS Systems Act of 1973, NHTSA defined the basic data types that should be collected by all EMS operations. Each EMS organization should be capturing the following data:

- Patient demographics
- EMS vehicle information
- EMS response and transport times
- Incident location and patients complaints
- Patients condition and mechanism of injury
- Patient treatments
- Patient outcome
- Receiving facility

MEASUREMENT INTERVALS

Several other organizations have defined measurements. The *NFPA 450 Guide for Emergency Medical Services and Systems* (National Fire Protection Association, 2009) has endorsed the common discrete time stamps, functional intervals, and process intervals to measure.

An EMS event has several different time stamps in which certain events occur. They are recorded to allow the QI system to measure intervals between events. The events are listed in Figure 5.4.

The time stamps define intervals. Each interval is the elapsed time between two time stamps. The interval from the time when a

1. Event occurs
2. Discovery of the event
3. Call for help
4. Phone rings
5. Phone answered at the primary public safety answer point (PSAP)
6. Phone rings at secondary PSAP
7. Phone answered at the secondary PSAP (if transferred)
   a. Interview
   b. Pre-arrival instruction start
   c. Pre-arrival instruction end
8. Interview ends
9. Response resources are identified
10. Dispatch time
11. Unit acknowledges
12. Wheels turning en route to scene
13. Wheels stopped
14. Time to the patient's side
15. En route to hospital
16. Arrived at hospital
17. Transfer of care
18. Available for service

FIGURE 5.4 ■ EMS intervals.

vehicle arrives to the time the crew arrives at the patient side and initiates treatment is an important area to measure, compared to the time on scene. There is value to measuring when exactly care is initiated, especially when it comes to defibrillation. Having a unit arrive, but having to walk across an arena or ascend a high-rise, sometimes delays actual care by minutes. In many communities, an EMS crew may have to traverse a large area, such as a mall, train station, or airport. In extremely dense urban areas, the ascent to upper-level floors creates a delay in patient care that is not accurately captured by using on scene as an equivalent to being at the patient's side. After identifying that cardiac arrest patients in tall buildings in the downtown Boston area had a low survival rate, EMS crews were empowered to meet with area businesses to facilitate placement of automatic external defibrillators (AEDs) in the buildings. In Las Vegas, the gap between patient contact and arrival of the EMS unit gave rise to the casino AED program, which places an AED within 90 seconds anywhere on the property in more than seventy hotels and casinos. The measurement of this interval should also include the cause of the delay.

TIME INTERVALS

A commonly measured time is on scene time. This measures when a unit arrives on scene, with or without patient contact, until the patient leaves the scene or the crew clears from the scene of a nontransport. Scene time can be prolonged by a standby due to an unsafe scene, crew performance, access problems, or any of a variety of other issues. Scene times for critically injured trauma victims is expected to be less than 10 minutes. This contrasts with the commonly accepted longer scene times (15–30 minutes) for patients with medical complaints. It is important to measure the scene time interval as it will be will be correlated to outcomes for certain types of patients. A few specific patient types (e.g., trauma requiring surgery, stroke, and STEMI) can benefit from short scene times, and EMS performance is critical to achieving a positive outcome.

Side Bar

EMS QI: Key Performance Measures and Software

The International Association of Fire Fighters (IAFF) key performance indicators and software systems are available to fire-based EMS leaders at the request of their local IAFF president's request to IAFF headquarters. The software is Web based and password protected. The power behind this system is the ability to compare performance of fire-based EMS operations on a national basis.

STATE EMS DIRECTORS PERFORMANCE MEASURES

In an attempt to incorporate a larger number of services in QI activities, state EMS directors and EMS managers have begun an initiative to define performance indicators that complement or include the International Association of Fire Fighters (IAFF) program. The state EMS directors look to incorporate an approach to quality from a traditional health care model that may be measured and improved in the following six dimensions:

- Competency and credentialing on both professional and organizational levels
- Appropriateness/accessibility
- Resource utilization and cost efficiency
- Effectiveness by assessing desired outcome, quality assurance
- Safety/risk management (medical/legal)
- Customer satisfaction

The performance measures were blended with the results from a survey of focus groups of paramedics that suggested that the fifteen EMS quality indicators listed in Figure 5.5 are important to providers.

Other performance measures suggested by paramedics in various focus groups convened by the National Association of State EMS Officials (NAEMSO) include crew and equipment appearance, accuracy of communication, and public confidence. Most of these suggested key indicators do not have established measurements. The use of valid performance measures cannot be substituted for when striving to improve quality in EMS systems. It is important to adopt validated criteria or to conduct research for validating new performance measures. When assessing call volumes and demand for services, analysis for EMS calls must have 20 weeks of data. Twenty weeks of data are needed to complete a **temporal analysis**. A temporal analysis pertains to time or limits in time which are identified with a suitable scatter graph that may reveal clusters with epidemiological significance.

- Patient satisfaction
- Managerial satisfaction
- Patient outcomes
- Dispatch accuracy
- EMS crew satisfaction
- Call quality
- Partner performance
- Response times
- Complaints
- Paramedic wellness/occupational illness
- Equipment practicality
- EMS cost-effectiveness
- Public confidence
- Crew and equipment appearance
- Innovations/research

FIGURE 5.5 State EMS officials' performance measures. *Source: Based on National Association of State EMS Officials publicly funded project.*

Measuring lack of quality is either a chance cause or must have an assigned cause. *Chance* is defined as those measured events that are beyond the ability to manage or control and external to the system and processes. EMS agencies and departments within agencies should not be penalized for recorded

Side Bar

Is It an EMS Model or Out-of-Hospital?

The measurement of an EMS interval should conform to four specific tests:

- Identification of patients with the specific condition is easy and unambiguous.
- Conditions are identified by readily obtainable risk adjustment measures.
- Pertinent final outcome is easy to obtain.
- Final outcome is solely based on the care rendered during the EMS intervals.

events that are out of EMS control. Assignable causes are those factors within the EMS system that contribute to a variance. There are five types of assignable clauses:

- Management
- Materials
- Methods
- Machines
- Manpower

MAKING MEASUREMENTS

Data constitute a set of collected facts. There are two basic kinds of numerical data. The first type is attribute data which is purely binary in nature (e.g. good or bad, yes or no), and no analysis can be performed. Attribute data must then be converted to variable data in order to be counted or useful. Variable data, the second type, is subject to change and is quantitative. Attribute data is qualitative data that can be counted for recording and analysis. Examples include the presence or absence of a required EPCR field, the absence or presence of a medication being administered.

A data measurement is the process of quantitatively comparing results to requirements. Measurements can be specified in any quality (length, weight, completion, etc.) and can be taken from any uniform sampling process.

A variable in EMS is any factor or influence upon the activity in an EMS response or outcome. There are three types of variables in experimental data or processes: dependent, independent, and controlled. Any event, attribute, interaction, treatment, or phenomenon that can vary or have different values is also referred to as a variable. Any factor or attribute that influences a variable prior to an EMS response or an aspect of the operation being measured is called an antecedent or antecedent variable. Precursors or activities required beforehand that may influence processes and outcomes—such as a vehicle checkout, EMS certification, battery exchange on a cardiac monitor—can also be antecedents.

In EMS, a **dependent variable** is any item that can be measured as having been applied or not, such as a treatment or action. For example, the Rescue 4 vehicle is on duty with Smith and Jones or it is not. An **independent variable** is a factor, treatment, or event that can be changed by a researcher or investigator. For example, the administration of nitroglycerin can change blood pressure, and the influence of traffic on a response may influence the deployment of Rescue 4. A **controlled variable** is a variable that is held constant when studying the effect of one particular independent variable, thus there is a need to eliminate the other factors affecting the outcome.

> **Side Bar**
>
> **Variables**
>
> A simple way to think about dependent and independent variables is to imagine a cup. The cup itself is the dependent variable. It is not going to change its structure, and you have no control over its parameters. What goes in the cup is the independent variable—for example, the liquid can be hot or cold. The change in temperature is the effect on the dependent variable.

Data are considered valid if they are representative of important aspects of service performance, determined to be important for successful service performance or outcome, and predictive of or significantly correlated with important elements of performance. Reliability is the other factor involved with measuring data. The data are reliable if the collection and interpretation methods can be trusted to be consistent and predictable. If the data collection is always performed in the same way using the same data collection tools and interpreted with the same definitions, the information is likely to be reliable.

One measurement is by observation. Observation is usually a process that determines the presence or absence of a variable. Observations are typically transcribed to a tally sheet or **check sheet**.

MEASURING INCREMENTS

Each item on a data collection tool should be filled out and engineered or reviewed to make sure a valid code is put in place. Accuracy is the extent to which the average value of the repeated measurement tends to be true to the value of what is being measured. Inputting or collecting data is an important process to manage.

Accuracy is also defined as to what degree something is measured. As in the case of response time, it is common to measure what is considered to be a fractal response. A fractile measure refers to how often a particular objective or benchmark is achieved. This is very appropriate in situations where there is a definitive "pass-fail" point or, in the case of emergency response, a time that is considered "fast enough" versus "not fast enough." A fractile measure can be used to evaluate the number of responses that pass (fast enough) against the number of responses that fail (not fast enough). A fractile measurement is a fraction of the minute or second of the time measurement. For example, a common response time measure is 7 minutes, 59 seconds. In many contractual or performance goals, a response of 8 minutes or less is called for. Using a fractile response time model, any measurement or 7:59 minutes meets this requirement. Progression above 7:59 minutes is deemed a late response. Often, the accuracy of this measurement means fines, compliance, and contractual issues with ambulance providers.

Often, accuracy is damaged by invalid or wrong inputs or measurements. There is a difference between an invalid code and wrong code. An **invalid code** means that the code is not on an approved list of possible choices. For example, a paramedic records pleurisy for a complaint of chest pain. A **wrong code** is simply incorrect input due to definitions or characters in a field, commonly an incorrect address or a letter in a field that is supposed to contain a number. A **null code** is when blanks or zeros appear. Many data collection or measuring tools allow for a zero because the data are not immediately available and will be recorded later. Zero often means that something was not entered or could not be determined.

For another example, consider what happens when there is an error in response times. A reversal of times can occur, which is when two times (e.g., dispatch time and arrival time) are reversed on a computer record or run report. Often, a records management system will allow entries in the system. Since the computer often calculates the response time, consider a dispatch time of 1107 and an arrival time of 1112 that should be 5 minutes. If the numbers are transformed, then the response becomes 1112 in the morning to 1107 at night—dramatically skewing the response time to nearly 12 hours. It only takes a few of these to make response-time calculations for a month or quarter incorrect.

A potential error in measurement can occur when information or actions are **anecdotal**. Anecdotal comments refer to process information that lacks specific methods, measures, deployment methods, evaluation and improvement details, or learning factors. Anecdotal information usually only describes individual activities or events, rather than describing a system process. Anecdotal comments are excellent tools for identifying events that will help narrow the focus or often trigger a further investigation to validate an observation.

EMS agencies must establish data-quality procedures to ensure that accurate information is documented. As little as ½ of 1 percent (0.5 percent) can skew data by three times the appropriate number. Data-quality procedures should include any response time over 15 minutes, any field with a zero or blank in it, and any time increment that is out of the norm greater than 20 percent. Independent samples are samples chosen from random that are not related to each other. For example, a random selection of charts that resulted in nontransport can be due to many reasons. Nontransport has significant risk to the organization, and understanding the exact causes requires a detailed review of the responses and proper analysis over time.

DATA DICTIONARY

The episodic model of measurement is the foundation of the Emergency Medical Services Outcomes Project (EMSOP). When interventions are dependent on a time interval and the relationship between the two is the key to survival, each interval or episode should be identified and measured to determine the influence on outcome. Medical and traumatic cardiac arrest, airway management, and most actions taken by EMS can fall into one or more episodes.

An indicator is an established measure used to determine how well an organization is meeting its customer or patient needs as well as other operational and financial performance expectations. Sometimes these can be used to measure length, commonly by dials. Clinical indicators are performance measures that include the identified standards. The Joint Commission (2008) defines a clinical indicator as something that measures conformance with a reasonable expectation as defined by the community served. Indicators consist of measurements of conformance to standards within a system.

The Out-of-Hospital Unit of Service Model is one of those intervals within the episodic model of care. It is specific to events or processes in EMS with little or no time dependency. For example, when a patient refusal or a call for lifting assistance is completed by an EMS unit, those events and the amount of time required have no effect on outcome.

KEY INDICATORS

A key indicator is a defined set of measurements for a process or structural indicator. Figure 5.6 lists a sample of the measurements in a key indicator for trauma destination

Indicator item	Percentage of injured patients who meet trauma triage criteria, and are not transported to a trauma center.
Data points	Inclusion criteria—any transported prehospital patient who is traumatically injured and meets trauma triage criteria.
Numerator (N)	Patients meeting trauma triage criteria with a destination other than a designated trauma center.
Denominator (D)	All patients who meet trauma triage criteria.
Reporting formula	N/D × 100 = %
Data elements	Age; chief complaint (injury); description of event; mechanism of injury met; anatomic criteria met; physiologic criteria met; comorbidity/special circumstances
Judgment	Documented reason for destination.
Destination	Facility
Reporting period	Monthly
Data source	Patient care reports

FIGURE 5.6 Key performance measures from a key indicator tool.

criteria. The measurement of this key indicator might be able to identify over- or undertriage of trauma patients.

UNUSUAL OCCURRENCES

Another measurement that needs to be made is any unusual occurrence. Unusual occurrences are signaled in a system by various means. Different from a sentimental event, an unusual occurrence may be any out-of-the-ordinary event experienced in the system. Often, unusual occurrences unearth a trend or can indicate further problems or adjustments needed in the system. For example, a teenager is brought into an emergency room and thought to be "just drunk." After a short time in the hospital, she dies from what later is found to be an overdose of prescription meds obtained at a "pharm party" (an event where children pool prescription meds from their homes and randomly pick a medication). When the emergency room reports this to the EMS supervisor, it is reviewed as an unusual occurrence, signaling not an error by the crew but a new event to report to law enforcement and about which to educate crews.

A mechanism for collecting and measuring unusual occurrences that could be risks to EMS systems should be developed as part of a QI system. In addition, a tally or collection of unusual occurrences and actions taken is required for accreditation standards from the Commission on Accreditation of Ambulance Services. Standard 202.05.01 requires a process to document, define, and identify what is required to be reported. This requires an investigation and feedback to the involved individuals with a mechanism to track and trend what is done with the information. An example of a classification system that can be used to track and trend unusual events is presented in Figure 5.7.

Level A	Reportable issue, low impact, low risk, trend only
Level B	Minor issue, low impact, low risk, trend only
Level C	Significant issue, possible system impact, medium to high risk, possible committee discussion, summary
Level D	Very outstanding quality of care issue, meritorious issue or issue with highly unique educational potential

FIGURE 5.7 Classification of unusual events matrix.

TYPES OF MEASURING/ REPORTING SYSTEMS

A system of measurement must have a level of discrimination or resolution that is capable of detecting and indicating even the smallest changes in the items being measured. An example is tracking return calls to an address within 24 hours or verifying that an address is not a nursing home or large apartment complex. This type of discovery sampling adheres to certain preestablished guidelines or areas to determine if problems are present. There are a number of different types of measuring/ reporting systems.

Side Bar

Discrimination Rule

The discrimination rule is a useful measure of item quality whenever the purpose of a test or measurement is to produce a spread of scores, reflecting differences in quality achieved so that distinctions may be made among the performances of the agency, crew, provider, and so on.

SATISFACTION MEASUREMENTS

Pay for performance is another movement that is being affected by measurements of medical quality. A movement in health care reform is increasing reimbursement for measurable satisfaction surveys. The Press Ganey survey, one such QI measurement for physicians, is commonly used in emergency rooms. A similar survey used by the EMS Survey Team is a version of the Press Ganey survey developed for EMS before it was decided the industry was not a market worth pursuing. Favorable ratings on the measurement in Press Ganey result in a slightly higher reimbursement rate for physicians. The Press Ganey system consists of the following categories:

- Teamwork and Climate
- Job Satisfaction
- Perceptions of Management
- Safety climate
- Working conditions
- Stress recognition

Press Ganey can easily be extrapolated to an EMS environment as many of the assessments of emergency room physicians also can be done for EMS crews. Some form of measure on perceived satisfaction of EMS services is required by most accreditation organizations.

In the hospital setting, patient satisfaction is considered a required quality measure. The Hospital Consumer Assessment of Healthcare Providers and Systems (HCAHPS) hospital survey, initially a voluntary program, became mandatory for hospitals in July 2007. Hospitals participating in the Medicare inpatient prospective payment system must now collect and submit patient satisfaction data in order to receive their full payment for inpatient stays. EMS performance can have a great impact on an HCAHPS score as a patient who is angered by EMS or receives poor patient care will arrive angry to the emergency room and affiliate both experiences.

SAMPLING

Samples are batches of data that are measured within a process. When measuring quality, size does matter. Having a sufficient sample size to make an accurate assessment of performance is important. You must determine how many patients or events you must measure in order to get results that reflect the target population as precisely as needed. This also affects the confidence intervals and overall confidence of the measurement. If the goal is to learn and improve, then the sample size needs to be just large enough to learn from and measure change, which is often much smaller than what a research agenda would require.

> **Side Bar**
>
> **Sample Size**
>
> Raosoft produces computer software that will estimate the size of a sample you need to accurately make a statistically significant change or impact.

Randomness

When assessing quality, you need to have randomness in the measurement at certain times. A random cause for a problem is a variation that occurs due to chance or is not assigned to any factor. When randomness is applied to EMS, it helps avoid possible bias due to influences in the system from known or unknown causes. For example, the physician medical director roving in a vehicle and randomly showing up for field observations introduces random assessment and measurements. Likewise, an EMS QI committee may randomly pull a subset of patients as a snapshot.

Random assignment and *randomization* are different terms that have one thing in common: randomness. A random assignment is selected by choosing from a population by use of a probability device or scheme—for example, a computer or a person manually selecting a certain procedure, medication administration, chart, or patient without regard to any specific crew, agency, station, or provider. An illustration of this principle is the **random assignment** to a clinical supervisor to review 10 out of 50 chest pain patients to determine if a 12-lead EKG was completed without identifying a specific provider or unit. This allows the QI supervisor to get a snapshot without singling out providers and helps reduce the culture of fear among providers. A computer program, when available, used to randomly select a list of subjects or people is the best way to ensure that bias is reduced or eliminated. In **randomization**, chance determines the assignment of the treatment. An example is assigning the application of a treatment to an even-numbered day of the month or withholding the treatment on an odd-numbered day for the purpose of evaluating the effectiveness of that event.

Field observations also must employ a degree of randomness. The schedule of most organizations allows for support staff such as EMS QI personnel or field supervisors to be staffed only during traditional business hours. However, EMS is a 24-hour operation and several studies have noted that clinical care is different, given the time of day or shift work. One study shows the number of intravenous starts are fewer on graveyard shifts than during day or evening shifts, despite the criticality of the patients being similar. Field supervision should have flexibility in their schedule to conduct in-field observations on every shift. This may mean having a 24-hours EMS captain or field supervisor sleeping in during the day and being out for graveyard shift to monitor the performance of field crews. As a best practice, this should be done monthly. Random observations should also be made on weekends and holidays. The randomness of this type of scheduling of field observation reinforces accountability for actions and discourages normalization of deviance.

Sample Selection Processes

Some QI measures are ongoing, such as the measurement of response times to every single event or recipient who calls for service. This is commonly called a blanket sample. **Blanket sampling** is helpful in identifying seasonal variations and disease-specific calls for help. A blanket sample can then be monitored as part of QI activities designed to assess other variables.

A stratified sample is obtained by dividing the measures into two or more segments. This selection or stratification process is often based on demographics, such as age or other variables, that lend themselves to division. Data need to be stratified if you are focusing on a certain segment of the data. If there is an idea that something is different, a stratified sample is necessary. For example, the time of day or night, new or veteran provider, or urban or rural environment all can be easily stratified. In EMS QI, the stratification of pediatric patients is a common technique. Multistage or cluster sampling is used when measurement is dispersed over a large area. In a situation where it is impractical to look at every call or EMS event, a cluster may be used. For example, a certain response district or neighborhood could be assessed for types of calls or response-time compliance to determine the need to move a station or add additional units. Analysis of a certain type of call can also help identify clusters. For example, an analysis of pediatric drowning in a city often can be isolated to certain neighborhoods. Further analysis may show that a cluster sample is in a neighborhood constructed prior to codes that required safety devices for pools (e.g., self-closing and self-locking gates, secondary barriers, certain fence heights).

Reducing Bias in Sampling

To avoid bias when sampling data, the sample should measure equally the most visible information and the more obscure portions of the data. For example, airway events that require intubation are commonly measured, yet an event where a choking victim received an abdominal thrust to dislodge an obstruction and did not require an advanced airway may not be included in the airway control statistics.

TOOLS FOR ACCURATE MEASUREMENT

Checklists are used as tools to ensure that all important steps or actions in an operation have been taken. Checklists contain items important or relevant to an issue or situation. Checklists are often confused with check sheets. A check sheet is a simple device for recording data, typically paper or, now more commonly, electronic. The check sheet is usually custom designed by the user to allow easy interpretation of the results. A check sheet can also be called a tally sheet.

Protocol compliance data are often compiled using a checklist or tally sheet and analyzed by EMS agency personnel. Reports are sent back to the provider agencies monthly to assist with improvement activities, such as additional training and education in the areas identified as noncompliant. This has been traditional quality assurance.

MACHINE MEASUREMENTS

More common now are **differential measurements**, which use a device that transforms actual movement into a known value. An example is the use of a CPR device connected to the monitor monitoring compressions.

Cardiac Monitors

Most versions of prehospital cardiac monitors have the ability to collect very detailed amounts of patient data. Cardiac monitors now measure several aspects of the EMS event. Most of the manufacturers offer software that assists in data collection.

The Physio-Control product CODE-STAT 7.0 is a data review software program with advanced CPR analytics. CODE-STAT can assist in QI in an EMS agency. CODE-STAT software allows an EMS agency to create benchmarking and trending reports for reviewing system performance. Individual reports are available to responders to explain and identify areas for further improvement in CPR delivery and cardiac arrest management. Embedded software in EKG devices with data collection and reporting capabilities helps keep patient files in a central location for easy access for analysis at a later date. This software organizes patient data in a single file and downloads from LIFEPAK defibrillators. CODE-STAT 7.0 data review software with CPR CODE-STAT 7.0 analytics is a post-event review tool that records chest compressions on the patient's continuous ECG report. The CODE-STAT 7.0 CPR report measures CPR performance (rate of compressions/ventilation) and identifies areas where improvement is needed. It calculates CPR statistics, such as compression rates and the amount of time the rescuers hands are off the patient, thereby interrupting CPR.

RescueNet Code Review is a resuscitation data management system from Zoll Data Systems that manages data collected from defibrillators and monitors. RescueNet Code Review can automate QI measurements by electronically capturing and organizing resuscitation data. It allows an EMS organization to measure and improve a reporting process by combining Utstein-style reports on cardiac arrests with ECG and vital-signs data collected from the complete family of ZOLL defibrillators. Utstein-style templates and reports enable fast and comprehensive review of resuscitation. A single patient record using this system measures information on ECG events, CPR, SpO2, EtCO2, 12-lead ECG,

NIBP, and more. This allows the QI staff and management to track the entire resuscitation process from the field to the hospital. An animated ECG and event playback system provide a complete record of all events, automatic time synchronization ensures accurate capture of event data, and optional audio recording provides detailed quality analysis of cardiac arrest data. Rescuers can offload data stored by the defibrillator and send it for clinical QA/QI, or they can download it to the RescueNet ePCR solutions. RescueNet Code Review also works seamlessly with RescueNet Billing, so management can capture accurate charges for used supplies, prove medical necessity, and automatically determine the ALS level of care to ensure appropriate reimbursement.

> **Side Bar**
>
> **Data Capture**
>
> The capture of treatment and diagnostic data has traditionally been thought of as necessary for QI purposes. The capture of this data is now required to justify billing and reimbursement.

Using the E Series and M Series Bluetooth option enables the transmission of the STEMI patient's 12-lead ECG and vital trends via the ZOLL Data Relay Server to unlimited destinations chosen by the medic in the field. The destination can be a fax machine in the emergency department or an email address. The 12-lead ECG can be sent to the cardiologist's PDA or iPhone, enabling quicker activation of the cardiac catheter lab. Real-time data can be transmitted to the on-call lab support personnel to speed up decision making, which can increase the patient's chance of survival.

The Event Review Pro from Phillips Electronics allows retrospective review of event summaries for quality audit purposes. This software allows QI personnel to debrief, run case and systemwide reports, and share findings. Event Review Pro is a data management solution that enables the measurement of system-wide QA/QI and supports continuous CPR training. This application provides a view of any resuscitation event, along with built-in, easy-to-use navigation to pinpoint key areas in a specific patient's cardiac event for education and QI efforts. Event Review Pro includes support for a variety of ALS data types (including invasive pressure, temperature, and vitals trending) and multi-waveform viewing. Philips has the advanced DXL 12-lead ECG algorithm that encompasses a clinical decision tool supportive of STEMI diagnosis. STEMI diagnosis assists the provider in confidently making decisions to help speed triage. Measurements are now so specific that the STEMI-CA (Culprit Artery) most likely responsible for the acute symptoms can be pinpointed, which can assist in directing care in the field and treatment in the cath lab. It generates critical values for four distinct life-threatening conditions (acute MI, acute ischemia, complete heart block, and very fast heart rate), all of which require immediate clinical attention. Measurements also provide enhanced gender-specific diagnostic criteria to improve recognition and interpretation of cardiac symptoms in women.

It is important to synchronize cardiac monitors with the dispatch clock. Most dispatch clocks are synchronized by software with the world's atomic clock. This public service is cooperatively provided by the two time agencies of the United States: the Department of Commerce's National Institute of Standards and Technology (NIST) and its military counterpart, the U.S. Naval Observatory (USNO). Readings from the clocks of these agencies contribute to world time, which is called Coordinated Universal Time (UTC). The time maintained by both agencies should never differ by more than

0.000001 second from UTC. The atomic clock standardizes the process of maintaining accurate time. The time sequence of therapies and events all have time stamps and must be matched with other processes, such as dispatch times. This is especially important if the event list from the EKG monitor is being downloaded into the electronic PCR.

Side Bar

It is important to synchronize cardiac monitors with the dispatch clock. The dispatch clock is synchronized with an atomic clock.

Measures by Electronic Patient Care Reports

Advancements in electronic patient care reports (PCRs) are now making measuring quality an automated function. Most electronic PCRs can be programmed to require certain fields to be filled in before the report will close. Pull-down menus standardize the terminology and choices that can be made in the selection of a measurement. This aids in the reduction of errors and helps make measurement uniform. Automatic QI reports can be generated, and many products have the ability to notify EMS supervision or the medical director by email. The use of an electronic PCR system eliminates having to reenter data. Many of the functions also have a "not report," which signals to supervision when a report is incomplete. Electronic PCRs should be robust enough that measurements entered into the system can be easily removed.

Electronic formats should download easily or have transfer capability to the national data collection systems. Databases of the future and the measurements that they hold need to be relational and have the ability to download material to the National EMS Information System and the National Fire Incident Reporting System. Outcomes and standardized measurements have the capability to enhance grants and target state and federal monies based on need.

Best Practice

King County Medic One Airway Data Collection

The King County Medic One program consists of a two-paramedic configuration in a two-tiered ALS-only response system. There are 7.5 medic units covering 700 square miles with a population of just under 700,000. Medic One paramedics intubate just over a thousand patients per year; roughly 66 percent of those are elective in nature with rapid sequence induction (RSI).

King County Medic One did not have a formal airway registry and only knew of airway QA/QI events when a failed airway (unable to mask ventilate/unable to intubate) occurred. The Medic One system had long since prided itself on generous RSI guidelines and a high degree of skill in airway management, but this proved to be anecdotal. To further the QA/QI processes, Medic One set out not only to develop an airway registry but also to quantify and qualify the registry.

After identifying the data to measure, the developers of the airway registry sought the input of anesthesiologists, critical care internists, and emergency medicine physicians. Once the registry development was complete, Medic One created a secure electronic form to be completed following an intubation; if it is not completed, the

Indication for Intubation (check all that apply)

- ☐ Unstable airway/Impending airway compromise
- ☐ Respiratory distress/ventilatory failure
- ☐ Neurological illness (e.g. coma, brain injury with agitation)
- ☐ Anticipated clinical course (e.g. severe facial and airway burn)
- ☐ Unstable patient (e.g. abnormal vital signs, cardiac arrest)
- ☐ Humanitarian indication (e.g. massive burn: 80% BSA)

Comments:

FIGURE BP5.1 Indication for Intubation section of the Airway QA Report. *Source: Excerpt from the Airway QA Report from Henderson Fire Department. Copyright © Henderson Fire Department. Used by permission of Henderson Fire Department.*

intubating paramedic does not receive credit for the skill. Once the paramedic logs into the Airway QA Report, the form automatically identifies the intubating paramedic's name, EMS number, email address (paramedics receive a confirmation email once the form is submitted), and date of the intubation. The paramedic then inputs the incident number and the Medical Incident Report form number. The form then asks for specifics about the patient: age, weight in kg, gender, and so on.

The next section of the form is the Indication for Intubation. (See Figure BP5.1). If the form does not adequately address the indication for intubation, the paramedic can further explain the reason for intubation in the comments section.

When feasible, patients who require endotracheal intubation should be assessed for potential difficult intubation or mask ventilation (e.g., Mallampati score, mouth opening, thyromental distance, mandibular and neck mobility, etc.). This is briefly addressed on page 2 of the form. (See Figure BP5.2).

The form also addresses any use of airway adjuncts and any overt challenges to an intubation attempt.

Page 3 of the form asks for premedications; induction agents; neuromuscular blockers; post-intubation sedation and doses administered; tube depth and size; time of tube placement; and processes used for confirming tube placement. (See Figure BP5.3). Page 3 also asks for pre- and post-intubation SpO2 and, when applicable, CO2 levels and transport destination. The final page of the Airway QA Report is the comments section, which is used to identify any adjustments necessary for successfully managing the patient's airway.

Once the completed form is submitted, the medical director receives an email informing him of the intubation. Furthermore, if there was a failed airway, an Unusual Incident Report must be submitted for immediate review by the medical director, the on-duty medical services officer (MSO), and the operations MSO.

This form and registry are accessed biannually for QA/QI purposes and descriptive statistics. If the medical director identifies any specific patterns or performance issues, he uses the opportunity to address individual paramedics or the organization as a whole in the form of training sessions, lectures, or specific guideline changes. Although there was some initial resistance to the form, it was dispersed when Medic One paramedics began to see that their first-attempt success rates paralleled those of the University Hospital Department of Anesthesiology. All data entered into the form are confidential and protected as a QA/QI document under the Revised Code of Washington (RCW 43.70.510).

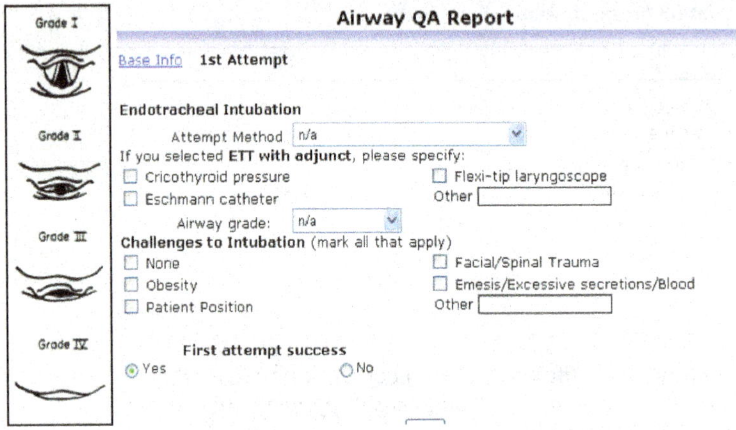

Airway QA Report

Base Info **1st Attempt**

Endotracheal Intubation

Attempt Method n/a

If you selected **ETT with adjunct**, please specify:

- ☐ Cricothyroid pressure
- ☐ Eschmann catheter
- ☐ Flexi-tip laryngoscope
- Other

Airway grade: n/a

Challenges to Intubation (mark all that apply)

- ☐ None
- ☐ Obesity
- ☐ Patient Position
- ☐ Facial/Spinal Trauma
- ☐ Emesis/Excessive secretions/Blood
- Other

First attempt success

◉ Yes ○ No

FIGURE BP5.2 ■ Page 2 of the Airway QA Report. *Source: Excerpt from the Airway QA Report from Henderson Fire Department. Copyright © Henderson Fire Department. Used by permission of Henderson Fire Department.*

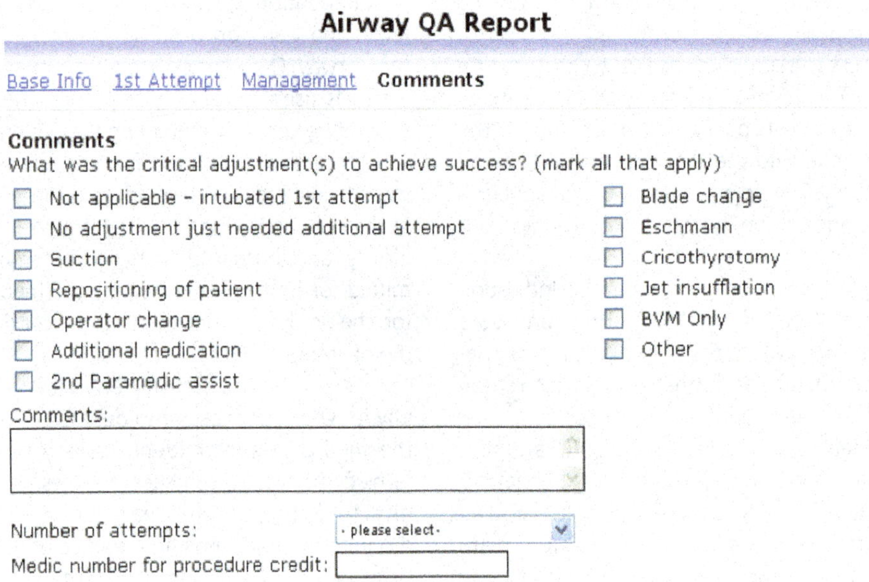

Airway QA Report

Base Info 1st Attempt Management **Comments**

Comments

What was the critical adjustment(s) to achieve success? (mark all that apply)

- ☐ Not applicable - intubated 1st attempt
- ☐ No adjustment just needed additional attempt
- ☐ Suction
- ☐ Repositioning of patient
- ☐ Operator change
- ☐ Additional medication
- ☐ 2nd Paramedic assist
- ☐ Blade change
- ☐ Eschmann
- ☐ Cricothyrotomy
- ☐ Jet insufflation
- ☐ BVM Only
- ☐ Other

Comments:

Number of attempts: - please select -

Medic number for procedure credit:

FIGURE BP5.3 ■ Page 3 of the Airway QA Report *Source: Excerpt from the Airway QA Report from Henderson Fire Department. Copyright © Henderson Fire Department. Used by permission of Henderson Fire Department.*

Measuring Vehicle Data

Technology now exists to measure the performance of an ambulance, including data collection on the abilities of the EMS provider operating the vehicle, video documentation of the road and the crew, and warning devices. RescueNet Road Safety is one available vehicle monitoring system that can evaluate and measure braking, speed, and cornering. An onboard system collects the data and can be collected for specific drivers. Typically, 5 percent of the employees are accountable for 95 percent of the crashes. These types of systems have increased vehicle life expectancy and decreased collisions.

EMS PREVENTION AND ACCESS

Prevention activities are a significant aspect of EMS operations. As the cost of the health care system continues to increase, it makes sense to place money and efforts on preventing injury and illness. Yet, when an event does not happen, it obviously cannot be measured—making it difficult to justify spending capital or resources on that activity. It is necessary to measure outcomes in terms of events—for example, the number of head injuries that occurred due to lack of a helmet or the residential fire fatalities rate per 1,000 or per capita without smoke detectors. The number of times a preventable injury occurs has to be tied to previous numbers of events and looked at over a longer period of time after a prevention initiative has occurred. If the outcome is something to which the EMS system makes a direct or significant contribution (e.g., sudden cardiac death survival rates and ST segment myocardial infarction), then it is helpful to measure it. If the outcome is more abstract (e.g., bicycle use or alcohol consumption), improvements may have no influence on outcome. Comparisons must be made before and after educational events and after public education campaigns.

The frequency of access to the EMS system and the appropriateness of the decision to make a call is another reflection of public education. Overutilization of the emergency response system is important to measure. Likewise, ensuring that life-threatening emergencies get into the system is important. Rapid notification is the key to many of the successful outcomes for EMS. Knowing the source of access to the system helps target public awareness campaigns.

The use of an AED is another important measure to make and tie to outcomes. The CARES program of the Centers for Disease Control and Prevention (CDC) measures the use of an AED and the performance of bystander CPR on cardiac arrest victims. The term *public access* encompasses the quickness of a call to 9-1-1 for a cardiac arrest victim and public access to defibrillation (PAD). This means making AEDs available in public and/or private places where large numbers of people gather, or where people who are at high risk for heart attacks live, and measuring the placement and use of AEDs.

MEASURING OPERATIONS

Although most quality measures focus on clinical indicators and processes, EMS operations is also a very important part of the overall process. Operations affect clinical care and influence the existence of the organization. Many EMS organizations neglect to include operational aspects in their QI process, such as how quickly a complaint is handled and if it has a one pass (meaning that the first employee to encounter the complaint solves the issue). An EMS system should measure operational issues, such as the availability of defibrillators to the community, extrication tools, specialty resources, and the number of times a hospital is on divert. Likewise, human resource issues are part of operations, and the turnover rate is another common quality measurement tool. The causes and effects of people leaving the organization should be reported. Ideally, costs associated with retraining or replacing employees should also be considered.

REPORTING SYSTEMS

Several events occur during an EMS operation that can trigger a report. This is an example of a stimulated reporting system where an error in an EMS call stimulates the creation of a record. A report of a negative event or deviations from normal operations stimulates a report. A sentinel event or error often requires a report. When the event or error occurs and falls in the reportable category, it is said to stimulate a report. A medication error is one such example. Stimulated reports often trigger further investigation by management or a root cause analysis by the EMS administration or QI team.

Automated processes (such as with each patient encounter or dispatch generating a record for additional information from a field provider) are part of the spontaneous reporting system. As more surveillance systems and artificial intelligence are placed into electronic PCRs, some spontaneous reporting of events can occur. The FirstWatch system has the ability to spontaneously report trends and events. In today's fast-paced EMS systems, "just in time" can easily turn into "just a little too late." FirstWatch's dashboards and operational reporting capabilities detect patterns hidden in EMS data and trends before they gain momentum. Real-time dashboard views and trend detection allow EMS field supervisors to access information typically not discovered until quarterly or monthly reports are run. Commonly known as a FirstWatch trigger, certain events can be mined off the dispatch computer. An immediate investigation can begin while events are fresh and people are available to interview.

Although confidential reporting systems have been in place for certain diseases (such as those that are sexually transmitted), blinding or keeping information being measured confidential is mandated by federal law. Breaches of personal information should lead to disciplinary or human resources actions. Confidential reporting of infectious patients is another common reporting system that remains under confidential guidelines of the Health Insurance Portability and Accountability Act (HIPAA).

A continuous sampling system is a plan to continue inspection of a process that has less than 100 percent inspection. Continuous sampling plans are common among high-risk, low-frequency EMS operations, such as difficult or failed intubation. Continuous sampling involves the automatic taking of measurements at closely spaced time intervals over a long period of time. The result is a series of measurements that can provide information on the pattern with which the concentration varied throughout the measurement interval. Some EMS systems and agencies review 100 percent of the intubations attempted in the system. Continuous sampling plans usually require that each time period (t) of a 100 percent inspection be continued until a specific number of individual assessments (I) are found clear of defects or errors. Any measurement that does not yield 100 percent requires an exception report. Exception reporting is the process of documenting those situations in which significant variances from specifications or from expected results have occurred.

MEASURING FINANCIAL OPERATIONS

There are essential performance measures for efficiency. As part of the QI process, a measurement of financial operations should incorporate cost per response, cost per unit hour, unit hour utilization ratio, and total system cost per capita. Compliance with budgets and tracking of expenditures, along with billing and accounts receivable, are critical to EMS operations and should be included in a QI program.

MEASURING UNIT COST AND PRODUCTIVITY

An ambulance's efficiency is measured by calculating the agency's cost per response, cost per unit hour, and unit hour utilization. When evaluated alongside quality measures, efficiency measures can be used to determine the

$$\text{Total Cost Per Response} = \frac{\text{Total Expenses}}{\text{Total Number of Responses}}$$

FIGURE 5.8 Cost per response formula. *Source: "Figure 9.6—Cost-Per-Response Formula" from MANAGEMENT OF EMS by Bruce E. Evans and Jeff T. Dyar. Copyright © 2009 by Pearson Education. Used by Permission of Pearson Education.*

relative performance of each agency or unit in the system. Regardless of provider type, EMS providers must calculate cost per response. Cost per response is determined by dividing each provider's total expenses by the total number of responses. To calculate cost per response, the complete cost of the service must be used (including overhead that is allocated in a 1-month period) by the total responses in the same 1-month period. This should also be done with an annual number of responses and yearly expenses using the formula in Figure 5.8.

The cost per response evaluates the system's cost from an external perspective and is used primarily for purposes of comparison to other service delivery models in EMS. The number is frequently used by county and city managers to compare cost of privatization of government services.

CALCULATING COST OF UNIT HOURS

Total cost per unit hour is a measure of the total cost of providing coverage during a given accounting period divided by the total number of unit hours of coverage provided during that same accounting period. This measurement can be used to identify whether unit hour costs are excessive, given the quality of care being delivered, in comparison to other similar EMS systems. If unit hour cost becomes excessive and response times are not being met, then EMS leadership should consider moving vehicles or adding unit hours. Other factors, such as top-heavy administration, high wages, poor economies of scale, and overtime pay, can drive up unit hour cost. The formula for depicting cost per unit hour is presented in Figure 5.9.

For example, a fire department has five ambulances covering a 24-hour period. Each ambulance is staffed with a firefighter/paramedic at \$23/hour and a firefighter/EMT at \$18/hour, including benefits. One shift supervisor earns \$28/hour. The cost to operate the vehicle, including fuel, maintenance, and hourly cost for the fixed facility to house the unit, is \$45/hour. Figure 5.10 portrays the numbers for a fire-based EMS unit.

Deploying an EMS supervisor in the system at a salary of \$28/hour adds an additional cost of \$672, which increases the cost per unit to approximately \$91/hour. Costs for dispatching, billing, and other personnel can be added to this same formula; however, most agencies share these resources or the resources fall under a separate budget item or agency budget.

Measurements of productivity are common in the industry, and the key term is unit hour utilization (U:UH). U:UH is measurement of workload for EMS agencies that was developed from a process called queuing theory. It is an excellent resource for EMS agencies to use to determine the line between too few ambulances and putting an ambulance on every corner. Queuing theory provides a

$$\text{Cost per Unit Hour} = \frac{\text{Total Costs of Providing Coverage During Given Accounting Period}}{\text{Total Number of Unit Hours Covered During an Accounting Period}}$$

FIGURE 5.9 Cost per unit hour. *Source: "Figure 9.7—Cost-Per-Unit Hour" from MANAGEMENT OF EMS by Bruce E. Evans and Jeff T. Dyar. Copyright © 2009 by Pearson Education. Used by Permission of Pearson Education.*

a. Units hours − 24 hours × 5 units = 120 units hours
b. Cost Paramedic salary: 24 hours × 23.00 × 5 = $2,760.00
Firefighter/EMT salary: 24 hours × $18.00 × 5 = $2,160.00
Vehicle operating cost: 24 hours × $45.00 × 5 = $5,400.00
Total cost for 24 hours = $10,320
c. Cost per unit hour: $10,320/120 = $86.00

FIGURE 5.10 Fire-based EMS utilizations. *Source: Excerpt from "Figure 9.8—Example of Cost Per Unit for a Five-Unit EMS Organization" from MANAGEMENT OF EMS by Bruce E. Evans and Jeff T. Dyar. Copyright © 2009 by Pearson Education. Used by Permission of Pearson Education.*

simple mathematical formula to determine the number of ambulances needed per hour, per day, and during seasonal fluctuations. To make calculations on U:UH, the EMS manager must know the number of EMS calls and the average amount of time a crew spends on an ambulance call. U:UH can determine how busy EMS units will be, based on an anticipated workload.

The formula can also be used to estimate the probability that a citizen will have to wait for an ambulance and the number of EMS units needed to meet the response time objectives of an EMS system. Another term for tracking utilization is in-service ratio.

Definitions often differ between the private ambulance industry and the fire service. U:UH is a measurement of productivity of the number of hours a unit is in service, resulting in revenue generation—essentially, looking to maximize revenue with fewer resources. Fire service measures this number based on totals calls versus private ambulances, measuring only actual calls that result in transport. This provides a skewed number, as the dry run rate or nontransported EMS calls in many systems can reach 50 percent or higher.

The U:UH ratio is calculated by dividing the total number of calls during a given accounting period by the total number of unit hours of coverage provided during the same accounting phase. (See Figure 5.11). The higher the utilization, the lower the cost per patient served. U:UH is commonly calculated on daily and weekly basis and is an indication of appropriate deployment of resources. It can be measured with two different formulas. Two examples are illustrated here. The first is a 24-hour ambulance running an average of 5.5 calls per day. An EMS manager who wanted to monitor the entire system or battalion of EMS units could compare unit hours and U:UH. This is one way of looking at vehicle deployment and the workload, allowing for proper budgeting for additional hours or personnel.

The lack of a response or unavailability of a unit or crew when requested or scheduled is another performance measure. For example,

$$\text{U:UH Ratio} = \frac{\text{Total Number of Calls Responded to During Accounting Period}}{\text{Total Number of Unit Hours of Coverage Provided During Budget Cycle}}$$

U:UH rate = 5.5 calls per day/24 hours =.22 U:UH

U:UH rate = (840 hours = 5 units staffed 24 hours a day, 7 days a week)
= 310 responses for the week/840
= .37

FIGURE 5.11 Calculating the U:UH ratio. *Source: From "Figure 9.10—Formula for Unit Hour Utilization with Example" from MANAGEMENT OF EMS by Bruce E. Evans and Jeff T. Dyar. Copyright © 2009 by Pearson Education. Used by Permission of Pearson Education.*

how often are calls passed to mutual aid or auto-aid providers. The mean downtime is a measure of maintainability derived by dividing the sum of the elapsed clock time that a unit, crew, or vehicle is unavailable due to failures by the number of occurrences over a selected time frame, such as hours weeks, months, or years.

BILLING AND REIMBURSEMENT –

In any EMS system, requirements for reimbursement are the lifeblood of the organization. Every agency involved in ambulance transportation should be generating a very detailed report for the financial aspects of billing and reimbursement. An EMS agency must include a minimum data set of features for measuring the effectiveness and flow of revenue and billing for ambulance transport. Reimbursement is critical to funding EMS operations. The payer mix or the sources of reimbursement (e.g., Medicare, private insurance, self-pay, etc.) are all aspects of reimbursement that must be plotted on a control chart. If you use a software company that specializes in the EMS industry, most basic features should include tracking of the following:

- Electronic billing and remittance from Medicare and Medicaid
- Preferred vendor rates and reimbursement from insurance clearinghouses
- Reimbursement from private and commercial insurance billing
- Detailed accounts receivable reports, including customized reports
- Billing cycles
- Number of secondary and tertiary billings
- Cash payments and write-offs
- Staff productivity with hours applied to billing and amount collected

Tracking financial reimbursement numbers without billing software can be challenging, and the inputs of cash, credit, and electronic transfer of fund must be tracked. The overall percentage of collection in general terms should be tracked monthly. It is important to track bad debt and uncollectible bills to be able to write off the debt and not carry it over to subsequent budgets or skew the operational budget.

CHAPTER REVIEW

Summary

Correctly measuring EMS activities requires knowledge of the processes of measurement and sampling. The measurement of EMS is a continuous process, starting with a service audit, proceeding through clinical parameters, and finishing with operational assessment and the effectiveness of the service. Measurement can be made at any of several locations, and the advance of technology makes measurements more automated. Data are now collected from electronic PCRs and cardiac monitors. How and when measurement is taken involves several parameters, such as randomness, selection of a sample, and accurate recording of a sample. Operational measurements are also important to determine billing success, vehicle deployment, and utilizations. Correct measurement is important to get a quality analysis. Measurement must be as accurate as possible.

WHAT WOULD YOU DO? Reflection

Checklists are a form of quality assurance, not of QI. Trend analysis is not conducted, and education tied to the identified deficiencies or improvement that could be made in patient care is not provided. No assessment is being made of the quality of care, just the application of care. In the c-collar example, more important questions should have been asked, such as "Was it applied correctly?" "Was its use indicated?" "Could a clearance protocol have been chosen instead?" "Was the size correct?" "Did the medic explain to the patient what was happening?"

What is not measured is not done. In this case, the QI staff is only on day shift. Several studies have alluded to the fact that the care changes throughout the shift. A redeployment of the staff to cover all hours of the day to ensure even and consistent measurement would provide for a more comprehensive look at the system's performance. Randomness is important in ensuring that staff perform to the highest level of performance and consistency.

Only one phase of the treatment is being measured. The outcome or matching of the care to the outcome has not been achieved; therefore, there is no assurance of the correct diagnosis and proper treatment. No feedback is being provided to the education department that would make it possible for continuous QI.

Review Questions

1. What is an antecedent variable? Provide an example.
2. What two factors are weighted heavily in order for data to be considered valid?
3. List examples of data collection tools and describe how they function.
4. Why is it important for EMS agencies to establish data quality procedures?
5. How does an indicator differ from a clinical indicator?
6. How does a checklist differ from a check sheet?
7. In order to make a statistically significant change or impact when measuring quality, what factor is necessary?
8. Why is randomness important?
9. Explain the difference between random assignment and randomization.
10. Should random observations be made on weekends and holidays? Why or why not?

References

Agency for Healthcare Research and Quality. (1998, March 12). "President's Advisory Commission on Consumer Quality in the Health Care Industry: Advisory Commission's Final Report." See the organization website.

Carey, R. C., and R. C. Lloyd. (1995). *Measuring Quality Improvement in Healthcare: A Guide to Statistical Process Control Applications.* New York: Quality Resources.

Davis, E. A., and A. J. Billitier, 4th. (1993). "The Utilization of Quality Assurance Methods in Emergency Medical Services. *Prehospital Disaster Medicine 8*(2), pp. 127–32.

EMS Insider. (2007, February). "Paramedics Activate Cath Lab for STEMI Patients in Some Areas." *Journal of Emergency Medical Services 25*(2).

Evans, B., and Dyar, J. (2010). *Management of EMS.* Upper Saddle River, NJ: Pearson Prentice Hall.

International Association of Firefighters/ International Association of Fire Chiefs. (n.d.). "EMS System Performance Measurements Operations Manual." Washington, DC: Author.

Jaffe, A. J., and H. F. Spirer. (1987). *Misused Statistics: Straight Talk for Twisted Numbers.* New York: Marcel Dekker.

Joint Commission. (2008). *Managing Performance Measurement Data in Health Care*, 2nd ed. Oakbrook, IL: Author.

Kane, R. (1998, August). "Managed Care as a Vehicle for Delivering More Effective Chronic Care for Older Persons. *Journal of the American Geriatric Society 46*(8), 1034–1039.

Karch, S., J. Graff, S. Young, and C. Ho. (1998). "Response times and outcomes for cardiac arrests in Las Vegas casinos." *American Journal of Emergency Medicine 16*(3), pp. 249–253.

Maio, R. F., H. G. Garrison, D. W. Spaite, et al. "Emergency Medical Services Outcomes Project I (EMSOP I): prioritizing conditions for outcomes research." *Annals of Emergency Medicine 33*, pp. 423–432.

Michael, J., and A. French. (2000, June). "EMS Education Agenda for the Future: A Vision for the Future of EMS Education." *Annals of Emergency Medicine 35*, pp. 623–624.

Moore, L. (1999). "Measuring Quality and Effectiveness of Prehospital EMS." *Pre-Hospital Emergency Care 3*, pp. 325–331.

National Fire Protection Association. (2009). *NFPA 450: Guide for Emergency Medical Services and Systems.* Boston: Author.

National Highway Traffic Safety Administration. (n.d.). "A Leadership Guide to Quality Improvement for Emergency Medical Services Systems." Washington, DC: U.S. Department of Transportation. See the organization website.

National Highway Traffic Safety Administration. (1994). "EMS Outcomes Evaluation: Key Issues and Future Directions." In *Proceedings from the NHTSA Workshop on Methodologies for Measuring Morbidity Outcomes in EMSi,* Washington, DC, April 11–12. Washington, DC: U.S. Department of Transportation.

National Highway Traffic Safety Administration. (1996). *EMA Agenda for the Future.* Washington, DC: U.S. Department of Transportation. See the organization website.

Professional Research Consultants. (2008). "National EMS Patient Perception Benchmark Study." Omaha, NE: Author.

Public Law 93-154, EMS System Act of 1973. Washington, DC, 1973.

Spaite, D. W., R. Maio, H. G. Garrison, J. S. Desmond, M. A. Gregor, et al. (2001, June). "Emergency Medical Services Outcomes Project(EMSOP) II: Developing the Foundation and Conceptual Models for Out of Hospital Outcomes Research." *Annals of Emergency Medicine 37*, pp. 657–663.

The President's Advisory Commission on Consumer Protection and Quality in the Health Care Industry. (1998, March). "Quality First: Better Health for All Americans: Final Report to the President of the United States." Washington, DC: U.S. Government Printing Office.

Vartanian, L., A. Avendano, G. Grieco, et al. (2008, October). "Paramedic Activated Cath Lab for STEMI Patients at Community Hospital Meets EMS Arrival-to-Intervention Guidelines with Low False-Positive Activation Rate." *Circulation 118*, S_968.

Key Terms

activity Any element of work required by a project and that uses resources and takes time to complete. Activities have expected duration, cost, and resources requirements and may be subdivided into task.

anecdotal Refers to process information that lacks specific methods, measures, deployment methods, evaluation and improvement details, or learning factors.

assessment Systematic process of collecting and analyzing data to determine the current, historical, or projected status of an organization, process, or project.

blanket sampling A type of sampling that captures every event being studied or every patient that meets a certain category of study. It is often used for compliance to standards of care or contractual operational requirements.

check sheet Simple data-recording device. The check sheet is usually custom designed by the user, which ready interpretation of the results. It may also be called a tally sheet.

controlled variable A variable that is held constant when studying the effect of one particular independent variable, thus there is a need to eliminate the other factors affecting the outcome.

dependent variable Those measured items in which there is a change between whether a treatment or action was applied or not applied.

differential measurement Use of a device that transforms actual movement into a known value—for example, the use of a CPR device that is connected to the monitor monitoring the compressions.

independent variable A variable that stands alone and is not changed by the other variables you are trying to measure.

invalid code The code is not on an approved list of possible choices.

measure A criterion, metric, or means by which a comparison is made with outputs.

null code A code or value that is entered as a zero or not recorded in a data field.

random assignment The use of chance procedures when conducting experiments or research to ensure that each participant or data point has the same opportunity to be assigned to any given group. Study subjects can be randomly assigned to different groups such as the experimental or treatment group.

randomization A method based on chance alone by which study participants or patients are assigned to a treatment group. This technique helps to minimize the differences among groups by equally distributing people with particular characteristics among all options being used to change an outcome.

risk adjustment A complicated topic; basically, a corrective tool used to level the playing field regarding the reporting of patient outcomes, adjusting for the differences in risk among specific patients.

service audit A measurement used to make an analysis of the EMS system for strengths and weaknesses, assessing what is being done and what level of performance or quality is being delivered.

temporal analysis Time or limits in time that are identified with a suitable scatter graph that may reveal clusters that are epidemiologically significant.

variable A characteristic of a unit being observed that may assume more than one of a set of values to which a numerical measure or a category from a classification can be assigned.

wrong code A wrong code is simply incorrect input of definitions or characters in a field, commonly an incorrect address or a letter in a field that is supposed to contain a number.

Databases and Data Collection

6 CHAPTER

Objectives

After reading this chapter, the student should be able to:

6.1 Describe a database.
6.2 Identify databases that are used to collect EMS-related information.
6.3 Evaluate the applicability of the National EMS Information System to an EMS organization.
6.4 Recognize relational databases containing EMS information.
6.5 Create a system that tracks a patient longitudinally through the health care system.
6.6 Identify how a database interacts with the GIS system.
6.7 Review and scrub data.

Key Terms

data scrubbing
describe
Health Level 7 (HL7)
object database
push
schema
Schematron
variable

WHAT WOULD YOU DO?

During a high school basketball game, a young sophomore paced the court in a very competitive game. Early in the day, a persistent cough and pallor had indicated sickness, yet the boy felt fine and did not want to miss the competitive game. Just past the second quarter, the student collapsed on the court. A frantic phone call to 9-1-1 summoned the local fire department. The event was reported as an unconscious person. As the first due engine arrived and entered the gym, a fever-pitch CPR was in progress mid-court. Another engine added itself to the call, after hearing the level of stress in the first-arriving captain's voice. The ALS transport was still a good distance away. Despite the efforts of the crew and aggressive resuscitation efforts by the pediatric intensivist at the local pediatric emergency center, the teen died.

Two months later, a teen the same age collapsed in a science classroom. Thanks to a quick response and aggressive CPR by the science teacher, the student made a complete recovery. This second patient was the same age as the basketball player who had died and also had been in cardiac arrest. It was assumed the two incidents had no connection to each other—or did they? No one in the department could recall having two teens collapse that close to each other in time. Other than trauma, overdose, or drowning, no one could remember such an alarming issue as what they currently faced. How could seemingly healthy kids be collapsing? The EMS field supervision opened an investigation and considered the deaths sentinel events.

Questions

1. Where would information on pediatric cardiac arrest be available?
2. Is this a developing problem or a fluke?
3. What other sources of information can help define this as a problem or rare event?
4. How can a database help this situation? Which database(s) should be created to assist in managing this situation?

INTRODUCTION

Government decision makers, payers, and consumers need objective evidence that they are receiving value and quality for the cost of EMS. The EMS system and its participants require objective feedback about performance that can be used internally to support quality efforts and demonstrate accountability to the government, oversight boards, and others stakeholders. This cannot be done without data and an accumulation and storage of that data to identify trends and provide for proper analysis.

Since the early 1970s, an assortment of publications and legislation has contributed to the development of emergency medical services information systems and databases. Many EMS systems differ in their ability to collect patient, clinical, and operational data and to put that information to use. As the health care system continues to look for efficiencies, evidence-based practice will eventually dictate whether the service or procedure is reimbursed. Those decisions will develop with the help of a body of evidence gathered from local, state, and national EMS databases. For this reason, a federal partnership—consisting of the National Association of State EMS

Officials (NASEMSO), the National Highway Traffic Safety Administration (NHTSA), and the Trauma/EMS Systems program of the Maternal Child Health Bureau of the Health Resources and Services Administration (HRSA)—developed a national database.

Although the collection of data are about the pursuit of the best clinical care, revenue is enhanced by proper documentation and being able to translate the data collected in a clinical patient care report (PCR) into a billing database. As ambulance billing drives the quest for better data and documentation, such a database would be useful in the following activities:

- Developing nationwide EMS training curricula
- Evaluating patient and EMS system outcomes
- Facilitating research efforts
- Determining national fee schedules and reimbursement rates
- Addressing resources for disaster and domestic preparedness
- Providing valuable information on other issues or areas of need related to care

No means currently exist to easily link disparate databases to allow analysis at local, state, and national levels.

WHAT IS A DATABASE?

A database consists of a well thought-out collection of data for one or more uses, normally in digital form. One way of classifying databases involves the type of its contents (e.g., bibliographic, document-text, or statistical). Digital databases are managed using database management systems, which store database contents, allowing data creation and maintenance, and search and other access. This collection of information is organized in such a way that a computer program can quickly select preferred pieces of data.

Traditional databases are organized by fields, records, and files. A field is a single piece of information; a record is one complete set of fields; and a file is a collection of records. For example, a telephone book is analogous to a file. It contains a list of records, each of which consists of three fields: name, address, and telephone number.

An alternative concept in database design is known as hypertext. In a hypertext database, any object, whether it is a piece of text, a picture, or a film, can be linked to any other object. Hypertext databases are particularly useful for organizing large amounts of disparate information, but they are not designed for numerical analysis.

A database management system makes it possible to access information from a database. This is a collection of programs that allow for entering, organizing, and selecting data in a database.

WHY COLLECT DATA?

Collecting data are the only reliable way to evaluate the responsiveness and effectiveness of emergency medical services. It identifies service areas that need improvement or further evaluation. It allows for dissemination of accurate public information and development of meaningful education and prevention programs. It promotes decision making and resource allocation that are based on solid evidence, rather than on isolated occurrences, assumptions, emotions, politics, and so on. In short, it makes it possible to know what has not been known.

HISTORY OF EMS DATABASES

In the Emergency Medical Services Systems Act of 1973, the Department of Health Education and Welfare identified fifteen essential elements of an EMS system. This was the first legislation to necessitate data collection or documentation of EMS services.

State EMS directors realized that they could not compare data from one state to another in any way or in any standard format or process and began to assign what should be measured. This set the stage for defining data points and items within these elements to be measured. In 1991, the Utstein databases began to proliferate in communities trying to equally measure cardiac arrest survival. In 1993, the first uniform data set from NHTSA defined 81 important elements of which 49 were considered essential and 32 desirable.

In 1996, NHTSA published the *EMS Agenda for the Future*, which included recommendations for developing 14 distinct attributes of EMS. One of the 14 components was Information Systems, which was addressed by the five recommendations noted in Figure 6.1.

In 1997, the National Center for Injury and Prevention Control established the Data Elements for Emergency Department Systems (DEEDS). This system extended the concept of linking the EMS data to the emergency department. A structured format is used to document each data element:

- A concise definition
- Description of uses
- Discussion of conceptual or operational issues
- Specification of the data type (and field length)
- Description of when data element repetition may occur
- Field values that designate coding specifications and valid data entries
- Reference to one or more data standards or guidelines used to define the data element and its field values
- Other references considered in developing the data element

- EMS must adopt a uniform data set to facilitate collaborative research.
- EMS must develop mechanisms to generate and transmit valid, reliable, and accurate data.
- EMS must develop and refine information systems that describe the entire event so that patient outcomes and cost-effectiveness can be determined.
- EMS should collaborate with other health care providers.
- EMS information system users must provide feedback to those who generate data.

FIGURE 6.1 *EMS Agenda for the Future* Recommendations for Information Systems. *Source: National Highway Traffic Safety Administration (1993)*

Data types and field lengths use **Health Level 7 (HL7)**, which is a widely used protocol for electronic data exchange. The current version of HL7, established in 2005, is version 3.0.

At the state and/or national level, many other data sets have been implemented that have potential for EMS linkage and interaction. These include, but are not limited to the following:

- Medical examiners' database, which catalogs deaths
- Trauma registries
- Vehicle accident reporting system through law enforcement
- Crash Outcomes Data Evaluation System (CODES) through NHTSA

Each of these should be investigated with the development of any EMS information system.

In 1998, NHTSA produced a follow-up document to the *EMS Agenda for the Future* entitled *The EMS Agenda for the Future Implementation Guide*. This document outlined suggestions or approaches to the development of the 14 components presented in the original agenda. Directly or indirectly, this follow-up document reinforces the need for a standardized information system for every one of the essential EMS components identified. The information system, in fact, is the backbone for the development of these components. The future of EMS will be based on information systems.

In 2001, a GAO report entitled "Emergency Medical Services: Reported Needs are Wide-Ranging, With a Growing Focus on Lack of Data" made an attempt to document the impact of EMS. The report started with the *EMS Agenda for the Future* report as there was little or no data to document EMS efforts subsequent to the National Academy of Sciences (1966) white paper entitled "Accidental Death and Disability: The Neglected Disease of Modern Society." Nevertheless, the report noted that four different federal agencies were involved in supporting and promoting EMS improvements:

- National Highway and Traffic Safety Administration
- Health Resources and Services Administration
- Centers for Disease Control and Prevention
- U.S. Fire Administration

None of these agencies imposes standards or enforces requirements on how EMS systems should operate. The failure of most EMS systems to collect reliable and valid data over time makes priority setting and improvement efforts difficult, if not impossible.

The Institute of Medicine (2006) published a landmark report entitled *Future of Emergency Care: Emergency Medical Services at the Crossroads*, which described the current challenges facing EMS as follows:

- Insufficient coordination
- Uncertain quality of care
- Lack of readiness for disasters
- Divided professional identity
- Limited evidence base

The IOM report recommended a direction for emergency care that envisioned a uniform systems approach "in which all communities will be served by well planned and highly coordinated emergency care services that are accountable for their performance" (Institute of Medicine, 2006, p. 5). A consistent theme of the IOM report is the development of regionalized, accountable systems of emergency care. (See Figure 6.2.)

REQUIREMENTS AND PREFERENCES

When placing data in a database for EMS purposes, several processes and procedures should be developed. Every database should have a data dictionary. The data storage method should also be defined. Every database requires rules for file naming and creation of a directory structure. Most rules for data have been established and exist to maintain accuracy. First and foremost, clocks in the system must be synchronized. Some medical devices, such as cardiac monitors,

FIGURE 6.2 Paramedic putting a call into an electronic PCR. *Source: Pre-Hospital Emergency Care 9th Mistovich*

seek out the National Institute of Standards and Technology's atomic clock to synchronize their internal clocks. Electronic patient care reports (ePCR's) and dispatch computers also need to be synchronized with the atomic clock.

Side Bar

Most computer clocks have the ability to synchronize with the National Institute of Standards and Technology's atomic clock.

When collecting data in a database, a unique identifier is necessary for each item being collected. This identifier is usually called a **variable** or database element. The identifier is called a variable because the data it contains (the data element) can vary depending on the individual record. For example, if an agency is collecting information about eye assessment for a research project, it may create a variable named "Pupil Size," which could have a value of constricted, normal, or dilated. These values are text values for the Pupil Size variable. A variable could also store numeric values, such as "1" for normal eyes, "2" for dilated eyes, or "3" for constricted eyes.

COLLECTION OF DATA

It is important to specify how data are collected and in what format. The National EMS Information System (NEMSIS) database requires that information be transmitted in XTML format, which is expected to handle a larger volume of data and be able to talk across multiple databases. However, many EMS systems specify more detail in how information must be reported. Data types include the following:

- Binary or graphics, such as a JPEG or PDF file associated with a graphic waveform from a medical device
- Date/time stamps that include the date and time of an incident's event or procedures
- Long integers, which are numeric data that are larger than the typical number or integer's data type
- Multiple-choice combinations that are a list of variables of which more than one can be selected
- Numbers that are numerical data (often called integer)
- Single-choice combinations that are a list of variables of which only one can be selected
- Text, which can be either alpha or numeric

Scrubbing and Cleaning Data

Data scrubbing, also known as data cleansing, is the process of cleaning up or amending data in a database that are incorrect, incomplete, improperly formatted, or duplicated. This could be due to poor data entry, including typos, misspellings, or transpositions. In some cases, the data are missing. There are tools to scrub data using computer programs and algorithms that look for flaws in the data. Many ePCR reporting programs have scrubbing tools that provide an indicator validating the reports before they can close out or save a report. An example of unclean data is a prehospital care report that does not include a Zip Code. Some scrubbing tools will find the Zip Code based on the address and town and add it or flag the field for an EMS worker to return to complete it.

Meaningful Variables

It is important to define the variables and what type of data elements they contain in a manner that will help those who are analyzing data to be able to quickly identify the type of information they are reviewing. When creating variables, it is strongly suggested that you create a variable that has meaning to you. In the example of pupil size, the variable "PS" is used because it is short and simple. When someone later reviews the database, it may be difficult to know what "PS" means. The variable should be easy to use and easy to remember but still meaningful.

Side Bar

The variable "Prfmc_Msr_1a" is difficult to type. Plus, it will have to be remembered that "Prfmc_Msr" is an abbreviation for "Performance Measure."

Variable Naming Conventions

A standard naming convention for database variables should be created. One-word variables are preferred. Do not use variables that contain spaces or uncommon characters, such as a slash, question mark, or numbers sign. Variables should be limited in length, as some software applications have restrictions on length (e.g., *carcrashwithimpactintowallcriticalinjury* vs. *carvsfixedobject*). Avoid generic names, such as Pupils, and use the underscore for spaces: Pupil_Size. Include the corresponding question numbers (for surveys): Q1_Pupil_Size. This practice will help users quickly identify the question number Q1 (question 1) on the actual survey. Be consistent and ensure that the naming convention is written down.

Null or Not

In every system of data collection, there will be fields that are not or cannot be reported. For data to be of value and reliable, an effort must be made to ensure that incomplete data are properly documented. The NEMSIS database requires that data elements that are entered electronically contain an explanation for every field, whether or not there is relevant information to enter into the program.

How to Handle Missing Data or Null Values

For any collection of data to be of value and reliably represent what was intended, a strong commitment must be made to correctly document incomplete data. When using the NHTSA data set, data integrity is ensured by the following method.

When data elements are being stored electronically in a database or moved from one database to another using XML, the following values should be applied to indicate a data element that is empty or contains a null value:

- *Not Reporting Code*—An EMS documentation or entry code indicating the information system from the agency is not using the data elements of the NHTSA data set for that field. The value "Not Reporting" should be inserted into the database and/or XML file for that data element. This value will be stored in the database to record that the EMS system was not using that data element when the EMS event or patient encounter was documented.
- *Not Recorded Code*—An EMS documentation entry code into the information system that has an empty field or for which nothing is recorded in any of the data elements of the NHTSA data set. The value "Not Recorded" should be inserted into the database and/or XML file for that data element. This value will be stored in the database to record that the EMS PCR did not have a value for that specific data element when the EMS event or patient encounter was documented, although the agency was using this code.

When data are being documented at the time of an EMS event or patient encounter and the EMS personnel or EMS system are unable to provide the information required to complete the data element, the following three values may be used:

- *Not Available Code*—At the time of the EMS patient care report documentation, the information was "Not Available" to the EMS personnel. This documents that the needed information did exist but that EMS personnel were unsuccessful in their attempt to obtain the information.
- *Not Known Code*—At the time of the EMS PCR documentation, the information was "Not Known" to the patient, family, or EMS

personnel. This documents that there was an attempt to obtain the information but that it was unknown by all parties involved.

- *Not Applicable Code*—At the time of the EMS PCR documentation, the information requested was "Not Applicable" to the EMS or patient event. This documents that there was not a need to document the information since it was not applicable. For example, it would not be necessary to document mechanism or injury-related information on a patient who was not traumatized.

STORAGE AND BACKUP

Files should not be more than 255 characters. In some cases, files longer than 128 characters may not allow information to be backed up onto CDs. Most systems are now backing up or saving data to external hard drives or remotely located hard drives or servers in another geographical area. Typically, folder names should not contain spaces or periods, aside from the file extension name.

Variables can store different types of information. This can vary among different software applications. Variable types are specifically set up for particular software applications. The following are some common variable types, followed by an example of usage:

- Text/String
  - Variable: "firstName"
  - Variable type: Text
  - Possible data element: "Joe"
- Numeric
  - Variable name: "age"
  - Variable type: Numeric
  - Possible data element(s): 1, 10, 100
- Date/Time
  - Variable name: "currentDate"
  - Variable type: Date (Short)
  - Possible Data Element: 06/25/06
- Boolean (True/False, Yes/No)
  - Variable name: "seatbelt used"
  - Variable type: Yes/No
  - Possible data Element: 1 = YES, 0 = NO

Managers of data must provide procedures for the sharing and achieving of data developed on an incident, including handling of sensitive data. Sharing data is a common requirement for EMS-related operations. The process of distributing data to other interested parties or agencies during the course of an incident is necessary.

Side Bar

Data Sharing

Several off-the-shelf database and ePCR systems allow for sharing. For example, an engine company could scan the patient's medications and driver's license and take a set of vital signs, then close the call and assign the material to transport unit personnel who in turn open the call to find most of the material automatically filled into their EMS report. Similar procedures could transfer data from law enforcement and EMS and from EMS to hospital staff.

It is necessary to archive data, meaning that long-term storage is needed. This requires the data to be stored in an area that is separate from the original drive, disk, or computer on which it was created. It is also necessary to have provisions in place for backing up data, which is a mechanism for securing current and active files or files that are resident on a local disk and actively in use. Backup makes it possible to recover the data in their most recent state in the event that they are lost during, for example, a power or hardware failure. It also enables recovery of a file or files lost by accidental deletion.

COMMUNICATING BETWEEN DATABASES

When information is routinely shared between databases, it is said to be a relational database. A relational database matches data by using common characteristics found within the data set. The resulting groups of data are organized and are much easier to understand. Relational databases have become a first choice for the storage of information in new databases used for EMS records because an EMS agency is part of the EMS system and must communicate data to other components of the EMS system (e.g., trauma centers and state highway traffic safety agencies). Relational databases have often replaced legacy hierarchical databases and network databases because they are easier to understand and use, even though they are much less efficient. As computer power has increased, the inefficiencies of relational databases, which made them impractical in earlier times, have been outweighed by their ease of use. However, relational databases have been challenged by the **object database**, which was introduced in an attempt to address the object-relational impedance mismatch in relational database and XML databases.

It is common for data from an EMS agency's database to be transmitted to a state EMS office; in turn, the state office reports to the National EMS Database. In many cases, fire reports are transmitted annually to the U.S. Fire Administration's National Fire and Emergency Reporting System. When information from one database is pushed to another, it is commonly called a **push**.

QUERYING DATABASES

Most databases can be queried using the structured query language (SQL). SQL allows users to access data in relational database management systems—such as Oracle, Sybase, Informix, Microsoft SQL, and Access—by allowing users to describe the data a user intends to acquire. In relational databases, data are stored in tables. SQL requires a selection of variables by name to be queried from a table. Therefore, proper naming of files, fields, and variable definitions are important for getting to the information accurately. The following are some of the common combinations of functions in a query other than just selecting one column are:

- And
- Or
- Combination of And and Or
- True and False, True and True, or False and False
- In and Between
- Like
- Joins
- Sum
- Average
- Max
- Min
- Count

XML AND SCHEMAS

Development of schemas and physical database schemas or models, as well as scripts to automatically create the database, is made available in different platforms. A **schema** is a collection of tables, indexes, views, and so on in a database. Most schemas are written in extensible markup language (XML) and are much like HTML, XML's counterpart. XML is a set of instructions that tells a program what to do with objects or text. XML marks up data. For example, if your EMS unit is Rescue 51 in XML, it would say <unit_name>Rescue51</unit_name>. XML has its own set of instructions maintained by the World Wide Web Consortorium (WC3), and users may make their own tags for data. This ability to tag data with XML allows users to exchange data in a format that not only contains the data but also contains the tag that reveals what the data are and how they are formatted. XML has its limitations in that with enormous amounts of data in a query, it gets slow. Databases such as Oracle, SQL, and DB2 have faster search engines.

An XML schema defines the structure of an XML document. An XML schema defines things such as the following:

- Which data elements and attributes can appear in a document
- How the data elements relate to one another

- Whether an element is empty or can include text
- Which types of data are allowed for specific data elements and attributes
- What the default and fixed values are for elements and attributes

A schema is also a description of the data represented within a database. The format of the description varies but includes a table layout for a relational database or an entity-relationship diagram. It is a method for specifying constraints on XML documents. The XML format was chosen as the standard for NEMSIS. It also was defined as the standard to move EMS data between local and state, or state and national, databases. XML's open format provides an easy way to pass data between different software formats. A solid data set and schemas are published on the NEMSIS website for integration. The Version 3.0 data set was created through a national consensus process to update and revise the standard focused toward EMS performance standards.

Data elements beginning with a "D" are associated with an EMS agency's demographic configuration and are typically collected once, with regular updates. Data elements beginning with an "E" are associated with the electronic medical record associated with an EMS event. The "E" data elements are collected in a PCR with every EMS event where the data element has relevance.

Side Bar

NEMSIS-TAC

In 2005, NHTSA, HRSA (EMSC), and the CDC saw the value from the pilot phase of the project and provided funding to create the NEMSIS Technical Assistance Center (NEMSIS-TAC). A contract was given to the University of Utah School of Medicine to operate the center. Utah partners with the University of North Carolina to handle all development and collection of data.

SETTING UP A DATA DICTIONARY

No matter how clear you think your definitions are, it always helps to have a roadmap or resource so you or someone else can view the setup of the database or how to interpret the database. Common definitions to include are these:

- Variable name
- Variable data type
- Description/purpose of the variable
- Possible "acceptable" values for the variable (helps to keep data clean)
- Checks or restrictions for the variable (helps to keep variables clean—e.g., text value not accepted, must be numeric)

Side Bar

Dates and Times

The ISO 8601 Standard Format specifies the most common forms of dates and times. Dates are configured as YYYY-MM-DD using the Gregorian calendar, where YYYY is the year, MM is the month between 01 (January) and 12 (December), and DD indicates the dates between 1 and 31.

Describes

Elements in a database require a specific code or description. A **describe** is a way to write a definition in computer language that creates a site for a piece of data or element to be placed in the database. From an operational perspective, state and national data elements are defined as follows:

- *State EMS Data Element*—A data element that should be collected by all fifty-six U.S. states and territories. State Data Elements are of value to state EMS officials in the description and measurement of EMS resources, service delivery, patient care, disparity, and performance within the state and its regionalized systems of care.
- *National EMS Data Element*—A data element that should be collected by all fifty-six U.S.

states and territories and submitted to the National EMS Database. National Data Elements are of value to the EMS industry and federal officials in the description and measurement of EMS resources, service delivery, patient care, disparity, and performance nationally.

Current NEMSIS software uses a newer process for data management that has open source architecture called **Schematron**. Schematron differs in basic concept from other languages that create schemas. It is not based on grammar but, rather, on finding tree patterns in the parsed document. This approach allows many kinds of structures to be represented, which is inconvenient and difficult in grammar-based schema languages. Using patterns versus grammar helps capture all the required data. For example, using Schematron the database can see patterns for patient care or responses of a chest pain patient which would indicate a field that includes, prompts, searches, or records an EKG.

NEMSIS uses a Web service application programming interface (API) to support transactions between distributed applications, ePCR software, and off-the-shelf software supporting NEMSIS messaging on version 3.0. The API definitions allow systems to communicate through a common interface to commercial software to transmit data to the NEMSIS database. API does not describe and does not instruct on what a component does with the data once it is received. It is merely a transmission formatting process.

LOCAL DATABASES

At the local level, the needs of EMS systems are wide ranging and diverse, reflecting the different environments in which they operate. However, the available data allow a better understanding about the kinds of problems reported than about their effects. The local level challenges faced by individual systems are often associated with variations in such factors as the characteristics of the population served and the geography of the area. The area served by an EMS system can range from isolated rural settings in mountainous terrain to a large metropolis. The variety of data collection and storage options are similar and require basic principles of records management. With the Internet, wireless systems, and hosted sites, every range of agency can collect, store, move, back up, transfer, and analyze data.

One of the simplest forms of a database is available to agencies that have Microsoft products. Both Excel and Access are designed for basic database functions. Each program makes it possible to create simple graphs and pie charts. Each carries the basic function of producing the building block of quality improvement (QI): a control chart.

Local databases can be as simple as information entered and stored on a small desktop to agency systems that send data to hosted sites. Often, the hosted sites also download material to a local server as a backup. This allows an organization to switch vendors and provides a backup in the event a vendor of a database experiences a catastrophic event at the vendor's storage site or a business failure.

STATE DATABASES

Many states have started creating databases in an effort to help secure grant money and respond on a state level to the *EMS Agenda for the Future*'s call for a collective database. Many of these projects were created by states with a strong state EMS office. Although almost every state has a data collection program, some of the early adopters are highlighted below.

Over the past 3 years, Colorado has developed its own data collection system called MATRIX. The system was written by Colorado government programmers. It allows agencies to enter data via Internet connection, PC utility (for agencies with slow connections), or by XML import from commercial software. More than half of the ambulance services in the state are participating and have collected more than 200,000 PCRs in the first year.

Connecticut began about 6 years ago to develop its own NEMSIS Software and got as far as the second round of beta testing. It became clear that the software on the shelf was far superior to what the agency was attempting to do. Connecticut state government now provides hardware, such as Toughbook computers. The services pick a NEMSIS "gold" vendor and submits to the Connecticut Department of Public Health/Office of EMS (DPH/OEMS) collector for download. The state facilitates getting the data in NEMSIS. Connecticut's Department of Information Technology requires Oracle, so it gets translated into an Oracle database. It then downloads the data into a comma delimited format and runs it through STATXFER for analysis. The data will then be linked with hospital discharge data to obtain outcomes and a definitive problem to check with EMT perception.

Florida has recently launched an EMS Tracking and Reporting System (EMSTARS). It is a custom-developed, in-house solution for collecting ePCR data from participating provider agencies in Florida. This program provides for the collection and analysis of incident-level data from EMS agencies for benchmarking and QI initiatives. Florida has been set up to upload state EMS data to the national database to become an official contributing state for NEMSIS.

Florida continues its commitment to providing quality EMS for its citizens and visitors, a service that is founded on the principles of QI to ensure that an optimal, uniform, and standard of prehospital emergency medical care is available to everyone in Florida. This program will make available to Florida's state EMS administrators, quality managers, educators, physicians, researchers, and public policy makers new facts and tools to measure and improve prehospital medical care for Florida's citizens and visitors.

EMSTARS collects a minimum set of data elements that provides specific, useful, actionable information to facilitate continued improvements in EMS service and patient care statewide. The following is representative of the data collection scope:

- All NHTSA national data elements for demographic data and EMS event data
- Other selected elements identified by participants and other stakeholders
- Demographic elements for the provider agency, its personnel, and patients
- Incident and unit times
- Situation and scene information
- Patient care information, including vital signs, injury assessment, trauma score, and intervention and procedural information
- Outcome and disposition information

Maine opted for an RFP process for its e-run reporting project and had a number of proposals for both commercial software and for custom-written applications. In the end, the most cost-efficient way was to go with one of the custom applications, which was ImageTrend. A vendor was chosen to ensure there was ongoing product support and improvement.

Maryland developed a Web-based patient care report called EMAIS, which feeds into the Maryland Ambulance Information System (MAIS). EMAIS is NEMSIS compliant as it was developed prior to the final NEMSIS definitions.

Minnesota uses a NEMSIS-compliant EMS data collection system: the Minnesota State Ambulance Reporting system (MNSTAR), which was developed by ImageTrend.

Montana has been developing a Web-based PCR for deployment. The Online Prehospital Information System (OPHI) complements another module called Online Prehospital Information System–Licensing (OPHI-L). This system was designed so that an EMS service licensing will be Web-based and electronic. Services will create rosters and be linked to the Board of Medical Examiners database so that only licensed EMTs can be on rosters. The medical director for the service approves EMTs to work on services, and then they are given access to OPHI. OPHI can also be used independently of OPHI-L. This version of OPHI enables a patient care record to be completed on any computer with internet access. A PCR can then be printed for medical records. Reports and a module to enable electronic transmission of billing data are available. OPHI is Health Insurance Portability and Accountability Act (HIPAA) compliant and meets the Silver NEMSIS compliance standard. Gold Systems, Inc., in Salt Lake City was the vendor. Gold Systems has an open source business model. Any development done on Montana data or software is available to other states at no cost.

Nebraska purchased a trauma registry system through ImageTrend, which is NEMSIS compliant. It was custom made for Nebraska. The Nebraska system has ambulance services utilizing the state prehospital data collection system to automatically feed patient information into the trauma registry.

North Carolina has had the Prehospital Medical Information System (PreMIS) for the past 5 years. It was built internally and is based on NEMSIS. The EMS office receives data from the entire state, which equates to about one million events per year and has a Web-based reporting system accessible by all EMS agencies. The state has integrated its credentialing system into this to cover personnel, agency, and vehicle licensure needs. The EMS Performance Improvement Toolkit Program is based on this structure as well. This is a targeted performance improvement initiative that assists local EMS agencies with quality management issues. All of these systems are supported by the EMS Performance Improvement Center. This technical assistance center supports the state EMS office.

Ohio's EMS Incident Reporting System (EMSIRS) was developed in-house in 2001, went online in 2002, and has been collecting data on over one million runs annually from more than nine hundred EMS agencies. Ohio is currently upgrading the system to align with NEMSIS standards.

Utah has a system called POLARIS, which was custom developed by a contractor using federal funding (HRSA BT/ASPR). The contract gives the state and the developer rights to the source code. The contractor, not the state of Utah, is responsible for going through the testing process and will hold the compliance certification.

Virginia has successfully launched a non-commercial EMS data registry; however, it is not NEMSIS compliant. Virginia is now replacing the data registry with a commercial Web-based system.

The Wyoming Office of Emergency Medical Services has a data collection system in place for EMS. The Wyoming Ambulance Trip Reporting System (WATRS) is built with the Centers for Disease Control and Prevention's epidemiology program. This is distributed to all EMS agencies in the state with computers at no cost to the agency. The agency has the choice to enter the data or send in paper trip reports to be entered by the EMS office. The program can be NEMSIS compliant with the XML format, although Wyoming has not made that conversion at this time.

The California EMS Authority is working to increase and improve local EMS agencies and state EMS data capacities and capabilities. The California EMS authority's intent is to standardize the collection of prehospital and trauma data in local EMS agencies with a robust data collection system to study the efficacy of EMS systems and traffic safety measures/

conditions and to reduce morbidity and mortality associated with traffic injuries in California by increasing the role/activity of EMS personnel in injury control activities. The goals and responsibilities of the California data collection include the following:

- Development and maintenance of an aggregated statewide prehospital database
- Establishment and maintenance of a core data set for California EMS
- Provision of guidance and technical assistance to local EMS agencies for the development and improvement of local EMS data collection systems
- Promotion of injury prevention and public information and education activities including citizen first-aid/CPR programs and appropriate EMS access
- Development and promotion of a pedestrian safety plan for California

The goal is to have all states reporting into the NEMSIS project. It is imperative for EMS to get an accurate picture of what activities are being conducted by EMS. Each agency should report to the state, which in turn should report to NEMSIS. With the complexity of database management, many states have opted to provide the service and platform for local EMS agencies.

REGIONAL DATABASES

Regional initiatives or cooperative organizations are in place in a few areas around the United States. The EMS Performance Improvement Center (EMSPIC) is located within the Department of Emergency Medicine at the University of North Carolina at Chapel Hill. The EMSPIC provides services and coordinates a three-state effort on data collection and QI. West Virginia, North Carolina, and South Carolina all have coordinated efforts through the EMSPIC. The following systems are currently maintained and supported by the EMSPIC:

- Credentialing Information System (CIS)
- EMS Toolkit Project
- Prehospital Medical Information System (PreMIS)
- State Medical Asset Resource Tracking Tool (SMARTT)

The North Carolina Office of EMS (NCOEMS) established a central location where, by regulation, incident data could be collected and maintained from all 101 North Carolina EMS systems/counties. This is accomplished by a contractual agreement in place since 1999. On January 1, 2008, the South Carolina Department of Health and Environmental Control (DHEC), Division of EMS and Trauma also entered into a contractual agreement with the EMSPIC to begin utilizing the systems in the preceding list. The EMSPIC is strategically placed to provide a high level of information technology (IT) support and quality management expertise. The EMSPIC supports state, regional, and local EMS service delivery from a patient care, resource allocation, and regulatory perspective.

The Duke Endowment supports three states' EMS data and QI initiatives. EMS agencies, software developers, West Virginia's OEMS, and the EMS offices of North Carolina and South Carolina have worked to accomplish one of the most substantial regional EMS data systems in the nation. Currently 100 percent of EMS events in West Virginia are being reported. The implementation of this system formed a ground-breaking level of participation, data collection, and data quality, swiftly placing West Virginia, North Carolina, and South Carolina regions among the top nationally submitting EMS data systems in the country.

The North Central EMS institute in Minnesota is sustaining a regional look at benchmarking and QI through a combination of several submitted databases. The North

Central EMS Institute has developed benchmark definitions for the ambulance industry with the intent of identifying some best practices based on information from a regional data repository. Several different sources of data are being collected, and partnerships with the National EMS Management Association and the Canadian EMS Chiefs are developing into ongoing projects on data and benchmarks.

NATIONAL DATABASES

EMS systems vary in their ability to collect patient and systems data and to put these data to use. There are currently several national EMS or EMS-related databases. There are three government-sponsored databases that are housed or sponsored by NHTSA and the U.S. Fire Administration. A fourth database is maintained through the Department of Health and Human Services for billing purposes and tracking medical cost as it relates to the reimbursement for Medicare, Medicaid, and other insurances. Several national quasi-governmental databases are collecting data as they are research oriented and operated under the management of associations or research organizations. These databases are fed by off-the-shelf software programs which transmit data from the user in the field or inputs in a station that go to an agency database and are then transmitted to a state portal and then up to a national database.

NHTSA Uniform Pre-hospital Dataset Version 3.3.0

In 1994, NHTSA founded the first Uniform Prehospital EMS Dataset, which would become known as NEMSIS Version 1.0. This was based on the realization that different data fields across all EMS systems exist for the same issue or event and that there is a need for standardization

In 2003, a memorandum of understanding (MOU) entitled *Member States Agreement to Conform to NHTSA Uniform Prehospital Dataset Version 2.0* recognized the need for EMS data collection at the national level. It also recognized the need for the assignment of specific definitions of a set of desirable data elements to collect on a national level. Fifty-two states and territories signed the memorandum. A 2-year project funded by NHTSA was established to develop a coding system for EMS as well as a uniform description of the reason for an EMS encounter. The MOU is based on EMS curricula and the NHTSA data set. The creation of a National Data Dictionary or (data set) provides information about each of the data elements, the variables, and the definitions associated with that data element as well as how to deploy the element in a database. The current data dictionary, as of January 2013, is Version 3.3.0.

NATIONAL EMS DATABASE

Currently, there exists an easy link for EMS databases that allows analysis at local, state, regional, and national levels. NASEMSO, with its federal partners at NHTSA and the Trauma/EMS Systems program of HRSA's Maternal Child Health Bureau and Centers for Disease Control and Prevention, developed a national EMS database known as the National EMS Information Management System. This database was developed to help accomplish the following:

- Focus nationwide EMS training curricula
- Evaluate patient and EMS system outcomes
- Facilitate research efforts
- Determine national fee schedules and reimbursement rates
- Address resources for disaster and domestic preparedness
- Provide valuable information on other issues or areas of need related to EMS care

EMS data systems, such as a state EMS database or the National EMS Database, use the NEMSIS data set in several ways. NEMSIS is designed to provide and build on a uniform national EMS data set, with standard terms, definitions, and values as well as a national EMS database, with aggregated data from all states on a limited number of data elements. Forty-eight of the states, the District of Columbia, and three territories signed a memorandum of agreement (MOA) documenting support for the NEMSIS project and expressing a desire for full implementation of the NEMSIS data set.

NEMSIS Structure

Data entered into the NEMSIS database can begin with 9-1-1 center data as dispatch computers have the ability to transfer patient and call information into an ePCR. Portable EMS equipment, such as cardiac monitors and other point-of-care devices, can transmit patient vital signs and other diagnostics to the ePCR. Local agencies then chose a patient care reporting system that is NEMSIS compliant at the silver or gold level in order to be able to transmit the data to a state database or portal that populates the NEMSIS database.

NEMSIS also provides a technical assistance center (TAC) to provide assistance to state, territory, and local EMS agencies. The NEMSIS TAC also provides assistance to commercial software vendors. Biannually, all states and territories are assessed to determine their capabilities to provide data to the national EMS database explanations and validity documentation. NEMSIS data are accumulated into what is known as the data cub. The cub contains national and state data that can be used to create a report. Each report allows the user to drill down and filter the material for more concise and accurate data.

EMS performance measures are often associated with patient encounters that are either time sensitive, treatment sensitive, or both. NEMSIS (and non-NEMSIS) variables may be used to build evidence-based performance assessments for sentinel patient conditions. The patient conditions currently addressed with NEMSIS templates are acute myocardial infarction (AMI), ST-segment elevation myocardial infarction (STEMI), acute stroke, and severe trauma. It is hoped that utilization of these lists of data variables will promote the development and standardization of performance measurement, leading to enhanced benchmarking and sharing of best practices.

FATAL ACCIDENT REGISTRY

Law enforcement uses a national database. In the future, this database may make it possible to communicate with an EMS database. For example, an EMS unit may transport a John Doe as a victim of a fatal accident. EMS may clear the scene quickly and not be able to obtain the information. The vehicle that transported the patient may have to return quickly to service, unable to get the demographics on the patient. Later, when accident investigators get the information and enter it into the system, it could populate the EMS database, filling in the missing information. The Fatal Accident Reporting System (FARS) contains data derived from a census of fatal traffic crashes within the fifty states, District of Columbia, and Puerto Rico. To be included in FARS, a crash must involve a motor vehicle traveling on a traffic way customarily open to the public and must result in the death of a person (occupant of a vehicle or a nonmotorist) within 30 days of the crash. In 1975 FARS was conceived, designed, and developed by the National Center for Statistics and Analysis (NCSA) of NHTSA to provide an overall measure of highway safety, to help identify traffic safety problems, to suggest solutions, and to help provide an objective basis to evaluate the effectiveness of motor vehicle safety standards and highway safety programs. All

FARS data on fatal motor vehicle traffic crashes is gathered from states' own source documents and is coded on standard FARS forms. The FARS database contains descriptions, in standardized formats, of each fatal crash reported. Each crash has more than 125 different coded data elements that characterize the crash, the vehicles, and the people involved. The analysts obtain the documents needed to complete the FARS forms, which generally include some or all of the following:

- Police accident reports
- State vehicle registration files
- State driver licensing files
- State highway department data
- Vital statistics
- Death certificates
- Coroner/medical examiner reports
- Hospital medical reports
- Emergency medical service reports

NATIONAL HEALTH OUTCOME DATABASES

In the future, the United States will develop a National Health Outcomes Database. Such a database will dramatically improve the quality and consistency of care delivered by the U.S. health system by ensuring that health care decision making reflects the best scientific information and outcomes research. A National Health Outcomes Database uses electronic health information from multiple data sources, such as the NEMSIS, to offer unbiased, evidence-based guidance on what treatments work best.

In order for a National Health Outcomes Database to work, it needs continuous updates of data. Personal electronic medical records, which the federal government has directed all doctors, hospitals, and medical providers nationwide to adopt by 2015, are the ideal source of health outcome data. Defining characteristics data such as age, height, and gender; treatment data such as surgeries and prescribed medications; and outcome data would be extracted from personal electronic medical records. All collected information would remain anonymous. Personal and confidential information, such as the patient's name, Social Security number, and address, would be stripped.

Crash Outcome Data Evaluation System

Crash data are an essential tool to help highlight how safety professionals can prevent and reduce injuries and deaths on America's roadways while maximizing the transportation system's efficiency. Information from crash forms and police accident reports (PARs) yields invaluable insights for planning traffic engineering, enforcement, and safety policy. The Model Minimum Uniform Crash Criteria (MMUCC) is a voluntary guideline that helps states collect consistent crash data for a wide range of traffic safety planning applications

CODES is the acronym for Crash Outcome Data Evaluation System. Twenty-three states receive CODES funding from the NHTSA. CODES uses statistically based techniques to link crash data with medical information, such as hospital discharge, emergency medical services, and hospital emergency department data. The system helps states by linking, and making available, data that can help to identify specific crash, vehicle, and behavior characteristics that lead to increased risk of injury severity and high health care costs in participating states.

New Hampshire is one state in the CODES Project unique from its inception because it focused on using project data to meet the day-to-day evaluation and planning needs of local communities and state agencies. All of the special studies and presentations developed by the New Hampshire CODES Project were in direct response to specific requests from local communities and agencies. In addition to the special studies, CODES is used to link data to generate a variety of reports examining various crash factors and their relationships to injury severity, inpatient charges, and length of stay in the hospital.

Congress has supported the improvement of crash data. In 2005, President Bush signed the Safe, Accountable, Flexible, and Efficient Transportation Equity Act: A Legacy for Users (SAFETEA-LU). To receive Traffic Safety Information System Improvement Grants, specified in Section 408 of SAFETEA-LU, a state must certify that it has adopted and uses model data elements identified by the Secretary of Transportation or that it will use Section 408 grant funds toward adopting and using the maximum number of such model data elements as soon as practical. The MMUCC elements were identified by the U.S. Department of Transportation (DOT) as one set of model data elements that apply to Section 408 (the other sets being NEMSIS for EMS data and Model Minimum Inventory of Roadway Elements [MMIRE] for roadway inventory data).

Implementation of MMUCC is a collaborative effort involving the Governors Highway Safety Association (GHSA), Federal Highway Administration (FHWA), Federal Motor Carrier Safety Administration (FMCSA), and NHTSA. The review and update of the MMUCC Guideline, 2nd edition (2003), was structured to obtain maximum input from all sectors of the highway safety community. Over a 12-month period during 2007–2008, feedback was obtained from meetings, phone, U.S. Postal Service mail, email, Internet, and so on before producing the MMUCC Guideline, 3rd edition (2008).

Data elements were developed and incorporated into MMUCC if they were deemed necessary (needed for highway safety decision-making purposes) and comprehensive (included all aspects of the issue or problem being described). The MMUCC Guideline is based on two other data standards: ANSI D16 (for classifying motor vehicle traffic crashes) and ANSI D20 (for promoting uniformity in the transmission of records between jurisdictions). MMUCC has also been developed in close association with NHTSA's FARS and National Automotive Sampling System (NASS), as well as the data elements mandated by the Federal Motor Carrier Safety Administration (FMCSA).

National EMS for Children Data Analysis Resource Center

The National EMS for Children Data Analysis Resource Center (NEDARC) operates a major database with website links to a wealth of reference materials and provides information on the services and workshops offered through NEDARC. NEDARC assists EMS for Children grantees and state EMS offices in developing and improving their capabilities to collect, analyze, and utilize EMS and other health care data to improve the quality of care in state EMS and trauma systems.

Utstein Style for Uniform Reporting of Data

In June 1990, an international group of scientists concerned with research involving out-of-hospital cardiac arrest met at the Utstein Abbey in Stavanger, Norway, published the first major document to specifically address EMS systems and their impact on patient outcomes. Participants debated the lack of uniform nomenclature and definitions as a key problem in research reports on cardiac arrest. A second meeting, the Utstein Consensus Conference, was held in December 1990 in Brighton, England. Recommendations from this follow-up conference were published simultaneously in American and European journals. The report included uniform definitions, terminology, and recommended data sets (the "Utstein style") to assist clinical investigators in reporting human resuscitation studies. (See Figure 6.3.)

NATIONAL FIRE INCIDENT REPORTING SYSTEM

The National Fire Incident Reporting System (NFIRS) is the world's largest national annual database of fire incident information. It is also an all-incident reporting system, collecting

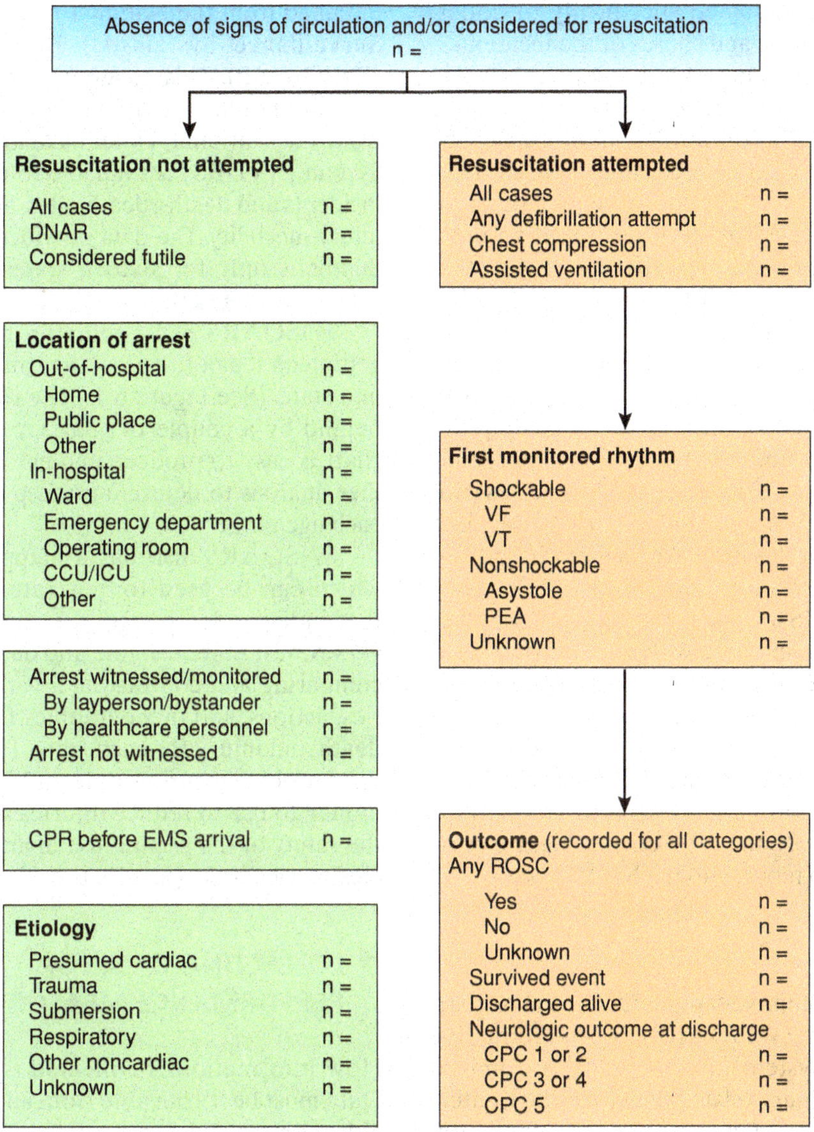

FIGURE 6.3 Report from an Utstein database. *Source: Utstein.*

data beyond fires to include the full range of fire department activity on a national scale. Fire departments may report through NFIRS electronically or by submitting paper forms. Each fire agency in the United States and its territories has a unique identifier.

After responding to an incident, fire department personnel complete one or more of the NFIRS modules or forms. The information in these modules describes the type of incident, where it occurred, the resources used to mitigate it and how, losses, and other information designed specifically to understand the nature and causes of the incident.

The Emergency Medical Services (EMS) is an optional module in NFIRS. It should be used when that option has been chosen by state or local authorities. This module is completed only if the fire department provides emergency medical service. If an independent provider performs EMS, this module is not used. The purpose of the EMS module is to gather basic data as it relates to the provision of emergency medical care to the community. It may be used by both responding EMS unit(s) and responding fire suppression unit(s) that provide emergency medical services. This module does not include patient care information; the data collected on this form are incident based, not patient based.

The EMS module is not intended to replace or otherwise interfere with state or local EMS patient care reporting requirements. Instead, the data elements contained in this module are viewed as "core elements" to be included in the design of upgrades or new EMS data collection systems. In most off-the-shelf software packages for EMS, the NFIRS data field can be extracted to report into the NFIRS system.

WISQARS

Web-based Injury Statistics Query and Reporting System (WISQARS) is an interactive database system that provides customized reports of injury-related data from the Centers for Disease Control and Prevention. WISQARS provides fatality data based on death certificate data obtained from the National Vital Statistics System: deaths, death rates, and years of potential life lost (a measure of premature death) by specific causes of injury mortality and common causes of death. National estimates of injuries treated in U.S. hospital emergency departments can be obtained from the National Electronic Injury Surveillance System-All Injury Program (NEISS-AIP). This program collects data to measure nonfatal and fatal injury rates. Data from the National Violent Death Reporting System (NVDRS) is available to track violent incidents and deaths, death rates, and causes of injury mortality. The data provided for violent deaths is only for sixteen states and is not nationally representative.

WISQARS is a good starting point for getting an idea of the leading causes of death in a state. (See Figure 6.4.) The database lags behind by a couple of years. A color-coded chart is easy to produce and can provide further analysis to determine cause of death for each age range.

WISQARS also has a mapping feature which can be used to generate state maps that indicate death rates for each county. A very robust search engine and database allow comparing and contrasting a variety of injuries, actions, and demographics for causes of death and injury for each state. This is a powerful tool for securing state and federal grant money to use to reduce injuries and increase the safety of the population in an EMS agencies service area. (See Figure 6.5.)

COLLECTING DATA FOR PERFORMANCE MEASURES

How information is collected is important. Data must be retrievable from and exchangeable with other databases to make reports. In many cases, data that are being transmitted will include comments provided to assist in the implementation of a database schema or instruction in how the information should be received. Often, this is more than is known by the EMS administrator and more within the scope of an information technologist who is familiar with relational databases

10 Leading Causes of Death, Colorado 2010, All Races, Both Sexes

	Age groups										
Rank		**1–4**	**5–9**	**10–14**	**15–24**	**25–34**	**35–44**	**45–54**	**55–64**	**65+**	**All ages**
1	Congenital anorralies 97	Unintentional injury 26	Unintentional injury 11	Unintentional injury 12	Unintentional injury 201	Unintentional injury 212	Unintentional injury 244	Malignant neoplasms 619	Malignant neoplasms 1,408	Heart disease 4,768	Malignant neoplasms 7,035
2	Short gestation 67	Congenital anomalies 11	Influenza & pneumonia ---	Suicide 10	Suicide 115	Suicide 133	Malignant neoplasms 151	Heart disease 336	Heart disease 753	Malignant neoplasms 4,756	Heart disease 6,038
3	Matemal pregnancy comp. 33	Homicide ---	Malignant neoplasms ---	Malignant neoplasms ---	Homicide 41	Malignant neoplasms 66	Suicide 150	Unintentional injury 311	Unintentional injury 252	Chronic low. respiratory disease 1,889	Chronic low. respiratory disease 2,199
4	SIDS 26	Malignant neoplasms ---	Chronic low. respiratory disease ---	Heart disease ---	Malignant neoplasms 23	Heart disease 43	Heart disease 109	Suicide 222	Chronic low. respiratory disease 236	Cerebro-vascular 1,357	Unintentional injury 2,106
5	Placenta cord membranes 23	Heart disease ---	Congenital anomalies ---	Cerebro-vascular ---	Heart disease 19	Homicide 39	Liver disease 58	Liver disease 188	Liver disease 188	Alzheimer's disease 1,317	Cerebro-vascular 1,607
6	Unintentional injury 16	Influenza & pneumonia ---	Benign neoplasms ---	Congenital anomalies ---	Congenital anomalies ---	Liver disease 26	Homicide 30	Diabetes mellitus 69	Cerebro-vascular 151	Unintentional injury 821	Alzheimer's disease 1,334
7	Neonatal hemorrhage 12	Five tied ---	Heart disease ---	Homicide ---	Cerebro-vascular ---	Influenza & pneumonia ---	Diabetes mellitus 21	Cerebro-vascular 67	Diabetes mellitus 144	Diabetes mellitus 479	Suicide 865
8	Necrotizing enterocolitis ---	Five tied ---	Homicide ---	Anemias ---	Influenza & pneumonia ---	HIV ---	Cerebro-vascular 18	Chronic low. respiratory disease 53	Suicide 140	Influenza & pneumonia 459	Diabetes mellitus 721
9	Circulatory system disease ---	Five tied ---	Septicemia ---	Septicemia ---	Chronic low. respiratory disease ---	Diabetes mellitus ---	Chronic low. respiratory disease 12	HIV 26	Viral hepatitis 54	Nephritis 367	Liver disease 599
10	Intrauterine hypoxia ---	Five tied ---	---	---	Meningo-coccal infection ---	Cerebro-vascular ---	Two tied 10	Homicide 26	Septicemia 43	Parkinson's disease 297	Influenza & pneumonia 550

WISQARS™ Note: For leading cause categories in this State-level chart, counts of less than 10 deaths have been suppressed (---), Produced by: Office of statistics and programming, National center for injury prevention and control, centers for disease control and prevention

Data source: National center for health statistics (NCHS), National vital statistics system

FIGURE 6.4 WISQARS chart for Colorado. *Source: Centers for Disease Control and Prevention (2013).*

Variables are associated with each data element, such as date and time of medication. Whether the data element is part of the medical record information (PCR) or is a quality management data element to be used internally by the EMS system and protected by peer review, it should be retrievable and transferable.

REQUIREMENTS OF STATE EMSC PROGRAMS

Performance measures represent a new priority and direction for Emergency Medical Services for Children (EMSC) partnership grantees for the next several years. Beginning in fiscal year 2007, state EMSC partnership grantees were required to provide baseline data for each

2004–2010, New Mexico
Death Rates per 100,000 Population
Transportation-related, Overall, Unintentional, All races, All ethnicities, Both sexes, All ages, Annualized crude rate for New Mexico; 21.50

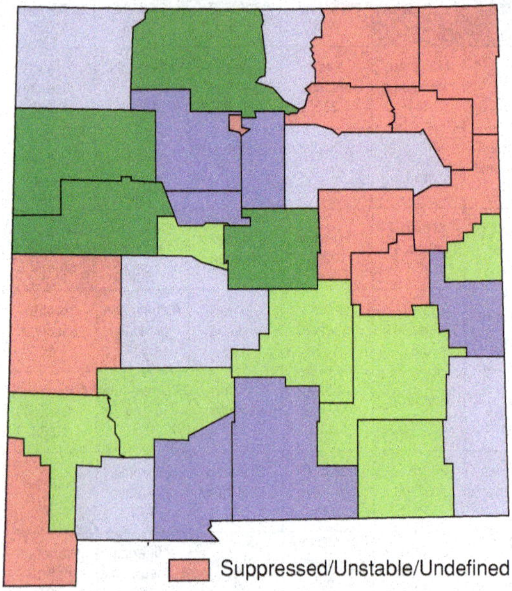

Reports for all ages include those of unknown age.
*Rates based on 20 or fewer deaths may be unstable. These rates are suppressed for counties (see legend above); such rates in the title have an asterisk.

FIGURE 6.5 WISQARS mapping of vehicle injuries per county in New Mexico. *Source: Centers for Disease Control and Prevention (2013).*

specific area of the performance measures, and annually thereafter through 2011. The details of how this is to be accomplished are contained in the implementation manual, but in essence grantees will report a simple number, percentage, or yes/no answer for each measure in the HRSA electronic handbook, followed by supporting documentation for each answer with submission of their grant continuation application. Many of these performance measures will require data collection.

> **Side Bar**
>
> **Data Managers Council**
>
> The Data Managers Council is a group of national leaders developing and maintaining a fully integrated and functioning National EMS Information System (NEMSIS) in all states and territories. The Data Managers Council provides a forum for communication, interaction, and networking among peers, other national organizations, and federal agencies with similar missions. This forum allows for the sharing of best practices, developing and encouraging mentoring programs, the joint resolution of obstacles and challenges, and the nationwide promotion of evidence-based decision making.

Cardiac Arrest Registry to Enhance Survival

Every minute counts during an out-of-hospital cardiac arrest (OHCA). To help EMS providers improve their performance in these situations and save more lives, the CDC created the Cardiac Arrest Registry to Enhance Survival (CARES) in collaboration with Emory University and the American Heart Association. CARES is a secure, Web-based data management system in which participating communities enter local data and generate their own reports. Communities can compare their EMS system performance to de-identified aggregate statistics at the local or national level and can discover promising practices that could improve emergency cardiac care. CARES helps EMS providers measure how well they respond to OHCA calls. The software creates graphs, charts, and maps for EMS providers to compare their performance with other participating communities in the United States. These reports can help guide decisions that will improve survival outcomes from OHCA.

The long-term goal of CARES is to save lives by improving emergency cardiac care at the community level and increasing public

Best Practice

Lost Unit Hours

The key performance indicator (KPI) of lost unit hours can serve on many levels of functionality. The first instinct of EMS is usually to see if units make it on time to their intended assignment. It could also assess whether the workforce is on time for its various shifts. Not showing up on time could be an indication of employee dissatisfaction. A dissatisfied employee tends to result in a bad attitude, poor care, lack of compassion, and decreased client satisfaction.

Employee tardiness is often an early indicator of a bigger problem to come. In addition, having a negative attitude in the field can become infectious. Conversely, tardiness could be an indication of a personal issue, where early recognition and employer intervention can yield a desirable outcome and a loyal employee.

This KPI is of critical importance! When a service schedules and anticipates that a unit is going to be in service but it is not, it costs the company money. Thus, when tracking lost unit hours, it is helpful to associate the financial loss along with hours lost. To track and trend this loss on a daily, monthly, and yearly basis will prove how the cost can mount up over time.

Lost unit hours can result from many causes, and knowing why is critical. Many items can be controlled, but some cannot. It is hard to control time lost when a unit is involved in a motor vehicle accident (MVA), but loss due to vehicle maintenance or employees' mixing up their start times can be controlled. When a service knows the reason for lost unit hours, it is up to the management team to develop a plan to limit these losses. Furthermore, it is critical to continually track losses to ensure that progress is being made toward their reduction.

The possibilities for determining KPIs are many. The ultimate goal is to determine what is important to your agency and begin tracking it. Once you have developed a pool of data, it is time to analyze it, develop a plan for change, continue to evaluate so you can determine if the changes have been effective, and then maintain the desired outcome through vigilance. Other KPIs that the Monmouth-Ocean Hospital Service Corporation (MONOC) tracks are on-time performance, critical vehicle failures, employee callouts, unit cancel rates, patient refusals, RMAs, overtime, lost staffing hours, intubation success rates, IV success rates, and return of spontaneous circulation (ROSC).

Joe Acciavatti
Operations Director, North Region Monmouth-Ocean Hospital Service Corporation (MONOC)
Elizabeth, NJ

---

awareness of the importance of prevention and emergency treatment of heart disease. Steps to meet that goal include improving the performance of EMS systems by providing opportunities for internal and external performance evaluation.

Trauma Registry

Trauma centers and systems are required to maintain registries of descriptive data as a quality management tool. The registry contains detailed information on the management of trauma patients as they progress through the trauma system. The National Trauma Data Bank (NTDB) is the largest collection of U.S. trauma registry data and is maintained by the American College of Surgeons in partnership with the U.S. Department of Health and Human Services. HRSA's Trauma-EMS Systems Program is designed to promote standardization of key trauma data and definitions and to enhance the state's collection and use of trauma data to improve trauma care outcomes. The NTDB has been generating reports on the nation's trauma patients. A comprehensive data dictionary, which is currently in version 5.0, is produced to enable users and trauma centers to collect uniform data. In 2002, the National Pediatric Trauma registry being managed by Tuft University was discontinued as most of the similar data are being recorded in the NTDB.

The NTDB has spawned numerous research organizations. The Society for Advancement of Violence and Injury Research is a nonprofit organization using the information collected from the NTDB to promote scholarly activity in the prevention, control, and rehabilitation of intentional and unintentional injuries.

Side Bar

Canada's Database System

The Canadian health care system has an equivalent trauma data bank called the National Trauma Registry. It is maintained by the Canadian Institute for Health Information.

MOTOR VEHICLE CRASH DATABASES

Motor vehicle crash databases are maintained through either the state department of transportation or state law enforcement agencies. NHTSA maintains the Crash Outcomes Data Evaluation System (CODES). As mentioned previously in this chapter, CODES is a collaborative approach to obtain medical and financial outcome information related to motor vehicle crashes for highway safety and injury control decision making. It evolved as the result of the Intermodal Surface Transportation Efficiency Act (ISTEA) of 1991, which provided funds to NHTSA to report to Congress about the benefits of safety belts and motorcycle helmets for persons involved in motor vehicle crashes. To measure benefits in terms of reducing death, disability, and medical costs, NHTSA determined that statewide data were needed that included all persons involved in police-reported crashes—those who were not injured, were injured, or died. In this manner, comparisons between those using and not using safety belts or motorcycle helmets could be made by identifying and contrasting the characteristics of the injured and uninjured persons within each of the restraint use group.

The National Center for Statistics and Analysis (NCSA) is an office of NHTSA responsible for providing a wide range of analytical and statistical support to NHTSA and the highway safety community at large, in the following general areas:

- Human, vehicle, environmental, and roadway characteristics, as they relate to crash frequency and injuries
- Injury mechanisms and associated crash dynamics in motor vehicle crashes
- Evaluations of the effectiveness of crashworthiness, crash avoidance, and traffic safety efforts
- Monitoring the magnitude of the traffic safety problem
- Quantifying the benefits resulting from proposed agency rules

The major data sources are NCSA's own FARS and the National Automotive Sampling System (NASS). NASS is composed of two systems: the Crashworthiness Data System (CDS) and the General Estimates System (GES). Both systems are based on cases selected from a sample of police accident reports. CDS data focus on passenger vehicle crashes and are used to investigate injury mechanisms to identify potential improvements in vehicle design. GES data focus on the bigger overall crash picture and are used to assess problem size and to track trends. In addition to data from FARS and NASS, NCSA uses data from other government agencies, as well as crash files from a number of states, to support analytical activities. NCSA conducts one-time and ongoing analyses of a wide range of safety issues. Examples of recent analyses include the following:

- Evaluation of the effectiveness of automatic occupant protection systems
- Monitoring and describing trends in female driver fatalities
- Analysis of the crash experience of vehicles equipped with antilock brakes
- Evaluation of primary enforcement and other provisions of safety belt use laws

NCSA also regularly produces a variety of fact sheets and reports that provide information on crashes at the national and state levels. Most are produced annually, including the following:

- *Traffic Safety Facts: A Compilation of Motor Vehicle Crash Data from the FARS and the GES*
- Traffic Safety Fact Sheets
- NASS Crashworthiness Data System Report
- Alcohol Involvement in Fatal Crashes Annual Summary

Fatal Accident Reporting System

Fatality information is derived from the Fatality Analysis Reporting System. FARS was established in 1975 and contains data on the most severe of traffic crashes, those in which someone was killed. FARS data are used to monitor trends in traffic safety and to evaluate motor vehicle safety standards. NHTSA has a contract with an agency in each state to provide information on fatal crashes. FARS analysts are state employees who extract the information and put it in a standard format. FARS includes motor vehicle traffic crashes that result in fatality to a vehicle occupant or nonmotorist within 30 days of the crash. The final FARS file is normally completed around Memorial Day (the end of May), at which time the final quality control procedures are implemented. When these procedures are completed, NCSA can begin to create fact sheets and release the new data.

FARS contains data on all fatal traffic crashes within the fifty states, the District of Columbia, and Puerto Rico. The data system was conceived, designed, and developed by the National Center for Statistics and Analysis (NCSA) to assist the traffic safety community in identifying traffic safety problems, developing and implementing vehicle and driver countermeasures, and evaluating motor vehicle safety standards and highway safety initiatives.

NCSA responds yearly to more than 3,000 requests for information and sends out more than 50 computer reports of FARS data each year. FARS data are used extensively within NHTSA, and requests are received from sources such as state and local governments, research organizations, private citizens, the auto and insurance industries, Congress, and the media. FARS data can be used to answer many questions on the safety of vehicles, drivers, traffic situations, and roadways. FARS data also can be accessed at the state level by the FARS analyst in response to state safety issues. To protect individual privacy, no personal information—such as names, addresses, or specific crash locations—is coded. Data are available for every year since FARS was established in 1975. Users can obtain FARS data in several ways:

- The FARS Query System enables users to perform their own custom queries, such as case listings, univariate tabulations, and cross-tabulations. It also makes it possible to download subsets of data based on selected fields of interest and a library of frequently requested tables. FARS documentation is also available via ftp.
- Fact sheets utilizing FARS data can be viewed as well as downloaded in PDF format and are also available from NCSA.

- *Traffic Safety Facts* utilizes both FARS and NASS GES data and is available by contacting NCSA. This annual report is a comprehensive overview of the year's data and includes some past years' data with comparative analyses.
- FARS data, reports, and documentation are also available for download via a FTP. Files on CD-ROM and computer tape are available in several formats amenable to analysis. This allows an agency to process the data on its own computer system.

Data Collected for FARS

Data on fatal motor vehicle traffic crashes are gathered from a state's own source documents and are coded on standard FARS forms. The analysts obtain the documents needed to complete the FARS forms, which generally include some or all of the following:

- Police accident reports
- State vehicle registration files
- State driver licensing files
- State highway department data
- Vital statistics
- Death certificates
- Coroner/medical examiner reports
- Hospital medical records
- Emergency medical service reports

FARS DATA

To be included in FARS, a crash must involve a motor vehicle traveling on a roadway customarily open to the public and must result in the death of a person (either an occupant of a vehicle or a nonmotorist) within 30 days of the crash. The FARS file contains descriptions of each fatal crash reported. Each case has more than a hundred coded data elements that characterize the crash, the vehicles, and the people involved. All data elements are reported on four forms:

- The *Accident Form* asks for information such as the time and location of the crash, the first harmful event, whether it is a hit-and-run crash, whether a school bus was involved, and the number of vehicles and people involved.
- The *Vehicle Form* and the *Driver Form* call for data on each crash-involved vehicle and driver. Data include the vehicle type, initial and principle impact points, most harmful event, and drivers' license status.
- The *Person Form* contains data on each person involved in the crash, including age, gender, and role in the crash (driver, passenger, and nonmotorist), injury severity, and restraint use.

CHAPTER REVIEW

Summary

A database is a complex and necessary tool for EMS agencies. The management of a database, including the naming, storage, design, and transmission of data, is important to an EMS system. A local EMS database that communicates to a state database or portal and then to the National EMS Information System is the optimal design for an EMS system. Data are placed into the system using a defined EMS data set. Certain processes in naming data and collecting data must be followed to ensure a uniform collection process. EMS data contribute or relate to other databases used in the EMS system (e.g., fatal accident database, trauma registry, cardiac arrest registries, crash outcomes). Data are a necessity in EMS as proving effectiveness and utilization is necessary to maintain or justify budgets, treatments, and service levels.

WHAT WOULD YOU DO? Reflection

Data on pediatric cardiac arrest should be available on the EMS-C website and within the EMS database. The local EMS database will also include the demographics and actions taken by the EMS crew. Patient care data could be obtained from the cardiac monitor and, perhaps, downloaded from an AED.

Depending on the population and the numbers reported per 100,000, this matter might need further analysis. Some analysis is important to ascertain what pediatric cardiac arrests have occurred before and what the etiology of any such cardiac arrests was determined to be. Extrapolating the data and looking at location or analyzing GPS could give a clear picture of the events.

First look at the WISQARS database to see how prevalent cardiac is as a cause of death in the state in which this occurred. Drilling down to the county level to look for common causes of death in this age group is also possible. State or national databases, including the CARES registry, could help further delineate this picture.

A database on pediatric cardiac arrest or creating a customized report from existing databases can help identify a specifically defined field highlighting, for example, causes of pediatric cardiac arrest. In some areas, pediatric patients in EMS systems vary in age. Some EMS systems consider pediatric patients as those 8 years of age and under whereas others use 12 or even 18 years of age as a threshold. Any report created from a database should consider the definition of what constitutes a pediatric patient. Stock reports form CARES and NEMSIS can also be run to identify patients and locate pediatric calls.

Review Questions

1. What is the WISQARS database system, and what information can be queried?
2. What criteria should be used when creating a naming variable for EMS units?
3. How can data collected in an EMS system be linked to other databases that would be relational to the EMS agency's data?
4. The FARS database and the NEMSIS database can perform a query on similar details. What are some examples?
5. Define a situation that would have a null value and a not value.
6. What data identified in cardiac arrest patients would be valuable to your organization?

Additional Midterm Exercises

1. Using WISQARS databases, identify the state and country within that state that has the highest rates of suicide, drowning, and vehicle accidents.
2. Create naming variables for all of your EMS units that reflect the principles of a naming convention.
3. Create a flowchart of how data are collected in your EMS system and include the areas that could be linked to other databases that would be relational to your EMS agency's data.
4. Access the FARS database and the NEMSIS database, and then perform a query on auto pedestrian crashes. Compare and contrast the statistics.
5. Define a situation that would have a null value and a not value.
6. Retrieve a month's worth of data, identify cardiac arrest patients, and place the numbers into the Utstein or CARES format.

References

Centers for Disease Control and Prevention. (2013). "Injury Prevention & Control: Data & Statistics (WISQARS™)." See the organization website.

Hoffer, J. A., M. B. Prescott, and F. R. Mcfadden. (2007). *Modern Database Management*, 8th ed. Upper Saddle River, NJ: Prentice Hall.

Idris, A. H., M. A. Berg, J. Bierens, L. Bossaert, C. M. Branche, et al. (2003). "Recommended Guidelines for Uniform Reporting of Data From Drowning: The Utstein Style." *Circulation 108*, pp. 2565–2574.

Institute of Medicine. (2006). *Future of Emergency Care: Emergency Medical Services at the Crossroads.* Washington, DC: National Academies Press. See the National Academies Press website.

McNally, B., A. Stokes, A. Crouch, and A. L. Kellerman. (2009). "CARES: Cardiac Arrest Registry to Enhance Survival." *Annals of Emergency Medicine 54*(5), pp. 674–683.

Mears, G., J. Ornato, and D. E. Dawsen. (2002, January–March). "Emergency Medical Services Information Systems and a Future EMS National Database." *Prehospital Emergency Care 6*(1), pp. 123–130.

National Academy of Sciences. (1966). "Accidental Death and Disability: The Neglected Disease of Modern Society." See the NHTSA EMS website.

National Highway Traffic Safety Administration. (1996). *EMS Agenda for the Future.* See the organization website.

National Highway Traffic Safety Administration. (1998). *EMS Agenda for the Future Implementation Guide.* See the organization website.

U.S. Government Accountability Office. (2001). "Emergency Medical Services: Reported Needs are Wide-Ranging, With a Growing Focus on Lack of Data." See the organization website.

Waien, S A. (1997, November). "Linking Large Administrative Databases: A Method for Conducting Emergency Medical Services Cohort Studies Using Existing Data." *Academic Emergency Medicine 4*(11), pp. 1087–1095.

Key Terms

data scrubbing Process for fixing or eliminating individual pieces of data that are incorrect, incomplete, or duplicated before the data are saved or analyzed.

describe Way of writing definitions in computer language that creates a site for a piece of data or element to be placed in the database.

Health Level 7 A widely used protocol for electronic data exchange of medical data.

object database A relational database that addresses the object-relational impedance mismatch in relational database and XML databases.

push Involves a cache of data or instructions being capable of receiving updates and modifications proactively sent to it from a remote server holding the source content data.

schema A cognitive framework or concept that helps organize and interpret information.

Schematron A rule-based validation language for making assertions about the presence or absence of patterns in XML data.

variable Identifier of data (the data element) that can vary depending on the individual record.

Data and Quality Analysis

7 CHAPTER

Objectives

After reading this chapter, the student should be able to:

7.1 Identify and calculate what the measures of central tendency are.

7.2 Interpret and apply test of correlation to determine causation and correlation with a set of data.

7.3 Identify patterns in statistics and apply formulas to identify and interpret those patterns as significant or correlating.

7.4 Select the proper displays and ways to communicate the results or analysis of the data, given a set of data.

7.5 Distinguish between comparative and noncomparative measurement scales.

7.6 Describe efficient ways of ordering, analyzing, and summarizing qualitative data.

7.7 Designate, at the end of data analysis, what additional activities are needed to test, confirm, and prove data validity.

Key Terms

analysis of variance
bimodal
causation
chi-square
Cronbach's coefficient alpha
data
descriptive statistical analysis
histogram
Likert scale
mean
measurement
measures of central tendency
measures of dispersion
median
mode
modulus
nonparametric
ordinal scale
outlier
PERT chart
phi coefficient
point bi-serial correlation
range
regression line
reliability
run
semantic scale
shift
standard deviation
trend
variable
variance

WHAT WOULD YOU DO?

A 32-year-old healthy man with a wife and young kids called EMS for a rapid heartbeat. Upon arrival, he was found by EMS to have unstable SVT (chest pain, hypotension). The patient received a synchronized shock at 100 joules that was refractory. Following protocol, another try at 200 joules resulted in the patient going into cardiac arrest. After a 60-minute resuscitation attempt, the patient died.

The code summary from the cardiac monitor revealed that the paramedic had failed to put the device in SYNC mode for the second shock, which resulted in the patient going into ventricular fibrillation. Following collection of the **data** from the cardiac monitor code summary, an analysis of the event revealed that the design allows for the device to silently leave the SYNC mode. The number of different monitors the paramedic had been trained on added to the omission.

As a proactive analysis in response to a one-time event with a catastrophic outcome, a study with fourteen paramedics was created to see if this is a common problem. Running the paramedics through the same situation revealed that 50 percent of the paramedics made the same error, and 71 percent of the paramedics did not know that they had made the error.

Questions

1. What test can be done on the results to ensure that this observation is accurate?
2. Are the findings valid and reliable?
3. Is there a possibility that the type of cardiac monitor causes a wider range or variation or a more reliable synchronized cardioversion? What is the opportunity for management to make a decision on this incident?
4. What tool or visual aid (e.g., chart, graph, picture) should be used to display the results of the test?

INTRODUCTION

Data analysis is a practice in which raw data are prepared and organized so that useful information can be extracted from it. The process of organizing and thinking about data is key to understanding what the data do and do not contain. There are a variety of ways in which people can approach data analysis, and it is easy to manipulate data during the analysis phase to push certain conclusions or agendas. It is important to decide before a project is started what process is trying to be improved. For this reason, it is important to pay attention when data analysis is performed and to think critically about the data and the conclusions that are drawn from it.

The objective of data analysis is to make better and more informed decisions in emergency services. Data have no value in a vacuum. Likewise fire and EMS reports have limited value if an organization does not make a change or act on the data analysis. Analysis turns data into information. For example, knowing individual call types and response times is common, but knowing average travel times allows identification of actual sources of delays or efficiencies in response. Reviewing travel times within the response time increases knowledge about what is going on in EMS incidents, units, and stations, which results, in turn, in more informed decisions within an EMS organization.

Statistical techniques must be applied to collected numbers for them to be useful—that is, the data typically collected by EMS organizations must be analyzed scientifically. Most EMS agencies collect a vast amount of data but do very little with it. Reports are completed on incidents daily, documenting the type of situation encountered, action taken, time of alarm, time of arrival, time spent en route to the hospital or at the scene, number of ambulances and first-response vehicles on scene, number of personnel responding, and who performed what skills. For clinical issues, the list also includes the nature of the complaint, vital signs, past medical history, and other diagnostics, such as an EKG or pulse oximetry reading.

The most common reason for these reports is a legal requirement for documenting incidents or to qualify for reimbursement. Patients, insurance companies, lawyers, and many others want copies of reports. These reports can, however, provide a more beneficial service by providing insight into the nature of calls and injuries in the jurisdiction. Typically, the number of EMS calls, the number and types of injuries, and the number of procedures are tracked. It is another story, however, if more probing questions are asked, such as the following:

- How many EMS calls took place on Sundays, Mondays, and so on, and at what time of day?
- How many illnesses or injuries took place during each hour of the day or month of the year?
- What was the average response time to calls about life-threatening and not life-threatening incidents?
- How much did response times vary by area, crew, shift, and time of day?
- What was the average time spent at the EMS scene on trauma versus medical?

Statistical techniques turn data into information by answering questions in a more detailed way. The techniques range from simple to complex. An EMS manager must be able to describe illnesses and injuries and make charts to provide more effective presentations about them. These charts may be beneficial to city or county officials who are dependent on the activities and needs of an agency. Discussions on the **measures of central tendency** (**mean**, **median**, **mode**) and **measures of dispersion** (**range**, **variance**, **standard deviation**) are important for EMS managers to understand. The use of the **chi-square** statistic is another statistical tool used in analyzing table data. The Pearson product-moment correlation coefficient and some additional correlation formulas are also important tools to find **causation** and how events in the EMS system are related even when it may not be obvious or, conversely, when it appears obvious but it is not related. These are all techniques that can reveal more about the nature of illness and injuries.

DATA ANALYSIS

Why should an agency go to all of this trouble to analyze data? Many decisions, such as personnel actions, grievances, promotions, and even decisions on how to handle an EMS call, do not require analysis. EMS and fire agencies cannot continue to operate in the same way they always have without doing a lot of analysis. As financial resources become scarce for operational issues, the cost versus benefit of a program or change will be dictated by the data-driven analysis of outcomes versus cost. Reimbursement for ambulance service is slowly moving toward outcome-based reimbursement, which requires analysis of data to determine performance.

The following are three excellent questions to consider when looking closely at data:

- Are we achieving the outcomes expected for the customer?
- Are the processes that are necessary to produce those outcomes reliable? If not, can we improve **reliability** for EMS?
- What training needs are present?

Probably the most compelling reason is that analysis gives insight into health care problems, which in turn can affect operations in the department. For example, the average time to respond to a cardiac arrest in an area is 8 minutes, compared to less than 5 minutes overall. This result may be helpful in justifying requests for more equipment; personnel; or another fire station, post location, or alternative action, such as a public access defibrillation program. As an example of improved resource allocation, statistical analysis of EMS calls can determine the impact of providing another paramedic unit in the field. Increasing the number of EMS units from four to five may, for example, decrease average response times from 5 minutes to 3 minutes, thus providing earlier defibrillation and advanced life support.

Another reason for analysis is to identify training needs. Most current EMS training is based on a curriculum that was taken as initial training years earlier or is from a standardized curriculum from the National Highway Traffic Safety Administration (NHTSA). Statistical analysis allows you to see how training matches the characteristics of EMS responses in a particular jurisdiction. Knowing more about the EMS problem in an area can improve the training. For example, if you are in an area with a large retirement population, the lack of pediatric patients may indicate a need for more frequent training to ensure readiness for encounters with pediatric patients. In addition, an analysis of personnel injuries may indicate a need for certain types of training.

A PROCESS FOR EVALUATING DATA

Data analysis is like cooking: You need to find a step-by-step process to follow to ensure that the end result is the right product. The following is a general process helpful in planning for evaluating data:

- Plan
- Assess
- Validate
- Clean
- Plan (again)
- Do

PLANNING THE ANALYSIS

The first step to data analysis is getting to know the data. This means learning the **variable** names, variable definitions, and what values are valid in each field. The next step is to plan what data will be collected from the various sources. It is then entered into a single data file. A plan for data analysis must address the need to accumulate data in one location so that all of the data can be analyzed in a consistent fashion.

The most convenient format for most data analyses is the variables-in-columns format. This format has the variable names in column headings and the values for the variables in the rows. The plan for analysis should include processes that are based on the data dictionary that contains the variable definitions.

Before using the data, the definitions should be well understood. The National EMS Information System (NEMSIS) has well-defined data. Local agencies must review their own additions to their data dictionary—for example, "What is a patient contact?" The data dictionary typically describes the following:

- The definition of each variable
- The valid values of the variable
- How missing values are represented
- The data type (numeric or alpha)
- The data format

The database and how the data are stored also must be understood. Original files should be saved in a safe place. All work should be done on a copy of the data. Getting halfway through a data analysis process and having a power surge, encountering a software glitch, or hitting a wrong key that damages or erases the process can be catastrophic and consume inordinate amounts of time.

Be mindful of time constraints related to the data analysis. In the planning stage, selecting the statistical test is the key step. Running statistical tests and preparing data are time-consuming activities. Planning often yields more questions and triggers many more questions or conclusions.

ASSESSING THE DATA

The type of data collected must be assessed to decide what process to use in the second phase of the planning. Qualitative data and quantitative data require two different processes. Which statistical test should be used and the resulting conclusions are also dependent on the type of data being analyzed. The quantity of data also must be assessed. The n, or number of samples or data points, must be assessed to determine if there are adequate numbers or samples to qualify the research as valid.

A sample size has to be large enough to establish reliability and accuracy, and it then becomes a precise measure. Assessing whether the sample is large enough to be precise uses a formula. Once the sample size is determined, a decision is required that begins with selecting either a 95 percent or 99 percent confidence level. Confidence levels established in this range are common for medical research due to the potential for a catastrophic outcome if there is an error. The confidence interval is a selection of the range (also called margin of error) that is either 5 percent or 1 percent in error in the minus or in error in the positive. For example, if you use a confidence interval of "5" and 47 percent of your sample picks an answer, you can be sure that if you had sampled the entire relevant population between 42 percent (47 – 5) and 52 percent (47 + 5) would have fallen in that category.

An analysis based on the standard normal distribution, more commonly known as the bell curve, typically encompasses a certain confidence that the data are within three standard deviations of the mean. The confidence interval is represented in the area located under the bell curve and to the left of a given z score. These areas represent probabilities and have numerous applications throughout statistics. When a normal distribution is used, a table such as the one in Figure 7.1 can be consulted to perform important calculations. If you need help reading the table, begin with the value of your z score. To use the table, the z score value should be rounded to the nearest hundredth. Find the appropriate entry in the table by reading down the first column for the ones and tenths places of your number, and along the top row for the hundredths place. For example, if $z = 1.67$, then you would split this number into $1.67 = 1.6 + .07$. The number located in the 1.6 row and .07 column is .953. Thus 95.3 percent of the area under the bell curve is to the left of $z = 1.67$. A score of 95 percent or higher is a sign of reliability or confidence the data is correct.

The table in Figure 7.1 may also be used to find the areas to the left of a negative z score. To do this, drop the negative sign and look for the appropriate entry in the table. After locating the area, subtract 0.5 to adjust for the fact that z is a negative value. The kinds of bell curves that are commonly appropriate to EMS in statistics are called normal probability distributions.

Despite the name "bell curve," these curves are not defined by their shape. A formula is used as the formal definition for bell curves. The only two numbers that are important are the mean and the standard deviation. The center of a bell curve for a given set of data is located at the mean. This is where the highest point of the curve or "top of the bell" is located. Sometimes the top of the curve can be shifted to the left or right of center. A data set's standard deviation determines how spread out the bell curve is. The larger the standard deviation, the more spread out is the curve.

Important Features of a Bell Curve

There are several features of a bell curve that are particularly important and distinguish them from other curves in statistics. A bell

STANDARD NORMAL DISTRIBUTION: Table Values Represent AREA to the LEFT of the Z score.

Z	.00	.01	.02	.03	.04	.05	.06	.07	.08	.09
0.0	.50000	.50399	.50798	.51197	.51595	.51994	.52392	.52790	.53188	.53586
0.1	.53983	.54380	.54776	.55172	.55567	.55962	.56356	.56749	.57142	.57535
0.2	.57926	.58317	.58706	.59095	.59483	.59871	.60257	.60642	.61026	.61409
0.3	.61791	.62172	.62552	.62930	.63307	.63683	.64058	.64431	.64803	.65173
0.4	.65542	.65910	.66276	.66640	.67003	.67364	.67724	.68082	.68439	.68793
0.5	.69146	.69497	.69847	.70194	.70540	.70884	.71226	.71566	.71904	.72240
0.6	.72575	.72907	.73237	.73565	.73891	.74215	.74537	.74857	.75175	.75490
0.7	.75804	.76115	.76424	.76730	.77035	.77337	.77637	.77935	.78230	.78524
0.8	.78814	.79103	.79389	.79673	.79955	.80234	.80511	.80785	.81057	.81327
0.9	.81594	.81859	.82121	.82381	.82639	.82894	.83147	.83398	.83646	.83891
1.0	.84134	.84375	.84614	.84849	.85083	.85314	.85543	.85769	.85993	.86214
1.1	.86433	.86650	.86864	.87076	.87286	.87493	.87698	.87900	.88100	.88298
1.2	.88493	.88686	.88877	.89065	.89251	.89435	.89617	.89796	.89973	.90147
1.3	.90320	.90490	.90658	.90824	.90988	.91149	.91309	.91466	.91621	.91774
1.4	.91924	.92073	.92220	.92364	.92507	.92647	.92785	.92922	.93056	.93189
1.5	.93319	.93448	.93574	.93699	.93822	.93943	.94062	.94179	.94295	.94408
1.6	.94520	.94630	.94738	.94845	.94950	.95053	.95154	.95254	.95352	.95449
1.7	.95543	.95637	.95728	.95818	.95907	.95994	.96080	.96164	.96246	.96327
1.8	.96407	.96485	.96562	.96638	.96712	.96784	.96856	.96926	.96995	.97062
1.9	.97128	.97193	.97257	.97320	.97381	.97441	.97500	.97558	.97615	.97670
2.0	.97725	.97778	.97831	.97882	.97932	.97982	.98030	.98077	.98124	.98169
2.1	.98214	.98257	.98300	.98341	.98382	.98422	.98461	.98500	.98537	.98574
2.2	.98610	.98645	.98679	.98713	.98745	.98778	.98809	.98840	.98870	.98899
2.3	.98928	.98956	.98983	.99010	.99036	.99061	.99086	.99111	.99134	.99158
2.4	.99180	.99202	.99224	.99245	.99266	.99286	.99305	.99324	.99343	.99361

FIGURE 7.1 ■ Standard normal distribution. *Source: Public Domain*

curve has one mode, which coincides with the mean and median. This is the center of the curve where it is at its highest. A perfect bell curve is symmetric. If it were folded along a vertical line at the mean, both halves would match perfectly because they are mirror images of each other. A bell curve follows the 68-95-99.7 rule, which provides a convenient way to carry out estimated calculations:

- Approximately 68 percent of all of the data lies within one standard deviation of the mean.

- Approximately 95 percent of all the data are within two standard deviations of the mean.
- Approximately 99.7 percent of the data are within three standard deviations of the mean.

VALIDATING THE DATA

The next step is to perform a quality check on the data. A quality check on the data uses graphical and numerical techniques. Typically, we are looking for data entry problems, unusual data values, missing data, or the wrong character in the field. A **modulus** is a check to ensure that there are no extra numerical fields. The modulus function is the magnitude of that number. For example, a systolic or diastolic blood pressure should not have four numbers for each field. A modulus flags or excludes a value that is above the magnitude of that number.

Two of the most useful tools for this step are the scatter plot and the **histogram**. A scatter plot reveals relationships or association between two variables. (See Figure 7.2.) Such relationships manifest themselves by any nonrandom structure in the plot. Running numerical summary statistics on all of the variables (both response and explanatory) also helps to identify data problems.

The purpose of a histogram is to graphically summarize the distribution of a univariate data set. The histogram graphically shows the following:

- Center (e.g., the location) of the data
- Spread (e.g., the scale) of the data
- Skewness of the data
- Presence of outliers
- Presence of multiple modes in the data

These features provide strong indications of the proper distributional model for the data and lend to its validation.

CLEANING THE DATA

A large part of becoming familiar with your data involves validating the variables in your data set. Therefore, you will need to validate your data. This means checking for bad or missing data. Ideally, the database also should

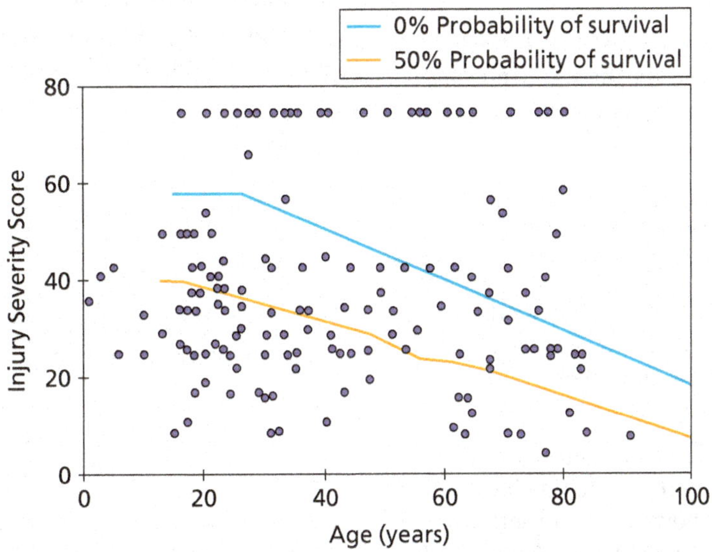

FIGURE 7.2 ■ Scatter plot of trauma data and the Injury Severity Score (ISS). *Source. Fictitious data provided by author*

indicate errors in data. The nature of EMS creates situations in which data are collected in the field and put into a database in times of high call volumes, by minimally trained staff, and without an appreciation for data accuracy. Often, EMS cannot collect the information due to a patient being unavailable due to a car crash or unconsciousness. Cleaning the data should serve to deliver accurate and useful end-user data. There are seven key purposes for cleaning data:

- Eliminating errors
- Eliminating redundancy
- Increasing data reliability
- Delivering accuracy
- Ensuring consistency
- Ensuring completeness
- Providing feedback for improvements

PLANNING YOUR ANALYSIS (AGAIN)

Planning an analysis often requires commitments of time and to following the process. Software also allows for scheduling or managing a project. Project management software is helpful in creating tasks and creating visual representations of the tasks that must occur. The time, cost per hour for staff, and supplies should all be figured into the planning process for analysis of a project looking at data.

Side Bar

Project Management Software includes Microsoft Project, Workengine, Tenrox, Teamwork, Severa, Proliance, Projecturf, Principle ToolBox, Oracle Project Management, and Genesis Inside.

A graph or chart commonly used to organize or control a project to initiate quality improvement is known as the program, evaluation, and review tool (PERT). A **PERT chart** is a project management tool used to schedule, organize, and coordinate tasks within a project.

A PERT chart presents a graphic illustration of a project as a network design consisting of numbered nodes (either circles or rectangles) representing events or milestones in the project linked by labeled directional lines representing a task. A PERT chart with an identification of the critical path is a powerful tool. A critical path is helpful for conveying to senior management the process and keeping the work flow managed on time and according to the proper sequence. The critical path is based on the most important tasks and the time frames to complete those tasks.

DOING YOUR ANALYSIS

The majority of data analysis only requires simple math to conduct a basic interpretation. Analysis also requires collecting or linking processes to outcomes to determine real quality improvement actions. Depending on the importance of the data and what is being examined, several layers of analysis can occur and various statistical tests run to get in-depth analysis and to confirm or refute conclusions with mathematics. This is commonly called **descriptive statistical analysis**. There are several types of descriptive statistical analysis:

- Counts
- Sums
- Measures of center
- Minimums and maximums
- Standard deviations

STATISTICAL SOFTWARE PROGRAMS FOR COMPUTERS

Data analysis is not an easy process. It requires careful data collection, attention to detail, and access to statistical software programs. Many different types of analysis are needed with regard to EMS data, such as how to calculate statistics; how to determine means and variances; how to do more advanced calculations, such as chi-square tests; and how to assign correlation coefficients. You will want to depend on computers with analysis programs to perform these calculations instead of doing them manually. Many calculations are time consuming and cumbersome, and the more advanced ones are all but impossible to do manually. Other software will be needed for the creation of several types of charts. Some commonly used charts are bar charts, column charts, histograms, line charts, and dot charts, all of which are often required for public presentation.

> **Side Bar**
>
> In EMS, the run chart is the secret weapon capable of analyzing the event and handling most interpretation of data in most QI projects.

Several good statistical software programs are available for both personal and mainframe or networked computers. Most of these programs can be used by novice statisticians. If you intend to apply the techniques, often it is more efficient to find a local statistician at a major university to calculate or proof your data when dealing with major decisions or publications.

The following is a list of such computer software programs:

- Microsoft Excel (can be used to do most statistical analysis for EMS)
- SAS
- SPSS
- Stata
- JMP™
- SPlus (R is the freeware version)
- Minitab

TYPES OF DATA ANALYSIS

Clearly, an important aspect of data analysis is the data, which can be of two different types: qualitative data and quantitative data. Qualitative data do not contain quantitative information, such as numerical information. Qualitative data can be classified into categories. In contrast, quantitative data represent an amount of something. For purposes of analysis, EMS variables can be divided into two types: qualitative variables and quantitative variables. Qualitative variables are classified into groups or categories. For example, EMS calls can be classified as trauma, medical, nontransport, canceled en route, and so on. Qualitative variables are also known as categorical variables (data) since they are not measured in quantity but are segregated into groups. Examples of categorical data for an EMS service include location, cause of injury or illness, treatment, transport destination, and so on. Most categorical variables that will be used in EMS data analysis will be found in the NEMSIS system.

Quantitative variables always reflect numerical values and some type of **measurement**. Quantitative variables can be discrete (exact) or analog (continuous). An example of a discrete variable is the number of days in the month or year (1 through 30 or 1 through 365) but no fractions of days. Time in hours, minutes, seconds, and fractions of seconds are an analog or continuous measurement. Other examples of quantitative variables are the number of EMS calls in a district over a period of time (discrete), the response time from alarm to arrival on the scene (analog), and the survival rate of cardiac arrest (discrete).

The distinction between data and variables should be noted. Data constitute a set of collected facts. There are two types of data: variable data and measurement data. A variable is a characteristic piece of data that varies or changes. Measurement data remains static and unchanging. Days of the week vary from Sunday through Saturday; months vary from January through December; and types of EMS calls vary, such as chest pain, shortness of breath, and traumatic injuries. Whenever observations are made on a variable, data are created for analysis. Each time an EMS report is completed, data for the listed variables are created. For example, by listing the day of the week, hour of day, month, type of situation found, and values for all other applicable variables in the NEMSIS reports, data are created. The data then can be summarized in a variety of ways, such as with tables, graphs, and charts. In this chapter, ideas about summarizing data are extended by expanding upon six basic descriptive measures: the mean, mode, and median as well as the range, variance, and standard deviation.

LIMITATIONS OF QUALITATIVE MEASURES

Qualitative data analysis cannot easily be measured with exactness because of the subjective nature of the data and the measurement. Items such as customer satisfaction and pain management are not easily measured due to their subjective nature and responses varying per individual. When subjective material is gathered and used to make management decisions, it should be converted into a numeric format by use of formulas, scales, and other types of rating systems.

Best Practice

Studying Response Time

The Santa Barbara Ambulance system was studied by the University of California, Los Angeles, statistics department. The intention was to identify what factors might be affecting response time in urban, suburban, and rural responses in the various zones in Santa Barbara County. The researchers identified the compliance requirements by legislation for the three types of areas within the service area (rural, suburban, and urban) within 20 kilometers. Ambulance response times in Santa Barbara County for 2006 were analyzed using point process techniques, including an advance statistical package called the kernel intensity estimates and K-functions. The goal was to investigate the dependence of ambulance response time on system load, to identify particular areas where improvements might have the most effect. For a fixed region with a finite number of ambulances, one may anticipate that response times may increase during times when a significant number of ambulances are unavailable due to previous emergencies.

Regression was used to investigate the relationship between the number of calls closely preceding any given incident and the percentage of violations. One aim of the present study is to look for evidence of spatial clustering of violation incidents, and in particular for clustering of violation incidents that had a positive number of preceding calls. Clusters of calls result in significantly higher response times, and this effect is quantified. In particular, calls preceded by other calls within 20 kilometers and within the previous hour are significantly more likely to result in violations of response times. This effect appears to be especially pronounced within semirural neighborhoods.

Of the 21,944 recorded emergency ambulance dispatch events in Santa Barbara County in 2006, 15,883 (72.4 percent) were Code 3 responses. Of these, 14,199 (89.4 percent) ambulances were to urban zoned areas, 1,382 (8.7 percent) to semirural zoned regions, and 302 (1.9 percent) to rural regions. Overall, 97.4 percent of Code 3 ambulance responses had response times within legislated limits. The research showed that the number of predecessor calls, within the previous hour and within a radius of 20 kilometers, for all Code 2 and Code 3 events in 2006 impacts response-time compliance. The majority (68.5 percent) of events have fewer than two predecessor calls, and less than 2 percent of calls have more than four predecessors. For calls without predecessors within 1 hour and within 20 kilometers, the proportion of response-time violations was 2.96 percent, whereas for calls with one or more predecessors, the proportion of violations was 4.56 percent. The increase in probability of not meeting response times associated with having predecessors is highly significant. As the predecessors increase, both the response time and the probability of a response-time violation were seen to increase. The fit of a logistic regression model to the relationship between violation and predecessors implies that on average, for each additional predecessor, the probability of violation increased by 19.1 percent.

The increase in response time is associated with an increase in predecessor calls, which shows that response time is a function of number of predecessors. The positive association between the differences in probability of violation associated with changing predecessors is seen to vary across response codes and district types. The increase in proportion of violations is most pronounced in semirural calls. The effect of load on the frequency of response time not being met appears to be especially pronounced within semirural neighborhoods in central Santa Barbara County, such as Solvang and Santa Ynez. Santa Barbra EMS officials were then able to adjust the deployment plan to add more ambulances to areas that appeared to be well covered, yet dramatically impacted if a predecessor call happened in that area.

TYPES OF SCALES USED FOR ANALYSIS

The nominal scale is often referred to as a categorical scale; basically, it puts things into categories. It is a system of classification and does not place the entity along a continuum. It involves a simple count of the frequency of the cases assigned to the various categories and if preferred numbers can be nominally assigned to label each category. **Ordinal scales** involve the ranking of individuals, attitudes, or items along the continuum of the characteristic being scaled. For example, if a researcher asked a paramedic to rank five scene-safety situations in order of most dangerous to least dangerous, he might obtain responses in a series of numbers used to indicate order.

NONCOMPARATIVE SCALES

Continuous ratings scales are used by respondents to give a rating by placing a mark at the appropriate position on a continuous line. The scale can be written on a card and shown to the respondent during the interview. Line marking scales are typically used to measure perceived similarity differences between products, brands, or other objects. Technically, such a scale is a form of what is termed a semantic differential scale, since each end of the scale is labeled with a word or phrase (or semantic) that is opposite in meaning to the other end. For some types of data analysis, the line-marking scale is an easier format because it uses discrete numbers (e.g., 5, 4, 3, 2, 1) to best reflect attitudes and feelings. The line-marking scale is a continuous scale that translates an opinion or feeling into a quantitative value by placing a number, therefore a value, to the feeling or opinion.

With an itemized scale, respondents are provided with a scale having numbers and/or brief descriptions associated with each category. They are asked to select one of the limited numbers of categories, ordered in terms of scale position, that best describes the product, brand, company, or product attribute being studied.

A **Likert scale** is a summated instrument scale. This means that the items making up a Likert scale are summed to produce a total score. In fact, a Likert scale is a composite of itemized scales. Typically, each scale item will

MISSION STATEMENT: To advance the Upper Pine River Fire Protection District vision by providing dedicated emergency and community services in a professional manner.

OUR DISTRICT, OUR PEOPLE, OUR DUTY

THE UPPER PINE RIVER FIRE PROTECTION DISTRICT
ORTHOPEDIC CUSTOMER SATISFACTION SURVEY

The 911 call was handled in a prompt, courteous, and competent manner:

❑ Outstanding ❑ Excellent ❑ Average ❑ Fair ❑ Poor

The 911 instructions given prior to the arrival of the EMS Crews were:

❑ Outstanding ❑ Excellent ❑ Average ❑ Fair ❑ Poor

The EMS Crew acted in a concerned, caring, and professional manner:

❑ Outstanding ❑ Excellent ❑ Average ❑ Fair ❑ Poor

The EMS Crews clearly explained the procedures performed:

❑ Outstanding ❑ Excellent ❑ Average ❑ Fair ❑ Poor

If you were lifted off the ground, the methods used by the EMS Crews to lift you were:

❑ Outstanding ❑ Excellent ❑ Average ❑ Fair ❑ Poor ❑ NA

If your injuries were splinted to stabilize your injury, the methods used by the EMS Crews were:

❑ Outstanding ❑ Excellent ❑ Average ❑ Fair ❑ Poor ❑ NA

The ride to the hospital in the ambulance was:

❑ Outstanding ❑ Excellent ❑ Average ❑ Fair ❑ Poor

How satisfied are you that your questions were answered and you were provided with adequate information or documents during your interaction with City of Upper Pine River Fire Protection District personnel?

❑ Very Satisfied ❑ Somewhat Satisfied ❑ Somewhat Dissatisfied ❑ Very Dissatisfied

How would you rate your overall experience with our services?

❑ Outstanding ❑ Excellent ❑ Average ❑ Fair ❑ Poor

Please circle the severity of your pain *when EMS Crews first arrived:*

1 2 3 4 5 6 7 8 9 10

None Mild Pain Moderate Pain Severe Pain

Please circle the severity of your pain *when EMS Crews delivered you to the emergency room:*

1 2 3 4 5 6 7 8 9 10

None Mild Pain Moderate Pain Severe Pain

Please provide any other comments or concerns regarding services provided by the Upper Pine River Fire Protection District: ______________________________

FIGURE 7.3 ■ The Likert scale in a customer service survey. *Source: "The Likert Scale in a Customer Service Survey" from Upper Pine River Fire Protection District. Copyright © Bruce Evans. Reproduced by permission of Bruce Evans.*

have five categories, with scale values ranging from –2 to +2 and with 0 as a neutral response. This explanation may be clearer from the example in Figure 7.3.

A **semantic scale** makes extensive use of words rather than numbers. Respondents describe their feelings about products or brands on scales with semantic labels. When bipolar adjectives are used at the end points of the scales, these are termed semantic differential scales.

QUALITATIVE MEASURES

Qualitative data consist of detailed descriptions of situations; events; interactions; direct quotations from individuals about their experiences, attitudes, beliefs, thoughts and excerpts; or entire passages from documents, correspondence, records, and case histories. Qualitative data are collected as open-ended narrative without predetermined or standardized categories. Qualitative analysis examines multiple groups to identify common themes that, having cross-confirmation, take on a greater significance. Qualitative data from this evaluation come from focus groups, open-ended survey questions, and written documents and records. The process for systematically analyzing the qualitative data collected for evaluation is summarized in the following steps:

- *Step one: Coding*—Involves coding recurring data or themes relevant to the evaluation question. This is done by reading through the open-ended responses to identify themes and patterns that are recorded on a worksheet. This step involves determining the basic unit of analysis and counting how many times each word, theme, or piece of data appears.
- *Step two: Categorization*—Involves creating meaningful categories to which the codes could be assigned. Categories are created and organized.
- *Step three: Classification*—Involves verifying that the codes could be easily and unambiguously assigned to the appropriate categories. This step emphasizes replication and reliability. Independent raters are found to classify a sample of the codes identified into the same categories.
- *Step four: Comparison*—Involves comparing the categories in terms of word-count frequencies and the performance of relevant statistical analysis.
- *Step five: Conclusion*—Involves drawing theoretical conclusions about the content in its context related to EMS or emergency medicine.

QUANTITATIVE MEASURES

Quantitative data analysis assesses information that can be measured or controlled. For example, the number of intravenous attempts and completed or cardiac arrest survivals are common quantitative measures. Making meaning of the quantitative measures requires looking at the patterns of data. You will often need to convert your data into other forms, such as graphs or charts. Plot your data, find a pattern, show the pattern, and evaluate the results. The number of data that do not fit the pattern should be small compared to the total data. A step-by-step process to analyze a quantitative measure is as follows:

- *Step one*—Involves a series of analyses to test the integrity of the data, commonly known as validity checks. Validity checks of the data are conducted to identify inconsistencies in the data within each data collection instrument, unreasonable entries, and impossible entries. These checks are conducted manually and by computer. All problems and errors are checked and corrected against the original instrument or sampling tool.
- *Step two*—Involves conducting descriptive analyses for each question. Descriptive statistics describe data in terms of measures of central tendency and measures of dispersion. These statistics are used to describe the location of the center of a distribution.

Measures of central tendency include mean, median, and mode. Measures of dispersion or spread include range, standard deviation, and percentiles.

- *Step three*—Involves cross-tabulation and comparison of information within and between target groups where sufficient sample sizes exist. Comparative analysis, or analysis of group differences, requires tests of statistical difference. A variety of tests are used to determine if real differences exist among certain target groups. For example, the **analysis of variance (ANOVA)** is used to determine differences in satisfaction ratings across three types of EMS calls: chest pain, shortness of breath, and orthopedic trauma. Statistical tests for differences between paramedics can be conducted on the data where sufficient sample sizes exist (e.g., patient surveys). The two most common tests to determine differences include the t-test and the chi-square test. The t-test determines whether there are significant differences between the means of two continuous variables. The chi-square test is used to determine whether or not there are significant differences between frequency distributions.
- *Step four*—Involves testing the reliability of questions measuring the provision of patient-centered care, the importance of patient-centered care, and customer satisfaction with emergency medical services. Questions can be constructed in a patient satisfaction survey. Reliability is a statistical measure of the reproducibility of survey data. Reliability is assessed by examining the internal consistency of the patient satisfaction survey questions. Internal consistency is measured by calculating a statistic known as **Cronbach's coefficient alpha**. Coefficient alpha measures internal consistency among a group of questions combined to form a single scale. It is a statistic that reflects the homogeneity of the scale. An alpha coefficient of .70 or higher is considered acceptable for social science research involving EMS where you are trying to identify consistency.
- *Step five*—Involves the determination of whether or not a relationship existed between variables of interest. The correlation coefficient, also referred to as the Pearson product-moment correlation coefficient, is used to indicate the strength of association between two continuous variables. The correlation coefficient has a range of +1 to −1.

Common Cause versus Special Cause

Two of the most important variations are common cause or special cause. This is the fundamental idea promoted by Shewhart and one of Deming and Juran's key messages. Common causes are those causes or data points in the system over time that affect everyone working in the system and affect all outcomes of the system. Special causes are those data points that are outside the normal limits and are not part of a system or do not affect everyone but arise from special circumstances. The rules and identification of special causes is the core of EMS QI activities.

A **trend** is a long series of consecutive data points ascending or descending. Typically five consecutive data points indicate a trend. Trend determination can also vary according to the data points.

A **run** is eight or more consecutive data points above or below the mean. An **outlier** is a data point or observation that lies an abnormal distance from other values in a random sample or population. Outliers can be found using graphical techniques, such as scatter and box plots, or using the Grubbs test. A special cause exists if a run contains too many data points (e.g., if the run is too long and beyond the upper or lower control limits). Control limits are set to areas that are typically three standard deviations above or below the mean. A **shift** is a significant event in data that involves six or more consecutive data points, either above or below the mean.

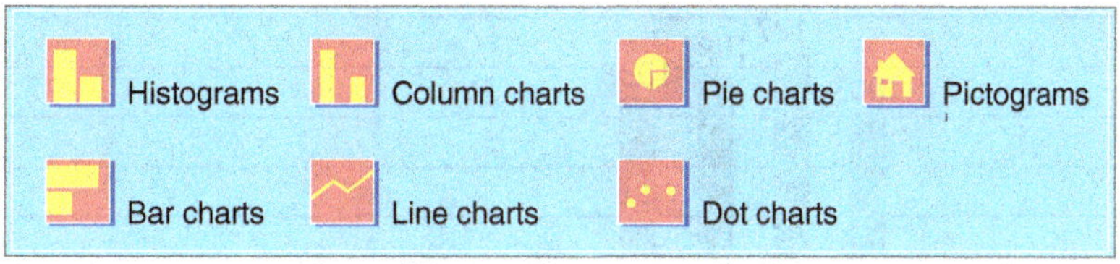

FIGURE 7.4 Collage of seven common types of charts. *Source: Fire Data Analysis Handbook by FEMA, pg. 9, http://upperpinefpd.org*

DESCRIBING THE DATA

Once a process has been completed on how the data are analyzed, there are six common types of charts to consider: bar charts, column charts, line charts, pie charts, dot charts, and pictograms. (See Figure 7.4.) The most important purpose of using any chart is to indicate conclusions more quickly and clearly than is possible with tables or numbers. It may be necessary to try several types of charts before the most appropriate one is found. Simplicity is the key. The message is what is important, so the chart form should not interfere with it.

DATA AS A DESCRIPTIVE TOOL

Numbers alone often do not tell a story. In the information age, data must be visual and must capture the attention of the intended reader to make a point or deliver a message. When presenting data, grabbing a viewer's attention and holding it require a visual aid. A variety of tools have been identified that can help with conveying a message and telling the story of what the data are describing. Each tool has a specific use and is most effective for certain kinds of data.

A bar chart should be used when categorical data is to be displayed and the objective is to show how the items in a category rank. Most EMS data are in categories, such as cause of illness, provider impression, and type of injury. These are reflected in the NEMSIS categories.

Use a column or line chart for data with a natural order, such as hours, months, or age groups. The chart will reflect the general pattern and indicate points of special interest, such as spikes, holes, gaps, and outliers.

A pie chart is beneficial when the objective is to show how the components relate to the whole. It is recommended that the number of components be kept to six or less and that the forming of several pie charts for comparison purposes be avoided.

A dot chart depicts the relationship between two variables. Generally, these variables are continuous, rather than categorical. The pattern between the two variables is the important aspect for a dot chart.

A pictogram is a pictorial representation of the data. Breakdowns by geographic areas, for example, are effectively shown by a pictogram.

HISTOGRAMS

"A picture is worth a thousand words" is an old saying that applies to numbers as well as words. The task of reaching conclusions from numbers is difficult, particularly when seeking trends and patterns in the data. A histogram and other charts are tools that can assist you in understanding data, since the human mind seems to comprehend pictures quicker than words and numbers. With graphic aids, we can answer several basic questions. For example, when are EMS calls most likely to occur? What are the primary causes of residential fires? Where do most of the serious motor

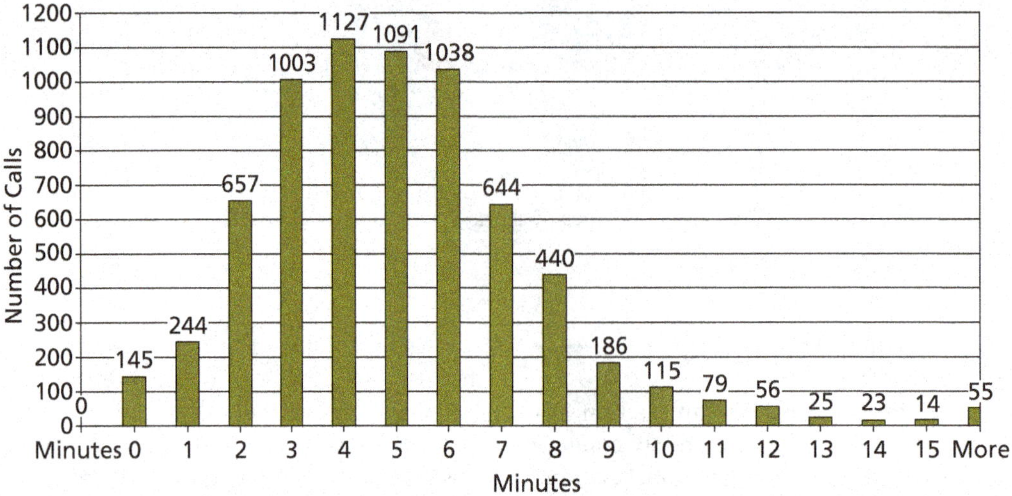

FIGURE 7.5 ■ Example of histogram showing call volume. *Source: "Figure 35.6—A Histogram: Emergency Responses" from CRITICAL CARE PARAMEDIC by Bryan E. Bledsoe and Randall W. Benner. Copyright © 2006 by Pearson Education. Used by permission of Pearson Education.*

vehicle accidents occur? How many bicycle injuries occurred last year by month? What are the ages of diabetics? What percentage of the emergency incidents have travel times less than 4 minutes? Less than 8 minutes? How many structure fires resulted in dollar losses greater than $50,000?

A histogram is a column chart in which the height of the columns indicates the relative numbers or frequencies or values of a variable. (See Figure 7.5.) The values may be numeric, such as travel times, or nonnumeric, such as days of the week. One of the most fundamental ways to describe response data is to show how calls are distributed by month, day of week, and hour of day—for example, showing the frequency of calls by hour of day or by day of the week. A list or array of numbers is almost always the starting point for a descriptive analysis. The numbers by themselves are not very useful. It is difficult to get a sense of what is happening by scanning a list of numbers. To grasp what the numbers are indicating, we can develop a frequency histogram. Frequency histograms show calls by day of week and month. When reviewing a frequency histogram, ask the following questions:

- Where are the low points and high points in the histogram?
- What groups of times (hours, days, or months) have similar frequencies?
- Is there anything in the histogram that runs counter to your experience?

With these histograms, we could begin to see a picture of the cardiac arrest problem in a community—for example time of day or, potentially, location. For example, a histogram showing location of cardiac arrest may identify common buildings or facilities where cardiac arrests are occurring, making it a target for CPR training or placement of an automatic defibrillator. Histograms allow for an easy descriptive and analytical procedure without having to think too much about the numbers themselves. Graphical displays should always strive to convey an immediate message, describing a particular aspect of the data. (See Figure 7.6.)

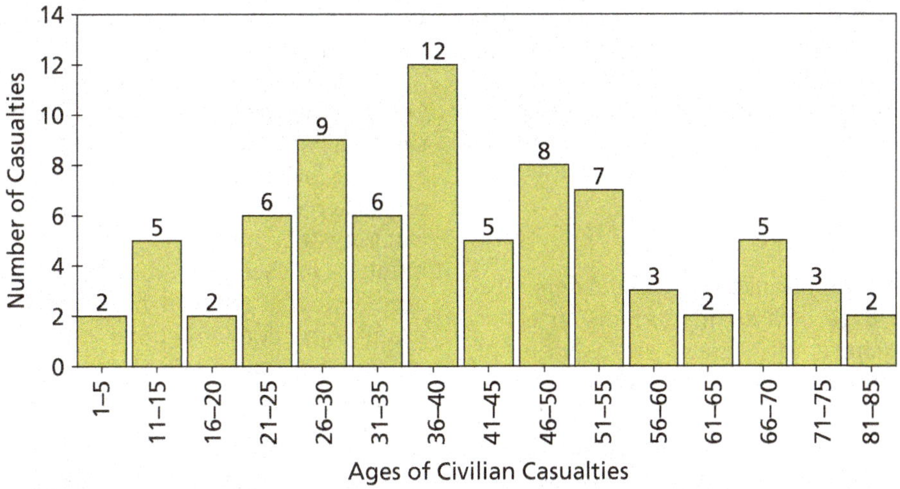

FIGURE 7.6 Frequency histogram of civilian injuries from fire or smoke, Blue Water County (2014).
Source: Fictitious data provided by author

Developing a Histogram

Making a histogram is relatively simple:

- Choose the number of groups for classifying the data. In most cases, five to ten groups are sufficient, but there are exceptions, such as histograms by hour of day. Sometimes the groups are natural, as in our exhibits by day of week and month. With other data, developing appropriate intervals will be necessary.
- Determine the number of events (fires, EMS calls, motor vehicle crashes, etc.) for each group.
- Define intervals for data, such as ages and response time. For these intervals, choose convenient whole numbers. That is, try to avoid using fractions and always make the intervals the same width. Intervals of 5 years are common for grouping the data. Data such as day of week do not require this step, since their intervals are naturally defined.
- Determine the number of observations in each group. Statistical packages are particularly useful in this step since they usually include routines for tabulating data.
- Choose appropriate scales for each axis to accommodate the data. Again, most statistical packages will do this with a default setting.
- Display the frequencies with vertical bars.

Do not expect to get a histogram, or any other type of chart, exactly right on the first try. Several tries may be necessary before the look of the histogram is satisfactory. The histograms presented in the previous section offer good examples of different characteristics for describing the data.

Histograms have certain characteristics that help define or analyze data:

- Peaks and valleys in a histogram indicate the values that appear most frequently (peaks) or least frequently (valleys).
- Spikes and holes are high and low points that stand out in the histogram.
- An outlier is an extreme value and/or point that is isolated from the main body of the data.
- Gaps are spaces that may reflect important aspects of a histogram.

- Symmetry results when a histogram is balanced along a central value. When this happens, the histogram is easier to interpret.
- The central value is both the mean (average) for the distribution and the median (half the data points are below this value and half above).

CHARTS

Often, it is important to extend the depiction of EMS data beyond histograms to other types of charts. Histograms are only one of many different ways of presenting data. It must be decided which type of chart best portrays the results that are to be represented. A histogram may serve as the best vehicle in some cases, but bar charts, line charts, pie charts, dot charts, and pictograms should also be considered. The following are two questions to bear in mind throughout this process:

- What are the main conclusions from your analysis?
- What is the best way to display the conclusions?

The audience may be an internal group of EMS managers, an outside association or group of citizens, or a city or county council. The audience itself influences the type of chart that is selected. The first step is to determine the key results from the data. Once they have been identified, a selection of the best type of chart to convey them must be made. Often, it is helpful to try different charts to determine the best presentation for a particular audience and data set. Each of the following sections describes a different type of chart.

BAR CHARTS

A bar chart is one of the simplest and most effective ways to display data. In a bar chart, a bar is drawn for each category of data, allowing for a visual comparison of the results. Some results can be determined relatively easily from the list of numbers. Although these comparisons can be made from the list, they work best to convey a message with a visual aid, such as a bar chart.

A bar chart presents the data in frequency order. As a general rule, the horizontal dimension in a bar chart is numeric, such as percentages or other numbers, and the vertical dimension shows the labels for the items in a category. It is not always necessary to include numbers in each bar, especially if there is an accompanying table or list, but they can be useful to readers unfamiliar with the data. If the numbers are omitted from the chart, a total number should be provided either in the title or a footnote.

Other Bar Charts

A Pareto chart, also called a Pareto distribution diagram, is a vertical bar graph in which values are plotted in decreasing order of relative frequency from left to right. Pareto charts are extremely useful for analyzing what problems need attention first because the taller bars on the chart, which represent frequency, clearly illustrate which variables have the greatest cumulative effect on a given system. For example, if we are measuring accuracy on assessment of a dozen patients with respiratory distress, we may expect a sequence of five processes followed: a pulse oximetry assessment, lung sounds, an EKG, a respiratory rate and quality, and a waveform or digital CO_2 reading. We may find that lung sounds and oximetry are almost always measured and are on the left of the Pareto chart, versus CO_2 being rarely measured and the last of the five processes with low frequency on the right side of the Pareto chart. This may indicate a need for additional training on CO_2 or capnometry with more emphasis on waveform interpretation. A Pareto chart provides a depiction of Juran's Pareto principle, which identifies that 80 percent of the outputs in a system is produced by 20 percent of the input. The Pareto chart is one of the basic tools of quality control. The independent variables on the chart are shown on the horizontal axis and the dependent variables are portrayed as the heights of bars. A point-to-point graph, which shows the cumulative relative frequency, may be overlaid on the bar graph. Because the values of the statistical variables are placed in order of relative frequency, the graph clearly reveals which factors have the greatest impact and where attention is likely to produce the greatest benefit. A clustered bar chart shows two categories in the same chart.

In Figure 7.7 for example, chest pain patients are distributed by treatment. One of the measurements in Figure 7.7 is the types of treatments that were required by protocol or a typical standard of care within an agency. This Pareto Chart indicates the treatments that were not initiated. It helps by identifying were the treatments are falling short. For example, in figure 7.7 a large discrepancy exist as 54% percent of chest pain patients did not get aspirin as compared to 100% got an IV. When a sequence of care is broken down into each treatment it can easily be identified as to what is causing poor outcomes or what is a target for a quality improvement initiative and where a limited resource can be applied to make a change. A Pareto helps focus on what needs attention and where the priorities are.

COLUMN CHARTS

When it is necessary to display change, data can be shown as a column chart. Column charts are particularly useful in demonstrating change over time. Where is the series increasing, decreasing, or staying about the same? If the analysis shows change over time, then column charts are particularly beneficial in presenting the changes. An example is EMS calls by hour of day. By looking from left to right, one can visualize the change over a 24-hour period. The horizontal scale shows the hours but is not really needed to get a "feeling" for the changes. Calls are low in the early morning hours, and they increase in the afternoon and evening hours. Column charts show frequency distributions that allow for easy identification of trends and other characteristics, particularly with time series data. The horizontal scale defines the natural groupings for the chart, and the columns give the frequencies.

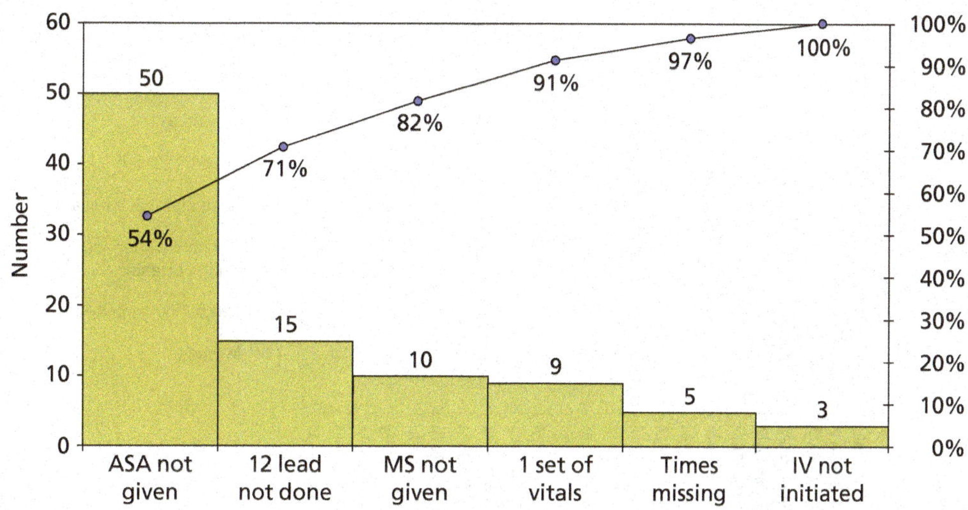

FIGURE 7.7 Pareto chart indicating compliance with chest pain protocol treatment compliance. *Source: "Figure 35.8—A Pareto Chart: Acute Coronary Syndrome Outliners" from CRITICAL CARE PARAMEDIC by Bryan E. Bledsoe and Randall W. Benner. Copyright © 2006 by Pearson Education. Used by permission of Pearson Education.*

LINE CHARTS

Line charts create an effective presentation of time series. Many statisticians believe that a line chart is the clearest way for showing increases, decreases, and fluctuations in a time series. Multiple line charts are great for comparing time series. For example, multiple stations can have their call volume compared over a period of time, as in Figure 7.8. Each station represented by a different color line, or by a line using a different geometry spaced throughout the line, can denote a 24-hour period for an entire department, thereby indicating the call volume for each station or unit. This is commonly called a run chart.

PIE CHARTS

A pie chart is an effective way of showing how each component contributes to the whole. In a pie chart, each wedge represents the amount for a given category. The entire pie chart accounts for all of the categories. Percentages are usually included with each wedge label because they aid in comparisons of the wedges. In developing pie charts, several rules should be followed:

- Convert data to percentages.
- Keep the number of wedges to six or less.
- If there are more than six wedges, keep the most important five and group the rest into an "Other" category.
- Position the most important wedge starting at the 12:00 position.
- Maintain distinct color differences among the wedges.

Although pie charts are popular, they are probably the least effective way of displaying results. (See Figure 7.9.) For example, it may be hard to compare wedges within a pie to determine their rank. Similarly, it takes time

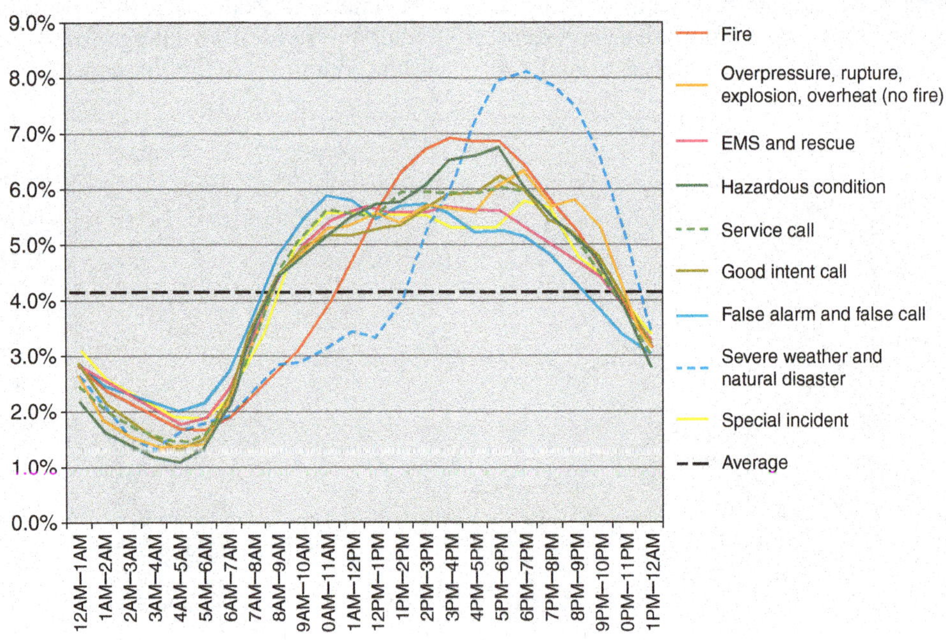

FIGURE 7.8 ■ Line chart for call volume for a 24-hour period. *Source: "Figure 35.9—A Control Chart: Sysytem Intubation Success Rate" from CRITICAL CARE PARAMEDIC by Bryan E. Bledsoe and Randall W. Benner. Copyright © 2006 by Pearson Education. Used by permission of Pearson Education.*

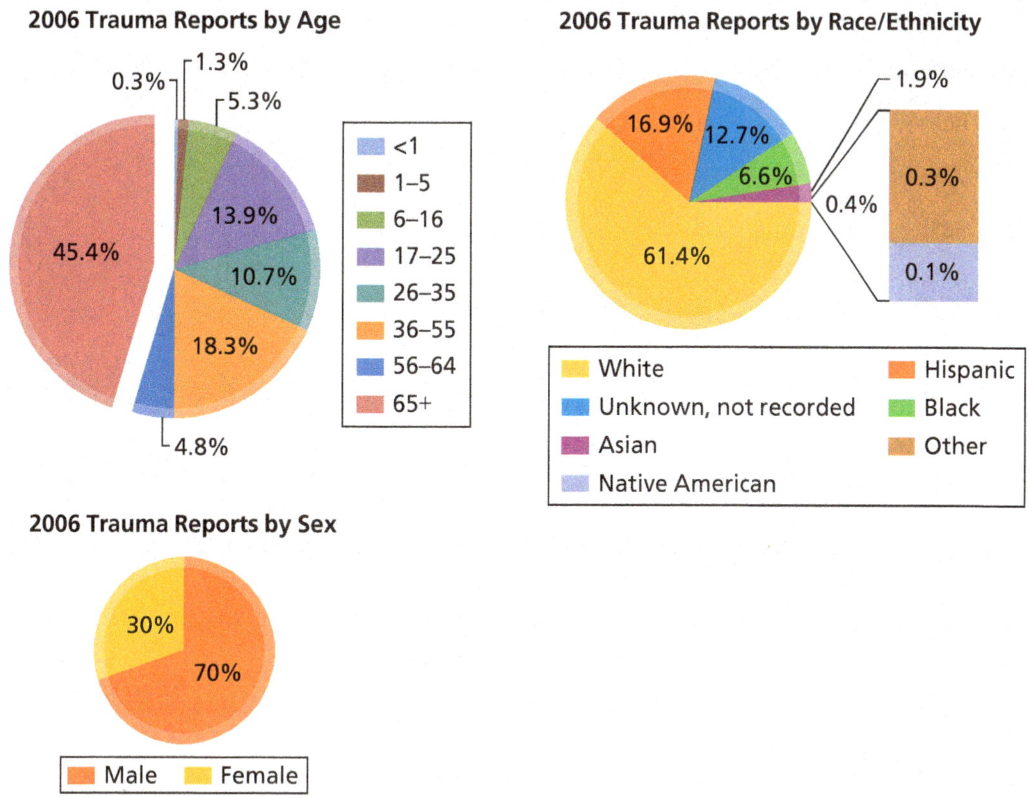

FIGURE 7.9 Pie chart as a snapshot of trauma for Central City Fire (2013). *Source: Fictitious data provided by author*

and effort to compare several pie charts because they are separate depictions. A removed or elevated wedge can be used to make a comparison or to highlight a specific segment to the data.

DOT CHARTS

Dot charts or scatter diagrams emphasize the relationship between two variables. For example, the 10-year trend in residential fires from 2000 to 2010 was generally a decrease from a high in 2000 of 15,000 to a low of 11,000 by 2010. During these years, a decrease in fire deaths also occurred. One would expect deaths to decrease with a decrease in fires.

Figure 7.10 is a dot chart for the success rates of inserting an IV on the first attempt based on years experience of the EMS provider. Years experience are along the horizontal or x axis, whereas success rates of inserting an IV on the first attempt are along the vertical or y axis. The pattern, rather than the individual dots, is the important aspect of a dot chart. The horizontal scale (x axis) should reflect the causation variable (independent variable), whereas the vertical scale reflects the resulting variable (dependent variable). That is to say that an increase in years of experience (the independent variable) results in an increase in success rates of inserting an IV on the first attempt (the dependent variable).

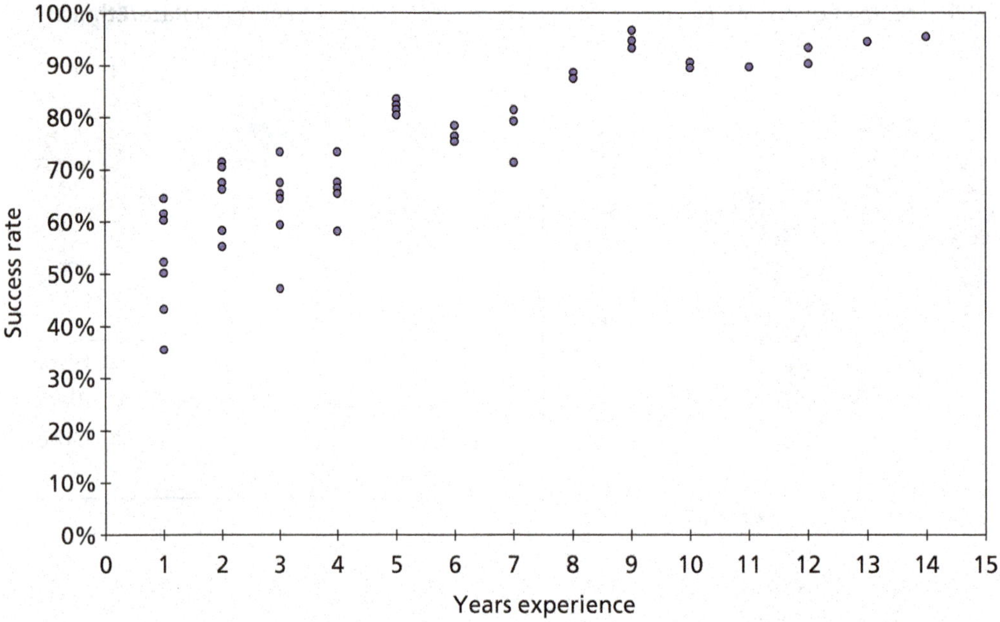

FIGURE 7.10 ■ Dot and scatter diagram for inserting an IV on the first attempt based on years experience of the EMS provider. *Source: "Figure 35.7—A Scatter Diagram " from CRITICAL CARE PARAMEDIC by Bryan E. Bledsoe; Randall W. Benner. Copyright © 2006, Pearson Education. Used by permission of Pearson Education.*

Another useful application of scatter diagrams is to identify outliers in the data. In Figure 7.10, we see that an EMS provider with 3 years of experience is averaging a 55 percent to 65 percent success rate, yet one dot is at 45 percent. Identifying an outlier from the general pattern can be useful in revealing an area of further data analysis that would account for this discrepancy from the rest of the data.

PICTOGRAMS

The final type of chart takes advantage of pictures to display data. Data by geographical areas, such as counties, census tracts, or EMS districts, can be presented on maps showing the boundaries of the areas. For example, a pictogram that shows the number of cardiac arrests in an EMS district can be created. By calculating the drive time from the EMS agency to these locations, the potential geographic area this EMS agency could effectively cover in regard to cardiac arrest would be shown. This pictogram could then help indicate potential locations where automatic external defibrillators should be placed due to longer drive times for the EMS agency to get to that specific area.

Other pictograms for state and local data are easily imagined. At the state level, data from individual counties may be collected. A pictogram provides a good way of depicting the county data by taking a state map showing county boundaries and developing problem or high call areas. Similarly, for a local jurisdiction, such as a city or a county, there may be data for individual fire districts. A jurisdiction map with fire district boundaries may be an effective way of presenting the data.

BASIC STATISTICS

Statistics commonly give people heartburn or grief, and the very thought of doing calculations that require formulas and mathematics often makes EMS managers reluctant to engage in analysis. Some simple calculations are common to most data analysis and can be easily handled with a common calculator or computer.

CUMULATIVE FREQUENCIES

Two types of important distributions are the cumulative frequency and the cumulative percentage frequency. A cumulative frequency is the number of data points that are less than or equal to a given value. A cumulative percentage frequency converts the cumulative frequency into percentages. Once we have the data, we can calculate the cumulative frequency and cumulative percentages for the response time data from a private ambulance contractor. (See Figure 7.11.)

The first entry under the Cumulative Frequency column is 129, which is the same as in the Frequency column. The second entry in the Cumulative Frequency column shows 335, which is 129 + 206, the sum of the first two entries in the Frequency column. By adding these two numbers, we determine that 335 incidents have response times of 2 minutes or less. The next entry is 1,094 (129 + 206 + 759), meaning that 1,094 incidents have response times of 3 minutes or less. The cumulative frequencies continue in this manner, with the last entry in the column always equal to the total number of incidents in the analysis. The last column, labeled Cumulative Percent, merely converts the cumulative frequencies into percentages. This step is accomplished by dividing each of the 11 cumulative frequencies by 5,394, which is the total number of incidents. The column shows that 2.4 percent of the incidents have response times under 1 minute, 6.2 percent under 2 minutes, 20.3 percent under 3 minutes, and so on. In general, cumulative

Response	Frequency	Cumulative Frequency	Cumulative Percent
Less than 1 minute	129	129	2.4
1 to 2 minutes	206	335	6.2
2 to 3 minutes	759	1,094	20.3
3 to 4 minutes	1,406	2,500	46.3
4 to 5 minutes	1,312	3,812	70.7
5 to 6 minutes	747	4,559	84.5
6 to 7 minutes	384	4,943	91.6
7 to 8 minutes	206	5,149	95.5
8 to 9 minutes	110	5,259	97.5
9 to 10 minutes	62	5,321	98.6
10 or more minutes	73	5,394	100.0
Total		**5,394**	**100.0**

FIGURE 7.11 Cumulative frequencies and percentages for Bayport EMS, Blue Water County (2014).
*Bayport EMS is meeting their contracted response time of 8 minutes or less 95.5 percent of the time.
Source: Fictitious data provided by author

percentages describe data in "more than" and "less than" terms. For example, about half of the calls have response times under 4 minutes, and about 95 percent have response times under 8 minutes. Response times exceed 10 minutes in only about 1 percent of the calls.

MEASURES OF CENTRAL TENDENCY

Measures of central tendency provide a single summary figure that describes the central location of an entire distribution. The three most common measures of central tendency are the mode, the median, and the mean. Each will be defined and the individual properties and uses for each will be discussed.

The mode is the value that occurs most frequently in a distribution. It is, therefore, easily recognized since no calculations are necessary. The mean is also known as the arithmetic mean or average. However, since the term *average* is sometimes used indiscriminately for any measure of central tendency, it should be avoided. Mean is defined as the sum of all values in a distribution divided by the total number of values. For example, suppose that travel times to nine incidents are 3 minutes, 2 minutes, 4 minutes, 1 minute, 2 minutes, 3 minutes, 3 minutes, 4 minutes, and 3 minutes. Adding these travel times gives 25 minutes in total; dividing by 9 yields a mean travel time of 2.78 minutes.

The third measure of central tendency is the median, which is defined as the middle value (50th percentile) of a distribution. To determine the median, the data must be ordered. The nine travel times from the preceding example would look as follows if arranged in order: 1, 2, 2, 3, 3, 3, 3, 4, 4. The median is the fifth or middle value, which is 3 minutes. There are four data values below and four data values above the median. In other words, 50 percent of the values lie on either side of the median, placing it at the 50th percentile.

If there had been an even number of data values, then the median would have been the mean of the two middle values. For example, if the on-site times for 10 EMS incidents were 12, 15, 17, 25, 27, 29, 32, 35, 37, and 42 minutes, then the two middle values would be 27 and 29. Totaling them and dividing by 2 (calculating the mean value) results in a median value of 28. Again the median splits the values, with five values below and five above.

Properties and Uses for Measures of Central Tendency

The mode is the only measure of central tendency that can be used for qualitative data. This is really its only use, other than to serve as an additional qualifier for a distribution. The mode by itself is an unstable measure of central tendency. Equal-size samples taken from a distribution are likely to have different modes. Distributions with more than one mode are said to be **bimodal**. This can be confusing; however, it really means that there are two areas in the data that cluster together to form two different peaks—that is, there are two distinct values that measurements tend to cluster around. Modes can also be multimodal and bivariate, with two or more peaks. An example is call volume statistics that are clustered in multiple areas around a city.

The median is a better choice than the mode for a measure of central tendency. Unlike the mode, the median cannot be used with qualitative data, but it can be used with quantitative variables. The median on scene time for fires or the median dollar loss for fires can be determined. However, the "median type of fire" or the "median cause of ignition" has no meaning since these are qualitative variables. Responding to how many values lie above and below the median, but not to how far away they are, is a less sensitive measure than is the relationship of the mean to the presence of a few extreme values.

Generally, the mean is the best choice for a measure of central tendency. Unlike the mode and the median, the mean is responsive to the exact position of each value in a distribution. It serves as a fulcrum point, balancing all of the values in a distribution. Consequently, the mean is very sensitive to extreme values (outliers) in a distribution. When a measure of central tendency must reflect the total of the values, the mean is the best choice since it is the only measure based on this quantity. Another of the more important characteristics of the mean is its stability over samples drawn from a distribution. This becomes especially important when further statistical computation is done.

MEASURES OF DISPERSION

Although measures of central tendency provide a summary of the values in a distribution, measures of dispersion provide a summary of the variability or spread of the values in a distribution. Measures of dispersion express quantitatively the extent to which the values in a distribution are scattered or clustered together. The three main measures of dispersion are the range, variance, and standard deviation.

The range is the most basic measure of dispersion. Its definition is simply the difference between the lowest and highest value in a distribution.

Another measure of the variability of a distribution is the variance. Variance is a measure of dispersion on observations based on the mean of the squared deviations from the arithmetic mean. The variance is the square of the standard deviation. To calculate the variance, it is necessary to first obtain what is known as the deviation values of a distribution. The deviation values are the difference between the values in a distribution and its mean. Since the mean is the balance point of the values in a distribution, the total of the deviation values would be zero. Therefore, in order to calculate the variance, it is necessary to first square the deviation values to eliminate the negative values, then divide the sum by one less than the total number of values (see the following discussion for why this is done).

If the variance is small compared to the mean, it indicates that the values are close to the mean, alternatively, if the variance is large compared to the mean, it indicates that the values are not very close to the mean. The final measure of dispersion is the standard deviation. It is obtained by taking the square root of the variance. This calculation will help to show how big or small the spread (variability) is around the mean. If the spread is not very large, then it shows the mean is a good descriptor of the data.

In our preceding calculation for the variance, the sum of the squared deviations was divided by the number of total values minus 1. This was done to correct for a statistical error that results when using inferential statistics. If the distribution is the entire amount of values being considered, then dividing by that number is perfectly legitimate. However, if the distribution is merely a sample of a larger distribution—which it usually is—then a better representation of the entire population of values can be obtained by subtracting 1 from the sample distribution.

Normal Distribution and Standard Score

Statisticians usually assume a normal distribution for any given set of values. As previously mentioned, a normal distribution is equally spread out in the general shape of a bell. This is commonly known as the bell curve. In a normal distribution, the mean, the median, and the mode are the same. Half the values are above the mean and half below. Most of the values, 68 percent, fall within one standard deviation on either side of the mean, 95 percent within two standard deviations, and fully 99.7 percent of the distribution is represented within three standard deviations.

By using a standard score, it is possible to compare values from different distributions on an equal basis. A standard score is a derived score that describes how far a given value in a distribution is from some reference point—typically the mean—in terms of standard deviation units. One of the most commonly used standard scores is the z score. Transforming the values of a distribution to z scores changes the mean to zero and the standard deviation to one, but it does not change the shape of the distribution. Refer back to the previous discussion in this chapter on z scores and see Figure 7.1 for an example of a table used to calculate z scores.

When to Use Measures of Dispersion

The range is ideal for preliminary work or in circumstances where precision is not an important requirement. It is not sensitive to the total condition of the distribution since only the two outermost values determine its calculation. Therefore, the range is of little use beyond descriptive analysis of direction toward further investigation.

Since the variance is the mean of the squares of the deviation values of a distribution, it is sensitive to the exact position of each value in a distribution. It can, therefore, be very important in inferential statistics because of its resistance to sampling variation. However, it is of little use in descriptive statistics because it is expressed in squared units.

The standard deviation, like the mean and the variance (from which it is derived), is responsive to the exact position of every value in a distribution. Because it is calculated by using deviations from the mean, the standard deviation increases or decreases as the individual values shift away from or toward the mean. Like the mean, it is influenced by extreme scores, especially with distributions that have a small amount of values. As the number of values increase, each individual value has less ability to shift the mean and the standard deviation. If the mean and the standard deviation of a distribution are known, a fairly accurate picture of the distribution can be obtained.

For example, suppose these are the travel times of an EMS agency to nine incidents: 3 minutes, 2 minutes, 4 minutes, 1 minute, 2 minutes, 3 minutes, 3 minutes, 4 minutes, and 3 minutes. The mean would be 2.78 and the standard deviation 0.973. Assuming a normal distribution, one standard deviation from the mean in both directions should cover 68 percent of the values. In this case, values between 1.807 and 3.753 include 2, 2, 3, 3, 3, and 3. Since there are nine values in the distribution, the six values that fall within one standard deviation from the mean account for 67 percent. Considering its small size, that is an extremely accurate picture of the distribution. It is also a good example of how powerful the combination of the mean and the standard deviation can be. Each is the best measure of its type (central tendency and dispersion), and both are used extensively in more sophisticated statistical calculations.

Skewed Distributions

Even though QI managers assume a normal distribution, not all distributions are normal or symmetrical. In a normal distribution, the mean, median, and mode are all the same. However, this is not the case with skewed distributions. As shown in Figure 7.12, distributions can be skewed positively or negatively. In a positive skew, the extreme scores are at the positive end of the distribution. This exhibits the "tail" on the right side and pulls the mean to the right. Since the median and the mode are less responsive to extreme scores, they remain to the left of the mean. So, in a positively skewed distribution, the mean has the highest value, with the median in the middle and the mode the smallest value. Conversely, in a distribution with a negative skew, the extreme values and the "tail" are at the

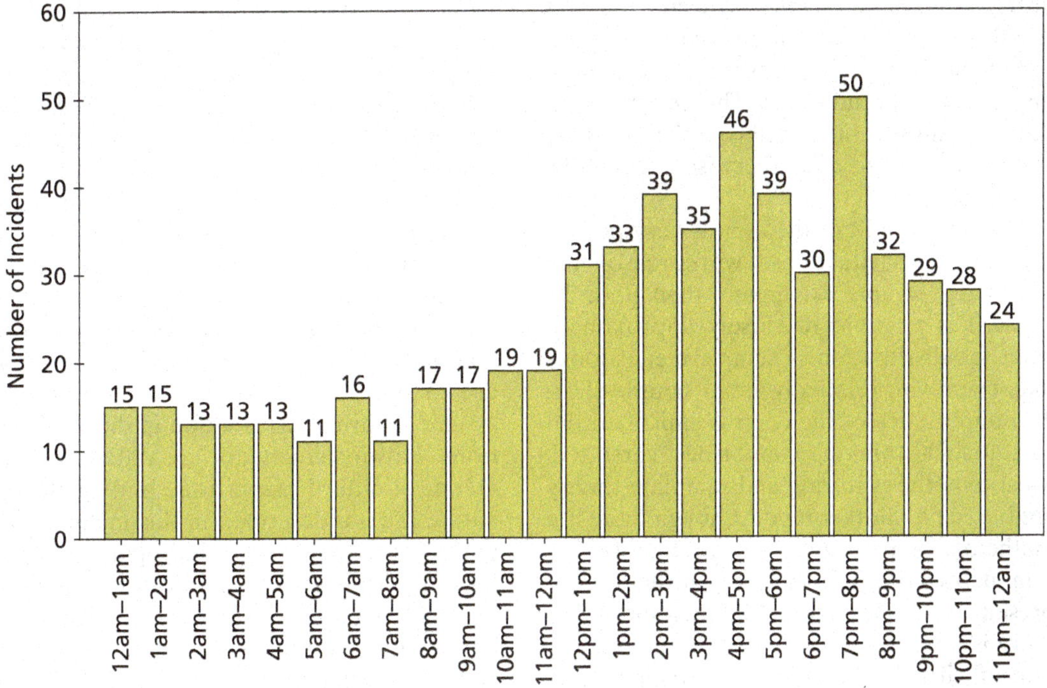

FIGURE 7.12 Skewed distribution of Harvest Junction Fire EMS responses (2014).
*Skewed Distribution commonly scene in suburban or commuter community. *Source: Fictitious data provided by author*

negative end, the mean is the smallest value with the median in the middle, and the mode is the largest value.

Side Bar

Management Focus for a Positive Skew

In modern QI theory, a positive skew and the people who perform in that right-shifted distribution become the focus of management. In a normal distribution, 20 percent fall within the top performers, 40 percent in the above average, 40 percent in the below average, and 20 percent in the poor performers category. When management focuses 80 percent of their efforts on the top 20 percent, the above average and below average performers desire the attention and the rewards provided by management and shift their performance, ultimately resulting in a positive skew. In most organizations, the focus is on disciplining or trying to correct the bottom-producing 20 percent, who typically never improve and consume much of the organization's resources.

Central Limit Theorem

To perform statistical tests and analysis, statisticians rely on their assumption of a normal distribution. However, as we have seen, this is not always the case. Fortunately, a rule allows them to make this assumption even when the distribution is not normal. The central limit theorem states that the sampling distribution of means increasingly approximates a normal distribution as the sample size increases. That is a distribution whose individual values are the means of samples drawn from the main distribution (population). The central limit theorem allows inferential statistics to be applied to skewed and otherwise normal distributions.

The central limit theorem is very powerful, and in most situations it works reasonably well with a sample size greater than 10 or 20. Thus, it is possible to closely approximate what the distribution of sample means looks like, even with relatively small sample sizes. The importance of the central limit theorem to statistical thinking cannot be overstated. Most hypothesis testing and sampling theory are based on this theorem. Although there is a mathematical proof for the central limit theorem, it goes beyond the scope of this text to present it. It is mentioned here to show that there is a solid statistical base for assuming a normal distribution for the statistical tests used in inferential analysis of fire and EMS data. With the proper sample size, the results will be valid even if the population distribution is not normal.

ANALYSIS OF TABLES

Most EMS data are qualitative (categorical) in nature. Examples of categorical data in EMS would include location of the emergency, nature of illness or injury, treatments, and so on. Since this type of data cannot be expressed in terms of the mean, median, and standard deviation, the number of each category can be used and listed in table form. It might be found, for example, that shortness of breath accounts for 26 percent of all EMS calls, 18 percent of vehicle crashes, and so on.

Several techniques for analyzing tables have been developed from categorical data. These include the development and interpretation of percentages for categorical data and the use of a nonparametric statistical test for comparing two independent samples in different population differences. All tests involving ranked data are nonparametric. The most common **nonparametric** statistical test is known as the chi-square. The chi-square is used to determine whether the percentage distribution from a table differs significantly from a distribution of hypothetical or expected percentages.

A nonparametric statistical test is one that makes little or no assumptions about the distribution. As stated previously, statisticians assume a normal distribution in their calculations. However, categorical data—such as mean, standard deviation, and such—by nature are not described in this manner. Statistical tests that have certain parameters to their use would not be appropriate for this type of data. The chi-square was designed to be used without these parameters and as such is ideal for categorical data.

CORRELATION

Correlation is a statistical measure that indicates the degree to which one variable changes with another variable. For example, EMS calls generally increase with population growth; as population increases, more medical service calls should be expected. This would indicate a positive correlation between population and EMS calls. The correlation measures the strength of the association between the two variables. If the population is healthy young people there might not be a correlation between calls and population.

If there is a correlation between two variables, then predictions that are better than chance can be made from an individual score (or whatever is being measured) on one variable to its predicted score on the correlate variable. Any problem in correlation requires two pairs of corresponding scores, one for each variable. Generally, the greater the association (correlation) between two variables, the more accurately a prediction can be made on the standing in one variable from the standing in the other. With relationships depicted in this manner, the usual terminology is to label one variable as the independent variable, and the other as the dependent variable.

It is important to emphasize two points about correlations. First, correlations assume an underlying linear relationship—that is, a relationship that can be best represented by a straight line. It should be noted that not all relationships are linear. There are curvilinear relationships where the points on a scatter diagram cluster about a curved line. Second, although correlation can be used for prediction, it does not imply causation. The fact that two variables vary together is a necessary, but not a sufficient, condition to conclude that there is a cause-and-effect connection between them. A strong correlation between variables is often the starting point for further research or investigation into a cause.

CORRELATION COEFFICIENT

The correlation coefficient measures the strength of association between two variables. The term *correlation coefficient* is used by most statisticians, but it is the same as the more commonly used *correlation*. The correlation is always between –1 and +1. A correlation of exactly –1 or +1 is termed a *perfect correlation*, meaning that all the points fall on a straight line. A correlation of zero indicates no relationship between the variables and would be represented on a scatter diagram as random points with no discernible direction. As a correlation coefficient moves from zero in either direction, the strength of the association between the two variables increases.

A positive correlation means that, as the independent variable increases, so does the dependent variable. In a negative correlation, the dependent variable decreases as the independent variable increases. The sign of the correlation indicates direction, not magnitude. Magnitude is indicated by the size of the number regardless of the sign. Therefore, a correlation of –.82 is greater than a correlation of +.63.

In the relationship between a scatter diagram and the correlation coefficient, the correlation coefficient is a number that indicates how well the data points in a scatter diagram closely parallel the straight line of best fit. With perfect correlations, all the data points fall exactly on a straight line that summarizes the relationship, and the value of the coefficient is +1 or –1. When the association between the two variables is less than perfect, the data points show some scatter about the straight line that summarizes the relationship, and the absolute value (regardless of sign) of the correlation coefficient is less than 1. The weaker the relationship is, the more scatter and the lower the absolute value of the correlation coefficient are.

Another important point to know is that correlations are not arithmetically related to each other. For example, a correlation of .6 is not twice as strong as a correlation of .3. Although it is obvious that a correlation of .6 reflects a stronger association than a correlation of .3, there is no exact specification of the difference. Subsequently, there is no relationship between correlations and percentages.

To make direct comparisons of correlations, the correlation coefficient must be converted to a coefficient of determination. The coefficient of determination is the square of the correlation multiplied by 100. This yields the percentage of association between the two variables. For example, a correlation of .50 would indicate a 25 percent (.50 ×.50 =.25 ×100 = 25) association between variables. A perfect correlation of 1.00 would be equal to a 100 percent coefficient of determination. So a correlation of 1.00 is four times as strong as a correlation of .50—not twice as strong, as might appear from comparing the correlations directly.

In addition, the differences between successive correlation coefficient values do not represent equal differences in degree of relationship. For example, the difference between a correlation of .40 and .50 does not represent the same difference as that between correlations of .90 and 1.00. This can be seen more clearly by examining the coefficients of determination and their corresponding correlations in Figure 7.13. There is more than double the difference between correlations of .90 and 1.00 than between .40 and .50 when the corresponding coefficients of determination are compared.

CALCULATING THE CORRELATION

Most pocket calculators include a program to calculate the correlation coefficient. In addition, virtually all statistical software packages calculate the various types of correlations. For those who must calculate a correlation by hand, and in order to show what factors make the coefficient positive or negative and what factors result in a high or low value, the deviation-score method will be used.

The most widely used correlation formula is the Pearson r or the Pearson product-moment correlation coefficient.

Correlation Coefficient	Coefficient of Determination
1.00	100%
.90	81%
.80	64%
.70	49%
.60	36%
.50	25%
.40	16%
.30	9%
.20	4%
.10	1%
.00	0%

FIGURE 7.13 Relationships between correlations and coefficients of determination. *Source: Fire Data Analysis Handbook by FEMA, pg. 60. exhibit 6-2, http://upperpinefpd.org.*

The Pearson Product-Moment Correlation Coefficient

The Pearson product-moment correlation coefficient or the Pearson r is the most common analysis conducted to prove correlation or cause and effect. When research refers to a correlation coefficient without being specific about which one is meant, it may safely be assumed it is the Pearson product-moment correlation coefficient. The Pearson correlation is used to find a correlation and strength between at least two continuous variables and the direction of the correlation. The value for a Pearson's can fall between 0.00 (no correlation), 1.00 (a perfect correlation), or –1.00 (negative correlation). A correlation that is above .80 is considered high and indicates a solid relationship between variables.

The term *moment* is borrowed from physics and refers to a function of the distance of an object from the center of gravity. With a frequency distribution, the mean is the center of gravity and, thus, deviation scores are the moments. The Pearson correlation is calculated by taking the products of the paired moments.

The computation of the Pearson correlation using the deviation-score method is summarized in the following steps:

1. List the pairs of scores in two columns. The order in which the pairs are listed makes no difference in the value of the correlation. However, if one raw score is shifted, the one it is paired with must be shifted as well.

2. Find the mean for the raw scores of each variable.
3. Convert each score in both variables to a deviation score by subtracting the respective mean from each.
4. Calculate the standard deviation for both variables. Since the deviation scores are already done, they need only to be squared and summed. Divide each of these totals by the number of pairs and take the square root of each.
5. Multiply each pair of deviation scores, known as the cross-product, and total the results.
6. Next, multiply the two standard deviations by each other and multiply that result by the number of pairs.
7. Divide the results of step 5 by the results of step 6. The result is the Pearson product-moment correlation coefficient.
8. Square this for the coefficient of determination.

The correlation obtained can be relatively high, indicating a measure of relationship between the variables. It does not mean that the relationship is necessarily causal, since there are usually many alternate and rational explanations for changes other than a causal one between two simultaneously changing variables.

The next step after obtaining a correlation that shows there is a relationship is to use it as a predictor. This is done by defining the **regression line**, which is the straight line around which the data points cluster. The regression line is defined algebraically, and the formula is used to make the predictions. The predictions become more reliable as the correlation increases. A discussion of the regression method is mentioned here to give meaning to the correlation coefficient.

OTHER TYPES OF CORRELATIONS

Although the Pearson correlation is by far the most commonly used, other types of correlations are derived directly or indirectly from the Pearson. These correlations are used with data points that are not continuous and quantitative as with the Pearson. The details of their computation and use are as follows.

Rank-order correlation is sometimes useful to categorize data by ranking. The largest gets a rank of 1, the second largest a rank of 2, and so on. When both variables consist of ranks, a rank-order correlation coefficient is calculated. It is sometimes called the Spearman rank-order correlation. It is found merely by applying Pearson's procedure to the ranks.

The bi-serial correlation is used for data in which one variable is continuous and quantitative and the other would be, except that it has been reduced to just two categories. An example is if the correlation between the number of chest pain patients and whether or not the number of STEMIs was above or below the median. This would require the use of the bi-serial technique, since one variable is continuous and the other is expressed dichotomously. **Point bi-serial correlation** would be used as in the bi-serial, except that the second variable is qualitative and divided into two branches and could not be expressed as continuous and quantitative. For example, there is often a correlation between the number of gunshot victims and the number of male versus female deaths. Males tend to suffer more self-inflicted injuries, whereas injuries associated with gun violence show more females as the victim.

The **phi coefficient** is the Pearson correlation coefficient for two variables that are both qualitative and divided into two parts or classifications. Partial correlation shows what the Pearson correlation coefficient between two variables would be in the absence of one or more other variables. For example, with the correlation of vehicle crashes to deaths, the relationship each has to the passage of time could account for the change in each rather than a relationship to each other. By doing a partial correlation between vehicle crashes and deaths for each month within a given year, time would be held constant. The resulting correlations would reflect a truer picture of the relationship between vehicle crashes and deaths. This is a great example, as new technology in vehicles has made a significant impact in fatalities, whereas the number of crashes has remained the same.

Other variations of correlations are used for determining variable relationships with different circumstances, but we have covered most of what is likely to be needed. All of these tools are readily available in various statistical packages. Most of them walk the user through the process with clear, understandable directions. The purpose of manually calculating these statistics in this chapter was to provide an understanding of the processes, which should make it easier to interpret the results when using a statistical package.

CHAPTER REVIEW

Summary

Once data have been collected, it is important that a step-by-step process be put in place to analyze the data to make an accurate conclusion. Making an assessment of the distribution of the data is very important. Conclusions on data must be tested to ensure the data are accurate, reliable, and significant as they relate to the actual conclusions being drawn from what the data indicate. During the analysis and after making a proper conclusion, the data must be accurately displayed for a person or group to understand the results. Presentation of data requires the use of certain bar graphs, pie charts, or another type of display. It is important to process data correctly to ensure that the information draws a clear picture of the events that were being measured and that management can decide on a course of action to improve on the system.

WHAT WOULD YOU DO? Reflection

An analysis of variance (ANOVA) and a quantitative step-by-step process can be conducted to determine if the failure in procedures is significant or a random error within the normal standard deviation of events related to ventricular tachycardia.

The findings are valid and reliable as this event has resulted in a sentinel event with the death of a patient from one interaction. Therefore, any event similar—as in the laboratory findings—is a significant finding.

The Pearson product-moment correlation coefficient could determine if one cardiac monitor is more likely to propagate the error than another, given that all paramedics are familiar or trained on each monitor. What is more important is if the training is correlated to the right type of cardiac monitor that the paramedic is most likely to use.

Histograms, pie charts, or bar charts are appropriate tools for displaying the results of the test.

Review Questions

1. What are the benefits and disadvantages of using certain visual displays, such as the histogram, pie chart, or column chart?
2. What are the benefits of and techniques used to establish mode, mean, and median?
3. When is a single mode used instead of a bimodal test for frequency of data?
4. What are four common patterns of data? What defines them?
5. How do you test for reliability? variance? correlation?
6. What are the differences between quantitative and qualitative data? List three examples of each.
7. What question could be answered about the results of an outcome of EMS delivery using a regression line?
8. What is the difference between a dependent variable and an independent variable?
9. What processes would be ideal for a positive skew and a negative skew?

References

Aczel, A. D. (1995). *Statistics: Concepts and Applications*. Chicago: Irwin.

Agresti, A., and Franklin, C. (2008). *Statistics: The Art and Science of Learning from Data*, 2nd ed. Upper Saddle River, NJ: Pearson-Prentice Hall.

Carey, R. G., and R. C. Lloyd. (2001). *Measuring Quality Improvement in Health Care: A Guide to Statistical Processes*. Milwaukee, WI: American Society for Quality.

Chang, J. C., and F. P. Schoenberg. (2009). "A Statistical Analysis of Santa Barbara Ambulance Response in 2006: Performance Under Load." *Western Journal of Emergency Medicine X*(1), pp. 42–47.

Coxon, A. P. M. (1999). *Sorting Data: Collection and Analysis.* Thousand Oaks, CA: Sage Publications.

Devore, J., and R. Peck. (2001). *Statistics: The Exploration and Analysis of Data*, 4th ed. Pacific Grove, CA: Brooks/Cole.

Gilbert, N. (1993). *Analyzing Tabular Data: Loglinear and Logistic Models for Social Researchers*. London: UCL Press.

Freedman, D., R. Pisani, and R. Purves. (1998). *Statistics*, 3rd ed. New York: W.W. Norton.

Harrison, T. R., S. E. Morgan, and Tom Reichert. (2002). *From Numbers to Words. Reporting Statistical Results for the Social Sciences*. Boston: Allyn & Bacon.

Jaffe, A. J., H. F. Spirer, and L. Spirer. (1998). *Misused Statistics,* 2nd ed., rev. and expanded. New York: M. Dekker.

Lewis-Beck, M. S. (1995). *Data Analysis: An Introduction*. Thousand Oaks, CA: Sage Publications.

Morgan, C. J., and A. F. Siegel. (1995). *Statistics and Data Analysis: An Introduction*, 2nd ed. New York: Wiley.

Mosteller, F., S. E. Fienberg, and R. E. K. Rourke. (1983). *Beginning Statistics with Data Analysis.* Reading, MA: Addison-Wesley.

Newton, R. R., and K. E. Rudestam. (1999). *Your Statistical Consultant: Answers to Your Data Analysis Questions*. Thousand Oaks, CA: Sage Publications.

Patton, M. Q. (2001). *Qualitative Evaluation and Research Methods*, 3rd ed. Newbury Park, CA: Sage Publications.

Provost, L. P., and S. Murray. (2011). *The Health Care Data Guide: Learning from Data for Improvement.* San Francisco: Jossey-Bass.

Stephens, L. J. (1998). *Schaum's Outline Theory and Problems of Beginning Statistics.* New York: McGraw-Hill.

Zelazny, G. (2001). *Say It with Charts*, 4th ed. New York: McGraw-Hill.

Key Terms

analysis of variance A basic statistical technique for analyzing data. It subdivides the total variation of a data set into meaningful component parts associated with specific sources of variation in order to test a hypothesis on the measurements of the model or to estimate variance in certain components.

bimodal Two areas in the data cluster together to form two different peaks; two distinct values that measurements tend to cluster around a measurement.

causation How events occur in the system or how they are related even when it may not be obvious, or conversely when it appears obvious but is not related. Causation is displayed on the horizontal scale or the X axis.

chi-square A test used to determine whether or not there were significant differences between frequency distributions.

Cronbach's coefficient alpha Measurement of internal consistency among a group of questions combined to form a single scale. It is a statistic that reflects the homogeneity of the scale.

data A set of collected facts. There are two types of data: variable data and measurement data.

descriptive statistical analysis Various statistical tests run to get in-depth analysis and to confirm or refute conclusions with mathematics. There are several types of descriptive statistical analysis, including counts, sums, standard deviation measures of center, minimums, and maximums.

histogram A column graph in which the height of the columns indicates the relative numbers or frequencies or values of a variable. The values may be numeric or nonnumeric.

Likert scale A summated instrument scale. This means that the items making up a Likert scale are summed to produce a total score as a composite on an itemized scale. Typically, each scale item will have five categories, with scale values ranging from –2 to +2, with 0 as a neutral response.

mean Also known as the arithmetic mean or *average*. However, since the term *average* is sometimes used indiscriminately for any measure of central tendency, it should be avoided.

measurement The act or process of quantitatively comparing results with requirements. Measurements may be in any quality and may be in any unit.

measures of central tendency The extent to which data gathered from a process tend to cluster toward a middle value somewhere between the high and low values of measurements.

measures of dispersion The tendency of values of elements in a sample to differ from each other.

median The middle value or the 50th percentile of a distribution. To determine the median, the data must be ordered.

mode The value that occurs most frequently in a distribution object from the center of gravity. With a frequency distribution, the mean is the center of gravity and, thus, deviation scores are the moments.

modulus A check to ensure that there are no extra numerical fields.

nonparametric A type of test for situations in which assumptions about underlying populations do not rely on normal distributions.

ordinal scale The ranking of individuals, attitudes, or items along the continuum of the characteristic being scaled.

outlier A data point or observation that lies an abnormal distance from other values in a random sample or population.

PERT chart A project management tool used to schedule, organize, and coordinate tasks within a project.

phi coefficient The Pearson product-moment correlation coefficient for two variables that are both qualitative and divided into two parts or classifications.

point bi-serial correlation Used as in the bi-serial correlation, except that the second variable is qualitative and divided into two branches and could not be expressed as continuous and quantitative.

range A plus/minus figure that encompasses data points above and below the mean that may be considered as part of the data set; also called margin of error.

regression line Formula used to make the predictions around which the data points cluster.

reliability A statistical measure of the reproducibility of data. Reliability is assessed by examining the internal consistency.

run Eight or more consecutive data points above or below the mean.

semantic scale A scale that makes extensive use of words rather than numbers. Respondents describe their feelings about the products or brands on scales with semantic labels.

shift Involves six or more consecutive data points either above or below the mean.

standard deviation Determines how spread out the bell curve is. The larger the standard deviation, the more spread out is the curve. This also calculates the distance in units from the mean in a positive or negative direction.

trend A long series of consecutive data points ascending or descending; typically the series is five (5) points, indicating a trend.

variable A characteristic or measurement that varies or changes.

variance A measure of dispersion on observations based on the mean of the squared deviations from the arithmetic mean; the square of the standard deviation, given by formula.

CHAPTER 8

Quality Improvement Program and Project Management

Objectives

After reading this chapter, the student should be able to:

8.1 Describe the characteristics of a quality improvement project or program.
8.2 Discuss how QI proposals are selected.
8.3 Identify the components of a well-designed project plan.
8.4 Explain how a QI project or program is controlled.
8.5 Develop and establish clear goals and objectives of a program or project.
8.6 Discuss how QI projects are scheduled and budgeted.
8.7 Identify the parts of the an effective written project plan.

Key Terms

checkpoints
coaching
crashing
critical path method (CPM)
event cost
Gantt chart
goal erosion
Kaizen
milestones
project charter
project proposal
root cause analysis
structural inhibitors

WHAT WOULD YOU DO?

The Central City Fire Department quality improvement (QI) team made up of an EMS field supervisor, a registered nurse (RN), and a key paramedic preceptor met with their counterparts at the regional private ambulance service. A joint QI initiative was being launched in response to a recently published study in *Prehospital and Disaster Medicine* that indicated patients being intubated with a pulse were desaturating during the procedure and had a 30 percent worse outcome when intubated by a combined ambulance/fire crew than when the procedure was done by a helicopter crew. A quick assessment of the data by the EMS chief at Central City Fire revealed an alarming parallel to the published study. Clear evidence and data from the CodeStat™ from the fire department cardiac monitors indicated clear evidence of desaturation of patients during a facilitated intubation in more that 40 percent of the patients treated by combined fire and Oceans Medical Response (OMR) teams on the scene with the most seriously ill patients. The participants all agreed that this was a problem and something needed to be done.

Direction was given by the EMS chief in concert with the OMR's operations director to come up with a solution to the problem. Repeated inquiries by the EMS chief indicated that the group was working toward a solution to the problem, yet specifics were never questioned and nothing appeared in writing during the process. After 3 months and numerous meetings, the group disbanded and the improvement desired in the system was never realized.

Questions

1. Why did the initiative fail? What components were missing that may have contributed to the failure?
2. If this was to be reattempted at a later date, what could be done to ensure the success of the program?
3. What distinguishes a team from a group of people?
4. What additional techniques or actions could be taken to motivate the group to achieve the desired results?

INTRODUCTION

A QI program should be made up of many different projects. A QI program is like a living document and should change according to the needs of the organization and as issues arise. Like any program in an organization, it must be managed and led. Programs must be constructed to make them functional and get results. A longstanding barrier to QI in EMS has been to have QI as a clinical-only initiative managed as an individual role or separate program. Yet, the emphasis should be on process improvement, organizational philosophy, and strategies that create a portfolio of projects to improve results. This requires EMS management to motivate a team, keep members on track, and set clear goals and objectives for the projects that make up a QI program.

ALIGNMENT AND INTERDEPENDENCY

As data become available, a manager may immediately want to respond to the numbers by instituting a change or responding to a quality issue. Before making any changes, good management technique requires that a project be thoroughly analyzed. A change in a program or operation can have an impact on other aspects of the EMS system. For every action, there will be a reaction as prehospital care involves a systematic approach and is interdependent. This is the premise of "Deming" the system, a common phrase when referring to the system of profound knowledge and systems theory that is applied to a process to optimize the work. In other words, an EMS system is made up of several interrelated components that require an outside assessment as it relates to Edward Deming's system theory.

Consider QI if your data reveal or you discover a lengthy door-to-drug time for ST elevation myocardial infarctions (STEMI) within an EMS system. The EMS provider could influence the time by recognizing and alerting the hospital; however, a bypass of the emergency room (ER) impacts reimbursement to the ER physician. A transmitted EKG to the ER for the doctor to read and then an alert to the cardiac lab could ensure that the system functions with optimal proficiency by aligning staff ahead of time. This process has an embedded barrier to improvement as reimbursement for the ER physician's direction requires the patient be seen and screened by the ER physician slowing the process of moving the patient to the treatment in the catheterization lab. A QI program is about removing barriers to quality care and focusing on the quality outcome verses maximizing reimbursement.

EMS is a system made up of several interdependent points of care that ideally result in a better outcome for the patient. QI proposals should consider the impact QI will have on the hospitals, dispatch, and first responder agencies. Internally, the interdependencies a proposal will have on standards of practice (SOP) development, logistics, or supply acquisitions as well as updates or changes to vehicle inventories all impact the project.

REASONS FOR CHANGE

Initiating a QI project is about change. Change comes from identified issues that may be from an internal influence or external event captured by the data in the system. Internal projects are designed to improve the planning process to show a direct or indirect budget savings. A change should be considered in response to data that indicates variation outside of the upper and lower control limits. This often indicates the need for an assessment or evaluation of the need for more resources or an allocation or reallocation of existing resources. Projects are often initiated to help justify items that meet the greater needs of organization, increased productivity, increased morale, recruitment, or retention.

External reasons for change could be due to tighter fiscal allotments, an expectation of tax cuts, or the rising cost of doing business. External forces in the future will require a higher degree of accountability of EMS resources and crews. External forces will require compliance to certain levels of clinical care and operational performance to meet contracts for service in communities or to maximize reimbursement. Market forces and competition from other EMS services can prompt QI projects. Many QI projects attempt to respond to actual and potential changes in patient care or public expectation of changes; often, these are triggered by demographics and technology. Whatever the reason, it is up to management to improve the accountability of EMS crews and resources in order to ensure compliance with what is expected.

REMOVING OBSTACLES

EMS managers or leaders will need to attempt to remove both external and internal obstacles. Lack of funding, political pressures, and culture are the most common obstacles to change. The organization may present some obstacles, especially the first time out, when few people are familiar with QI techniques or experienced in the process. Often, a lack of experience and fear of change become catalysts for obstruction.

Personal motives may be another obstacle. For example, if a leader who is perceived as an expert becomes obsolete with the change or someone in power loses power, he may raise obstacles. If the change will potentially alter the allocation of budgets, resistance to the project should be anticipated. It is important to learn how to read body language and understand a person's posture, which may indicate nonsupport for the process.

FOCUS ON QI PROJECT MANAGEMENT

Organizations must have ongoing QI projects because they support the mission of providing quality patient care and moving organizations toward their goals. An organization with no ongoing projects lacks long-term focus and then becomes rooted in day-to-day operations without an opportunity to move forward. Poorly managed QI projects waste time and money and demoralize team members.

A project typically has three characteristics: performance, cost, and time. QI projects should be prioritized according to the cost-benefit, priorities, impact, and alignment with the organization. For most EMS agencies, a QI project will be a first-time endeavor as most EMS organizations simply do chart review. A first-time project should be well planned and be given every chance for success.

PROJECT PROPOSAL

A **project proposal** is a document that provides clear information concerning the goals and objectives that a particular project hopes to achieve. A project proposal discusses how the project supports the overall mission, goals, and objectives of the organization. An effective proposal provides readers with insight into what must be accomplished and how that will be achieved. Including a clearly stated mission, goals, and objectives associated with a specific QI project in a proposal helps to sell it. A project proposal contains specific components: an introduction, background information on the problem, and the need for the project. It also outlines the task, financial requirements, administrative support, and logistical support. Too often the entire cost of an EMS project is not identified. A missed opportunity to stop or reinforce a project is often not acted on due to this missing piece of the project. Proposals also name key individuals associated with the project, including the project leader. A project proposal creates a general understanding of the following:

- What is needed
- What must be done
- Why it must be done
- Who is going to do it
- When it will be done
- Where it will be done
- How much will be done
- How much it will cost

An organization would be well served to maintain a checklist for the components that should be in a proposal.

Several processes or theorists have proposed step-by-step procedures for project implementation. Several approaches identify the causes that trigger the need for a QI project or proposal. The implementation of a proposal becomes a project. More commonly, this is a management process that incorporates change, or is essentially QI.

One of the more modern ideas comes from management professor J. P. Kotter (2012), who developed an eight-step plan for implementing a QI process or programs. This is based on the principles of change management. Kotter's eight-step processes include the following:

1. Establishing a sense of urgency or creating a compelling reason for change.
2. Forming a team or coalition with enough power to make the changes.
3. Creating a new vision with achievement strategies.
4. Communicating the vision throughout the organization.
5. Empowering people to act on the vision.
6. Planning for and rewarding short-term wins.
7. Consolidating improvements, reassessing, and making adjustments.
8. Reinforcing the changes by demonstrating the relationship between new behaviors and organizational success. (p. 33 and ff.)

The application of these eight steps requires some accountability. For example, always communicate the need for changes. Never assume that the key stakeholders of the EMS system understand and know the reason for change. When forming a team, consider incorporating those who oppose change as it often can help overcome the resistance. We frequently build teams with key stakeholders and people who can be constructive champions. There is no value in including resisters unless they can be constructive and know they are being included as part of the team so they can contribute. When establishing the new goals of the program, it is important to ensure that the team is empowered to act. In many cases, it is important to pause to check on a quality process in order to get a fresh set of eyes on the project to ensure it is moving in the right direction.

EFFECTIVE PROPOSALS

A proposal is used to make a case for leadership in a project. A project team must have a charter that holds the team members accountable and assists in promoting ownership of the QI project. A charter for a QI project is a written document that identifies the process to be studied and outlines the parameters of the QI project. It will establish **milestones** and dates.

Selecting Goals and Objectives

Goals are an important component of a QI project. It is important for any team to help set the goals of the project. The team has a much better chance of attaining goals that are created by the team. Goals must be specific, measurable, attainable, realistic, and timely (SMART). In other words, SMART goals must be achievable and have manageable and appropriate benchmarks. Goals should be sequential. When people are asked for input, there is better buy-in and ownership in the solution if people had a hand in creating the goals. Goals can be divided into steps in order to maintain small victories and move a large project forward. Benchmarks for goals are derived from best practice in the literature or reported by EMS industry or historical internal data.

> **Side Bar**
>
> **The Aim Statement**
>
> An aim statement is the common tool used in health care QI projects when trying to establish goals. Often referred to as a charter, it asks, "What is to be accomplished?" Without an aim statement, a team can quickly get off track.

Goals are incorporated within a QI project and should be linked to the strategic plan, defining boundaries and any special factors. Goals help to identify what will be accomplished and create commitment among the participants and focus on the project. Goals are accomplished more often when they are written down.

FOSTERING SUCCESS OF QI PROPOSALS

The success of a proposed implementation of a project or any aspect of a QI program depends on several factors. One important aspect is the duration of the project and the time between intervals of when the milestones are reviewed. A milestone is a long-term or major event that has been or must be completed for a project. Typically, a series of tasks must be achieved before a milestone is achieved. Milestones differ from **checkpoints**, which are smaller events used to judge how far a project is from completion.

The *D*uration, *I*ntegrity, *C*ommitment, and *E*ffort (DICE) method from the Boston Consulting Group is a process by which an EMS manager can evaluate the success of a project.

The DICE method is based on a mathematical formula:

$$D + (2 \times I) + (2 \times C1) + C2 + E$$

D = Duration
I = Integrity
C = Commitment
  C1 = Commitment of top management
  C2 = Commitment of effected employee
E = Effort

Each of the letter variables has a score of 1-4. This formula results is a score of between 7 and 28.

When taken together and considered properly, the four DICE components help determine the probability of successfully completing a QI initiative. This is a quick and easy way to assess a project's success prior to beginning, whether it is a short project with an experienced team or a lengthy project with a weak team.

The duration (D) score is based on the length of time for the project: less than 2 month scores a 1; 2-4 months scores a 2; 4-8 months scores a 3; if the project is greater than 8 months it scores a 4.

The integrity (I) score is based on team performance. If the historical performance is very good it scores a 1; good to very good 1.5; good 2; average to good 2.5; average 3; poor to average 3.5; poorly performing teams receives a score of 4.

Commitment (C) is broken down into two categories;

C1 indicating management's commitment to the project and C2 the employee's commitment to the project. Under the C1 category if management's commitment is strong and clearly communicated it scores a 1; reasonably communicated 1.5; seems to want success 2; neutral to seems to want success 2.5; neutral 3; reluctant to neutral 3.5; reluctant 4. In the C2 or employee's commitment, if the employee's are eager the score is 1; willing to eager 1.5; willing 2; reluctant to willing 2.5; reluctant 3; strong reluctance to reluctant 3.5; or strongly reluctant they receive a 4.

The additional effort (E) is based on how much extra the organization will have to put forward and is based on additional commitments of less than 10 percent indicating a score of 1; 10-20 percent indicating a score of 2; 20-40 percent indicating a scoare of 3; and greater than 40 percent indicating a score of 4. The formula using the four DICE components uses a scoring system that ranges from 7 (best) to 28 (worst). The scores are classified as "win" 7-14 meaning a high probility of success; "worry" 15-17 when a project success is unpredictable; and "woe" 17-28 meaning it is likely to fail.

COMPONENTS OF AN EFFECTIVE PROJECT PLAN

Once a proposal is accepted, the framework or foundation of the project plan must be created. Complex operations need a written project plan. Often, in the amount of time it takes to write a plan for smaller projects, the program can be easily implemented. However,

CASE STUDY: Dice

A large EMS operation considered restructuring the vehicle checkout and resupply operations after the QI system identified some supply failures and lack of equipment on certain calls. The QI director identified several events that led to a trend. A QI project was requested by the operations director and the EMS field supervisors who agreed with the goals and objectives. At the same time, each field supervisor had a different view on whether the results could be achieved, though they all seemed to want to succeed. A meeting using the DICE method distilled a 2-day discussion into a 2-hour discussion.

There was a minimal time commitment for key stakeholders to put their inputs into the system. It was discovered that changes could not take place without a SOP and vendor change that would take 4–8 months to get through parallel processes, and there were no clear milestones upon which to base a review. The team that was put together to carry out the design of the restock process had a good performance record. However, the staff were not committed to changing the process as the field crews would be required to use more of their time to check their vehicles and that would result in the loss of several stocking technicians who currently stock and clean the vehicles. Therefore, the commitment of the employees was poor. The reassignment of crews and staff plus a financial outlay required 10-20 percent of the organization's effort. Overall, the score was 21, which rated in the "woe" category.

This resulted in the leadership being able to identify exactly what and where to strengthen the project. The leadership divided the project into two separate categories: securing a new and more reliable vendor for supplies and establishing a new procedure for restocking. Now no employees would be eliminated, but rather they would be reassigned. This increased the commitment of the staff so the score was raised to 3. In addition, the program was shorten to 2 months, and some specific milestones were placed into the project to improve reliability of the EMS supplies for patient care. This changed the overall score to 11, which shifted the project status to a "win" category.

DICE allows for a project to be dynamic and open to feedback to ensure success in a project that involves change. Since project teams are composed of people, there is often a variety of opinions, ideas, and perspectives regarding a project. If the team has an influential leader, sufficient time, and clear objectives with milestones at appropriate intervals, the project is likely to succeed. When embarking on a QI project, a series of questions is helpful for determining to move forward:

- What is the investment to implement this improvement?
- What is the return?
- What are the project benefits?
- How long will the project take to complete?
- How will the return on investment be measured?

if not formalized in writing, the record of the process and its implementation may be lost, and future generations within the organization and in other agencies will be unable to use it. This is a common source of variation when processes and programs are not written down to ensure consistency. The use of a template can make recording, processing, and archiving the plan easier to achieve. Projects have three objectives: meeting the budgetary requirements, completing the project on schedule, and meeting the performance improvement goals of the organization. However, no project plan ever goes exactly as intended and often must be modified.

Project plans include specific information about the mission and specific goals and objectives supporting the mission and its goals. The tasks that are required to meet the goals and objectives must be recorded in the project plan. The mechanics of who, what, where, when, why, and how must be listed in as much detail as possible. A schedule that outlines the time needed to support each aspect of the plan and what resources are required to support the plan should be completed. A cost and value analysis that looks at the outlay in time, money, and personnel versus the potential benefit of the project to the organization should be calculated. Often this is measured in cost savings, reduction in the illness or injury, or increases in positive outcomes. The personnel requirements including who is needed for each part of the plan and their responsibilities and assignments are a key part of the written plan. How the project will be evaluated and the milestones or checkpoints should be listed to keep things on track. An assessment of what can go wrong and a contingency plan also should be noted.

Schedules

After the milestones are created from the goals, a QI project must have a schedule. A schedule for both the operation of the project and the anticipated results should be provided to the EMS leadership or providers. Timeliness is an important aspect of any QI project to ensure that the project effectively provides current and accurate information. Scheduling a project plan helps translate projects into operational time frames.

A **Gantt chart**, the program evaluation and review technique (PERT), and the **critical path method (CPM)** are excellent tools for monitoring the complex links of activities associated with a QI project. A Gantt chart displays the flow and completion of each item using time and task of each division that is needed. The CPM gets it name by being able to identify the longest interrelated events that must be completed in a project or the critical path. These tools are available as part of the Microsoft Project™ software and help visualize the team's task.

The PERT is used to show relationships between tasks for a QI project. It involves making a list of activities and tasks, determining the relationship, and then constructing a diagram from the end working backward to the beginning. Each event or task is a node on the diagram. Related nodes are linked. Once the nodes are linked with their subtask, they are placed together as a frame of the entire project.

A CPM builds on the PERT by adding the cost per unit time. The critical path requires that estimates of times and costs be done. Certain aspects of the path can be accelerated if there is a reason, and certain nodes or path can have their time frames moved up. This is called **crashing** a project so that certain activities can be done more quickly.

SELECTING A TEAM FOR THE PROJECT

A group of people does not make a team, and people in a group do not always get along or work together. The success of a team requires proper selection. For those being considered for a QI team, several key factors should be assessed.

The personal identity of team members can often inhibit a team's performance. If a team member does not feel like he fits in, he is likely neither to engage in the process nor assist the team. Rather, allowing each team member to have a say and developing their trust in the project are both management techniques that can lead to good teamwork.

EMS workforces are becoming more diverse, and working together requires that team members develop a relationship. This sharing or finding of common ground is important, and when team members begin to care about each other, they will go to great lengths to support one another. The team should fit into the organization, too, as a team member still must identify with the organization and not feel alienated from it by being on the team.

When putting together a team, there are often more people to choose from than are needed. A typical team should contain no more than twelve members; and six to eight team members are more effective as a team. Subject-matter experts can be used to supplement team strengths and keep the team size manageable. The following are twelve characteristics that commonly describe successful team members:

- Honesty
- Selflessness
- Dependability
- Enthusiasm
- Responsibility
- Cooperativeness
- Initiative
- Patience
- Resourcefulness
- Punctuality
- Tolerance/sensitivity
- Perseverance

As a manager or team leader, it is important to assess the team needs, identifying the characteristics of good team players and teamwork. A team leader must understand the motivation of each team member. Is the motivation financial, for promotional experience, a genuine interest in a topic, or a feeling of responsibility to the agency leadership? Ensure that trust is demonstrated within the group and by everyone selected for the team.

It is the team leader or management's responsibility to make the job more complete by empowering people to make real decisions. The QI team's work must seem real and meaningful. Encourage someone to become an expert specializing in a certain aspect of the program. For example, if the team's goals are to improve emergency airway control in the EMS setting, one member may want to become an expert in the various technologies to assess end tidal carbon dioxide.

Get rid of slackers and remove nonperformers before they destroy the mission or zap the energy of the team. Insubordinate attitudes are not to be tolerated as the cost, success, and future of QI initiatives can be compromised by such actions. Drive out fear and preserve people's dignity, which often involves communicating appropriately.

ENHANCING TEAM COHESIVENESS

Building a cohesive QI team primarily requires building trust, showing appreciation, communicating, being ethical, and seeing team members as assets. To build trust in the team starts with setting an example. It is imperative that a team leader share information and explain any personal motives. A leader should avoid personal criticisms and personal favors; instead, he should hand out sincere rewards and recognition. People have to be appreciated as assets by respecting their thoughts, feelings, and fears associated with a QI project.

Despite a leader's best attempts, team members often create barriers between themselves and the people with whom they work. When placed into a team, those barriers can hamper the team's goals. Breaking down bias in a team can be accomplished by conducting a cultural audit—that is, by looking at the personalities, values, and individual differences among team members.

It is important to look at each person's needs as part of the team. They should be there to help achieve the team's aim. Secondary goals should be complementary to the work. For example, a firefighter/paramedic may be looking to gain experience in the group for promotional reasons. A staff person may have a genuine interest in the EMS agency confronting a disease process due to a family member's illness. Someone may be assigned to a light-duty situation due to an injury or mandated to participate, which may create a culture clash. Likewise, religious, ethnic, and age- or gender-related factors may polarize a team. Management of the team and leading others requires a complete understanding of the makeup of the members.

Cultural clashes or motivations must be recognized and perhaps confronted. Stress from the goals and interpersonal dynamics can create coping mechanisms that result in one of three types of behaviors: fleeing or withdrawing from the team, accepting the ideas, or becoming confrontational in the face of team stresses. These responses often call for one of two strategies: problem oriented or emotionally oriented.

COACHING

In many instances, a team involved in an organization's QI project is participating as a team for the first time. Like any team, there is a need for a coach. EMS leadership in the organization must provide **coaching**. Coaching varies greatly from managing as it has a specific cycle:

- Observation to identify a gap or opportunity to improve
- Discussion and agreement
- Active coaching
- Follow-up

Coaching is about human performance, and management involves ensuring that processes are working correctly. Coaching requires a coach to help people and teams to develop skills. Coaches achieve this by showing or demonstrating skills and allowing people to develop a variety of outcomes. (See Figure 8.1.)

COMMON CAUSES OF POOR TEAM PERFORMANCE

There are **structural inhibitors** to teamwork. A structural inhibitor is an administrative procedure, organizational principle, or cultural element that works against change. One common structural inhibitor is the unit structure. The traditional paramilitary structure in EMS organizations may not work. A QI team must be cross-functional and will work outside the traditional boundaries of the traditional unit structure.

Accountability and unit goals work best when the focus is on the overall process. The responsibility for team work must be communicated to members to ensure that personnel are held responsible for the performance of the team. Team and individual achievements also need recognition; when it is unilateral, it can inhibit team performance. Teams often cite unclear goals, bad processes, and personnel problems as excuses for poor performance.

Management Focus	Coaching Focus
Telling	Exploring
Directing	Facilitating
Authority	Partnership
Immediate needs	Long-term improvement
A specific outcome	Many possible outcomes

FIGURE 8.1 Coaching versus management.

Goal erosion occurs when people reduce their goals in response to experiencing failure and adversity. Often, people give up on an important goal or lower their standards to such a low level that the accomplishments of the team bring no sense of satisfaction. Shifting the burden from short-term solutions to correct problems with seemingly happy immediate results ultimately will cause poor performance as a long-term solution never is achieved. People also rarely appreciate the delays involved in striving to reach a goal. They give up prematurely, or they work so hard to overcome delays that they resent the work.

Side Bar

ISO 9000

The ISO 9000 is a family of standards representing an international consensus on good quality management practices. It consists of standards and guidelines relating to quality management systems and related supporting standards. ISO 9001:2008 is the standard that provides a set of standardized requirements for a quality management system, regardless of what the user organization does, its size, or whether it is in the private or public sector. It is the only standard in the family against which organizations can be certified—although certification is not a compulsory requirement of the standard. The other standards in the family cover specific aspects, such as fundamentals and vocabulary, performance improvements, documentation, training, and financial and economic aspects.

ROOT CAUSE ANALYSES AND ACTION PLANS AS PROJECT

A **root cause analysis** can become an individual project that gets assigned to a team. It is often called a failure mode effective analysis (FMEA). To be done correctly, the root cause analysis must have certain characteristics. The analysis focuses on a project attempting to solve a problem that focuses primarily on systems and processes, not on individual performance. The analysis progresses from special causes in clinical processes to common causes in organizational processes. The analysis repeatedly digs deeper by asking "Why?" When answered, "Why?" is asked yet again, and so on. A root cause analysis can include or identify changes that could be made in EMS systems. These processes can be either through redesign or development of new systems, processes, or protocols that would improve the quality issues the project team was setting out to complete.

A root cause analysis should be thorough and credible, determining the human and other factors most directly associated with a sentinel event or problem that has been trended by statistical analysis. This focuses on changes to the processes and or systems related to its occurrence. An analysis of the underlying EMS systems and processes should be asked through a series of "Why?" questions to determine where a redesign might reduce patient errors or provide more efficient care. An identification of the causes and their potential contributions to the type of event the project team is attempting to correct can be supplied by a good statistical analysis. Statistical analysis can determine the potential for improvement in processes or systems that would tend to decrease the likelihood of such events in the future or—a rare determination—after an analysis concludes that no opportunity for improvement exists.

To be credible, the root cause analysis must include participation by the EMS leadership of the organization and by individuals most closely involved in the EMS processes and systems under review. For a root cause analysis to be internally consistent (i.e., not contradict itself or leave obvious questions unanswered), it should follow standardized processes every time, resisting jumping to a conclusion with only limited information. This includes casual factors and near root cause items that should be charted. This can be done by providing an explanation for all findings of "not applicable" or "no problem." Included in a root cause analysis should be any relevant literature to support the project or the project outcomes.

An action plan will be considered acceptable if it identifies changes that can be implemented to reduce risk or formulates a rationale for not undertaking such changes. An action plan also identifies, in situations where improvement actions are planned, who is responsible for implementation, when the action will be implemented (including any pilot testing), and how the effectiveness of the actions will be evaluated. A slower or gradual process is known as **Kaizen**. Kaizen is a Japanese approach to a quality process that encourages a 1 percent change over 100 days to get a 100 percent change rather than a more disruptive change of 100 percent over a short period or one day. This can be an approach to an action plan that can be effective and easier to manage.

Best Practice

Medstar Mobile Healthcare DMAIC Process

Control charts are a powerful tool, and this case demonstrates the results of a Six Sigma–DMAIC improvement process intended to increase daily response time compliance. This was achieved by removing variability and by aligning supply and demand with a geographic buffer. The defined problem was inconsistent unit hour utilization (UH:U), by day of the week and hour of the day, producing higher variation in compliance. The control chart represents daily compliance observations based on a 24-hour period showing upper control limits (UCL) and lower control limits (LCL). The goal was to reduce variability and increase daily compliance. This was done with three specific improvements:

1. Better align supply and demand.
2. Test a smoothed average of peak staffing against the mean plus 2× standard deviation compared to the time frames for the highest percentage of missed response times.
3. Added a geographical buffer based on time of day and day of week.

Three phases are represented in the preceding control chart. Old stage represents the schedule prior to a non-DMAIC, non-data-driven decision to move hours off weekends onto weekdays. This resulted in increased variability day to day and decreased overall compliance demonstrated in the Weekend stage. The Old stage secondarily was used as a control variable to test the improvement of moving from a two standard deviations (2xSD) of deployment to "smoothed" average peak with a geographic buffer producing favorable results.

The continuous improvement model using a DMAIC process produced a new schedule that better aligned resources and geographical buffers, produced an overall increase in compliance by 3 percent on the daily average, and reduced the number of individual days on which the agency missed its 90 percent compliance. The primary measurement was overall system compliance. However, it is worth noting that priority one—hot responses—actually saw a greater increase in compliance that is not represented in the graph. All response time metrics increased by at least 4 percent.

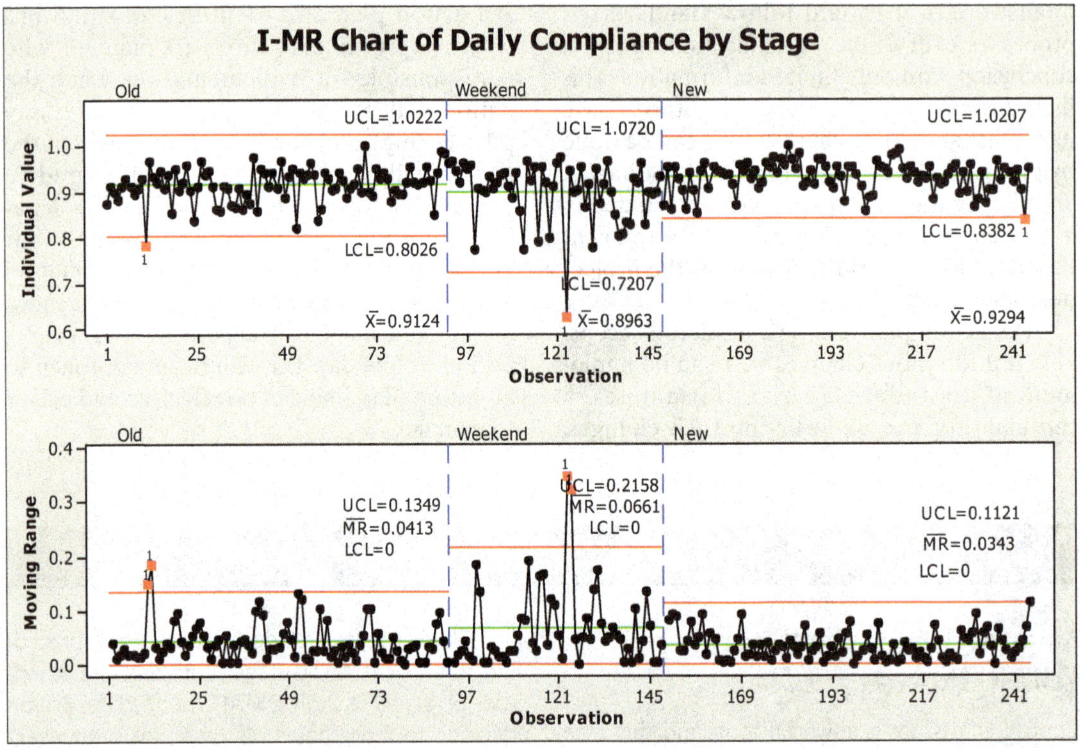

FIGURE BP8.1 I-MR Chart of Daily Compliance by Stage. The chart demonstrates the upper control limits (UCL) and lower control limits (LCL) of response times for Medstar Mobile Healthcare. It demonstrates a variance of quality on the weekend shifts by focusing supervisor efforts to increase coverage to meet performance requirements. The average (X) and the moving range (MR) are related as the control limits or deviations should be within the moving range plus or minus the MR. *Source: This Data Created by Medstar Mobile Health Care, Fort Worth TX.*

DMAIC AS PROJECT

The *D*efine, *M*easure, *A*nalyze, *I*mprove, *C*ontrol (DMAIC) method is the QI model promoted through the Six Sigma process. Six Sigma has long been a process used by Fortune 500 companies to improve manufacturing and decrease defects. In recent years, Six Sigma has been found to be equally effective in the service industry and provides a step-by-step process on how to manage a project. DMAIC put things in sequence and is designed to improve on improvement processes.

DEFINE PHASE

Defining an opportunity or identifying a problem is the first step. Observations must be taken beyond a simple observation or anecdotal assumption. In the define phase, a **project charter** is made. A project charter is a document format used for proposing a performance project and is brought before the senior management team to evaluate the project. Project charters can be clinical, operational, financial, or political. The senior management team is expected to prioritize and evaluate the QI projects. Once the project is approved, the proposal is refined along with any other project details. This ends the define phase, and the project team is ready to proceed.

MEASURE PHASE

The main function in the measurement phase is to understand how the process is currently operating and know the numbers, or the performance. Specifically, this phase identifies what is going to be adjusted by establishing baseline data. Often, this will require the team to document the process or the flowchart. Performance measures are employed and the levels of performance or how efficiently the process is working will be documented to establish a baseline. Once the baseline studies are completed, the measure phase is completed.

ANALYZE PHASE

In the analyze phase, the main goal is to identify what is holding the system from achieving higher performance. This involves using fishbone diagrams, Pareto charts, and other graphics. Once what is limiting or inhibiting the performance has been identified, the project proceeds to the improve phase.

IMPROVE PHASE

The improve phase in the DMAIC process involves creating solutions to the problem. There may be several solutions to the problem, and each should be evaluated for its ability to make a change, have the most significant impact, and improve on the process. As there can be multiple solutions to a problem, the improve phase may involve other projects. Data analysis will be ongoing at this point to determine if the change achieved the desired level of performance. Once a solution is found that achieves the desired layer of improvement, the control phase can begin.

CONTROL PHASE

The control phase is about sustaining process improvement. It also involves gathering information on the process to reference for future projects or to share with other fire or EMS providers. Data points must be set to identify any return to the processes' original configuration and to alert the project team. Often, there are problems not foreseen in the improve phase that require more analysis or review of the work. The critical path method can help ensure that the process is controlled, stays on timelines, and meets critical milestones and benchmarks.

FADE OR FADEE AS PROJECT PATH

Many hospital QI programs follow the *F*ocus, *A*nalyze, *D*evelop, and *E*xecute (FADE) model for QI project management. This process was used at Duke University and was developed from the Organizational Dynamic Institute (ODI), which is best known for helping organizations implement successful Total Quality Management (TQM) strategies, leadership training, management training, and organizational alignment.

The FADE model for taking action on a project involves first evaluating the impact of your change. You then drill down further, analyze the problem to find the root cause(s), develop methods for further improvement, execute the change and reevaluate, further examine the process, and repeat the process until the goal is achieved.

Using a FADE model, an EMS manager may focus on the cleaning cycle of an ambulance and how the crews get an ambulance back in service. For example, staff analyze the way cleaning is handled and find that the disinfecting process seems to be inefficient. A team of EMS providers develops a step-by-step process for washing, drying, disinfecting, and designing surfaces that would be expected to speed up the process and eliminate wasted effort. The team then executes the process with the agency staff and will evaluate for effectiveness on a weekly basis.

There are four broad steps to the FADE QI model. In some examples, a fifth step of "evaluate" is added:

- *Focus*—Define and verify the process to be improved
- *Focus*—Collect and analyze data to establish baselines, identify root causes, and point toward possible solutions
- *Develop*—Based on the data, develop action plans for improvement, including implementation, communication, and measuring/monitoring
- *Execute*—Implement the action plans on a pilot basis
- *Evaluate*—Install an ongoing measuring/monitoring (process control) system to ensure success

Side Bar

Instituting a Near-Miss Protocol

The national near-miss system has been in place for almost a decade. A near-miss is often a sentinel event indicting the need for a project or program. Although the perception has been that the national near-miss program is a fire reporting system, it is quite the contrary. There are several EMS near-misses routinely reported. A near-miss can initiate a QI project. Near-misses can be surveyed at the National Fire Fighter Near-Miss Reporting System or the EMS Voluntary Event Notification Tool (E.V.E.N.T) which are a voluntary, confidential, nonpunitive, and secure reporting systems with the goal of improving firefighter safety. Submitted reports are reviewed by fire service professionals. Identifying descriptions are removed to protect agency and personal identity. The reports are then posted online for other fire and EMS personnel to use as a learning tool.

BUDGETING FOR QI PROGRAMS —

When initiating a QI project, it is important to plan for a detailed budget. (See Figure 8.2.) The effect a QI program has on a certain process and the process of applying a program to an organization has a cost. Although not all attempts to increase quality will be met with success, the majority of QI program efforts must be successful in reducing the cost to the organization. Many of these costs are in errors, lost time, or inventory issues. A poor performance on a medical call can result in a death or injury and a multimillion-dollar loss. Operationally, a QI program implementing a safety or prevention campaign can also result in savings elsewhere in the health care system. Therefore, the cost of a program must be monitored and a cost-benefit analysis conducted at the end of the event.

Most important is the tracking and costing of personnel detailed to a QI program. Each person's hourly rate or salaried per hour cost should be recorded as this is typically the largest expense in the QI program. Looking at the cost for personnel at meetings emphasizes the efficiency needed for running a meeting and sticking to an agenda. Meetings may require overtime for personnel, especially if mandated by contract or labor law.

Printing costs, promotional materials, and copying costs also should be tracked. Custom printing for slogans or posters can vary greatly, and tracking this cost can provide a benchmark for future costs and a base for comparing vendors. Costs should also be included for computer time, software programs, information technology support, and hardware or computers. The cost for educating crews about changes must be recorded (typically, the cost per hour and any instructor time, including the preparation time).

Comparing the overall project budget to the cost of one event that results in a loss, or additional medical expenses that could be

2010

Stroke QA/QI Committee Budget Proposal

PROJECTED Expenses for 2009 (Calendar Year 2010)	Budget	$4,780
	Additional Allowance	$0
	Total Budget	**$4,780**

ACTUAL Expenses for 2009 (Calendar Year 2010)	Budgeted Expenses	$0
	Unbudgeted Expenses	$0
	Total Actual Expenses	**$0**

STAFF COSTS	Projected Cost	Actual Cost	Difference
Admin Staff (24hrs @ $30/hr) × 4 meetings	$2,880		$2,880
Prof. Staff (8hrs @ $50/hr) × 4 meetings	$1,600		$1,600
Subtotals	$4,480	$0	$4,480

PRINTING/MAILING	Projected Cost	Actual Cost	Difference
Associated Printing/Mailing $75 × 4 meetings	$300		$300
Subtotals	$300	$0	$300

PROJECTED BALANCE (Projected income minus expenses)	**$4,780**
ACTUAL BALANCE (Actual income minus expenses)	$0
DIFFERENCE (Actual minus projected)	($4,780)

TOTAL PROJECTED COST	**($4,780)**
TOTAL ACTUAL COST	**($0)**
TOTAL DIFFERENCE	**($4780)**

FIGURE 8.2 Sample budget on QI project.

prevented, is often where the biggest improvement can be seen. For example, trending the events and applying an educational process to increase awareness of dangerous areas of EMS operations can prevent a patient on a gurney from being dropped. An **event cost** associated with a poor medical outcome is an estimate of the annual social cost of an adverse medical event based on what people are willing to pay to avoid such risks in non–health care settings. Designing a QI program should take into account all the costs that an EMS agency, medical provider, or hospital might be required to bear through the tort liability system: patient care expenses, lost income and household production, future medical expenses, burial costs for fatal injuries, and noneconomic losses (e.g., pain and suffering).

Other costs, such as changing medications or not applying a piece of equipment or conducting a procedure, can also result in cost savings that can justify a QI project outside of preventing a loss. A better way of conducting EMS operations can justify a QI program. A different rotation for a preventative maintenance program of ambulances that reduces out of service time is an example of how a QI program focused on management processes versus clinical outcomes can improve efficiency. Consider, for example, the choice of using a $125 intraosseous device with a needle on a cardiac arrest versus using a peripheral intravenous catheter costing less than $5. The QI process identifies that after a year in operations, there is no statistical difference in the outcome.

The following are some other examples of cost-benefit analysis in operational quality:

- How often cardiac equipment is available or used
- How often extrication equipment is available and needed
- How often ancillary resources are available to support operations
- Identifying diverted or unavailable resources
- Evaluating vehicle and equipment performance

Management/administrative quality is another program area. How often is there compliance with protocol? How many run reports are reviewed? How long does it take to process a report? A common measurement in the service industry is how long and how many people an inquiry or complaint passes through until it is resolved. Other management measurements subject to QI initiatives are turnover rates and the delivery of the number of EMS training hours. Some other issues may include the following:

- Communication breakdowns
- Presence or lack of teamwork
- Working conditions, including problematic environmental or safety issues
- Trend medication error type and specialty
- Trends related to procedures
- Trends related to access and flow of process

CHAPTER REVIEW

Summary

A comprehensive QI program starts with aligning the organization with a proposal for a QI project. The proposal process is key to developing a clear understanding of the goals and objectives of a QI program. Proposals contain a charter, milestones, and checkpoints to ensure a program will stay on track. Project management can follow several different models. A schedule, budget, and team formation are all part of a good program. A root cause analysis is commonly used in industry failure or complex problems. The DMAIC process is a program management technique recommended by Six Sigma. The FADE or FADEE process is commonly used in hospital QI programs. Teamwork, team selection, and the leadership of a QI team comprise an important aspect of any QI program. A QI team and project management for each topic are core functions for a QI program.

WHAT WOULD YOU DO? Reflection

In this scenario, there was no coaching from the leader to get the group through a new process. When an inexperienced team is asked to handle a complex topic, it may be difficult to achieve success. In fact, the expertise on process is often very limited.

A team leader or EMS manager should have ensured clear goals and a cohesive team. It is important to ensure an expert is on the team to help guide the other participants.

One way to make the team more successful is to establish SMART goals and ensure that the proposal is well defined. There was no proposal, and the lack of such a document to outline the process resulted in failure to produce a checklist or other tools to steer the group.

This is a more of a group than a team due to the lack of team cohesiveness. This group displays some of the problems with establishing a team. There are unclear goals, goal erosion, and no commitment to the issue as a problem by either organization.

The EMS manager should reward team members for small victories and ensure that milestones and checkpoints are used to track a project. The EMS manager should determine the critical path and use a PERT or Gantt chart(s) to visualize progress.

Review Questions

1. Define coaching, and list at least two differences between coaching and managing.
2. What specific information does a project plan include?
3. What should a leader avoid when building trust within a team?
4. What is the DICE method?
5. What is a charter?
6. List common control tools to keep a project on track.
7. What are some of the common items placed in a program or project budget?

References

Goetsch, D. L., and S. B. Davis. (2010). *Quality Management for Organizational Excellence: Introduction to Total Quality.* Upper Saddle River, NJ: Prentice Hall.

Joint Commission on Accreditation of Healthcare Organizations. (1991). *An Introduction to Quality Improvement in Health Care*, pp. 56–58. Oakbrook, IL: Author.

Kotter, J. P. (2012). *Leading Change.* Boston: Harvard Business School Press.

Kotter, J. P., and D. S. Cohen. (2012). *The Heart of Change: Real Life Stories of How People Change Their Organizations.* Boston: Harvard Business School Press.

Mello, M. A., D. M. Studdert, E. J. Thomas, et al. (2007). "Who Pays for Medical Errors? An Analysis of Adverse Event Costs, the Medical Liability System, and Incentives for Patient Safety Improvement." *Journal of Empirical Legal Studies 4*(4), pp. 835–860.

Robbins, S. P., and T. P. Judge. (2007). *Organizational Behavior*, 12th ed. Upper Saddle River, NJ: Prentice Hall.

Summers, D. (2009). *Quality Management*, 2nd ed. Upper Saddle River, NJ: Pearson Education.

Key Terms

checkpoints Smaller events used to judge how far a project is from completion.

coaching Varies greatly from managing as it has a specific cycle; a coach helps a person or team develop skills by demonstrating and allowing for a variety of outcomes.

crashing Management term used when certain aspects of the project can be accelerated if there is a reason and certain nodes or paths can have their time frames moved up in a project schedule.

critical path method (CPM) Analysis that determines the longest series of interrelated events that must be completed in a project.

event cost All costs associated with a poor medical outcome or adverse medical event that an EMS agency, medical provider, or hospital might be required to bear through the tort liability system: patient care expenses, lost income and household production, future medical expenses, burial costs for fatal injuries, and noneconomic losses (e.g., pain and suffering).

Gantt chart Displays the flow and completion of each item using time and task of each division that is needed.

goal erosion Occurs when people reduce their goals when they experience failure and adversity; often, people give up on an important goal or lower their standards to such an extent that the accomplishments of the team bring no sense of satisfaction.

Kaizen A Japanese approach to a quality process that encourages a 1 percent change over 100 days to get a 100 percent change.

milestones Long-term or major events that have been or must be completed for a project.

project charter Document format used for proposing a performance project and brought before senior management to evaluate the project; can be clinical, operational, financial, or political.

project proposal Document that provides clear information concerning the hoped-for goals and objectives of a particular project.

root cause analysis Identifies changes that could be made in EMS systems and processes.

structural inhibitors Administrative procedure, organizational principles, or cultural elements that work against change.

Creating and Maintaining a Culture of Quality

9 CHAPTER

Objectives

After reading this chapter, the student should be able to:

9.1 Apply techniques to help create a cultural change for quality improvement (QI).
9.2 Assess culture in an organization.
9.3 Identify the components of a high-reliability organization.
9.4 Use standardized assessments to determine the attitudes and beliefs in an organization.
9.5 Differentiate between values, beliefs, and attitudes.
9.6 Identify sample reward systems to promote a system of quality.
9.7 Recognize the components of a "just culture."
9.8 Integrate the necessary parts to bring an organization into alignment.

Key Terms

agapao
alignment
attitudes
attribution error
beliefs
cherry picking
culture
customer service
highly reliable organization
human error
just culture
mission statement
normalization of deviance
organizational culture
reckless behavior
search satisfying
servant leadership
values
values statement
vision statement

WHAT WOULD YOU DO?

Rescue 11 is covering the resort corridor and has responded to a person down on the sidewalk. Upon arrival, the patient is found sitting on a bus bench. He states he does not want any help and has been drinking. A release is signed, and the man returns to his vacation and walks away.

An hour later, E-12 and a private ambulance respond to a man acting strangely. After encountering the same patient who produced a patient refusal from the previous EMS response, the engine cancels the private ambulance.

Yet again, an hour later, a third call is received a mile down the resort corridor from the previous two calls. Rescue 12 arrives, assesses the patient who seems intoxicated, and offers to get him an ambulance. A full set of vitals is taken and are within normal values. The patient is told he should go to the hospital. When the private ambulance arrives, it is the same unit as on the call with E-12. When responders advise that the patient was seen by E-12 and R-11 earlier, the tone changes among three of the four EMS providers. Despite a small bump on the frontal skull, the man is released.

Forty-five minutes later, a call is received for a man unconscious on a bus bench about a half mile down the resort corridor from the previous call. It is handled by R-11. Once again, the same patient is found by R-11. The patient sits up and appears slightly more intoxicated than when he had been seen earlier. Belligerently, he refuses care. A dressing is placed on the patient's head, and one of the paramedics from R-11 writes in pen on the tape across the bandage, "DO NOT CALL 9-1-1. JUST DRUNK."

Fifteen minutes later, the patient makes it to the next bus bench and lies down, triggering another call to 9-1-1. A police officer arrives, sees the message, places the patient in the squad car, and starts to the jail. En route, the patient appears to have trouble breathing and is quickly diverted to the emergency room. The officers arrive with the patient in respiratory arrest in the back seat. Quick treatment and a more thorough assessment find an empty bottle of Lortab, which was combined with alcohol, resulting in a multidrug overdose.

Questions

1. What attitudes and beliefs affected the patient outcome?
2. Why were various levels of assessment done on the patient?
3. Was any bias placed on this patient? How do you overcome bias?
4. How would you ensure reliability in future patient encounters?

INTRODUCTION

Creating a culture of quality can be the most daunting task for an EMS leader or manager. Most EMS organizations have operated under a culture of fear—not typically the fear of oppression but more commonly the fear of being singled out, hazed by peers, labeled, or opened up for potential liability. Simultaneously, the lack of feedback and the difficulty of middle managers to hold people accountable often provides no feedback to help build, learn, and achieve quality results. Creating a culture of quality requires defining the current culture and then creating values and beliefs that reflect quality. Changing culture can take years and often occurs only with significant effort and dedicated leadership. It requires an organization to hire the right people with a servant's attitude and to promote responsible leaders.

Most public safety providers are drawn to this profession and come to work every day wanting to do a good job. However, improvement does not happen in a vacuum. Having systems that provide feedback and offer EMS providers the opportunity to become better, while—ideally—seeing positive results, can change culture. The best designed program can never achieve results without being connected to a workforce embracing quality. If employees value and believe that quality improvement efforts make a difference, even the smallest of quality efforts can light a fire in an organization.

QUALITY CULTURE DEFINED

The mechanical features of an organization's quality management tools, processes, and objectives still remain dependent on the human factor of culture. EMS is a service-oriented profession, and it is about the care that people receive and give. Creating a culture of quality where people's **beliefs**, **values**, and **attitudes** come in line with the organization's **mission statement** and **vision statement** is a key element in any successful quality improvement (QI) initiative.

A belief is a principle, degree of conviction, or idea accepted as true. It then becomes a challenge to maintain this alignment and become a highly reliable organization or to maintain quality. Part of a quality system, then, is to create and maintain a system with a culture of quality that has integrity in the process.

When speaking of quality in an organization, there are often policies and procedures that are not followed and thereby affect the outcomes of quality in the organization. The quality management process should begin with hiring for success or selecting people based on similar beliefs in quality and customer service. Many times, this does not occur in EMS because the expectations of how to meet the standards in the organization have not been conveyed to the line EMTs and paramedics. The expectation of field supervision to enforce ideas about cultural expectations and organizational values is another area often found to be weak in most agencies as a visit from the supervisor is often more reflective of the negative than the positive.

Normalization of deviance is a long-term phenomenon in which individuals or teams repeatedly accept a lower standard of performance until that lower standard becomes the so-called norm. Usually, the acceptance of the lower standard occurs because the individual or team is under pressure (e.g., budget, schedule, call volume, etc.) and perceives it will be too difficult to adhere to the expected standard. Their intention may be to revert back to the higher standard when this period of pressure passes. However, after bypassing the standard without consequences or a negative outcome the deviation becomes routine. Over time, the individual or team fails to see actions as deviant. For teams to maintain their high standards of performance they must have repetitive planning and practice to automate processes to the expected level of performance. Managers need to connect the dots to ensure that errors are not signs of entrenched normalization of deviance in critical processes.

DEFINING CULTURE

Culture is a pattern of shared beliefs and values that provides the members of an organization with rules of behavior or accepted norms for conducting operations. Culture helps remove uncertainty for personnel and provides a context for doing the organization's work. Culture provides personnel with cues that guide them in performing their functions. These cues often originate with top management and pervade all parts of the organization. Thus, culture influences personnel behavior by providing cues as to what is and is not appropriate behavior. The influence of culture on all personnel throughout the organization will affect the organization's overall performance. The values, beliefs, and assumptions that underlie the organization's culture, coupled with the strength of that culture, will determine whether an organization will successfully continue to meet the challenges posed by the environment.

Culture can be made up of artifacts, behaviors, values, beliefs, and underlying assumptions that are developed by a given group of people as they learn to cope with internal and external problems of survival and prosperity. The members of the organization have a common set of values and beliefs that enable them to come together to communicate and work together effectively. Values are those things we regard as having ultimate importance, significance, or worth. Attitude is a variable in culture. Attitude is a manner, disposition, feeling, or position with regard to a person or thing. Culture is rooted in the community in which the agency serves.

An organization defines its culture of quality by first stating its beliefs through the mission, values, and vision statement. For EMS QI to be successful in an organization, a just culture must be developed and nurtured. A **just culture** is one in which people can report mistakes, errors, or waste without reprisal or personal risk. This does not mean that individuals are not held accountable for their actions but it does mean that people are not held responsible for flawed systems in which dedicated and trained people can still make mistakes. All personnel must feel empowered to identify errors, defects, and system failures that could lead to bad patient outcomes. Policies should reflect these statements, and the leaders of the organization should support them and promote the vision.

Culture is a body of learned behaviors specific to a given agency or EMS organization and acts like a template (i.e. it has predictable content or actions), shaping behavior and conduct within an agency from generation to generation. Culture resides in all learned behavior which also shapes the organization's template or behaviors. The "cultural template" can or should be formed in initial EMS training or new employee orientation.

This shaping of a cultural EMS template and body of learned behaviors might be further divided into the following categories, each of which is an important element of cultural systems. A system of meaning is a set of relationships between one group of variables (e.g., words, behaviors, physical symbols, slang, etc.) and the meanings that are attached to them. Relationships in meaning systems are unique. For example, there is no particular reason why the word bus should refer to an ambulance. However, when an organization agrees upon certain relationships between these variables it becomes embedded in the culture and is hard to change. Language, labels, and slang are perhaps the most formal of meaning systems. Similarity certain behaviors also gain meaning like using an automatic blood pressure cuff verses a manual cuff, or walking patients verses placing them on a gurney. All of these complex meaning systems become part of a complex and established system of meaning that influences the **organizational culture**. Another example is that many EMS organizations allow or do not discourage the use of derogatory terms for certain types of patients such as *troll* or *gomer*, which dehumanizes the patient or is the result of an emergency response to a social, mental, or chronic health problem for which they do not have the solutions.

Leaders and managers often set the stage for culture by establishing the mission, vision, and goals that give the organization direction. Given their position of authority, leaders are often able to influence the organization's culture; they have the ability to ensure that the founder's vision is passed on to future generations (e.g., they may be responsible for socializing new employees). Leaders also can use their power to change organizational culture by creating new mission statements, new visions, and new goals. Leaders must often do just that in response to changing economic conditions. Because the culture can facilitate or inhibit the organization's performance, the leaders role in shaping and transmitting the culture is an important one.

DEFINING THE ORGANIZATION—

Leaders are responsible for creating change in the organization. A mission statement is designed to turn an agency's vision into practice. The mission statement is the one that will actually do the work. A mission statement should be actionable and not considered to be a job that cannot be done. The mission is the doing part and is what the agency will do to bring that vision to reality. It is powerful to talk about QI and what you will do. It is more powerful to talk about it in the context of why you are doing that work to achieve quality in the organization.

VISION STATEMENT

A QI team and an organization must have a vision. A vision statement is a statement of what is possible; it is the picture of the future that the QI team wants to create. The critical questions for an EMS organization are "To whom does the vision apply?" and "What will be affected?" The EMS organization's ability to accomplish a certain level of service for the community should be reflected in the agency's mission statement. The answers to the preceding questions must be that your organization's vision is for the future that you want to create for the community, process, or that part of emergency services you wish to affect.

> **Side Bar**
>
> **Vision**
>
> An effective vision statement will tell the world what change you wish to create for the future of your community.
>
> Our vision is a community where ________.
>
> Our vision is a community that ________.

An EMS agency is all about serving communities. An organization's vision statement is the picture of the future you want for the organization. In a for-profit company, that definition of a vision statement identifies what a company is meant to do. For example, providing quality medical transportation may be part of the EMS organization's mission statement. When the purpose of an organization is community service, its vision must be for the community, not for itself. Creating significant improvement in our communities is what the vision should be about. Exactly what the agency wants its vision to be should be wrapped around care and quality. The dream of our communities should be for the highest potential for quality emergency services.

As you create an agency's mission statement consider starting with your vision statement as the lead-in to your mission statement:

> Our vision is an EMS agency where ______________. To bring that vision into reality, we ______________________.

MISSION STATEMENT

To expand on the practical part of your mission statement, you might add where you do your work, and for whom, to further describe what you do:

> Our vision is an organization where _______________. To bring that vision into reality, we _______________ for _______________ in the _______________ (region/area/township/etc.).

Mission statements should not be overblown or impossible to accomplish. A mission statement for a particular QI initiative should reflect the actual work or project goal. Making an accurate mission statement should take little time and effort. If it is taking a committee 6 months to rewrite a mission statement, the result is likely to be poor. Keep it simple and to the point. (See Figure 9.1.)

> The Memphis Fire Department Quality Improvement Program is dedicated to both the employee and the citizens that we serve. We will strive to identify areas within the Department, policies, protocols and overall patient care processes that require modification, changes, training and/or remediation so that we continually strive to provide the best resources to the employee and the citizens that we serve.
>
> This mission is only accomplished by the support, guidance and feedback by all employees of the Memphis Fire Department. And we will accomplish these goals by receiving active support from the Command Staff, Medical Director, QI Coordinator, B/C's, Lieutenants, and all field personnel

FIGURE 9.1 Memphis Fire Department mission statement. *Source: "Memphis Mission Statement" from Memphis Fire Department. Copyright © by City of Memphis. Used by Permission of City of Memphis.*

VALUES STATEMENT

Whether effective or ineffective, mission statements and vision statements are relatively common to EMS agencies, but that is where most organizations stop. Vision and mission statements indicate where a particular organization is headed, and what the personnel will do to get there. It is the rare organization that takes the time to then define how they will do that work.

The only way an agency can achieve a remarkable culture of quality in EMS for a community is if the work is done in a way that reflects the universally shared values defined by a well developed mission, vision and **values statement** that represents the community's values and culture. This ensures that valuable staff time and resources are not squandered in rationalizing QI actions. It helps to ensure that an agency is not potentially eroding or losing the public trust. If the goal is to create a future EMS operation, then the EMS manager will want to ensure that the work reflects the values desired by the EMS organization and seen in the QI initiative.

A values statement provides the tools for the organization to accomplish that. First, the values statement will look outside the organization to establish and scan the environment to move toward a visionary outcome that leadership may want to create for the EMS organization and/or the quality processes. The following are some questions that help narrow the vision into a more concise statement:

- What values will be needed in the EMS agency's management team or the QI team for the agency or QI team's vision to come to pass?
- What values must the organization emphasize to make the QI team successful? What values would have to be the norm?

An organization's values statement must look within the organization to see how the management team's approach will model those values. A values statement must allow QI teams and educators to teach those values or demonstrate by example. This can only be done if there is a clear definition and concise statement of the values of the organization or QI team that can be translated into actions:

- How will your work reflect those values?
- How will you ensure you are modeling those values to the community and the staff?

- When you have a tough decision to make on quality, will you always err on the side of those values?
- Fill in the blank: We always want the community to be able to say _________ about the way we provide EMS.

Most EMS and QI programs never talk about how issues of quality relate to the overall values of the organization or the work group. A few organizations or QI teams often simply designate a list of core values or have a single values statement to complement their mission and vision statements. It is important to ensure that mechanisms for ensuring the stated values are used in their work. There should be a way of translating beliefs into decisions that a team will be involved with as part of a QI process and the actions they take every day. That is the power of what a values statement can do. It tells the world outside and inside the organization what the organization believes and how it acts, but it can also provide the tools for measuring whether or not the organization is indeed walking its talk or operating with integrity.

When the organization or the QI team begins talking with organizations about creating a values statement, management can get mixed reactions. One of the most common reactions is "We don't need this. We already know what our values are." When we ask a few key questions, though, it becomes clear that although everyone on the board believes they have a shared core of values, in fact each member simply believes that everyone has shared similar values. One of the other common reactions when the issue of values is raised is that a discussion of the values becomes little more than a checkbox with no practical application to the work that the organization does. The truth is directly opposite, emergency service agencies face values-based dilemmas daily during operations and on almost every call. A values-based decision must be made any time that a crew or QI team is faced with the question of "What is important here?" Any discussion that focuses on the question "What's more important—this or that?" is a discussion of values. And without prior discussion of what values will guide decisions, each of these discussions has no context for the decision.

All these issues are important reasons for addressing core values in the form of a formal statement. If an EMS organization is absent a set of core values for decision making, groups are more likely to default to fear-based decision making, which goes directly against eliminating the culture of fear in EMS when it comes to QI. And had we talked about those fear-based decisions first, it is likely we would have crossed the very lines we thought we could not cross. The only defense against making fear-based decisions or having QI processes go down the wrong path is to have a discussion about core values ahead of time. A values statement will start with your vision and mission, and will then talk about how you will ensure that work is done to model the behaviors you want to see in the community.

Side Bar

Normalization of Deviance

The *Challenger* tragedy is a hallmark case in normalization of deviance. Under tremendous schedule and budget pressures and over multiple launches, the NASA team accepted a lower standard of performance on the solid rocket booster O-rings until that lower standard became the norm. At the time of the *Challenger* disaster, the NASA team had become so comfortable with seeing occasional O-ring damage and getting away with it that the original standard, in which *any* O-ring damage was defined as intolerable, was marginalized. Some engineers had a gut feeling that an O-ring disaster loomed, but management refused to react to instincts. EMS managers should investigate instinctual fears to determine if, in fact, they are rooted in reality. Although the *Challenger* was a disaster in front of the world, the same thinking and culture have the potential to create the same disaster on a personal level with every patient.

ORGANIZATIONAL ALIGNMENT —

Once the leadership has determined the mission and vision statements that are necessary to direct the organization toward a level of quality, the hard work of alignment begins. The process of aligning the resources of the department or agency should be given just as much consideration as setting the direction of the organization's quality initiative. Often, the biggest challenge is to align the people in the organization.

Alignment is the state of agreement and cooperation between persons, groups, and divisions with a common cause and viewpoint. Although an EMS division may have great mission, vision, and values statements at the department level, the overarching organization (e.g., a county government) must also be in alignment with those mission, vision, and values statements. Alignment occurs when context, strategy, people, structure, processes, and leadership uniformly line up with the vision of the organization.

Assessing and aligning an organization with a QI program and the vision and mission of the organization require a step-by-step process. First, you must study the context of the research or quality initiative, understanding every aspect of the environment that could affect the purpose. Has the hospital been consulted? Are employee labor groups aware of the impact a QI program will have?

Embracing change and developing a culture of change create an expectation of alignment activities. There are many change management models, and any program is acceptable as long it is planned for and used. Instituting organizational change that deals with values and mission is a critical step in the process that can be the root of failure in an alignment process. For example, implementing a process too quickly may be disruptive or result in a critical step being overlooked. Implement too slowly, and the perception may be that the program is not viable.

QI initiatives must cross the social barriers connecting the community and the organization. The community is made up of both internal and external customers who are immersed or will be in the QI initiatives. The people affected by a QI program must become aligned with the mission and vision of the program.

The mechanics of a QI program require development and statistical changes to be selected from a vast amount of data and QI tools that are available. Choose a strategy for changing processes and make or employ a technology adjustment (e.g., new fields in an electronic patient care report). A variety of processes and programs can be used to make changes in quality. It is important to identify those as among the processes that must be brought into alignment.

Flexing the structures of the organization is required for alignment. The core of a QI program has always been structure and process equals outcome. Structural changes may be as simple as adding or subtracting staff members, or they may be more complex, requiring changes in leadership. Realigning people into a QI team or replacing ineffective or poor leadership are changes that may need to be made in the process. The right people in the right positions, and adjusting or aligning organizational leadership, are key to the success of any QI project.

Identifying core purposes and empowering leadership to reinforce those values are important in bringing all the parts into context with the mission. Measure core values by monitoring performance and reporting back changes to help establish the brand of the quality initiative. Establishment of the QI processes brand is necessary to establish the recognition that the culture, mission, vision, and goals of the QI program have achieved alignment.

BRANDING

A brand as it relates to an EMS quality initiative is the entire experience personnel and patients have with an EMS agency. It is what the agency's QI program or projects stand for, a promise made to the community or the personnel, and the culture the agency conveys. For example, becoming a "Heart Safe Community" as part of a QI effort to raise cardiac arrest survival awareness in the community or the organization is a way to brand a QI process. Although it may include a program name, creative elements such as caricatures, color palette, logos, and slogans also convey the brand of a QI project. The brand lives in every day-to-day interaction with EMS providers and patients:

- Images the program conveys
- Messages delivered on the agency's website
- Interaction between EMS personnel and customers
- Customer opinion of the service or programs

Branding is crucial for the success of a program. It is also important to brand a program because it helps QI stand out from other programs. It positions the QI programs as a certain "something" in the mind of your personnel, stakeholders, and patients. Your brand consistently and repeatedly tells your staff and patients why and what the QI program is trying to achieve. If you want to bring significant attention to the goals of a QI initiative, start with a strong and unique brand identity for the QI program. It is important that QI become a management approach, not just a department or people. Building distinctive relationships with employees and patients is what branding is about. Some important tasks to consider include the following:

- List the features and benefits of the QI program/initiative. A feature is an outcome, a configuration or process, or key personnel.
- Determine which benefits are most important to each of the people involved.
- Identify which benefits are emotional. The most powerful brand strategies tap into emotions of the people, such as successes with cardiac arrest or STEMI survivors.
- Look at the emotional benefits and boil them down to one thing that the stakeholders should think of when they think of this particular QI program. That is what the agency brand should represent.

A corporate brand stands for the relationship that an organization has with its personnel, as much as it represents the relationship that it has with the patients or the stakeholders through its patient care and services offered. For a brand to come to life with customers, the organization must be internally aligned to deliver a promise of a level of quality through the organization's culture, reward systems, key success activities, and structure. Personnel must live the brand values in their day-to-day interactions. EMS management must demonstrate its commitment to these values through behavior and agency communications, demonstrating sincerity—not just rhetoric. Benchmark EMS agencies signal their commitment to their declared brand values in various ways:

- They effectively use internal communications to raise personnel morale and commitment through shared beliefs and vision.
- They provide managers and staff a deeper understanding of the brand promise and the behaviors and values the promise demands and train them to adapt their behavior.

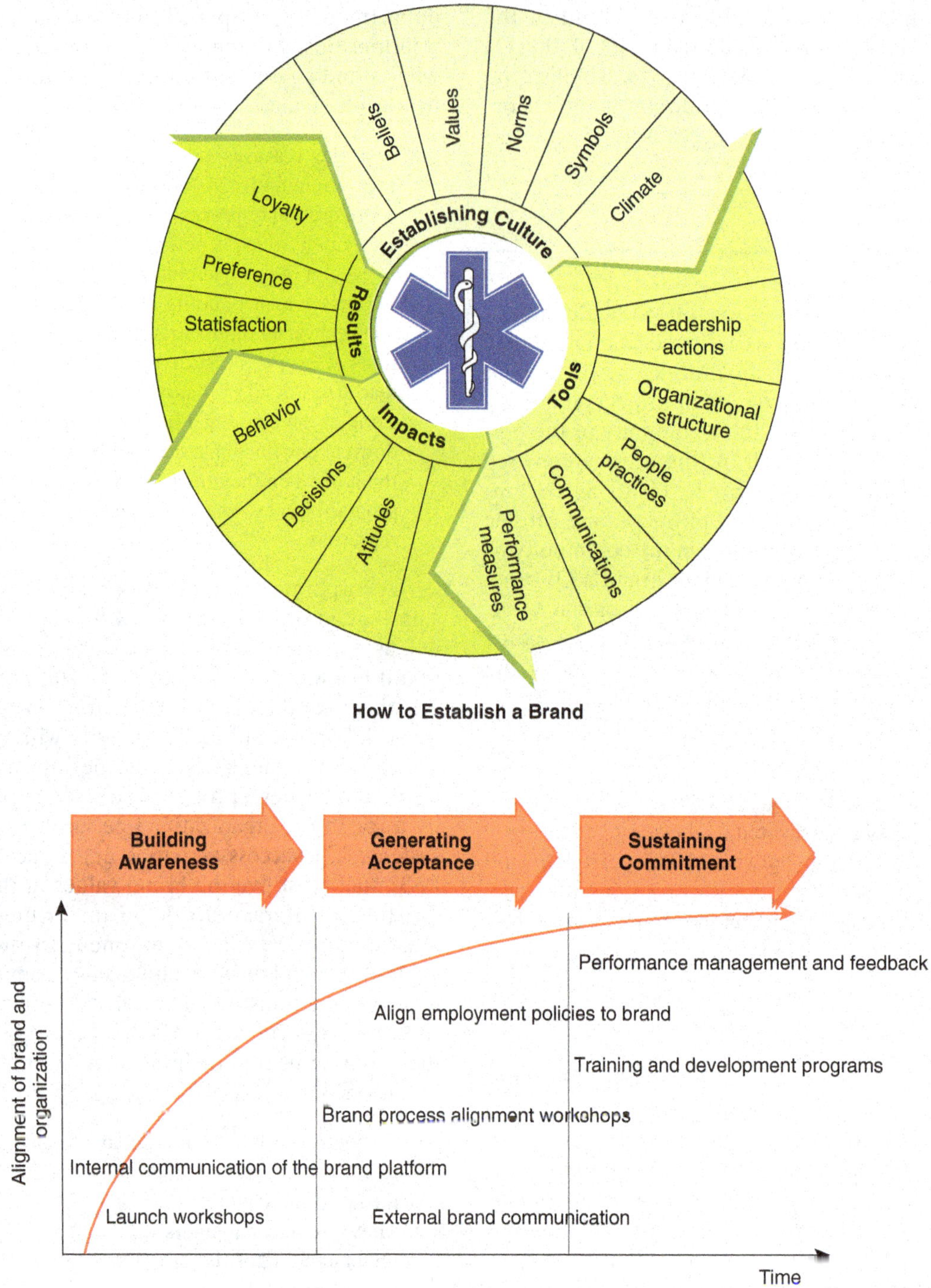

FIGURE 9.2 ■ How to establish a brand.

Best Practice

Medic One

Nowhere is the brand of EMS more significant than in the Seattle and King County MedicOne programs. Most of the brand loyalty comes from an effective campaign to treat cardiac emergencies. The MedicOne system promotes good CPR, rapid BLS, and clinically competent ALS. The MedicOne Foundation also tracks cardiac arrest and STEMI survivors during and after their hospital stay. On the anniversary of their event and until their passing, survivors are called and followed up. The patients are tracked and provided ongoing information about cardiac disease. The community is acutely aware of the capabilities and goals of the MedicOne system in maintaining one of the highest levels of cardiac arrest in the United States.

- They enable all personnel to understand how their own work processes and responsibilities contribute to delivering the brand promise to customers.
- They change agency policies (e.g., recruitment, training, rewards) so that the organization is behaving in line with its brand promise.

The cover diagram shows how the alignment process works to deliver a strong brand performance. (See Figure 9.2.) When personnel understand and accept that the values are genuine, they align their attitudes and behavior to the brand values. The result is greater satisfaction for both patients and personnel, leading to personnel and patient preference and loyalty.

CREATING THE CULTURE OF SERVICE

What do you think of when you hear the term **customer service**? Do you, the crews you have working on QI programs, and your field providers view your agency as a provider of services? Customer service is the ability to provide a service or product in the way that it has been promised. To understand the basic practices of customer service, we must understand the details of customer service and how that relates to EMS. We also must appreciate the fact that a patient who is ill or injured is not your typical customer. A patient does not have a choice or opportunity to shop around when calling for EMS. A patient is in his most vulnerable state when calling for EMS. EMS providers must be mindful of this, and although we recognize that patients are indeed customers, they are also often in a fragile state and require an up-close, empathetic, and personal approach, not an aggressive decision process in which they are not able to agree or disagree in the course of the events.

We put it all together by concentrating on a concept that has its roots in private industry and is well established in the business community. Companies known for their excellent products and services rely on their ability to capture and hold a market share. When it comes to creating quality, the personnel and management team must believe your agency and its QI processes are about the people and that it is a service industry.

ORIENTATION FOR CUSTOMER SERVICE

The public accesses EMS processes based on an emergency need, and rarely do they have a choice of provider. Because of the realities of EMS system design, providers and management tend to become complacent when it comes to marketing their services and striving to provide the best service on a consistent basis. When a new member arrives at an organization, a design should be in place to orient people to the mission, vision, and values statements of the organization and what the expectations are for customer service.

New hires should be informed of the tools management is using to monitor service, with an eye toward transitioning from data collection and analysis to the expectations of action points to ensure quality care. Often seen in the first pages of any EMS textbook is a picture of a uniformed EMT or paramedic in perfect attire, stethoscope around his neck, holding a blood pressure cuff with this caption: "A professional appearance inspires confidence." With the advent of customer care surveys, professional appearance does rank high. However, customer service practice goes deeper, into the caring and compassion provided to a customer.

Customer service is any contact, whether active or passive, between a customer and a company that causes a negative or positive perception by a customer. There has been a renewed interest in how the consumer wants or expects to be treated. The advent of electronic patient care reports and online survey systems, such as Zoomerang or SurveyMonkey, allow for member feedback from internal and external customers that is close to point of service and anonymous. Most EMS organizations can quickly measure quality service. Not only is it important to listen to what the customer wants, it is equally important to stay the course and reevaluate the agency's efforts to see if the EMS care is providing a change in outcomes and allows for change to keep up with the times.

So, how do you know what the public and personnel want or expect? First, you must define the customer. In the prehospital setting, our customers include, but are not limited to, the following:

- The patient
- The patient's family
- Supervisor
- Personnel
- Paramedic and EMTs
- Nurses
- Doctors
- Hospital clerical staff

EMS leadership, QI teams, and EMS providers must remember that in public and private service, anyone must be considered a customer. Service quality and conduct are being judged every day. We have come to realize that the public perception of what we do has long been identified with the media's portrayal of our profession.

From a public service perspective, stakeholders hold the provider agency or EMS program accountable under the pretext of the holders of the public trust. The public can demand change through the legislator or community council. Mergers or disbanding agencies can affect the provider's morale. For-profit companies can simply be dropped for an alternative service.

There are some simple principles of customer service that EMS providers should follow:

- Make everyone feel comfortable.
- Smile and introduce themselves.
- Be courteous and try to go the extra mile.
- Be professional and dress the part.

Always remember that the primary principle of a QI program is to handle patients with care. Imagine yourself in the situation faced by your patient and family. Respecting privacy is not only mandated but is also needed to maintain the confidence of the patient. It is the bedrock of any culture of quality.

IS EVERYTHING OKAY?

All EMS providers are also consumers of many types of service when it comes to QI. The key is to treat the patients entering into some aspect of the quality processes the way you expect you and your family to be treated. Certainly, open-ended questions may lead to verbose responses, and appropriate close-ended responses may be useful. Asking the patient/customer questions about the care and attention received will convey to him that you are concerned about his well-being. The following are examples of questions you might ask:

- Has the service met your expectations?
- Did you receive and understand the information given to you?
- Do you have any questions about the care you have received or will receive?

MANNERISMS AND NONVERBAL COMMUNICATION

If you dial 9-1-1 and receive services from EMS but an error is made, it is believed that this was not intentional. If an error is identified and brought to the attention of the EMS provider, who responds, in an apathetic tone, "See the EMS supervisor," this becomes a QI event. Either the experience becomes representative of quality or the sequence of the contact with the EMS manager starts the QI cycle, and the process will be measured. The other option is to continue to be enraged that this mistake occurred and could not be rectified by the provider. What kind of messages do we send with our actions, and not our words? Does your body language exude confidence and a general interest in what you are doing, or does your body tell the patient that his emergency is a nuisance in your day?

SERVANT LEADERSHIP

Often the level of quality and the delivery of EMS are reflective of the leadership of the organization. A term for this, **servant leadership**, was first coined in 1970 by Robert Greenleaf. Servant leadership is necessary for the delivery of quality: EMS leaders must demonstrate that they serve the line EMT or paramedic and determine the needs of the organization.

The servant leader is servant first, which begins with the natural feeling that one wants to serve. Following the desire to serve may be a conscious choice that brings one to aspire to lead. The leader-first and the servant-first are two extreme types of leaders, with the servant-first leader making sure other people's highest-priority needs are being served. Much of servant leadership is based on the concept of **agapao**, which refers to a moral love, or doing the right thing at the right time for the right reason. More specifically, agapao means to love in a social or moral sense, embracing the judgment and deliberate assent of the will as a matter of principle, duty, and propriety. The basis for agapao love is to consider each member or follower as a total person with needs, wants, and desires. In demonstrating agapao love, the leader focuses on the member first, the talents of the member second, and the benefit to the organization third.

APPROPRIATE EVALUATION OF ADVERSE EVENTS AND DISCIPLINE

A thorough and appropriate evaluation of adverse events is necessary to help prevent future occurrences. Actions taken in response to adverse events can be administrative or disciplinary, as well as safety related. These actions must not only be fair—they must be perceived to be fair; otherwise, future reporting of events may be discouraged. Such an approach is consistent with a culture of safety and is symbolic of a just culture. A just culture is not wholly blame free. There are tools and techniques that can help organizations examine an adverse event and determine if disciplinary action is appropriate. Blameless acts are particularly important sources of information about system vulnerabilities. Understanding how blameless (as well as blameworthy) acts and weak defenses interact to result in an adverse event is a vital part of the learning an organization should gain following an adverse event investigation.

Edward Deming was the father of modern QI and the creator of the Plan-Do-Check-Act cycle. Deming's focus was to improve the system. Deming estimated that 95 percent of defects are system/process related. EMS still assumes that the provider's actions are to blame for the majority of error or poor quality. Often, there is a lot of talk about nonpunitive actions or fixing quality issues with education; however, the coaching or counseling of a member without fixing the problem is often seen as punishment.

JUST CULTURE

Patient safety and quality dominate the discussion on values in an organization pursuing quality, but they cannot be the agency's only values. In the delivery of health care, the complex interaction of diagnostics, protocols, and treatments of a variety of injuries or illnesses exposes the patient to an imperfect system. A machine cannot get fatigued, forgetful, distracted, rushed, or bored. People, on the other hand, are susceptible to multiple opportunities from the influences of many factors to make an error. Robust systems that operate in high-risk industries expect or predict human variability in critical circumstances. Organizations should have a transparent and equitable disciplinary process that takes into account personal responsibility and accountability. Just culture refers to a values-supportive model of shared accountability. It is a culture that holds organizations accountable for the systems they design and for how they respond to staff behavior in a fair and just manner. EMS providers in this environment are accountable for the quality of their choices and for reporting both their errors and system vulnerabilities. Just culture is not protection of incompetent or misbehaving team members. It assumes that personnel understand they have a duty to act, to follow procedural rules, and to avoid causing unjustified risk.

Side Bar

Terminating or failing to support an employee who self-reported an adverse event is not a principle of just culture. The National Quality Forum Safe Practices includes "Care of the Caregiver" to address respectful and compassionate support of health care providers involved in serious unintentional harm and tp use the providers first hand knowledge of the event to help identify the risk, determine the cause, or supply ideas to mitigate activities to avoid a repeat event. In EMS, self-reported errors should not be subject to discipline unless they involve reckless or deviant behavior.

The inconsistent application of just culture policies are noticed by field crews and are correctly interpreted as only paying lip service to patient quality and safety. Therefore, a systematic approach to responding to certain behaviors is a key factor in ensuring a just culture. A provider may injure a patient, yet a root cause analysis of the situation shows that it was the organization's equipment, processes, systems, or work environment, not the member, at fault. Just culture recognizes three different types of human behavior—human error, at-risk behavior, and **reckless behavior**—that can be categorized when diagnosing errors in human performance. A consistent and appropriate response by the QI team or the EMS leadership is paramount to maintaining and establishing a just culture. It requires that the leadership facilitate the ability to console human error, coach at-risk behavior, and punish reckless behavior.

HUMAN ERROR

Generally, problems caused by humans are classified as *human error*, but this term is too broad. To be more specific, **human error** is inadvertently doing other than what should have been done. When human error occurs, the response is to console the person who made the mistake, but it is also important to help people make better choices. Consider redesigning the system or managing the risk. Examining the human error rate through review of reports, audits, and near misses can help a QI and management team improve the system.

AT-RISK BEHAVIOR

Certain aspects of EMS operations are prone to at-risk behavior. For example, failing to take a complete set of vital signs, failing to wear a seat belt, or failing to confirm a medicine dose with another provider all can be at-risk behavior. At-risk behavior is a choice that increases risk when the risk is not recognized or is mistakenly accepted as justified. The concept of normalization of deviance employs at-risk behavior. At-risk behavior requires a counseling or coaching response and for the QI team to examine more closely the choices that were made in the behavior. This also requires removing the barriers to following the rules or promoting incentives. It is important to examine the norms with both the individual and the group determining what role these may have played in the choices that led to at-risk behavior. Punishing at-risk behavior only serves to drive self-reporting underground, with errors reported only when they cannot be hidden.

RECKLESS BEHAVIOR

Reckless behavior is consciously choosing to disregard rules or procedures that can have a substantial and unjustifiable risk. The response should be to discipline the person who knowingly disregards the process or procedure, regardless of the outcome. Again, discipline should be consistent and evenly applied. The QI team and EMS leadership should be intolerant of reckless behavior, such as restraining a patient facedown or running a red light when responding to an emergency.

Expecting perfection in patient care through a just culture has a price and requires effort and consistency. It starts with understanding the value, setting expectations to align those values, and designing robust systems so it enables personnel involved with quality initiatives to make the right choice. Just culture is about good design of processes and people. (See Figure 9.3.)

The response to an event or a near miss is tied to the mechanism of error. An isolated human error is an opportunity to correct a system weakness. Repetitive problems are often caused by system weakness but sometimes are individual performance issues, particularly when coaching or additional training has not improved the problem. For example, repetitive human errors may be an indication that the individual is not capable of safely performing his job. Repetitive at-risk behaviors may be due to impairment (e.g., drug abuse) or unwillingness to follow proper procedures.

COMMON CULTURE ERRORS

In EMS, there is a group of common practices which indicate that the culture may be a barrier to quality and must be adjusted. **Search satisfying** occurs when an agency or QI committee stops looking for reason for failures once something is found. **Cherry picking** is a condition in which the team explains away things once the decision is made by focusing on item(s) that indicate an acceptable outcome, ignoring the indicators of error. The crew continues to move down the path, even though in error. An **attribution error** occurs when the crew becomes judgmental and blames the patient for his

Human Error	At-Risk Behavior	Reckless Behavior
Product of our current system design and behavioral choices	*A Choice: Risk believed insignificant or justified*	*Conscious disregard of substantial and unjustifiable risk*
Manage through changes in: • Choices • Processes • Procedures • Training • Design • Environment	Manage through: • Removing incentives for at-risk behaviors • Creating incentives for healthy behaviors • Increasing situational awareness	Manage through: • Remedial action • Punitive action
Console	Coach	Punish

FIGURE 9.3 ■ Just culture in EMS QI.

condition, inferring that the actions of the patient were responsible for the condition.

An EMS field supervisor welcoming complaints or opportunities to intercede before a situation results in a formal complaint may turn a negative situation into a positive. The supervisor must connect with the customer in the same manner as the provider. When faced with the unhappy customer, the supervisor should correct the situation at hand and then work with the complainant to identify the root cause of the circumstance. It is important to determine if the problem was personal (individual based) or procedural (agency based). Having complainants involved empowers them, and they are likely to have an enhanced opinion of the service controls. This becomes a sentinel event for assessing quality and acting as an indicator of whether the culture and values of the organization are being upheld.

Remember, as an agency or regional leader or manager, the EMS provider is one of your "customers." In this relationship, feedback to the provider is necessary for successful customer service. Negative feedback should be given at appropriate times and never in front of the patient/customer. Telling the patient/customer that the employee is wrong without investigation will damage the relationship between the provider and supervisor.

MOTIVATION TO ADOPT CULTURAL CHANGE

It is important to understand how staff members expected to carry out quality activities are motivated. In one of Deming's fourteen points, it is noted that leadership must remove barriers that rob people of their right to pride of workmanship. Each generation of personnel has unique characteristics and ways in which it receives and processes information. When approaching culture change, how that message is conveyed is dependent on the generation to which employees belong.

The silent generation chooses formality over informality, often calling EMS managers and leaders by titles and surnames. They communicate face to face or on a regular telephone, rather than by electronic forms of communication, such as email or text messaging. They often ask for things to be explained logically to them and respond to traditional forms of recognition, such as plaques, awards, or pictures with their boss or supervisor.

Baby boomers are goal oriented and take steps to achieve those goals. Boomers state objectives in people-centered terms, and they look to engage in activities where successful positive attitudes are found and focus their efforts on those ideas and beliefs. They respond to inspirational speeches and function well in most team-centered activities. Boomers see widespread recognition from newsletters or press releases as an incentive.

Generation Xers need a leadership style that does not micromanage. Xers will operate with little instruction, once told what must get done and when. They are great at multitasking. For this group, provide frequent feedback, keep the work environment fun, and ask for their opinions and reactions. Free time or additional time off is the best motivator for Generation X.

Generation Y workers must be constantly challenged with continuous learning and building skills. Know their personal goals and try to match up tasks with those goals. They respond best to coaching and upbeat messages through informal routes of communication (Lindsey, 2005).

To sum it up, the EMS and QI managers' approach to building bridges across generational gaps to maintain a culture of quality in the organization involves an ongoing conversation, asking "What can I do for you?" and sharing "What I need from you. . . ." EMS managers will always have a bias, and it is important not to let those biases turn into prejudices. The rewards of doing so are enormous. It starts with analysis of the job and creation of a sound job description.

RECOGNITION

Too often, the QI team and EMS management try to change culture by describing the vision and desired behaviors that would align the two together. Frequently, the actions do not match the words due to the lack of rewards tied to the goals and objectives. Having a way of knowing how well the QI project is progressing and how the provider's performance is impacting that project is important.

Reward systems should recognize achievement. Although the work of Alfie Kohn (1992, 1993) indicates that incentives can corrupt QI processes, recognition of a member making change is a powerful tool for quality activities. It is equally important that personnel have some input in designing or establishing a recognition process in order to highlight outstanding customer service activity. This recognition is important to tell everyone that it is not okay just to have a customer service or QI initiative, but it is in your mission to meet that objective.

REWARD PROGRAMS

Each agency must create a system of rewards and recognition programs. Although rewards and recognition rank behind having input and being part of the decision-making process, they are still powerful motivators. Agencies should create a variety of reward programs to complement their quality processes. Some specific rewards for individual EMS providers include having delivered a baby or having participated in the successful resuscitation of a cardiac arrest.

EMS Week

EMS Week is held each year, typically in May. It is promoted through the American College of Emergency Physicians (ACEP) and the National Association of EMTs. It is an ideal time to have a survivors' reunion or recognition, BBQ, or banquet to promote the results of the QI processes and highlight what matters most. It reinforces the human piece to the process and provides a date to launch or reset quality improvement initiatives.

It is also important to create an annual report to the public. Annual results of QI programs should be published in pamphlet form or, more economically, in newspaper format. This should also highlight EMS providers and report response times and other key processes that define the department's performance.

NATIONAL AWARDS

A number of EMS awards from national organizations are available. However, no specific awards are known to exist solely for the recognition of excellence in QI. Awards for management teams, providers, and agencies can encompass QI activities as a reason for the award in a more general category. There are also research awards given through the Prehospital Care Research Forum and the Prehospital Care Research Summit that directly relate to QI activities. Despite the lack of a specific award for QI activities, an agency should pursue national awards. Often, competition for outside awards rallies the staff, reduces internal conflict, and establishes a target for the organization. Once an award is secured, living up to the symbolism of the award helps change culture.

Malcolm Baldrige National Quality Award

The highest award for quality in the United States is the Malcolm Baldrige National Quality Award. The award is named after the former Secretary of Commerce and is awarded by the president of the United States. It is given to four organizations from industries representing manufacturing, health care, education, and/or service. The award is managed by the U.S. Department of Commerce's National Institute of Standards and Technology. Similar quality awards are offered by state governments based on the Baldrige QI criteria. The Baldrige QI criterion are organized according to the seven categories displayed in Figure 9.4.

- Leadership involves efforts by senior leadership and management leading by example to integrate QI into the strategic planning process and throughout the entire organization and to promote quality values and QI techniques in work practices.
- Information and analysis concerns managing and using the data needed for effective QI. Since quality improvement is based on management by fact, information and analyses are critical to QI success.
- Strategic quality planning involves three major components: (1) developing long- and short-term organizational objectives for structural, performance, and outcome quality standards; (2) identifying ways to achieve those objectives; and (3) measuring the effectiveness of the system in achieving quality standards.
- Human resource development and management involves working to develop the full potential of the EMS workforce. This effort is guided by the principle that the entire EMS workforce is motivated to achieve new levels of service and value.
- EMS process management concerns the creation and maintenance of high-quality services. Within the context of quality improvement, process management refers to the improvement of work activities and work flow *across* functional or department boundaries.
- EMS system results entails assessing the quality results achieved and examining the organization's success at achieving quality improvement.
- Satisfaction of patients and other stakeholders involves ensuring ongoing satisfaction by those internal and external to the EMS system with the services provided.

FIGURE 9.4 Seven Baldrige categories for health care organizations. *Source: Text compiled by author from U.S. Department of Commerce, National Institute of Standards and Technology, www.nist.gov/baldrige/publications/criteria.cfm*

Health care organizations that follow the Baldrige program have the option of asking for an external review of their progress. The benefits gained by simply applying the Baldrige guidelines and recommendations include improvements in service and patient care delivery, economic efficiency and/or profitability, patient and community satisfaction and loyalty, and health outcomes.

Side Bar

For more information regarding the Malcolm Baldrige National Quality Award, contact the National Institute of Standards and Technology.

NAEMT Awards

The National Association of EMTs (NAEMT) bestows several awards, including separate awards for EMT, Paramedic, Educator, and EMS Executive of the Year. In addition to individual awards, the Dick Ferneau Paid EMS Service of the Year award recognizes outstanding performance by a paid EMS service, and the Impact Volunteer EMS Service of the Year award recognizes outstanding performance by a volunteer EMS service. The most prestigious award granted by NAEMT is the Rocco V. Morando Lifetime Achievement Award, sponsored by the National Registry of Emergency Medical Technicians. Applications are not accepted for this award; rather, an outstanding professional working in the field of EMS is chosen. In all of these awards, QI can be or should be a part of the award process; however, recipients are chosen based on consensus.

Canadian EMS Award

In 2011, the Canadian EMS Chiefs created the Award of Excellence for a Quality Workplace Strategy for any person or team involved in emergency medical services in Canada, or for a process, method, or program that shows extraordinary achievement in creating a quality workplace strategy within the last 3 years. It is one of the most comprehensive assessments, using objective grading criteria. All submissions should address how the initiative creates a quality workplace.

The work environment consists of social, physical, and technical components. Because each component affects the other, all must be taken into consideration simultaneously, along with the financial effects, to create a cohesive plan. The program's implementation should define service quality indicators to measure efficacy. The submission also must explain actions taken to ensure sustainability of the initiative. In addition, the submission should demonstrate that all the partners were involved and describe any shared contributions that add to the success of the initiative. Points are awarded based upon the number of partners and the depth of their contribution to the project.

The submission or award winner should demonstrate the potential for the initiative to make a positive impact on creating a quality workplace. There are many ways that this can be accomplished and measured; some are more qualitatively defined than objective and numerically based. At the core of this criterion are assessment of value/return on investment, effect on the workplace, and effect on operations. The submission should state how the project is innovative or progressive. The project is required to clearly demonstrate elements of progressiveness and innovation in advancing the development of best practices in creating a quality workplace.

STATE EMS AWARDS

Almost all fifty states, and U.S. territories, have state-sponsored EMS awards. In most of the state EMS systems, the awards are ALS and BLS providers or EMS agency of the year. Only a few states recognize quality efforts in EMS. The state of Oregon is one, with the Commitment to Quality Medal honor given to an EMS system or individual EMS agency, or subunit of an EMS agency, that has demonstrated commitment to the principles of QI, customer service, and excellence in EMS. To maintain the integrity of the award, it is not given every year. It is bestowed only when a worthy candidate or agency is verified to meet the requirements. A statewide system to support quality programs would be an excellent addition to any state EMS award systems.

EMS INNOVATORS AWARDS

The EMS 10: Innovators in EMS initiative was created and sponsored by JEMS/Elsevier Public Safety and Physio-Control Inc. to recognize ten individuals who have earned the respect of their colleagues and often taken great risks to advance the art and science of prehospital emergency care. Started in 2008, the award recognizes ten individuals who have progressive ideas that are recognized at the EMS Today Conference and whose efforts are an inspiration and a challenge to the rest of the EMS community.

HIGHLY RELIABLE ORGANIZATIONS

The concept of a **highly reliable organization** relies on human culture and interactions for flexibility when there is uncertainty about how to proceed with a process and when there is time dependency. The choices EMS providers make are dependent on how reliable they believe the QI and support system are. A highly reliable organization can be defined as an organization that has fewer accidents than is normal. This occurs in most EMS and emergency service operations. High reliability is a culture that is built on values, beliefs, and behaviors.

A highly reliable organization has five characteristics. First, it has in place a system of ongoing audits that recognize anticipated problems as well as unexpected ones. Second, it has a reward system that encourages desired behaviors, rather than focusing on punishment. Third, it ensures quality by maintaining the essential quality of the system. This involves constant evaluation of performance, its capabilities, and its goals. Fourth, there is a perception of risk as well as knowledge of how that risk is mitigated. Fifth, the organization has command and control systems in place that place decisions in the hands of the most experienced person, regardless of rank. The command and control system also has redundancy built into systems, with strong situational awareness and rules that allow for flexibility. This results from training that focuses on common objectives and collective behavior.

BUILDING ORGANIZATIONAL RELIABILITY

Building on top of solid QI processes, an organization can become a highly reliable organization by employing certain processes. Culture is the foundation for the vision and strategy for high reliability. Transparency is key to changing the culture of an organization in order to move toward a highly reliable environment.

CHAPTER REVIEW

Summary

Once the mechanical aspect of QI has been constructed, it is time to move beyond charts and graphs and look to ensure that the alignment of the organization with the QI initiative can be accomplished. The organization's mission and vision statements and values must be linked to QI. Fostering quality has its roots in customer service, and establishing processes to focus on customer service helps align employees with quality initiatives. Personnel are internal customers and integrate best with a culture of quality when a just culture exists. A just culture helps build a highly reliable organization. Proper rewards, and management focused on people by addressing behavior and motivation issues with servant leadership, help maintain a highly reliable organization and lead to quality.

WHAT WOULD YOU DO? Reflection

An event that is created by the lack of an assessment and complete set of vital signs displays the phenomenon of normalization of deviance and the frustration of routine medical calls that involve intoxicated patients in a high-volume district. Not completing a thorough patient assessment on every patient is another example of normalization of deviance. The actions of a field crew that create a bad outcome often indicate that the people and processes of the organization are not aligned with the mission and values statement of the organization.

Bias is easily created, and although alcohol is a frequent issue, the multiple drug overdoses, the high risk for closed head injury, and/or a diabetic problem are all potential underlying issues that were never evaluated due to bias. Bias is overcome by education, orientation of new employees, reinforcement of messages, and using just culture to allow for review and learning without fear of reprisal.

Reliability is defined in the culture and mission relating it to customer service and a level of quality of care. An EMS organization must build a culture of service and align the mission with policies, procedures, and people who have beliefs and values that reflect the mission of quality and consistency of following procedures.

Review Questions

1. How do leaders translate the vision and mission of quality into day-to-day operations?
2. How can the Malcolm Baldrige National Quality Award help an organization become more effective?
3. Why is it important to translate the vision and mission into day-to-day operations?
4. What are the characteristics of a highly reliable organization?
5. What techniques can be employed to bring an organization into alignment with the mission and values set forth by the leadership?
6. What are the components of culture in an organization? How do these components relate to quality improvement?
7. Identify circumstances in your organization that may give rise to normalization of deviance.

References

Bigley, G. A., and K. H. Roberts. (2001, December). "The Incident Command System: High-Reliability Organizing for Complex and Volatile Task Environments." *Academy of Management Journal 14*(6), pp. 1281–1299.

Institute of Medicine. (1999). *To Err Is Human: Rebuilding a Safer Health System*. Washington, DC: National Academies Press.

Kohn, A. (1992). *No Contest: The Case Against Competition.* New York: Houghton Mifflin Harcourt.

Kohn, A. (1993, September). "Why Incentive Plans Cannot Work." *Harvard Business Review 71*(6), 42–43.

Lindsey, J. (2005). *Fire Service Instructor.* Upper Saddle River, NJ: Prentice Hall.

Patterson, K. A. (2003). "Servant Leadership: A Theoretical Model." Doctoral dissertation, Regent University, Virginia Beach, VA (UMI No. 3082719).

Russell, R. F. (2001). "The Role of Values in Servant Leadership." *Leadership & Organization Development Journal 22*(2), pp. 76–84.

Key Terms

agapao Refers to a moral love, doing the right thing at the right time for the right reason.

alignment The state of agreement and cooperation between persons, groups, and divisions with a common cause and viewpoint.

attitudes Manners, dispositions, feelings, or positions with regard to a person or thing that encompasses the tendency or orientation.

attribution error When the crew becomes judgmental and blames the patient's actions for his condition.

belief Principle, degree of conviction, or idea accepted as true.

cherry picking A condition of explaining away things once a decision is made by focusing on item(s) that are acceptable while ignoring the indicators of an error.

culture Pattern of artifacts, behaviors, values, beliefs, and underlying assumptions developed by a given group of people as they learn to cope with internal and external problems of survival and prosperity.

customer service Ability to provide a service or product in the way that it has been promised.

highly reliable organization An organization with fewer accidents than normal.

human error Inadvertently doing other than what should have been done.

just culture A culture in which people can report mistakes, errors, or waste without reprisal or personal risk.

mission statement Document designed to turn an agency's vision into action.

normalization of deviance Long-term phenomenon in which individuals or teams repeatedly accept a lower standard of performance until that lower standard becomes the "norm."

organizational culture Way in which people act and think.

reckless behavior A choice to consciously disregard rules or procedures, which can have substantial and unjustifiable risk.

search satisfying When an agency or QI committee stops looking for reason for failures once something is found.

servant leadership Leadership philosophy that actions taken by the leader are primarily intended to ensure that other people's highest-priority needs are being served.

values Those things regarded as having ultimate importance, significance, or worth.

values statement Document that starts with a vision and a mission, and then talks about work that will be done to model the desired behaviors.

vision statement Statement of what is possible for the future.

10 CHAPTER

Legal Considerations and Corrective Action

Objectives

After reading this chapter, the student should be able to:

10.1 Describe the types of legal and regulatory influences on the quality improvement process.
10.2 Identify existing statutes and laws from the various states outlining those processes that shall be utilized in the quality assurance process.
10.3 Identify the statutory protections for quality improvement processes protected from disclosure.
10.4 Outline the steps necessary for remediation and due process for quality improvement.
10.5 Explain the regulatory and legal structures for quality improvement.
10.6 Identify the legal process progress in the discovery phase and quality improvement issues related to civil litigation generally protected from discovery.
10.7 Discuss HIPAA events that indicate the need for discipline.
10.8 Identify the progression of a lawsuit and the responsibilities of an EMS manager in that process.

Key Terms

answer
authority have jurisdiction (AHJ)
briefs
contingency
counseling
counterclaims
declaratory judgment
defendant
deposition
discovery
due process
injunction
interrogatories
judgment

lawsuit
motion to dismiss
plaintiff
pleading
progressive discipline
proof of service
punitive damages
remediation
summary judgment
summons
Weingarten rights

WHAT WOULD YOU DO?

An EMS crew arrived at the scene of a hotel where the husband of a female patient stated that she was suicidal. After a brief discussion, the patient was determined to be awake, alert, and oriented to time, place, and event. Although the crew documented she had been drinking, the patient's story was that she had just had a fight with her husband and was not suicidal. The crew had the patient sign a release and then left the scene to some protest by the husband. The patient was left with her husband and hotel security. Twenty minutes later, the patient jumped from the twelfth story to her death.

The family filed a lawsuit, stating the crew was unprofessional and derelict in its duties. The call was captured by the QI team as all patient refusals are reviewed by the quality team in this organization. The quality team identified that the documentation of the patient "had been drinking" potentially disqualified the patient from being able to sign as a competent adult. Other seasoned providers on the quality team also noted that the patient was on antidepressants. Both of these elements were noted on a feedback form from the committee to the crew. No further action was taken to the crew as the release was signed and the patient met the criteria for being alert and oriented to time, place, event, and person with no obvious suicidal gesture.

The family continued to pursue the litigation. Several months later, a district court ruling absolved the EMS crew of responsibility, citing that the patient was competent to refuse care. The documentation was deemed adequate, meeting the orientation standard. The issues of alcohol and antidepressant therapy surfaced; however, those issues were not seen as key issues and were outweighed by the crew obtaining the refusal and documentation that the patient was oriented to date, time, and event.

Questions

1. How would the use of the quality team findings potentially affect this case?
2. What process was in place for risk management? What strategies were employed to avoid judgment or legal award?
3. What legal statutes, administrative rules, or regulations could be put in place to protect the organization and the crews, yet keep the patient protected medically within ethical constraints?

INTRODUCTION

Prehospital care is often administered in an uncontrolled environment and involves a considerable amount of uncertainty. It can result in loss; the pain and anguish experienced by a grieving family may prompt an attempt to place blame. That often places EMS in the legal arena, defending actions or simply providing documentation on a job well done, yet with a poor outcome. EMS lends itself to the public eye as patients are being treated and transported in view of the public or the family. Much of EMS is about taking care of people, and when a family member or patient is not addressed in a courteous and professional manner with protection of dignity, it can result in closer scrutiny of the call and a higher probability of a **lawsuit**.

Consider the patient who is being moved out of his home and is wheeled to the ambulance uncovered, where the neighbors watch as the patient's backside is hanging out. This immediately angers a family member. Later, an error in moving the patient or a misdiagnosis starts the legal process as the family was already upset about poor protection of the patient's dignity.

The best way to avoid litigation or a lawsuit is first be nice, then be competent. Errors will be made occasionally by every member of the staff, and as long as the crews are polite, respectful, and professional, the public and patient are often very forgiving. However, when a catastrophic outcome is the result of an injury or an illness—despite EMS following the exact procedures and processes—families may have no resources to care for a disabled person. Often, this triggers the litigation process as suing for damages is the only means possible for the family to survive.

Legal aspects of QI have a broad spectrum. They require EMS managers to understand where they stand in their state and jurisdiction in regard to protective QI processes, the authority or mandate to do QI, and what due process procedures may be required for the labor force. It is important to understand how a lawsuit progresses and what steps must be taken to manage litigation against an agency.

THE QI PROCESS LIABILITY

A QI coordinator or review committee commonly reviews and evaluates the professional medical competency of emergency medical technicians and paramedics under the jurisdiction of an organization or regulatory authority. In an EMS agency with a "just culture," a climate exists where errors are self-reported as a committee or coordinator cannot be aware of all processes and performance, especially in a busy urban EMS system. As information comes back to the organization, a cause is assigned and corrections are made. The cause may identify a problem with the system, a procedure, or the performance of an individual or crew. Most accreditation organizations require that a QI process identify causes and then tie them back to an education plan. Although education is often indicated, it is only a foundation to build upon versus first determining that processes and proper system design need priority. The quality assurance (QA) process must incorporate a feedback process. That information is then compiled at the system management level to determine if the standard set by the local EMS counsel or **authority having jurisdiction (AHJ)** has been met. If it has not been met, how will improvements in the response system be made?

> **Side Bar**
>
> **Ambulance Standards**
>
> The independent Commission on Accreditation of Ambulance Services (CAAS) established a comprehensive series of standards for the ambulance service industry. CAAS accreditation signifies that your service has met the "gold standard" determined by the ambulance industry to be essential in a modern EMS provider. These standards often exceed those established by state or local regulation. The CAAS standards are designed to increase operational efficiency and clinical quality while decreasing risk and liability to the organization.

PROTECTING THE PROCESS

We all wonder why we spend so much time reviewing our past performances and medical responses. Many times, we feel as providers that we did a great job taking care of that cardiac arrest, MVA, or slip and fall. We especially believe that when we respond to children or the elderly. We shine in our medical performance as the outcomes are generally good, the patient or family is thankful, and we feel as though we had a good shift. What we fail to realize is that although we may have done well, our colleagues may not be as well versed on those medical issues as we are, or we missed something on the elderly patient call because we went to the home at least ten times over the past month and all we wanted to do was to quickly treat and transport.

What could we have missed? It could have been the subdural hematoma that was making the elderly patient confused and possibly combative, marked down as an unknown change of behavior. It could have been the epiphyseal fracture in a young child who fell from her bicycle and complained of knee pain. It could have been the individual who slipped and fell in the grocery store and complained of elbow pain that we thought was a sprain and referred the patient to his personal physician.

What can we learn from these calls? Plenty—if we take the time to review these calls with a medical program director or through the efforts of a peer-driven QI committee in sessions that review the performance on the call. This is an important component in the improvement of quality EMS services and has a variety of names, but all mean the same thing. These sessions are also good for the recognition of outstanding performances and picking up the subtle signs of underlying injuries or disease, identifying a teaching point, and passing that knowledge on to other EMS providers. A quality and comprehensive quality review program in place within the organization or system may also contribute to preventing or mitigating a successful lawsuit.

Every type of business has QA programs—from the cars we drive, the food we eat, the computer software we use, or the airplanes in which we fly. We certainly feel safer when the airplane actually flies and lands without incident or the car starts out and arrives at a destination in good mechanical shape. Our patients feel the same way: They expect that when we arrive on the scene of their medical emergency, we are capable and qualified to deliver a certain quality of care. We obtain this "quality of care" through initial training, continuing education, experience, street smarts, and QI reviews. For information on performance to be forthcoming and self-reported in a "just culture" environment it must be protected. Otherwise the culture of fear spreads and opportunities decline for improvement based on crew information.

It should be noted that QI starts with establishing or identifying a process and then testing or measuring variations by tracking time series data (i.e., run charts) until you create reliable processes. This helps ensure that the organization is protected. Then, a QI process can be used to learn about outliers and to spot-check the process steps and ensure continued adherence to techniques that avoid variation. The data are then rolled into future improvements.

What has just been described is not the norm for the majority of EMS providers. It is part of improvement work, but this is where the majority of leaders waste most of their time. The theory behind it is that if providers are the source of most defects, inspecting their work and providing feedback may prevent that defect from repeating, and inspection keeps us on target. This approach is absent of the theory of systems and variation.

LEGAL PROTECTIONS

The cost of a medical error is often immediately encumbered by the patient or the organization. Often, relief from the additional financial resources that must be committed or the long-term consequences of the event are provided through litigation. QI requires comprehensive legal protections in many areas. Employee discipline, the discovery of records, consistency and approval of policies and procedures, and the process by which errors are identified with the resulting outcomes all require legal protection.

PROTECTING QI ACTIVITIES AND OTHER REVIEW PROCESSES

Deviations from medical practice or the standard of care all have the potential to result in litigation or a lawsuit. The very nature of QI is to discover errors and find solutions or to improve care. The mechanics of a QI process essentially do the same thing that the **discovery** phase of a lawsuit does: It looks to find cause and responsibility. Since the QI process gives validity to causes of errors and identifies them, this information is valuable to lawyers and those looking to benefit from medical errors. Therefore, it is important to ensure that the results of QI improvement activities are protected from discovery and used for internal purposes only. Many states have laws that prohibit access to or exempt the QI results from discovery in litigation. Figure 10.1 depicts an example of state law protecting QI information.

PROTECTING QI PROCESSES

QI activities must be protected from legal proceedings. Protected documents have certain features and, generally, three types of protection. The first protection is immunity from litigation, meaning that any cause and effect that arises from the quality processes should be immune from discovery or being entered into legal proceedings.

An agency should mold its QI efforts to produce documents that meet these criteria. Although these criteria might seem cumbersome (such as the requirement that a document be created by an entire quality committee), they arguably create an effective QI program. Given the increased likelihood that a document will be protected from disclosure to a **plaintiff** in litigation if it has the features described in the following paragraphs, the awkwardness might pay off in terms of reduced liability exposure. Incorporating these features into a document will not guarantee that a court will protect the document's confidentiality because the law governing these matters is not clearly established. Protected documents are generated by a QI committee. The fact that a quality committee generates a document does not by itself give it protected status, but it is a factor the courts may consider. Protected documents contain analyses of quality of care. An analysis is a product of reviewing facts and is not the facts themselves. For example, census data and outcome data contain only facts, but by comparing them one can come up with a conclusion as to whether there are enough staff and units to cover a community's population. That conclusion, which is not found in the source data themselves, is an analysis.

There are several general features of protected documents. As previously stated immunity for bringing forth QI issues and identifying improvement needed is a common piece of legislation present in most states. The need for confidentiality is also a common assurance that should be placed in administrative law or legislation and should protect medical providers and organizations involved in the quality process. Figure 10.2 is sample legislation from the New York State EMS regulations.

PROTECTING AND DOCUMENTING THE PROCESS

Protected documents contain evaluations of quality of care. Evaluations, like analyses, are based on source data but are not found in the

Emergency medical services quality assurance; immunity from liability.
(3)(a) There shall be no monetary liability on the part of, and no cause of action shall arise against, any person, including any person acting as a witness, incident reporter to, or investigator for, an emergency medical review committee for any act or proceeding undertaken or performed within the scope of the functions of any emergency medical review committee if such action is taken without intentional fraud or malice.

The provisions of this section shall not affect the provisions of s. 768.28. Except as provided in subsection (3), this section shall not be construed to confer immunity from liability on any person while performing services other than as a member of an emergency medical review committee, or upon any person acting as a witness, incident reporter to, or investigator for, an emergency medical review committee for any act or proceeding undertaken or performed outside the scope of the functions of such committee.

The records obtained or produced by a committee providing quality assurance activities as described in subsections (1)-(4) are exempt from the provisions of s. 119.07(1) and s. 24(a), Art. I of the State Constitution, and committee proceedings and meetings regarding quality assurance activities are exempt from the provisions of s. 286.011 and s. 24(b), Art. I of the State Constitution. The investigations, proceedings, and records of a committee providing quality assurance activities as described in subsections (1)-(4) shall not be subject to discovery or introduction into evidence in any civil action or disciplinary proceeding by the department or employing agency arising out of matters which are the subject of evaluation and review by the committee, and no person who was in attendance at a meeting of such committee shall be permitted or required to testify in any such civil action or disciplinary proceeding as to any evidence or other matters produced or presented during the proceedings of such committee or as to any findings, recommendations, evaluations, opinions, or other actions of such committee or any members thereof. However, information, documents, or records provided to the committee from sources external to the committee are not immune from discovery or use in any such civil action or disciplinary proceeding merely because they were presented during proceedings of such committee nor should any person who testifies before a committee or who is a member of such committee be prevented from testifying as to matters within the person's knowledge, but, such witness shall not be asked about his or her testimony before a committee or information obtained from or opinions formed by him or her as a result of participating in activities conducted by a committee. If the defendant prevails in an action brought by a health care provider against any person who initiated, participated in, was a witness in, or conducted any review as authorized by this section, the court shall award reasonable attorney's fees and costs to the defendant. (Title XXIX PUBLIC HEALTH, Florida Revised Statute Chapter 401 . . . 401.425)

FIGURE 10.1 Protections from Florida Statutes Chapter 401.425.

data themselves. A QI committee might evaluate an employee's performance as being either good, bad, or in between. The evaluation could contain observations about which areas of an employee's performance are acceptable, which areas need improvement, and how to improve in these areas. Such conclusions not found in the source data themselves are evaluations.

Protected documents are not administrative documents. Administrative documents that reflect routine operations of a facility, such as a provider's records or a contract with a regular care provider, are not protected from disclosure to plaintiffs. Protected documents deal with distinct care issues that might arise from process issues. Although a QI committee's task in this regard is ongoing, it is not

1. Immunity from suit. Any person who participates in the activities of any emergency medical services quality assurance committee approved by the board is immune from civil liability for undertaking or failing to undertake any act within the scope of the committee. [1991, c. 588, §23 (AMD).]

2. Confidentiality. All proceedings and records of proceedings concerning the quality assurance activities of an emergency medical services quality assurance committee approved by the board and all reports, information and records provided to the committee are confidential and may not be obtained by discovery from the committee, the board or its staff. Quality assurance information may be disclosed to a licensee as part of any board-approved educational or corrective process. [2003, c. 559, §6 (AMD).]

3. Assistance of information; immunity. Any person, health care facility or other emergency services organization which assists in the activities of an emergency medical services quality assurance committee approved by the board which provides information to an emergency medical services quality assurance committee approved by the board shall be protected by the provisions of section 93 as though that assistance of information were provided to the board itself.

FIGURE 10.2 New York Administrative Code 92-A: Records of quality assurance activities.

a routine task, such as the matters reflected in records concerning the ambulance or the EMS service's daily operations.

QI committee members, and not facility management or administrative staff, should be responsible for addressing quality issues so that the documents generated in connection with quality review processes will be from the quality committee and not be considered administrative documents. A protected document's purpose is to improve the quality of care rendered by the EMS agency. The document's purpose should be the same as the committee's purpose: to improve the quality of care provided by the agency. Such a document may contain suggestions on how to improve care. It may also contain an analysis of a problem that helps the reader understand the problem's context and gives suggestions on how to solve it. The purpose of a protected document is not simply to report facts but also to describe a process in an EMS organization. Protected documents reflect a committee investigation of a process that establishes a standardized process. A protected document is prepared to address a specific problem in the quality of care and can contain the results of a committee's investigation into such a problem. A protected document may contain facts relating to the problem that will help the quality committee evaluate the problem and generate a response to it.

PROCEDURES FOR CREATING DOCUMENTS

Statutes and rules both have the force and effect of law. Statutes are enacted by a legislative body, whereas rules become law through an administrative process initiated by a state or federal agency. In order for a state or federal agency to promulgate rules, there must be a law in place that authorizes the agency to develop rules (enabling legislation). Administrative rulemaking is used by agencies to specify requirements that may be too detailed to be included in statute or are within the expertise of the regulating agency.

All QI documents should be created using the procedures listed for each document's use. All QI documents related to QI processes whose protection under the law is uncertain should have a disclosure statement. Quality committee meeting minutes are not addressed here because they are generally found to be protected. Each of the documents should have a caption at the bottom indicating that it is a protected document, such as:

> This document has been created by the quality assurance committee for the purpose of monitoring and evaluating the quality of care in the facility. It is protected from discovery by Evid. Code [Section] 1157 and by the work product privilege.

Each of these documents should also be kept in a single filing location along with all other QI documents (such as the QI policies and procedures, committee minutes, lists of committee members and their duties, etc.). The following procedures should be part of the committee's policies and procedures. Some of the procedures call for the creation of draft documents before a final version is created. The format of these draft documents should make it easy for committee members to add comments. Drafts should be double-spaced and have 1.5-inch margins. Committee reports should be generated by the QI committee members. Appointment letters offering a provider a committee position should be generated to officially empower and sufficiently cover the provider's involvement. If a provider already serves the agency or already serves on the committee, he should be made an integral part of the committee via an appointment letter officially explaining the QI process. Everyone who has a relationship with the EMS agency must be officially noticed on privacy requirements and liability.

The entire committee should participate in the creation of agency reports. The most efficient way to accomplish this is to have a specialist who is in charge of a specific area (such as a pediatric physician or nurse) circulate a draft report to the committee before a meeting. Each committee member should review the draft, comment on it, and return it to the committee either before or during the committee meeting. The committee should then incorporate everyone's comments into a document that reflects the entire committee's findings and that should be signed by all committee members.

For liability purposes, it is best not to generate reports if they are not required by a regulation because a plaintiff may obtain access to them under the current uncertain status of the law. If a committee report is generated, a facility should have a clear plan for destroying it at an appropriate time.

INCIDENT REPORTS

When an event that should generate an incident report occurs, the witness to the incident should report it to a QI committee member. That QI committee member should describe the incident in the incident report and include any other information that might be helpful, such as an evaluation of the actions of the witness or responsible party, an analysis of how this incident may be related to other incidents, and so on. That report should then be submitted to the quality committee and discussed by the committee, whose members may add more comments to the incident report, if necessary. Once the entire committee has had an opportunity to review and discuss the incident report and add any comments, each committee member should sign the report. Figure 10.3 is an example of legal requirements to report incidents that can have an effect on quality and that typically require management involvement with a backup from regulation. This type of regulation is often developed in states and jurisdictions with strong labor agreement that may attempt to prevent full processing of medical errors or bad behavior.

STATE MANDATES FOR QI

In many states and counties, a mandate exists for an EMS agency to conduct some form of QI. The authority or mandate can take

Part 800

CERTIFIED AMBULANCE SERVICES

800.21 GENERAL REQUIREMENTS

An ambulance service shall:

(q) upon discovery by or report to the governing authority of the ambulance service, report to the Department's Area Office by telephone no later than the following business day and in writing within 5 working days every instance in which:

1. a patient dies, is injured or otherwise harmed due to actions of commission or omission by a member of the ambulance service;
2. an EMS response vehicle operated by the service is involved in a motor vehicle crash in which a patient, member of the crew or other person is killed or injured to the extent requiring hospitalization or care by a physician;
3. any member of the ambulance service is killed or injured to the extent requiring hospitalization or care by a physician while on duty;
4. patient care equipment fails while in use, causing patient harm;
5. it is alleged that any member of the ambulance service has responded to an incident or treated a patient while under the influence of alcohol or drugs;

On or in a form approved by the Department, maintain a record of all unexpected authorized EMS response vehicle and patient care equipment failures that could have resulted in harm to a patient and the corrective actions taken. A copy of this record shall be submitted to the Department with the EMS service's biennial re-certification application.

FIGURE 10.3 Model Legislation: Title 10 of the New York State Codes, Rules and Regulations Part 800.21 (q) and (r).

multiple forms. In some circumstances, it can be by state statute and be part of law. This is in contrast to areas where the law authorizes a program, but the enforcement and implementation are handled by administrative regulations often determined by a county regulatory authority or some other empowered government or quasi-governmental agency. Figures 10.4 and 10.5 provide examples of state law authorizing or mandating QI activities.

DISCIPLINE

One of the most fluid areas within the scope of practice of the physician medical director is the role in discipline. Medical directors are tasked to make certain that EMS providers are delivering quality patient care. Medical directors as employees of the jurisdiction are given that responsibility; however, they have a limited capacity to recommend or administer discipline to employees. Case law has established that a medical director has the ability to limit the practice of a paramedic or EMT under the license of the medical director. In a Minnesota case, *Hennepin County v. Hennepin County Association of Paramedics and Emergency Medical Technicians*, the medical director was able to limit the practice of a paramedic although it was unclear whether the medical director had the authority to terminate employment. No organization or person does the right thing every time. By its nature, EMS requires paramedics and EMTs with an incomplete knowledge of the situation to make complex life-or-death decisions very rapidly and during continuous distraction. It is a tribute to EMS professionals that, through dedication and training, they get things right the vast majority of the time. When mistakes happen, the challenge of the medical director is to decide a course of action. Several considerations must be assessed prior to taking action. Prior to any decision, it is imperative that the investigative process be completed. To help focus the investigative process, the physician must decide generally one of four actions to be considered:

- If, given the situation faced by the medics, the mistake is understandable

Section 3006. Quality Improvement Program

1. By January first, nineteen hundred ninety-seven, every ambulance service and advanced life support first response service shall establish or participate in a quality improvement program, which shall be an ongoing system to monitor and evaluate the quality and appropriateness of the medical care provided by the ambulance service or advanced life support first response service, and which shall pursue opportunities to improve patient care and to resolve identified problems. The quality improvement program may be conducted independently or in collaboration with other services, with the appropriate regional council, with an EMS program agency, with a hospital, or with another appropriate organization approved by the department. Such program shall include a committee of at least five members, at least three of whom do not participate in the provision of care by the service. At least one member shall be a physician, and the others shall be nurses, or emergency medical technicians, or advanced emergency medical technicians, or other appropriately qualified allied health personnel. The quality improvement committee shall have the following responsibilities:

(a) to review the care rendered by the service, as documented in prehospital care reports and other materials. The committee shall have the authority to use such information to review and to recommend to the governing body changes in administrative policies and procedures, as may be necessary, and shall notify the governing body of significant deficiencies;

(b) to periodically review the credentials and performance of all persons providing emergency medical care on behalf of the service;

(c) to periodically review information concerning compliance with standard of care procedures and protocols, grievances filed with the service by patients or their families, and the occurrence of incidents injurious or potentially injurious to patients. A quality improvement program shall also include participation in the department's prehospital care reporting system and the provision of continuing education programs to address areas in which compliance with procedures and protocols is most deficient and to inform personnel of changes in procedures and protocols. Continuing education programs may be provided by the service itself or by other organizations; and

(d) to present data to the regional medical advisory committee and to participate in system-wide evaluation.

2. The information required to be collected and maintained, including information from the prehospital care reporting system which identifies an individual, shall be kept confidential and shall not be released except to the department or pursuant to section three thousand four-a of this article.

3. Notwithstanding any other provisions of law, none of the records, documentation, or committee actions or records required pursuant to this section shall be subject to disclosure under article six of the public officers law or article thirty-one of the civil practice law and rules, except as hereinafter provided or as provided in any other provision of law. No person in attendance at a meeting of any such committee shall be required to testify as to what transpired thereat. The prohibition related to disclosure of testimony shall not apply to the statements made by any person in attendance at such a meeting who is a party to an action or proceeding the subject of which was reviewed at the meeting. The prohibition of disclosure of information from the prehospital care reporting system shall not apply to information which does not identify a particular ambulance service or individual.

4. Any person who in good faith and without malice provides information to further the purpose of this section or who, in good faith and without malice, participates on the quality improvement committee shall not be subject to any action for civil damages or other relief as a result of such activity.

FIGURE 10.4 Excerpt from Article 30, Section 3006 of the New York State Public Health Law.

Subtitle 03 EMS OPERATIONAL PROGRAMS

Chapter 04 Quality Assurance Authority: Education Article, §13-509, 13-510, and 13-516, Annotated Code of Maryland

30.03.04.01. 01 Scope. This chapter governs the requirements for quality assurance in an EMS operational program.

30.03.04.02. 02 Quality Assurance Plan.

A. Every EMS operational program shall have a written quality assurance plan approved by its medical director.

B. The quality assurance plan shall include provisions for:

1) Reviewing data concerning patient care rendered by EMS providers affiliated with the EMS operational program;
2) Identifying and analyzing trends in EMS care rendered by EMS providers affiliated with the EMS operational program;

30.03.04.03. 03 Medical Review Committee.

A. Every EMS operational program shall have a medical review committee.

B. The EMS operational program in conjunction with the EMS operational program medical director shall select the medical review committee.

C. The medical review committee shall be a committee established in MIEMSS subject to the confidentiality and immunity provisions of Health Occupations Article, §1-401, Annotated Code of Maryland, as well as the other provisions of that statute.

30.03.04.05. 05 Direct Treatment Quality Assessment and Quality Improvement.

A. For the purpose of quality assessment and quality improvement, an EMS provider licensed or certified by the EMS Board under Education Article §13-516, Annotated Code of Maryland, who has or has had a direct treatment relationship with a patient, may request and receive follow-up data or information on that patient pertinent to the treatment relationship from the facility to which the patient is.

30.03.04.08. 08 Quality Assurance Officer.

A. Each EMS operational program shall designate a Quality Assurance (QA) Officer in concurrence with the EMS operational program medical director.

B. Qualifications of an EMS operational program Quality Assurance Officer. An EMS operational program Quality Assurance Officer shall:

1) Be certified or licensed as an EMT-B, CRT or EMT-P in Maryland.
2) Either: a) Successfully complete a QA officer course as defined by MIEMSS.

FIGURE 10.5 Excerpt from Title 30 Maryland Institute for Emergency Medical Services (MIEMSS).

- If the mistake at hand indicates a need for further training
- If the mistake was simply an anomaly
- If a specific medic or the entire service must be addressed about the mistake

All possible information should be gathered before action is taken to handle a potential problem situation. Feedback should be collected from everyone involved, including the medics, physicians, and nurses at the receiving hospital and, perhaps, the patients and their families. Obtain patient care records (PCRs), emergency department reports, and, when relevant, inpatient care records and autopsy records. Obtaining courtesy privileges at all hospitals to which a service transports often gives the medical director access to a patient's medical record. Often, what initially appeared to be a dangerous mistake turns out to be a reasonable decision based on the information available to the medic at the time.

Many states give the medical director the right to limit the practice of EMS workers under his direction. The medical director can only discipline an EMS worker by suspending, terminating, or adhering to a contracted set of circumstances and subsequent actions. In fire-based EMS systems, the medical director's authority is influenced by the public employee's property right in the job. Public employees are entitled to **due process** rights when faced with disciplinary charges that may affect their continued employment. Due process includes notification of the employee regarding the pending decision, a hearing during which the employee has the opportunity to present his side, and representation by legal counsel at a hearing if the employee so chooses. In *Brodie v. Connecticut 401 U.S. 371* these rights were guaranteed, and only when there is an immediate threat to safety or health can the hearing be postponed. Discipline must be suitable for the offense and not be subjective to the individual. Employers must develop—in a collaborative fashion with the labor unit—policies and procedures concerning discipline and the boundaries within which the medical director will operate.

Many states have collective bargaining, and the labor union will be required to represent and protect the employee under the labor agreement. Terminations under such a system must be for cause. *NLRB v. Weingarten, Inc. 420 U.S. 251* established that the grievant may also have **Weingarten rights** during interviews where management is investigating the employee for disciplinary actions. An employee must make a clear request for labor union representation when being investigated and cannot expect retribution for requesting the representation. Any labor union officer can be called to represent the employee and has the right to counsel him on the answers, engage in private conversation prior to the interview, and ask the employer to clarify a question. Feedback from medical directors can strengthen an EMS system and an employee's performance and, ideally, will focus on QI activities, not employee discipline.

Best Practice

EMS Task Force–Continuous Improvement: Washington, D.C., Fire and EMS

Washington, D.C. (DC), introduced a Patient Bill of Rights that has been developed and implemented by the DC Fire and Emergency Medical Services (FEMS) Department. In concert with a strategic plan based on the comprehensive recommendations of the EMS task force, DC FEMS has made, and will continue to make, systemwide improvements and operational adjustments.

A Bill of Rights for each patient is one of the improvements instituted by DC FEMS. Annually, FEMS responds to about 160,000 emergency calls for service. Over 130,000, or 80 percent, of these calls are medical in nature. FEMS has employed several solutions to problems with the system, including the Street Calls program, which identifies those patients who call frequently and regularly. This program finds solutions other than a transport to the emergency room and has resulted in a 50 percent reduction of repeat transports for patients involved in the program. In an effort to measure customer or patient satisfaction with FEMS, recent surveys or customer-satisfaction ratings among patients transported indicates that 95 percent were "very satisfied" or "satisfied" with EMS delivery and service.

To bring these efforts full circle and help clarify patients' expectations, DC FEMS's Patient Bill of Rights was implemented. All patients have the right to expect competent and compassionate service from FEMS, including timely and appropriate medical services; to be transported in a clean and properly maintained ambulance; that FEMS will never refuse to transport them; that FEMS personnel will check vital signs; that FEMS personnel will protect health information; that FEMS personnel will dress and act in a professional manner; that FEMS personnel will explain what is being done to assist patients; that FEMS personnel will be polite, compassionate, considerate, and respectful; and that a patient's privacy and comfort will be of utmost concern to FEMS personnel.

The Bill of Rights was brought on-line in DC FEMS after the release of the health care bill of rights concept from 1997, when President Bill Clinton established an Advisory Commission on Consumer Protection and Quality in the Health Care Industry, which developed a Patient Bill of Rights. The Nashville Fire Department is credited as an early adopter of the Patient Bill of Rights concept for EMS. Most EMS patient bill of rights, including DC FEMS, are based on Nashville's template. In 1999, the Nashville Fire Department established a Patient's Bill of Rights created by its medical director, and the bill is still in active use.

The DC FEMS Patient Bill of Rights was developed in part because of an EMS run on February 10, 2010, during which a 2-year-old girl with breathing problems was not initially transported to the hospital. She was transported several hours later after a second 9-1-1 response and subsequently died at the hospital of pneumonia. DC FEMS has taken a very positive step in developing its Patient Bill of Rights.

THE LEGAL PROCESS

The legal process starts with a concerned party contacting legal counsel or a lawyer. A lawyer may take a case on a **contingency** basis, meaning that the services are free until there is an award. A lawyer's experience will often dictate the decision to take a case on contingency based on past awards, case law, or in cases of gross negligence, potentially where there is media interest. In most cases, there will be fees involved by the law firm and the plaintiff will be charged. These fees, known as **punitive damages**, may ultimately become part of the award. Punitive damages are often limited in some states.

THE BEGINNING OF LITIGATION

A lawsuit is typically called litigation and is a civil action brought in a court of law in which a plaintiff or a party who claims to have incurred loss as a result of the actions of a **defendant** demands a legal or equitable remedy. A lawsuit may involve dispute resolution of private law issues between individuals, business entities, or nonprofit organizations. A lawsuit may also enable the state, city, county, or any government agency to be treated as if it were a private party in a civil case, as if it were a plaintiff or defendant regarding an injury, or as having a civil cause of action to enforce certain laws. A person typically makes a legal claim for monetary compensation or damages. The term *equitable relief* is commonly used in an **injunction** and/or another request for relief, such as pain and suffering. When a person files a complaint with a court, the next step is to serve a copy of that notice of intent to get relief. This is known as a **pleading** or a **summons** to the other party. The summons is a command to respond to the complaint. Which court the complaint is filed in will depend on several things. Part of the fees associated with filing a lawsuit pertain to the filing of a summons and a pleading, which is also called a case or action.

Once the plaintiff has served the summons and complaint to the defendant and, if needed, filed **proof of service** with the court, typically by a sheriff or constable hand-delivering the summons, the defendant has a certain amount of time in which to serve and file an answer to the complaint or, in some circumstances, a **motion to dismiss** the complaint for any number of several reasons. The **answer** to a complaint can be as straightforward as a denial of each and every claim in the complaint or can be more complex, with explanations denying the complaint or citation of statutes indicating immunity or reasons for dismissal. An answer can contain **counterclaims** by the defendant against the plaintiff, either related or unrelated to the plaintiff's claims. If the court grants a motion to dismiss (at the start of the case or at any time), the lawsuit ends. The granting or denial of almost any motion can be appealed to a higher court.

THE DISCOVERY PHASE

Once the pleadings have been served and filed, the case moves into the discovery stage. Because the goal of a lawsuit is to get to the truth of the matter at issue, the rules of every jurisdiction require an open exchange or disclosure of relevant information and documents so that both sides can prepare for trial completely. Several different discovery devices are available to each party to a lawsuit.

Each party may serve **interrogatories** (written questions) on the other. Each party may serve requests for admission. Each party may serve document demands. Each party may ask questions of the other party in person, under oath, at what is often called a **deposition**. Persons who are not party to the lawsuit can also be examined under oath in certain circumstances, through the service of a subpoena. Each discovery device has its own rules, which vary from state to state and sometimes from court to court. It is common to request EMS reports and incident reports and to interview the witnesses or people involved in the incident.

It is not unusual for a court to confer with the parties' lawyers (in person or by phone) to make sure that discovery is moving along smoothly and on schedule. If there are problems, the court will try to resolve them in this conference. Very often, when discovery is complete, one party or both parties will move for **summary judgment**. In essence, the party is asking the judge assigned to the case to rule, giving that party all or some of what he is asking for in his complaint without the necessity of a trial because the relevant facts are not in dispute and the law, when applied to those facts, is in the moving party's favor. A motion for summary judgment is a difficult thing to win because summary judgment deprives the other side of his day in court. A judge might require the lawyers to argue the motion in person.

PREPARING FOR LITIGATION

Once it appears that a lawsuit will progress out of the discovery phase and get to a trial, it is important to ensure that legal counsel coach or counsel the EMS employee as to what will be said and what immunities are to be afforded a person or organization. It is also important to ensure that employees understand how to respond to objections and interrogatories. Volunteering additional information, or information not supported by facts, and other common missteps in a trial or interrogatories, such as speculation, should be explained to the personnel involved in the case. Often a legal team and management will put employees through a mock deposition and review responses. The appropriate dress and conduct also must be explained to the employee. For example, will the employee appear in uniform or in dress clothes?

THE TRIAL

When all pretrial motions have been made, one party or the other will inform the court that the case is ready for trial. The court will set a date for the trial, setting aside a certain number of days for the proceedings, based on the lawyers' estimates of how long it will take to have all the witnesses testify. The court will usually ask the parties to submit pretrial memoranda or **briefs**, which set forth each side's position and cite relevant laws and previous lawsuits. These pretrial submissions enable the judge to know what to expect to hear at trial, but the judge will not make up his mind about the merits of the case before all the evidence has been presented.

Other motions might be made before trial, usually very close to the start date. These motions typically concern the evidence to be offered. One side might ask the judge to prohibit the other side from offering certain pieces of evidence, for any of a variety of reasons. This is typically where organizations can seek protection if the organization is in a jurisdiction that has immunity laws for QI processes. One of the most common reasons is that the other side did not produce the information or documentation in response to a discovery request. Courts frown on surprise litigation tactics. If the parties do not settle the case out of court, then the parties will appear in court before the judge (and/or a jury in some cases) and present their cases in turn, each side putting its witness(es) on the stand to be asked questions by the parties' lawyers. When all the evidence has been presented, the judge (or the jury) will render a verdict, effectively deciding what the factual "truth" of the matter is. The judge will then apply the appropriate law to the verdict and issue a **judgment**. (See Figure 10.6.)

THE JUDGMENT

If the plaintiff is successful, a judgment will be given in the plaintiff's favor, and a variety of court orders may be issued to enforce the judgment. The judgment can have different components. The most common is an award of money and/or an order requiring someone to do or not do something by imposing a temporary or permanent injunction to prevent an act or compel an act. A **declaratory judgment** may be issued to prevent future legal disputes. Once a judgment has been entered, it can be enforced. Although not as common, lawsuits may also refer to a criminal action, criminal proceeding, or criminal claim.

LEGAL CASES AND ARTICLES

Several prominent cases have been established and processes put in place that are standard assumptions in EMS QI. Case law establishes many of these practices and builds a path for practice. The QI process will occasionally find fault that may arise from at-risk or deviant behavior. Often, this requires an employment action and an assumption of due process and progressive discipline. **Progressive discipline** is a system of increasingly harsh penalties for each time an employee is disciplined for work-rule violations. Typically, the progression goes from oral warnings to written warnings to suspension and, finally, to termination. On occasion, an organization will have a decision-making leave as a final step in progressive discipline. For a decision-making leave, a person is given a paid day off and sent home as a final step before termination. During this time an employee is to decide whether he wants to continue employment

FIGURE 10.6 ■ Medic on a courtroom stand. *Source: From Emergency Care, 12 ed. by Limmer, Figure 4.4 on page 84*

with the organization. Often this is a chance to resign rather than being terminated.

DUE PROCESS

In the United States, criminal prosecutions and civil cases are generally governed by explicit guarantees of procedural rights under the Bill of Rights. Most of these rights have been incorporated under the Fourteenth Amendment to the states. Among those rights is the constitutional right to procedural due process, which has been broadly construed to protect the individual so that statutes, regulations, and enforcement actions must ensure that no one is deprived of "life, liberty, or property" without a fair opportunity to affect the judgment or result. Due process is the legal principle that the government must respect all of the legal rights that are owed to a person according to the law. Due process holds the government subservient to the law of the land, protecting individual persons from the state. When a government harms a person without following the exact course of the law, it constitutes a due process violation which offends against the rule of law.

Due process has also been frequently interpreted as limiting laws and legal proceedings so judges, instead of legislators, may define and guarantee fundamental fairness, justice, and liberty. This interpretation has proven controversial and is similar to the concepts of natural justice and procedural justice used in various other jurisdictions. This interpretation of due process is sometimes expressed as a command that the government must not be unfair to the people or abuse them physically.

The due process clause prohibits state and local governments from depriving persons of life, liberty, or property without certain steps being taken to ensure fairness. This clause has been used to make most of the Bill of Rights applicable to the states, as well as to recognize substantive and procedural rights.

PROCEDURAL DUE PROCESS

This protection extends to all government proceedings that can result in an individual's deprivation, whether civil or criminal in nature, from parole violation hearings to administrative hearings regarding government benefits and entitlements to full-blown criminal trials. This would include the possibility of decertification of medical licensure.

According to the courts, it includes an individual's right to be adequately notified of charges or proceedings, the opportunity to be heard at these proceedings, and the right to impartiality of the person or panel making the final decision on the matter. When an individual is facing a deprivation of life, liberty, or property, procedural due process mandates that he is entitled to adequate notice, a hearing, and a neutral judge. In cases of EMS quality where there is an identified failure in the **remediation** process, coaching and **counseling** that results in the discharge of the employee due process must be followed.

The U.S. Supreme Court has formulated a balancing test to determine the rigor with which the requirements of procedural due process should be applied to a particular deprivation, for the obvious reason that mandating such requirements in the most expansive way for even the most minor deprivations would bring the machinery of government to a halt. The Court set out the test as follows: Specific means test for due process generally requires consideration of three distinct factors:

1. The private interest that will be affected by the official action.
2. The risk of an error being made that can or did result in the deprivation of such interest through the procedures used, and the probable value of additional or substitute procedural requirements that could have been used as safeguards.
3. The Government's interest, including the function or legal and administrative oversight the government may have. (This would include the fiscal and administrative burdens that the additional or substitute procedural requirement would entail.)

At some point, the effort put forth by an agency can be discontinued once the proof of procedural due process can be well documented.

Procedural due process has also been an important factor in the development of the law of personal jurisdiction, in the sense that it is inherently unfair for the judicial machinery of a state to take away the property of a person who has no connection to it whatsoever. A significant portion of U.S. constitutional law is therefore directed to what kinds of connections to a state are enough for that state's assertion of jurisdiction over a nonresident to conform with procedural due process.

Side Bar

Disciplining and Limiting a Practice

In a Minnesota case, the medical director as an employee of the jurisdiction is given the responsibility for medical quality; however, he has a limited capacity to recommend or administer discipline to employees. Case law has established that a medical director has the ability to limit the practice of a paramedic or EMT under the license of the medical director. In a Minnesota case, *Hennepin County v. Hennepin County Association of Paramedics and Emergency Medical Technician*, the medical director was able to limit the practice of a paramedic, although it was unclear whether the medical director had the authority to terminate employment. In many cases, a paramedic's license is revoked and the provider is downgraded to an EMT or moved to a position within the organization that does not have patient contact.

SUBSTANTIVE DUE PROCESS

The term *substantive due process* (SDP) is commonly used in two ways: first to identify a particular line of case law, and second to signify a particular attitude toward judicial review under the due process clause—for example, the application of whether or not a Good Samaritan defense could be used. The term *substantive due process* began to take form in legal casebooks of the 1930s as a categorical distinction of selected due process cases and, by 1950, had been mentioned twice in Supreme Court opinions.

SDP involves liberty-based due process challenges that seek certain outcomes instead of merely contesting procedures and their effects. In such cases, the Supreme Court recognizes a constitutionally based "liberty" that then renders laws seeking to limit said "liberty" either unenforceable or limited in scope, or the tactics of SDP decisions typically assert that those liberties ought to be left to the more politically accountable branches of government. Courts have viewed the due process clause, and sometimes other clauses of the Constitution, as embracing those fundamental rights that are implicit in the concept of ordered liberty. Just what those rights are is not always clear, nor is the Supreme Court's authority to enforce such unremunerated rights clear. Some of those rights have long histories or are deeply rooted in American society.

LIBERTY INTEREST AND FIRST AMENDMENT RIGHTS

In many legal cases, the right of the individual to earn a living remains a legal consequence from trial and arbitration hearings when an employee is discharged for quality issues or performance. Although discharge from an organization has been upheld in many cases, decertification has often been reversed. The Equal Protection Clause of the Fourteenth Amendment to the United States Constitution provides that "no state shall . . . deny to any person within its jurisdiction the equal protection of the laws." The Equal Protection Clause can be seen as an attempt to secure the promise of the professed commitment of the United States to the proposition that all men are created equal by empowering the judiciary to enforce that principle against the states. The Fourteenth Amendment Equal Protection Clause applies only to state governments, but the requirement of equal protection has been read to apply to the federal government as a component of Fifth Amendment due process.

More concretely, the Equal Protection Clause, along with the rest of the Fourteenth Amendment, forced a shift in U.S. constitutionalism. Before the enactment of the Fourteenth Amendment, the Bill of Rights protected individual rights only from invasion by the federal government; however, after the Fourteenth Amendment was enacted, the

Constitution also protected rights from state leaders and governments, even including some rights that arguably were not protected by the federal government. In the wake of the Fourteenth Amendment, the states could not, among other things, deprive people of the equal protection of the laws.

In many cases, the constitutional right in the Fourteenth Amendment guaranteed a person to earn a living or pursue wealth in all lawful ways; to live and work where he will; to earn his livelihood by any lawful calling; to pursue any livelihood or avocation, and for that purpose to enter into all contracts that may be proper, necessary, and essential to carrying out to a successful conclusion the purposes above mentioned. In *Truax v. Raich* (239 U.S. 33, 41), the Supreme Court, evoking the Fourteenth Amendment, supported that the right to work for a living in the common occupations of the community is of the very essence of the personal freedom and opportunity that it was the purpose of the Amendment to secure.

In a Washington State case, *Bryan Braswell v. Shoreline Fire Department (WA) and Dr. Gary Somers*, a paramedic sued the fire department and the medical director after he was suspended from paramedic duties for anger management issues. The court rules that the plaintiff was properly dismissed but could seek to prove that he was given due process by the fire department. On September 16, 2010, the U.S. Court of Appeals for the Ninth Circuit in San Francisco, 2010 U.S. App. LEXIS 19308, held that a federal judge in Seattle properly dismissed the firefighter's claim that the medical director tortuously interfered with his employment, since the firefighter did not have a sufficient "property interest" in his job to support such a claim. The Court of Appeals, however, in an unusual decision, remanded the case for further discovery against the fire department on the claim that the department breached his "liberty interest" in finding a future paramedic position with another fire department.

An EMS run led to suspension of duties when on November 30, 2005, Plaintiff and his paramedic partner were dispatched to the residence of Tommy Davis, who had called emergency services complaining of chest pain. As part of the examination, Plaintiff asked whether Mr. Davis had used any recreational drugs that evening. Mr. Davis became agitated. Plaintiff administered a lung exam and instructed Mr. Davis to breathe deeply. However, Mr. Davis either would not or could not comply. Plaintiff bent down and spoke directly into Mr. Davis's face, instructing him repeatedly to breathe deeply. After several requests, Mr. Davis became angry and asked Plaintiff what his problem was. Plaintiff repeated his instructions and asked Mr. Davis to give him "a little less attitude."

The exchange between Plaintiff and Mr. Davis led to a verbal altercation. Mr. Davis stood up and threw a file folder on a desk so forcefully that papers and objects flew off the desk. Mr. Davis told the paramedics to leave. Plaintiff asked Mr. Davis to fill out a release form stating that he did not consent to treatment. Mr. Davis replied, using profanities, that he would not sign the form. In the course of the altercation, Plaintiff asked whether he should call the police, and Mr. Davis responded that he would give Plaintiff a reason to throw him in jail. Feeling physically threatened and suspecting that Mr. Davis, who was rummaging through desk drawers, might be looking for a weapon, Plaintiff and his partner left without treating Mr. Davis or obtaining a release form.

The next day, Plaintiff met with his fire department supervisors and two union representatives to discuss the incident. Several days later, the plaintiff met with the chief of the fire department, the deputy chief, and Dr. Somers. Dr. Somers, after having reviewed written statements from witnesses, stated that Plaintiff had an anger management problem, that he failed to identify medically significant symptoms in

Mr. Davis, and that he abandoned Mr. Davis. Dr. Somers told Plaintiff that Plaintiff was no longer authorized to practice medicine under Dr. Somers's medical license. The firefighter resigned his paramedic position: Because Dr. Somers had revoked Plaintiff's ability to practice under his medical license and Plaintiff could not legally practice medicine with the Shoreline Fire Department. For that reason, Shoreline reassigned Plaintiff from a paramedic position back to a firefighter position. Shoreline then froze Plaintiff's salary at the higher paramedic level until his firefighter salary caught up to that level. Plaintiff's paramedic certification was not revoked, but it lapsed in 2007 when Plaintiff failed to seek recertification.

The Court of Appeals agreed that the claim that the medical director tortuously interfered with the firefighter's employment was properly dismissed. The U.S. Supreme Court has defined the boundaries of a "property interest" in the context of the Fourteenth Amendment. Plaintiff failed to demonstrate that Washington law creates a property interest in the statutorily required supervision by having a physician medical director delegate the practice. Plaintiff pointed out that no Washington statute or regulation was present that limits a medical director's discretion to revoke a paramedic's permission to practice under his or her license. Without such a limit on a medical director's authority to revoke a paramedic's permission to practice, Plaintiff could not have a "legitimate claim of entitlement" to that permission. The court found the firefighter has a federal "liberty interest" in future employment and that the fire department violated his liberty interest in pursuing his profession as a paramedic when it revoked his, however the medical director does.

LEGAL LESSONS LEARNED

Fire departments that are considering revoking a firefighter's EMS duties for a substantial period of time, or terminating the firefighter from either a career, part-time, or volunteer agency, should consider providing the employee with an administrative due process hearing audio- or videotaped before making the final decision.

1983 SUITS

A lawsuit involving a process commonly used in public safety labor argument was filed in federal court under Title 42 U.S.C. § 1983 (a so-called "1983 suit"). Title 42 U.S.C. § 1983 was enacted in 1871 after the Civil War, to allow lawsuits in federal court against state and local agencies when their officials violate the rights of U.S. citizens. The statute provides that "[e]very person who, under color of any statute, ordinance, regulation, custom, or usage, of any State or Territory or the District of Columbia, subjects, or causes to be subjected, any citizen of the United States or other person within the jurisdiction thereof to the deprivation of any rights, privileges, or immunities secured by the Constitution and laws, shall be liable to the party injured in an action at law, suit in equity, or other proper proceeding for redress." These "1983 suits" have long been filed against police agencies, where plaintiffs allege police were inadequately trained or supervised, leading to death or injury or false arrest of another. Increasingly, "1983 suits" are being filed against fire and EMS departments. A local government cannot be sued under Title 42 U.S.C. § 1983 for injuries caused by its employees or agents unless it is the "execution of a government's policy or custom, whether made by its lawmakers or by those whose edicts or acts may fairly be said to represent official policy" that causes the injury (*Monell v. Department of Social Services*, 436 U.S. 658, 694 1978). Maintaining detailed training records of fire and EMS personnel, including periodic reviews of EMS protocols and standard operating guidelines (SOGs) and documented corrective actions, are essential in the defense of a "1983 suit."

DISMISSAL BASED ON A QA PROGRAM

A paramedic was properly terminated for not promptly disclosing a medical mistake when a cardiac patient was administered dextrose, instead of epinephrine, down the endotracheal (ET) tube. The paramedic did not advise the transport crew, the emergency room, or the officer in charge.

On March 31, 2006, in *Snyder v. Beavercreek Township*, 2006 Ohio 1612, 2006 Ohio App. LEXIS 1460 (2nd Appellate District; Greene County), the Ohio Court of Appeals upheld the termination of a paramedic. The court rejected the paramedic's argument that this discipline was too severe, given her lack of previous disciplinary problems or medical mistakes. The court held that termination was appropriate since the paramedic "failed to inform anyone that she had made a mistake."

A fire department responded on a run on August 30, 2004, for a cardiac arrest at a local restaurant. The first crew to arrive started CPR. The second crew hooked up a monitor. Paramedic Snyder was on the third crew to arrive, along with a more senior paramedic who was the officer in charge (OIC). Snyder spoke to the patient's wife, as others started an IV line. The patient's wife advised Snyder that her husband was an insulin-dependent diabetic. Paramedic Snyder informed the rest of the crew, and she took a glucometer reading of 41 milligrams. She informed the OIC that the team needed to "look at" the blood sugar level as a possible cause of the cardiac arrest. The OIC told Snyder to first assist with inserting an ET tube. Snyder assisted with inserting the ET tube, and then Snyder administered the first dose of epinephrine down the ET tube. Snyder then retrieved an ampoule of dextrose 50% solution (D50) as well as another dose of epinephrine.

The female paramedic kneeled by the patient's head, with the two drugs on the floor by her knees. She then mistakenly administered 50 ml of the D50, instead of the epinephrine, down the ET tube. She then performed a second blood sugar check—it had risen from 41 to 79 milligrams. The transport crew drove the patient to Miami Valley Hospital, where he was pronounced dead. A few hours later, Snyder received a call from another paramedic who had been on the run. He told her that she needed to document the fact that she had administered the D50 down the ET tube. The court's opinion states, "At that point, Snyder explained, 'Oh, my God, I must have done that. I did that, didn't I?'"

The township board of trustees brought administrative charges of "misfeasance and gross neglect of duty" and held a hearing. They voted to terminate the paramedic and issued several written findings, including this one: "Regardless of whether Ms. Snyder actually realized she was making a mistake while pushing the D50 down the ET tube while she was doing it, the Board finds that Ms. Snyder unequivocally knew, immediately after pushing D50 down the tube, that she made a mistake." The Township also found, "Ms. Snyder knowingly failed to inform the emergency transport crew that the D50 had been administered improperly."

The trustees also found that under the Greater Miami Valley EMS protocol, the D50 was to be administered by IV only, since it is known to "have a necrotic effect on tissue and could seriously injure or kill a patient if administered down the ET Tube and into the lungs. Further, 50 ml is five times the amount of liquid medication that can be safely administered through an ET Tube. This was an egregious error by Ms. Snyder."

After her termination, Snyder filed an appeal to the Court of Common Pleas for Greene County, which affirmed her termination based on the administrative record. On appeal to the three-judge Court of Appeals, her legal counsel claimed there was no support in the record for the township trustees' finding that she "knowingly" failed to inform others of her mistake, since she may not have even been aware of her mistake when the patient was transported. The Court of Appeals disagreed, citing Snyder's testimony before the trustees: "when asked whether Snyder had told the patient's widow that she administered the D50, Snyder answered affirmatively. The widow of the patient also testified that Snyder had informed her that she administered the D50."

Ms. Snyder on appeal also contended that the Trustees erred by finding that she demonstrated a lack of proficiency with respect to department policies and procedures. However, given that she administered a drug in an improper manner and that she failed to inform anyone of the mistake, her argument was found not to have merit. The lesson learned is not to compound a mistake by covering it up: Promptly disclose it, document it on the run report, and establish a corrective action plan that includes continuing education.

HEALTH INSURANCE PORTABILITY AND ACCOUNTABILITY ACT

The Health Insurance Portability and Accountability Act (HIPAA) of 1996 does not prevent the use of privileged health information or QI activities within the institution and its business partners, such as an ambulance service that transports to a hospital. The hospital and the ambulance can share information for QI purposes. It is expected that data collected will be collected as de-identified data. Typically, dates are the most commonly used data elements that create concerns. The Privacy Rule allows a date of birth to be recorded as a year, an age, or an age range. Year of birth or actual age cannot be used if the patient is older than 89 years; all patients older than this cutoff age must be grouped. The use of age ranges would appear to be an easy solution to this problem, but can result in problematic data loss unless previous work has indicated the relationship of age to the study outcomes in question. In general, it is preferable to collect a year of birth or an actual age in years with a way, such as a check box, to indicate that a patient is older than 89 years. Although this solution appears straightforward, during clinical care it can be difficult for clinicians or staff to write down a year of birth for some patients and to check a box for others. Electronic data collection systems can help in this regard. Dates of care are also a restricted data element and can cause considerable difficulty in longitudinal studies.

Unlike treatment situations where you normally share an entire record with other treating health care providers, a "minimum necessary" standard applies to most QI activities. This standard essentially limits the information disclosed to the minimum necessary information needed to accomplish the task. For example, a patient's name, age, and sex would not be necessary to share when reviewing the frequency and thoroughness of vital sign assessments. Typically, your notice of privacy practices (NPP) tells patients that you will use their personal health information (PHI) for QI reviews. Specific authorization from the patient is not necessary.

There are several exceptions to permitted uses of PHI, and a few are worth highlighting here. Reports to public health authorities of communicable diseases; reports of child abuse or neglect; notifications of drug or medical equipment failure or safety hazards; and reports for the purposes of government oversight such as licensure and disciplinary actions are all usually allowed without authorization from the patient and without opportunity for the patient to agree or object to the disclosure (45 CFR 164.512). It is important to understand, however, that state laws do not necessarily supersede HIPAA restrictions.

A provision in the Field EMS Quality, Innovation, and Cost Effectiveness Improvements Act of 2010 provides for a clarification of

HIPAA. The exchange of information related to the treatment of patients is specifically addressed, with the federal language stating,

> Nothing in HIPAA privacy and security law (as defined in section 3009(a)(2) of the Public Health Service Act (42 U.S.C. 300jj-19(a)(2))) shall be construed as prohibiting the exchange of information between field EMS practitioners treating an individual and personnel of a hospital to which the individual is transported for the purposes of relating information on the medical history, treatment, care, and outcome of such individual (including any health care personnel safety issues such as infectious disease).

The law directs the Secretary of Health and Human Services to establish guidelines for exchanges of information between field EMS practitioners treating an individual and personnel of a hospital to which the individual is transported to protect the privacy of the individual while ensuring the ability of such EMS practitioners and hospital personnel to communicate effectively to further the continuity and quality of emergency medical care provided to such individual.

Nothing in HIPAA privacy and security law (as defined in section 3009(a)(2) of the Public Health Service Act (42 U.S.C. 300jj-19(a)(2))) shall be construed as prohibiting a field EMS agency from submitting EMS data to the state EMS office for the purpose of QI and data collection by the state for submission to National EMS Information System (NEMSIS), or the state EMS office from submitting aggregated nonindividually identifiable EMS data to the National EMS Database maintained by the National Highway Traffic Safety Administration (NHTSA). (See Figure 10.7.)

PEER QI COMMITTEES LEGAL ISSUES

Whatever you call it in your agency, the purpose of peer review is to accomplish several purposes. Mostly, it is an opportunity for the physician, EMS personnel, and their supervisors to accomplish the following:

- Review medical responses
- Provide oversight for the medical control physician to see what the EMTs are doing in the field as it relates to following protocols
- See changes in medical responses in order to possibly incorporate additional training to meet new challenges
- Ensure that the EMTs and paramedics are following protocol and to make corrective actions for those individuals not adhering to a protocol-based EMS system

The purpose of making peer review privileged or confidential is to promote honesty, truthfulness, and confidentiality in the peer review process in order to foster aggressive critiquing of medical care and qualifications by an EMT's peers.

Most of us know and understand several examples of legally privileged communications, such as attorney–client privilege and conversations between a physician, nurse, or psychologist and their patient. Generally, the conversations between domestic abuse or sexual assault patients and/or their victim advocates are privileged conversation unless there is grave danger to the patient from their abusers that requires law enforcement interaction. It is possible that counselors can work with the police in providing an additional level of protection without breaching the confidentiality of those conversations. In addition, privilege extends to communication between a husband and wife and communication to clergy. In some cases, privileged communication requires a signature statement at the opening of a peer meeting.

In most states, the QI processes are protected from discovery under various legislative protections as we have described elsewhere in this chapter. There are no cases that have involved the disclosure of an EMS QI committee or peer review action. That is not to say

Medical Control and Quality Management Program

The King County Medical Control and Quality Management section is responsible for the medical direction and oversight of the prehospital provision of Advanced Life Support and Basic Life Support Services. In addition, this section supports quality management programs to assure excellent patient care.

King County Medical Program Director

The Medical Program Director (MPD) is responsible for providing medical oversight and guidance to Emergency Medical Services Technicians and Paramedics. The MPD must develop or adopt written prehospital patient care protocols to direct Emergency Medical Services personnel in patient care as per the Washington Administrative Code 246-976-920.

Medical direction is provided by the Medical Program Director who coordinates with hospital emergency departments, dispatch centers, the Director of Paramedic Training at Harborview Medical Center, and the agencies and fire departments who employ EMTs and Paramedics.

King County Quality Management Program

Mission and Values: It is the mission of the Emergency Medical Services Division to increase survival and reduce disability from out-of-hospital medical emergencies in King County. This is achieved through partnerships with other agencies, providing the highest quality of patient care and innovative leadership. The mission is best accomplished through the application of organizational values. These values can be expressed as follows:

A commitment to quality, beginning with a goal of providing quality patient care. We endeavor to achieve quality in virtually every program or service we provide.

Providing services in an efficient, systematic, and fiscally responsible manner is a value that helps to ensure we receive the respect and support needed to accomplish our mission.
Using innovation, creativity, evaluation, and research to guide our mission, we search for ways to improve how services are delivered and how patient care is provided.

This system is a unique and complex blend of county, cities, fire districts, hospitals, individual paramedics, emergency medical technicians (EMTs), dispatchers, physicians, private ambulance companies, citizens, elected officials, and countless others dedicated to emergency medical services. Maintaining open communications and a commitment to cooperation and consensus building with these entities is essential to our continued success.

Individual success equates to organizational success. When individuals within the system succeed in their role, the system as a whole succeeds. The EMS Division encourages and supports individual excellence.

Service to the citizens of King County and our partners in the EMS community is a strongly held value. For some, the service is to provide direct patient care. For others, the service is to support the regional network of providers delivering care.

Our EMS system has always valued scientific research, evaluative studies, and data analysis. We actively participate in the gathering of this kind of information for possible application in the field of EMS.

Quality Management Organization:

The following summarizes the general EMS quality management infrastructure in King County as depicted in the EMS Division's 2005 Quality Management Plan (PDF). This plan has been reviewed and approved by the Washington State Department of Health and reflects the complex, interactive

FIGURE 10.7 Sample agency regulation for QI program. (*Continued*)

nature of providing EMS care in the region. There are five major sections: Regional Medical Control, Advanced Life Support (ALS) Program, Basic Life Support (BLS) Program, Emergency Medical Dispatch, and Regional Services.

Regional Medical Control

The Medical Program Director (MPD) is responsible under the Washington Administrative Code (WAC) and Revised Code of Washington (RCW) for medical control and direction of all certified EMS personnel in King County. This is accomplished through a delegation of medical oversight to individual medical directors of paramedic programs and emergency room-based, on-line medical control for ALS personnel. The MPD also oversees the development of policies and procedures related to the provision of ALS and BLS services, and provide written treatment guidelines for BLS personnel.

Advanced Life Support (ALS) Program

The goal of quality improvement in ALS is to ensure the provision of the highest level of paramedic services in King County, an internationally recognized program. There are a variety of components to the paramedic program that create a solid foundation based on standardized training, provide ongoing program oversight, and establish a system of quality management.

Major quality improvement activities for ALS services in King County:

Paramedic Assessment and Oversight
Sentinel Event and Inquires
ALS Medical Incident Report Form (MIRF) Review

These activities are monitored by the individual medical program directors and supported by the King County Medical Program Director (see Section A. Regional Medical Control). Paramedics are required to complete a standardized training program and recertify on a regular basis. The following sections detail the specifications.

Basic Life Support (BLS) Program

The goal of quality improvement in BLS is to ensure the provision of the highest level of basic life support services in King County. There are a variety of components to the BLS program that create a solid foundation based on standardized training, provide ongoing program oversight, and establish a system of quality management. They include Emergency Medical Technician (EMT) Training and Certification, EMT Competency Based Training, and EMT/Defibrillation oversight.

Emergency Medical Dispatch (EMD) Program

The goal of EMD Quality Improvement is to increase the incidence of appropriate dispatching for EMS units and enhance the EMD program and training for dispatch agencies. The Dispatch Review Committee (DRC) regularly reviews both trending and sentinel event data to monitor dispatch activities. Results are used to evaluate the quality and impact of EMD training provided by the EMS Division and the consistency and appropriateness of the use and application of the Criteria Based Dispatch (CBD) Guidelines. These guidelines offer a mechanism for providing standardized dispatching across the county. The QI process includes a feedback system to dispatchers, supervisors, and the EMS Division. It also provides an opportunity to conduct QI in key areas and conduct system-wide review in areas where there is over-utilization of ALS services.

FIGURE 10.7 Sample agency regulation for QI program. (*Continued*)

Regional Services Programs

The EMS Division is committed to providing exceptional regional emergency medical services in King County. The following programs reflect a commitment to a comprehensive regional quality improvement approach to service delivery.

Center for the Evaluation of Emergency Medical Services (CEEMS)

The CEEMS program seeks federal grants and private donations to support research in the field of pre-hospital emergency care for cardiac events. CEEMS collaborates with faculty, residents, and students from the University of Washington. The focus of CEEMS research has been to evaluate each of the links in the chain of survival.

Administrative Quality Assurance Programs

The EMS Division oversees a variety of quality assurance activities to ensure appropriate and efficient administration of EMS personnel, finances, and long-term planning. This includes the administration of contracts, risk management, financial monitoring and forecasting, strategic planning, and data management.

FIGURE 10.7 Sample agency regulation for QI program. (*Continued*) *Source: "Sample Agency Regulation for QI Program" from Medical Control and Quality Management Program. Copyright © by King County Medical Examiner's Office. Used by Permission of King County Medical Examiner's Office.*

that the discipline action is not discoverable if there is discipline of an EMT or paramedic as a result of this peer committee action. This chapter does not address that facet of discovery and privilege; those questions should be directed to your agency's legal counsel regarding the protection of employee personnel files. As a general rule, all QA peer review actions are immune from discovery. A good example of this legislation is found in many states' legislative tenets. In Washington State under Revised Code or Washington (RCW) 70.41.200 (3) Information and Documents:

> including the analysis of complaints and incident reports, created specifically for, and collected and maintained by, a quality assurance committee are not subject to discovery or introduction into evidence in any civil action, and no person who was in attendance at a meeting of such committee or who participated in the creation, collection, or maintenance of information or documents specifically for the committee shall be permitted or required to testify in any civil action as to the content of such proceedings or the documents and information prepared specifically for the committee. This subsection does not preclude: (a) In any civil action, the discovery of the identity of persons involved in the care that is the basis of the civil action whose involvement was independent of any quality improvement committee activity; and (b) in any civil action, the testimony of any person concerning the facts which form the basis for the institution of such proceedings of which the person had personal knowledge acquired independently of their participation in the quality assurance committee activities.

As with any EMS delivery system, the public has a strong interest in effective and quality services and equally strong interest on supporting those services. What the public also deserves is a transparent system to ensure that the quality of a service remains strong and any errors in the delivery are fully evaluated. There is also strong public interest in supporting and protecting the process of an effective medical QA review of programs and activities.

The protections of privilege alleviate the fear of revealing the content and discussions or the potential liability involved in those deliberations that would not only discourage participation by the EMS professionals in these QA committees, but also would quash candor and impair objectivity in these peer review sessions. A solid QA process can also be used as an important educational tool to provide an understanding of the care delivered by the EMTs and paramedics and provide a teaching mechanism to enhance the quality of field delivery by those and other EMTs and paramedics. As indicated previously, all fifty states and the District of Columbia have statutes in place to protect those communications. Much of the legislation is directed at hospitals—a highly regulated industry—and EMS is included in those regulations, most likely under different sections of the legislation specifically addressing EMS issues.

Statutes related to EMS are generally open ended as to the detail of conducting those sessions and rely on the governing or authority having jurisdiction (AHJ) with attorney input to place into action those protections under the applicable law. Those statutes generally convey immunity to a participating agency but do not define how that occurs.

On the hospital side, the legislation tends to include several elements:

- A section defining the peer review process and a definition of peer review or medical review committee
- The legislation conveys immunity for the peer review participant from suits that may arise as a result of the participant's involvement in the peer review process
- Privilege or confidentiality of the records, documents, communications in the peer review process and protection from disclosure to third parties as well as protection from discovery during litigation and trial

As found in *Sw. Cmty. Health Servs. v. Smith*, 755 P.2d 40, 44 (N.M. 1988), almost every state puts the burden of proving entitlement to peer review protection on the party seeking these protections. This case states that when a party seeks to invoke the protection of the peer review statute, it must prove that the "information was generated exclusively for peer review and for no other purpose, and that opinions were formed exclusively as a result of peer review deliberations."

What does this mean for an EMS agency? Remember the terms *privilege* and *confidentiality*. Confidentiality protects QI material from disclosure to third parties. For example, if you are a member of this committee, the confidential aspect prevents you from disclosing the information gained during the meetings with other paramedics, EMTs, providers, and certainly with opposing counsel. Privilege, however, deems peer review materials not discoverable between the parties in the course of litigation and cannot be used in trial. The question remaining is, what is discoverable and not privileged? To start, any documents commonly found in simple research or other sources, including those that have been used in a peer review process, are discoverable. A good example is the protocols that may be used in the cardiac resuscitation of a patient in the field. Those are commonly found in most textbooks or in the latest cardiac arrest protocol published by the American Heart Association. Another example is if a patient requests a copy of his medical records from an EMS agency.

In a request for records that includes material produced during QI sessions, the defendant EMS agency has the burden to prove facts sufficient to establish the claim of privilege. This is a high bar to jump over, and the process starts at the beginning of a QI session. The EMS agency must think of the protection of this material at the outset. This is a good time to bring in an attorney to discuss this issue of privilege. Defendants claiming privilege have the burden to prove that the privilege applies and that the privilege has not been waived. Some courts have ruled that there can be an express waiver of the privilege or an implied waiver by conduct. Express waiver is done in writing, specifically waiving privilege. Waiver by conduct may be found in a deposition during which a party or member of the QI committee compelled to attend the deposition and asked specific questions related to the findings or deliberations of the committee work is protected by the privilege or, in some circumstances, by other state law.

In many, if not all, cases where you are required to produce records, the court will take a stronger role in determining the viability of protection and privilege. "In camera" review is conducted by a judge in a closed session and a determination is made after a review if the privilege or protections remain in place. Courts may conduct an "in camera" review to determine if records should remain protected.

Documents prepared in the ordinary course of business may also be discoverable despite the fact that they may be possessed by a peer review committee. Merely adding to a letter, memorandum, report, or minutes of various hospital committee meetings—including minutes of departmental meetings—a statement such as "This information is privileged under the medical studies act of the state and therefore free from discovery and is not to be admissible as evidence" is insufficient to warrant immune status.

In a variety of cases courts have considered other types of documents and information in the peer review process, and have found them to be privileged in some cases and not privileged in others, and some courts could not make a determination. A final word of advice as these discussions relate to protection and privilege: It is wise to seek advice from the agency's legal counsel to determine a process. Because states vary widely in terms of the types of peer review protections available, counsel for the health care entity or practitioner is strongly advised to review applicable state peer review and related statutes, along with case law interpreting the same.

The following are a few things to remember in the protection or privilege of your session in a QA committee:

- If there are criminal proceedings, your QA sessions and the records produced during a QA session are not protected. Prosecutors can subpoena those documents.
- Records kept in the normal course of business (e.g., the medical incident report form or PCR) are not protected from discovery.
- If you are deposed, information that may be transmitted during this process may waive the ordinary protections of privilege of a QA session.
- The PCR or incident report is not deemed to be work product, as when you write your medical records you are not anticipating litigation. It remains the defendant EMS agency's burden to establish that the PCR or incident report was created in anticipation of litigation. This is hardly a defendable position claiming privilege, especially if the response was a number of years ago but still within the acceptable statutory period. If the burden is not met, the objection to production based on the theory of work product will be overruled.
- For records to be deemed privileged, the records must be created for the committee in its investigative or deliberative process. Merely stamping a record as confidential does not mean automatic protection. An example is a cardiac arrest where an approved protocol was not followed and a death resulted from the action of the paramedic. The question is, was it due to the medical condition of the patient that the outcome of death was predicable or were there breaches in established protocol? The records must be created for the exclusive use of the review or QA committee, but the report created by the paramedic is not protected under these rules. Remember the caveat that records produced in the ordinary course of business are not protected or privileged.

- Documents or evidence gathered by a peer review committee after its deliberations are not protected.
- Discipline of a paramedic or EMT resulting from an investigation as a part of a QA session is discoverable, as are most public records sought under a correctly formulated public records request.

In addition, the requirements for establishing privileges and protections related to a QA session occur long before the request for records occurs. It is incumbent upon the EMS agency to involve legal counsel early on to establish those steps necessary to protect documents reviewed in QA sessions.

FEDERAL MANDATES FOR QI

The Field EMS Quality, Innovation, and Cost Effectiveness Improvements Act of 2010 was introduced into Congress in November 2010 and continues to survive in debate. It was designed to ensure high-quality, cost-effective EMS systems. It requires readiness, preparedness, medical direction, oversight, and innovation throughout the continuum of emergency medical care through federal, state, and local multijurisdictional collaboration and sufficient resources for EMS agencies and providers. This action was based on numerous recommendations from several significant national reports. Documents have demonstrated the need in multiple areas for substantial improvement for emergency medical services provided in the field, including recommendations in the Institute of Medicine's report entitled *EMS Agenda for the Future*. In general, the act calls for the administrator to establish a grant program to improve field EMS system performance, integration, and accountability; to ensure preparedness for field EMS at the state and local levels; and to enhance physician medical oversight of field EMS systems. This bill was designed to improve coordination between regional field EMS systems and integration of such regional field EMS systems into the larger health care system; to enhance data collection and analysis to improve, on a continuing basis, the field EMS system; and to enhance standardization of national EMS certification of emergency medical technicians and paramedics. It was designed to use grant funds to enhance preparedness and coordination of medical first response for pandemic influenza and all-hazards EMS, to improve cross-border collaboration and planning among states, and to collect data with regard to the following:

- NEMSIS
- Field EMS education
- Field EMS workforce
- Cardiac events, including STEMI and sudden cardiac arrest
- Stroke
- Disasters, including injuries and illnesses
- Ambulance diversion and patient parking
- Trauma (in a manner that is complementary and not duplicative of other trauma data collection, such as the National Trauma Data Bank)
- Data determined necessary by the state office of EMS for oversight and coordination of the state field EMS system
- Any other data that the administrator specifies

This bill was also designed to implement and evaluate systemwide QI initiatives, including medical direction at the state, local, and regional levels; to integrate field EMS with other health care services as part of a coordinated system of care provided to patients with emergency medical conditions; and to help ensure that the right patient receives the right care by the right crew in the right vehicle and at the right medical facility in the right amount of time, including by enhancing regional emergency medical dispatch.

REPORT ON DATA INTEGRATION TO PROMOTE QUALITY CARE

The Field EMS Quality, Innovation, and Cost Effectiveness Improvements Act of 2010 bill is designed so that within 18 months after the date of the enactment of this act, the Secretary of Health and Human Services, acting through the head of the Office of the National Coordinator for Health Information Technology, in collaboration with the Federal Interagency Committee on EMS (FICEMS) and the administrator of NHTSA, as appropriate, and taking into consideration input from relevant stakeholders, shall submit a report (including recommendations) on issues, impediments, and potential solutions. The idea is to incorporate EMS PCRs into patient electronic health records, taking into consideration the extent to which field EMS PCRs are presently created in electronic format and the potential for elements of such reports to be incorporated into patient electronic health records. Incorporating data elements of EMS PCRs that promote quality and efficiency of care into patient electronic health records is the final step to integrating EMS into the health care system.

The stage is set for modifications to the Medicare and Medicaid programs under Titles XVIII and XIX, respectively, of the Social Security Act or other federal health programs (including potential modifications to the HITECH Act [Title XIII of Division A of Public Law 111-5]), including modifications to the entities included as eligible for incentive payments under Section 1848(o), 1853(l) (to the extent that such section 1848(o) is applied), or 1903(t) of the Social Security Act. Criteria is set for technology requirements for determining meaningful use of technology for purposes of providing appropriate reimbursement and financial incentives for EMS agencies to maintain field EMS PCRs in a structured electronic format; to otherwise adopt and use electronic health records; and to offer potential modifications to the Health Information Technology (HITECH) Act. The HITECH Act provides incentives to eligible hospitals under Section 1886(n), 1853(m) (to the extent that such section 1886(n) is applied), or section 1814(l)(3) of the Social Security Act to incorporate appropriate data elements of field EMS PCRs into patient electronic health records.

Federal recognition includes the incorporation of PHI created by field EMS emergency care that has been uploaded into NEMSIS. Federal incentive programs take into consideration what types of medical information created by field EMS emergency care can be linked to hospital data (such as outcomes information or information regarding subsequent care and treatment). If NEMSIS data can be linked to the hospital record it will be potentially useful in evaluating and improving the quality of EMS care. How best to integrate such information into NEMSIS and the potential modifications to the HITECH Act to require eligible hospitals, as defined in section 1886(n)(6)(B) of the Social Security Act, for purposes of incentive payments under 1886(b)(3)(B)(ix) and 1886(n) of such Act, to develop or report relevant data to NEMSIS or other appropriate State or private registries, will be further influenced by the Affordable Care Act. There will be potential modifications to the Medicare and Medicaid programs under titles XVIII and XIX, respectively, of the Social Security Act or other federal health programs to provide appropriate reimbursement and financial incentives for field EMS agencies to develop or report relevant data to NEMSIS or other appropriate state or private registries. These changes to the incentives system are what have given rise to community paramedicine and mobile integrated health services. Much of the information generated from this legislation will facilitate a different type of reimbursement for EMS based on quality, outcome, and efficiency.

CHAPTER REVIEW

Summary

Most states have some form of mandated QI or reporting for EMS. QI programs do present some risk to an organization if proper law, regulation, or administrative code is not in place to protect the process. It is the responsibility of the authority having jurisdiction to ensure protection from litigation is in place for the process, people, and the organization. Compromising the process's confidentiality will reduce the honest efforts to improve EMS care. The legal process has a discovery, a trial, and an award or ruling phase. HIPAA does not preclude the sharing of information for the purpose of QI. Findings in the QI process that cannot be corrected by coaching, counseling, or education must have due process to ensure that fairness in the process does not create a culture of fear. Although impending federal legislation may require a QI initiative to receive payment from Medicare or Medicaid sources, the majority of legal statutes that mandate QI are state level.

WHAT WOULD YOU DO? Reflection

The QI process would use the QI team findings that have identified how often a complete set of vital signs and assessment of level of consciousness and potential for suicide were completed. The potential for the person not to be mentally competent, supported by documentation of the alcohol consumption, was a clear flag in this case. A person who cannot answer accurately his name, location, time, and events regarding the incident is not competent to refuse care. A person whose judgment is impaired by drugs or alcohol must be evaluated to the above criteria. Failure to evaluate the person and document his ability to reason and his level of orientation predisposes the course of events to a potentially negative outcome.

To help avoid a judgment or legal award, it is necessary to document the history and obtain a release form after assessing the level of consciousness and if the patient was a legally consenting adult. To help reduce the risk a standardize algorithm for refusing care and a standard response by law enforcement to further assess the situation would be best practices. Mandatory signature and witnesses on the refusal should be under constant review to demonstrate compliance and cover risk management issues.

Most states and organization have case law, administrative rules, regulations, or policies and procedures that have been established to help identify the level of orientation that must be documented before a refusal. If not defined by statute, level of orientation should be defined by the agency. The current number and compliance with patient refusals should be an ongoing QI process, as it poses the largest risk.

Review Questions

1. What three areas are commonly protected in EMS QI?
2. What are the three phases of, or the progress of, a lawsuit?
3. What are the provisions of sharing EMS information under HIPAA?
4. Explain the differences between substantive and procedural due process.

5. What is the difference between summary and declarative judgments?
6. What is the purpose of due process? Does your agency meet the means test for due process?
7. What are the potential benefits identified in the Field EMS Quality, Innovation, and Cost Effectiveness Improvements Act of 2010?
8. What are Weingarten rights, and when do they apply to EMS QI?
9. What are the differences between an interrogatory and a deposition?

References

Bennett, L. T. (2005). *Fire and EMS Law for Officers: Employment Best Practices.* Stillwater: Oklahoma State University, Fire Protection Publications.

Bennett, L. T., (2007). *Fire Service Law.* Upper Saddle River, NJ: Prentice Hall.

Bremer, W. D. (1999). *Scope and Extent of Protection from Disclosure of Medical Peer Review Proceedings Relating to Claim in Medical Malpractice Action,* Annotation, 69 A.L.R. 5th 559.

King County, State of Washington. (n.d.). "Medical Control and Quality Management Program." See the organization website.

Morgan, D., W. R. Trail, and V. A. Trompler. (1985, April–June). "Liability Immunity as a Legal Defense for Recent Emergency Medical Services System Litigation." *Prehospital and Disaster Medicine 10*(2), pp. 82–90.

New York State. (2012, November). "EMS Rules & Regulations, 10 NYCRR Parts 18, 80 and 800, & BEMS Advisories." See the organization website.

Key Terms

answer In law, a defendant's written defense against charges.

authority having jurisdiction (AHJ) Agency or individual having statutory authority, such as federal, state, regional, or local department; fire chief, fire marshal, or fire bureau chief; building official or electrical inspector; and so on.

briefs Written document that concisely states the issues of a lawsuit, what brings the parties to court, relevant laws, and arguments that explain how the law applies to the case facts.

contingency Arrangement for payment for an attorney's services, in which the attorney is paid out of the recovery awarded to the client.

counseling Service that renders evaluation and therapy.

counterclaims Assertions that the defendant could have made by starting a lawsuit if the plaintiff had not already begun the action.

declaratory judgment An opinion declaring the rights of each of the parties involved; differs from other judicial rulings in that it does not require that any action be taken.

defendant Person or institution against whom an action or claim is brought in a court of law.

deposition Sworn testimony recorded for use in court at a later date.

discovery Compulsory disclosure of relevant documents in a party's possession.

due process An established course for judicial proceedings or other governmental activities designed to safeguard the legal rights of the individual.

injunction A court order prohibiting a party from a specific course of action, or an equitable remedy in the form of a court order that requires a party to do or refrain from doing certain acts.

interrogatories Written questions asked by one party to a suit, to which the other party has to give written answers under oath.

judgment Legal document stating the reasons for a judicial decision.

lawsuit Comprehensive term for any proceeding in a court of law whereby an individual seeks a legal remedy.

motion to dismiss Party's request to a court to dismiss a case because of settlement, voluntary withdrawal, procedural defect, or claim for which the law provides a remedy.

plaintiff Person who initiates a court action by filing a complaint with the clerk of the court against the defendant(s) demanding damages, performance, and/or court determination of rights; sometimes called a petitioner.

pleading Complaint and answer; reply to a counterclaim; an answer to a cross-claim; third-party complaint and answer.

progressive discipline System of increasingly harsh penalties for each time an employee is disciplined for work-rule violations, typically progressing from oral warnings to termination.

proof of service Document or court paper filed in a court as evidence that process has been successfully served on a party or a witness in a lawsuit.

punitive damages Awarded in a lawsuit as a punishment and example to deter others from malicious, evil, or particularly fraudulent acts.

remediation Affording a resolution by giving the means of obtaining redress that is intended to remedy wrongs or abuses, abate faults, or supply defects.

summary judgment Decision made without a trial on the basis of statements and evidence presented in legal pleadings and documents filed.

summons Paper issued by a court informing a person that a complaint has been filed against him.

Weingarten rights Derived from the Supreme Court's 1975 Weingarten decision, in which the Court recognized union employees' rights to representation at investigatory interviews.

Glossary

accountable care organizations (ACOs) Combinations of hospitals, primary care physicians, and possibly specialists associated with a defined population of patients accountable for the total Medicare spending of that patient population.

activity Any element of work required by a project and that uses resources and takes time to complete. Activities have expected duration, cost, and resources requirements and may be subdivided into task.

agapao Refers to a moral love, doing the right thing at the right time for the right reason.

alignment The state of agreement and cooperation between persons, groups, and divisions with a common cause and viewpoint.

American National Standards Institute (ANSI) A private, nonprofit organization that administers and coordinates the U.S. voluntary standardization and conformity assessment system. It is the U.S. member in the International Organization for Standardization.

analysis of variance A basic statistical technique for analyzing data. It subdivides the total variation of a data set into meaningful component parts associated with specific sources of variation in order to test a hypothesis on the measurements of the model or to estimate variance in certain components.

anecdotal Refers to process information that lacks specific methods, measures, deployment methods, evaluation and improvement details, or learning factors.

answer In law, a defendant's written defense against charges.

assessment Systematic process of collecting and analyzing data to determine the current, historical, or projected status of an organization, process, or project.

attitudes Manners, dispositions, feelings, or positions with regard to a person or thing that encompasses the tendency or orientation.

attribution error When the crew becomes judgmental and blames the patient's actions for his condition.

authority having jurisdiction (AHJ) Agency or individual having statutory authority, such as federal, state, regional, or local department; fire chief, fire marshal, or fire bureau chief; building official or electrical inspector; and so on.

belief Principle, degree of conviction, or idea accepted as true.

benchmark A standard against which something is measured. In most cases, there is a reference point or organization that has been identified as "best in class."

benchmarking Using known results of similar data measurements or tests as an impetus for achieving or surpassing a desired goal for improvement.

best practices Using the best-known results of similar data measurements of similar tests for similar systems or operations as an impetus for achieving or surpassing a desired goal for improvement.

bimodal Two areas in the data cluster together to form two different peaks; two distinct values that measurements tend to cluster around a measurement.

blanket sampling A type of sampling that captures every event being studied or every patient that meets a certain category of study. It is often used for compliance to standards of care or contractual operational requirements.

briefs Written document that concisely states the issues of a lawsuit, what brings the parties to court, relevant laws, and arguments that explain how the law applies to the case facts.

causation How events occur in the system or how they are related even when it may not be obvious, or conversely when it appears obvious but is not related. Causation is displayed on the horizontal scale or the X axis.

check sheet Simple data-recording device. The check sheet is usually custom designed by the user, which ready interpretation of the results. It may also be called a tally sheet.

checkpoints Smaller events used to judge how far a project is from completion.

cherry picking A condition of explaining away things once a decision is made by focusing on item(s) that are acceptable while ignoring the indicators of an error.

chi-square A test used to determine whether or not there were significant differences between frequency distributions.

coaching Varies greatly from managing as it has a specific cycle; a coach helps a person or team develop skills by demonstrating and allowing for a variety of outcomes.

contingency Arrangement for payment for an attorney's services, in which the attorney is paid out of the recovery awarded to the client.

controlled variable A variable that is held constant when studying the effect of one particular independent variable, thus there is a need to eliminate the other factors affecting the outcome.

counseling Service that renders evaluation and therapy.

counterclaims Assertions that the defendant could have made by starting a lawsuit if the plaintiff had not already begun the action.

crashing Management term used when certain aspects of the project can be accelerated if there is a reason and certain nodes or paths can have their time frames moved up in a project schedule.

critical path method (CPM) Analysis that determines the longest series of interrelated events that must be completed in a project.

Cronbach's coefficient alpha Measurement of internal consistency among a group of questions combined to form a single scale. It is a statistic that reflects the homogeneity of the scale.

culture Pattern of artifacts, behaviors, values, beliefs, and underlying assumptions developed by a given group of people as they learn to cope with internal and external problems of survival and prosperity.

customer service Ability to provide a service or product in the way that it has been promised.

data A set of collected facts. There are two types of data: variable data and measurement data.

data scrubbing Process for fixing or eliminating individual pieces of data that are incorrect, incomplete, or duplicated before the data are saved or analyzed.

death The patient did not survive to hospital discharge or was pronounced at the scene of the incident.

declaratory judgment An opinion declaring the rights of each of the parties involved; differs from other judicial rulings in that it does not require that any action be taken.

defendant Person or institution against whom an action or claim is brought in a court of law.

dependent variable Those measured items in which there is a change between whether a treatment or action was applied or not applied.

deposition Sworn testimony recorded for use in court at a later date.

describe Way of writing definitions in computer language that creates a site for a piece of data or element to be placed in the database.

descriptive statistical analysis Various statistical tests run to get in-depth analysis and to confirm or refute conclusions with mathematics. There are several types of descriptive statistical analysis, including counts, sums, standard deviation measures of center, minimums, and maximums.

destitution A monetary measurement for the patient and for the service.

differential measurements Use of a device that transforms actual movement into a known value—for example, the use of a CPR device that is connected to the monitor monitoring the compressions.

disability The patient's level of function as a result of the injury or as a result of the patient care rendered.

discomfort Accessing whether there was an improvement in the patient's symptoms (e.g., alleviation of pain, improved breathing).

discovery Compulsory disclosure of relevant documents in a party's possession.

disease A pathological condition of a part, organ, or system of an organism resulting from various causes, such as infection, genetic defect, or environmental stress, and characterized by an identifiable group of signs or symptoms.

dissatisfaction Negative assessment by the patient (and/or patient's family) of services rendered.

DMADV An improvement system (*D*efine, *M*easure, *A*nalyze, *D*esign, *V*erify) used to develop new processor products at Six Sigma quality levels.

DMAIC An improvement system (*D*efine, *M*easure, *A*nalyze, *I*mprove, *C*ontrol) for existing processes falling below specification and looking for incremental improvement.

due process An established course for judicial proceedings or other governmental activities designed to safeguard the legal rights of the individual.

event cost All costs associated with a poor medical outcome or adverse medical event that an EMS agency, medical provider, or hospital might be required to bear through the tort liability system: patient care expenses, lost income and household production, future medical expenses, burial costs for fatal injuries, and noneconomic losses (e.g., pain and suffering).

external benchmarking A process that requires a comparison of work with external organizations in order to discover new ideas, methods, products, and services.

flowchart A schematic representation of a sequence of operations, as in a manufacturing process or service.

Gantt chart Displays the flow and completion of each item using time and task of each division that is needed.

goal erosion Occurs when people reduce their goals when they experience failure and adversity; often, people give up on an important goal or lower their standards to such an extent that the accomplishments of the team bring no sense of satisfaction.

Health Level 7 A widely used protocol for electronic data exchange of medical data.

highly reliable organization An organization with fewer accidents than normal.

histogram A column graph in which the height of the columns indicates the relative numbers or frequencies or values of a variable. The values may be numeric or nonnumeric.

human error Inadvertently doing other than what should have been done.

iatrogenic Induced inadvertently by the medical treatment or procedures or activity of a health care provider. The term is now applied to any adverse condition in a patient occurring as the result of treatment by a physician, nurse, or other health care professional, especially infections acquired by the patient during the course of treatment.

independent variable A variable that stands alone and is not changed by the other variables you are trying to measure.

indicators Objective behaviors or outcomes that can be measured to determine compliance with a standard.

injunction A court order prohibiting a party from a specific course of action, or an equitable remedy in the form of a court order that requires a party to do or refrain from doing certain acts.

internal benchmarking Involves two-way communication and sharing opinions between departments within the same organization or between work areas of the organizations operating as different units.

International Organization for Standardization (ISO) A network of national standards institutes from 148 countries working in partnership with international organizations, governments, industry, and business and consumer representatives to develop and publish international standards.

interrogatories Written questions asked by one party to a suit, to which the other party has to give written answers under oath.

invalid code The code is not on an approved list of possible choices.

judgment Legal document stating the reasons for a judicial decision.

just culture A culture in which people can report mistakes, errors, or waste without reprisal or personal risk.

Kaizen A Japanese approach to a quality process that encourages a 1 percent change over 100 days to get a 100 percent change.

lawsuit Comprehensive term for any proceeding in a court of law whereby an individual seeks a legal remedy.

Likert scale A summated instrument scale. This means that the items making up a Likert scale are summed to produce a total score as a composite on an itemized scale. Typically, each scale item will have five categories, with scale values ranging from −2 to +2, with 0 as a neutral response.

managed care Systems and techniques used to control the use of health care services, including reviews of medical necessity, incentives to use certain providers, and case management. It is a body of clinical, financial, and organizational activities designed to ensure the provision of appropriate health care services in a cost-efficient manner.

mean Also known as the arithmetic mean or average. However, since the term *average* is sometimes used indiscriminately for any measure of central tendency, it should be avoided.

measure A criterion, metric, or means by which a comparison is made with outputs.

measurement The act or process of quantitatively comparing results with requirements. Measurements may be in any quality and may be in any unit.

measures of central tendency The extent to which data gathered from a process tend to cluster toward a middle value somewhere between the high and low values of measurements.

measures of dispersion The tendency of values of elements in a sample to differ from each other.

median The middle value or the 50th percentile of a distribution. To determine the median, the data must be ordered.

medical errors Errors or mistakes committed by health care professionals that result in harm to the patient. They include errors in diagnosis (diagnostic errors), delivery of drugs and other medications (medication errors), performance of procedures, use of other types of therapy, use of equipment, and interpretation of laboratory findings. Medical errors are differentiated from malpractice in that the former are regarded as honest mistakes or accidents, whereas the latter is the result of negligence, reprehensible ignorance, or criminal intent.

medication errors Any preventable events that may cause or lead to inappropriate medication use or patient harm while the medication is in the control of the health care professional, patient, or consumer. Such events may be related to professional practice, health care products, procedures, and systems, including prescribing; order communication; product labeling, packaging, and nomenclature; compounding; dispensing; distribution; administration; education; monitoring; and use.

metric Standard for measurement or evaluation method.

milestones Long-term or major events that have been or must be completed for a project.

mission statement Document designed to turn an agency's vision into action.

mode The value that occurs most frequently in a distribution object from the center of gravity. With a frequency distribution, the mean is the center of gravity and, thus, deviation scores are the moments.

modulus A check to ensure that there are no extra numerical fields.

motion to dismiss Party's request to a court to dismiss a case because of settlement, voluntary withdrawal, procedural defect, or claim for which the law provides a remedy.

National Quality Forum (NQF) A unique, multistakeholder organization that has been instrumental in advancing efforts to improve quality through performance measurement and public reporting.

nonparametric A type of test for situations in which assumptions about underlying populations do not rely on normal distributions.

normalization of deviance Long-term phenomenon in which individuals or teams repeatedly accept a lower standard of performance until that lower standard becomes the "norm."

null code A code or value that is entered as a zero or not recorded in a data field.

object database A relational database that addresses the object-relational impedance mismatch in relational database and XML databases.

ordinal scale The ranking of individuals, attitudes, or items along the continuum of the characteristic being scaled.

organizational culture Way in which people act and think.

outcome indicator The measurement of the sum of structural and process indicators within a system.

Changes in structure and/or processes have direct effect on outcomes.

outcomes Results of structure and process.

outlier A data point or observation that lies an abnormal distance from other values in a random sample or population.

patient-safety incidents (PSIs) Any unintended or unexpected incidents that could have or did lead to harm for one or more patients receiving health care.

patient-safety organizations (PSOs) Established under the Patient Safety and Quality Improvement Act of 2005, Pub. L. 109-41, 42 U.S.C. 299b-21—b-26 (Patient Safety Act). The Patient Safety and Quality Improvement final rule (Patient Safety Rule) establishes a framework by which hospitals, doctors, and other health care providers may voluntarily report information to PSOs, on a privileged and confidential basis, for the aggregation and analysis of patient safety events.

peer review organizations (PROs) Individuals or organizations who review projects or performance. They have equivalent knowledge and background but do not hold a superior position or role to the person or operation being reviewed.

performance-based reimbursement Financial incentives based on the utilization of resources and application of procedures or medications as indicated by evidence-based medicine.

PERT chart A project management tool used to schedule, organize, and coordinate tasks within a project.

phi coefficient The Pearson product-moment correlation coefficient for two variables that are both qualitative and divided into two parts or classifications.

plaintiff Person who initiates a court action by filing a complaint with the clerk of the court against the defendant(s) demanding damages, performance, and/or court determination of rights; sometimes called a petitioner.

pleading Complaint and answer; reply to a counterclaim; an answer to a cross-claim; third-party complaint and answer.

point bi-serial correlation Used as in the bi-serial correlation, except that the second variable is qualitative and divided into two branches and could not be expressed as continuous and quantitative.

process A set of interrelated work activities involving people, materials, machines, methods, energy, and environment.

process indicator Measurements of activities occurring within a system.

progressive discipline System of increasingly harsh penalties for each time an employee is disciplined for work-rule violations, typically progressing from oral warnings to termination.

project charter Document format used for proposing a performance project and brought before senior management to evaluate the project; can be clinical, operational, financial, or political.

project proposal Document that provides clear information concerning the hoped-for goals and objectives of a particular project.

proof of service Document or court paper filed in a court as evidence that process has been successfully served on a party or a witness in a lawsuit.

punitive damages Awarded in a lawsuit as a punishment and example to deter others from malicious, evil, or particularly fraudulent acts.

push Involves a cache of data or instructions being capable of receiving updates and modifications proactively sent to it from a remote server holding the source content data.

quality Subjective term for which each person has his own definition. In technical usage, quality can have two meanings: (1) the characteristics of a product or service that bear on its ability to satisfy stated or implied needs and (2) a product or service free of deficiencies.

quality assurance system All of the planned and systematic activities and related results to comply with planned arrangements and whether these arrangements are implemented effectively and are appropriate to achieve the objectives.

quality control All the planned and systematic activities implemented within the quality system that can be demonstrated to provide confidence that a product or service will fulfill requirements for quality.

quality council Group driving the quality improvement effort that usually has oversight for the implementation and maintenance of the quality management system; operates in parallel with the normal operation of the business; also called quality steering committee.

quality gap Differences between health care processes or outcomes observed in practice and those thought to be achievable with the most current and effective professional knowledge.

quality improvement (QI) The formal approach to the analysis of performance and systematic efforts to improve it.

quality improvement organizations (QIOs) Organizations that represent, promote, and/or validate the actions taken to increase the value to the customer by improving the effectiveness and efficiency of processes and activities throughout the organizational structure.

quality improvement system A formalized system that documents the structure, process, and responsibilities required to achieve effective customer satisfaction or the delivery of quality products and services to the patient or the public.

quality management Oversight and application of quality principles in a management system used to guide overall operational process to achieve maximum customer satisfaction at the lowest overall cost to the organization while continuing to improve the process.

quality of health care The degree to which health services for individuals and patient populations increase the likelihood of desirable health outcomes and are consistent with current professional knowledge.

quality planning Establishing and developing objectives and requirements for quality and the requirements for application of the quality system. According to Juran, these steps should include a quality council, quality policies, strategic quality goals, deployment of quality goals, resources for control, measurement of performance, and quality audits.

quantitative approach A systems approach to quality that is continuous and designed to keep a process within a range.

random assignment The use of chance procedures when conducting experiments or research to ensure that each participant or data point has the same opportunity to be assigned to any given group. Study subjects can be randomly assigned to different groups such as the experimental or treatment group.

randomization A method based on chance alone by which study participants or patients are assigned to a treatment group. This technique helps to minimize the differences among groups by equally distributing people with particular characteristics among all options being used to change an outcome.

range A plus/minus figure that encompasses data points above and below the mean that may be considered as part of the data set; also called margin of error.

reckless behavior A choice to consciously disregard rules or procedures, which can have substantial and unjustifiable risk.

regression line Formula used to make the predictions around which the data points cluster.

reliability A statistical measure of the reproducibility of data. Reliability is assessed by examining the internal consistency.

remediation Affording a resolution by giving the means of obtaining redress that is intended to remedy wrongs or abuses, abate faults, or supply defects.

risk adjustment A complicated topic; basically, a corrective tool used to level the playing field regarding the reporting of patient outcomes, adjusting for the differences in risk among specific patients.

root cause analysis Identifies changes that could be made in EMS systems and processes.

run Eight or more consecutive data points above or below the mean.

schema A cognitive framework or concept that helps organize and interpret information.

Schematron A rule-based validation language for making assertions about the presence or absence of patterns in XML data.

search satisfying When an agency or QI committee stops looking for reason for failures once something is found.

semantic scale A scale that makes extensive use of words rather than numbers. Respondents describe their feelings about the products or brands on scales with semantic labels.

sentinel event An unexpected occurrence involving death or serious physical or psychological injury, or the risk thereof.

servant leadership Leadership philosophy that actions taken by the leader are primarily intended to ensure that other people's highest-priority needs are being served.

service audit A measurement used to make an analysis of the EMS system for strengths and weaknesses, assessing what is being done and what level of performance or quality is being delivered.

shift Involves six or more consecutive data points either above or below the mean.

Six Sigma A model for improvement deriving from the statistical use of the Greek letter sigma to denote standard deviation from the mean. Six sigma is equivalent to 3.4 defects or errors per million.

special cause variation Difference in outcome of a process that required investigation in order to ensure quality and maximize productivity.

standard A generalized goal that is an achievable model of excellence and is used to define expectations.

standard deviation Determines how spread out the bell curve is. The larger the standard deviation, the more spread out is the curve. This also calculates the distance in units from the mean in a positive or negative direction.

standards Can be developed for inputs, processes, or outcomes; can be clinical or administrative.

structural indicator Measurement of an expectation of people, places, or things within a system.

structural inhibitors Administrative procedure, organizational principles, or cultural elements that work against change.

summary judgment Decision made without a trial on the basis of statements and evidence presented in legal pleadings and documents filed.

summons Paper issued by a court informing a person that a complaint has been filed against him.

system A network of interdependent components.

temporal analysis Time or limits in time that are identified with a suitable scatter graph that may reveal clusters that are epidemiologically significant.

trend A long series of consecutive data points ascending or descending; typically the series is five (5) points, indicating a trend.

trending The process of showing by plot or process control chart, the upward, downward, or level movement of an activity over a specified period of time.

values Those things regarded as having ultimate importance, significance, or worth.

values statement Document that starts with a vision and a mission, and then talks about work that will be done to model the desired behaviors.

variable A characteristic or measurement that varies or changes.

variance A measure of dispersion on observations based on the mean of the squared deviations from the arithmetic mean; the square of the standard deviation, given by formula.

vision statement Statement of what is possible for the future.

Vital Few Term coined by Joseph Juran to describe his use of the Pareto principle. This principle suggests that most effects come from relatively few causes; that is, 80 percent of them come from 20 percent of the possible causes. The 20 percent of possible causes are referred to as the "vital few."

Weingarten rights Derived from the Supreme Court's 1975 Weingarten decision, in which the Court recognized union employees' rights to representation at investigatory interviews.

wrong code A wrong code is simply incorrect input of definitions or characters in a field, commonly an incorrect address or a letter in a field that is supposed to contain a number.

Index

L

M

Q

R

T

U